Democracy in Africa

Carolina Academic Press
African World Series
Toyin Falola, Series Editor

Democracy in Africa

Political Changes and Challenges

Edited by

Saliba Sarsar

Julius O. Adekunle

CAROLINA ACADEMIC PRESS

Durham, North Carolina

Library of Congress Cataloging-in-Publication Data

Sarsar, Saliba G., 1955-
 Democracy in Africa : political changes and challenges / Saliba Sarsar and
Julius O. Adekunle.
    p. cm. -- (African world series)
 Includes bibliographical references and index.
 ISBN 978-1-61163-002-2 (alk. paper)
1. Democracy--Africa. 2. Africa--Politics and government--1960- 3. Political
participation--Africa. I. Adekunle, Julius. II. Title. III. Series: Carolina Aca-
demic Press African world series.

 JQ1879.A15S29 2011
 320.46--dc23

                                                 2011023910

                        CAROLINA ACADEMIC PRESS
                              700 Kent Street
                        Durham, North Carolina 27701
                          Telephone (919) 489-7486
                            Fax (919) 493-5668
                            www.cap-press.com

                   Printed in the United States of America

For Dr. Kod Igwe
distinguished professor,
renowned sculptor, and
generous donor.

Contents

Tables

Abbreviations

ACF	Arewa Consultative Forum
ADI	Independent Democratic Action
AFL-CIO	American Federation of Labor-Congress of Industrial Organizations
AJM	Association of Journalists and Media Workers
AME	African Methodist Episcopal
ANC	African National Congress
AP	Associated Press
ASP	Afro-Shirazi Party
ASU	Arab Socialist Union
AU	African Union (formerly Organization of African Unity OAU)
AZ	Agenda for Zambia Party
BAWATA	*Baraza la Wanawake Tanzania* (Tanzania Women's Council)
BMA	British Military Administration
BMM	Brigade Mixte Mobile
CAN	Christian Association of Nigeria
CCM	*Chama Cha Mapinduzi*
CCM	*Centre for Cinématographique Marocain* (Moroccan Cinema)
CD	Campaign for Democracy
CdIA	Camp of the Autonomous Islands
CDT	*Confédération democratique de travail*
CENER	*Centre National des Etudes et des Recherches*

CGEM	*Association Marocaine D'Employeurs* (Moroccan Employers Association)
CNRR	Coalition for National Reconciliation and Reconstruction (CRRN in French)
CNU	Cameroon National Union
CODO	Democratic Coalition of the Opposition
CPC	Countries of Popular Concern
CPDM	Cameroon's People Democratic Movement
CPNC	Cameroon People's National Convention
CRC	Convention for the Renewal of the Comoros
CSF	Central Security Forces
CUF	Civic United Front
DP	Democratic Party
DRC	Democratic Republic of the Congo
DTA	Deutsche Turnhalle
EDA	Eritrean Democratic Alliance
EFCC	Economic and Financial Crimes Commission
ELECAM	Elections Cameroon
ELF	Eritrean Liberation Front
EPLF	Eritrean People's Liberation Front
EU	European Union
FBI	Federal Bureau of Investigation
FCFA	Francs (currency) of the Bank of Central African States
FEDECO	Federal Electoral Commission
FGM	Female Genital Mutilation
FJA	Freelance Journalists Association
FNJ	National Front for Justice
GDP	Gross Domestic Product
GIS	Geographical Information Systems
GNP	Gross National Product
GNPP	Great Nigerian Peoples Party
GUMW	General Union of Moroccan Workers
HDI	Human Development Index

HRW	Human Rights Watch
ICFTU	International Confederation of Free Trade Unions
IMF	International Monetary Fund
ISD	Information Services Department
JET	Journalism for Environment in Tanzania
KNC	Kamerun National Congress
KNDP	Kamerun National Democratic Party
KPP	Kamerun People's Party
LPF	Liberal Progressive Front
MAP	*Maghrib abd Arabe* (Maghrib Arab Press)
MDFM	Force for Change Democratic Movement
MDR	Mouvement Démocratique Républicain
MDR	Movement for the Defense of the Republic
MEND	Movement for the Emancipation of the Niger Delta
MINAT	Ministry of Territorial Administration
MISA	Media Institute of Southern Africa
MLP	Mauritian Labour Party
MLSTP	Movement for the Liberation of Sao Tome and Principe
MMD	Movement for Multiparty Democracy
MMM	Mauritian Militant Movement
MpD	Movement for Democracy
MSM	Militant Socialist Movement
MTD	Democratic Labour Movement
MUC	Movement for Union of Cameroon
MWU	Moroccan Workers Union
NDP	National Democratic Party
NEC	National Electoral Commission
NEO	National Electoral Observatory
NEPA	National Electric Power Authority
NGO	Non-Governmental Organizations
NLC	Nigerian Labor Congress
NP	National Party

NPN	National Party of Nigeria
NPP	Northern Peoples Party
NR	National Radio
NRC	National Republican Convention
NUEW	National Union of Eritrean Women
NUPF	National Union of Popular Forces
OPEC	Organization of the Petroleum Exporting Countries
PAICV	African Party of Independent Cape Verde
PARMEHUTU	Parti du Movement de l'Emancipation Hutu
PCD-GR	Democratic Convergence Party-Reflection
PDP	People's Democratic Party
PJD	Justice Development Party
PF	Patriotic Front
PFDJ	People's Front for Democracy and Justice
PGE	Provisional Government of Eritrea
PMSD	Mauritian Social Democratic Party
PRP	People's Redemption Party
PSD	Social Democratic Party
RND	National Rally for Development
RPF	Rwandan Patriotic Front
RTLM	*Radio et Television Libres des Mille Collines*
RTM	*Radio-Television Marocaine* (Moroccan Broadcasting Network)
SADR	Saharan Arab Democratic Republic
SAP	Structural Adjustment Programs
SCAF	Supreme Council of the Armed Forces (in Egypt)
SDF	Social Democratic Front
SDI	Status of Democracy Index
SDP	Social Democratic Party
SEDOC	*Service des Etude et de la Documentation*
SNP	Seychelles National Party
SPPF	Seychelles People's Progressive Front

SUPF	Socialist Union of Popular Forces
SWAPO	South West Africa Progressive Organization
TAJA	Tanzania Journalists Association
TAMWA	Tanzania Media Women Association
TANU	Tanganyika African National Union
TASWA	Tanzania Sports Writers' Association
TLP	Tanzania Labour Party
TPA	Tanzania Photographers' Association
TUC	Trade Union Congress
UDC	Cameroon Democratic Union (as translated in English)
UDP	United Democratic Party
UGTM	Union Général des ouvriers marocainas
UMT	*Union des ouvriers marocains* (Union of Moroccan Workers)
UN	United Nations
UNDP	National Union for Democratic Progress
UNIA	United Negro Improvement Association
UNIP	United National Independent Party
UNMEE	United Nations Mission to Eritrea and Ethiopia
UNMT	*Syndicat national du Maroc* (National Union of Morocco)
UPC	Union of Populations of Cameroon
UPN	Unity Party of Nigeria
UPND	Unity Party for National Development
UR	Union for the Republic
WDC	Workers Democratic Confederation
ZADECO	Zambia's National Congress Party
ZCTU	Zambia Confederation of Trade Unions
ZDM	Zambia Daily Mail
ZNP	Zanzibar Nationalist Party
ZUJ	Zambia Union of Journalists

Series Editor's Preface

The *Carolina Academic Press African World Series*, inaugurated in 2010, offers significant new works in the field of African and Black World studies. The series provides scholarly and educational texts that can serve both as reference works and as readers in college classes.

Studies in the series are anchored in the existing humanistic and the social scientific traditions. Their goal, however, is the identification and elaboration of the strategic place of Africa and its Diaspora in a shifting global world. More specifically, the studies will address gaps and larger needs in the developing scholarship on Africa and the Black World.

The series intends to fill gaps in areas such as African politics, history, law, religion, culture, sociology, literature, philosophy, visual arts, art history, geography, language, health, and social welfare. Given the complex nature of Africa and its Diaspora, and the constantly shifting perspectives prompted by globalization, the series also meets a vital need for scholarship connecting knowledge with events and practices. Reflecting the fact that life in Africa continues to change, especially in the political arena, the series explores issues emanating from racial and ethnic identities, particularly those connected with the ongoing mobilization of ethnic minorities for inclusion and representation.

Toyin Falola
University of Texas at Austin

Foreword

I commend this book to readers for the significance of the subject matter and the innovative approaches adopted in various chapters. Today, we are all witnesses to the monumental changes in the northern part of the continent. Street protests in Egypt and the full-scale war in Libya demonstrate the extent of those struggles, and the demand for democracy and accountability.

Since the mid-twentieth century, when most African states gained independence from colonial rule, the practice of democracy has been an issue. Africa is a plural society with different political systems, making the practice of democracy, in its liberal definition, a challenging one. While elements of democracy existed among the various polities in the pre-colonial period, the introduction of the Western political system, through colonialism, brought about significant political changes with which Africans had to grapple. Changing from the old political order of monarchy to the parliamentary system, African leaders and peoples have faced the challenges of implementing the Western form of democracy. While colonialism helped to introduce a new political framework in Africa, it was not necessarily in the context of democracy.

As the euphoria of independence died down, and the reality of governance dawned on the emerging political leaders, it became important to fashion politics on the Western model, align with the democratic states of the world, and adopt democratic principles. It did not take long for many independent African states to be engulfed in ethnic conflicts, economic problems, and political instability, all spurred on by bad governance and corruption. These, and other issues, led to military intervention, which delayed or completely halted attempts to integrate democratic practices into African political culture. The military in politics is a fundamental violation of a democratic system, since military rule is by decree, not by law. As the military gained political control, they suspended democracy, especially between the 1970s and 1990s. Politics will be more democratic and stable if there is a balanced interaction between the government and the people. African states are experiencing pervasive unrest and political explosions partly because of the wanton violation of democratic ideals.

People need to be politically empowered; they should be able to enjoy their fundamental rights, and derive the benefits of democracy.

The contributors to this important book have demonstrated the changes and challenges that are associated with democracy in contemporary Africa. Drs. Saliba Sarsar and Julius O. Adekunle and their contributors are aware of the complexities of the principles and practices of democracy; they have clearly examined how the African countries represented in this book deal with the challenges of democracy. Other African nations have similar political and democratic conditions as those discussed in this book. What gives this book its uniqueness is the adoption of the Status of Democracy Index (SDI), which has been used to analyze and measure the level of democracy in Africa.

This book is a novelty in its approach and depth of analysis. It offers a new, interesting, and informative path to understanding the dynamics and intricacies of democracy in Africa. The book reveals the hitherto unrecognized extent of the weakness of democracy and brings issues to our attention with unprecedented clarity and precision. It is an eye-opener that urges African political leaders to focus on the various aspects of governance that will promote democracy and political stability.

Toyin Falola
University of Texas at Austin
Vice President, International
Scientific Committee
UNESCO's Slave Route Project

Acknowledgments

Democracy in Africa is the result of a collaborative effort among scholars who are deeply interested in understanding and strengthening the democratic structures and processes in Africa. The authors' names appear atop the individual chapters; their ideas provide a fresh look at the concept and practice of democracy, and how its challenges can be overcome. We extend to them our heartfelt thanks for their incisive analyses and their patience during the process of editing and producing this book. We are grateful to Dr. Toyin Falola for his strong interest in our work, as well as for authoring the Foreword. We also wish to express our gratitude to Ms. Maria Geiger for her great assistance in meticulously editing and proofreading the manuscript. Along with the contributors, we thank Carolina Academic Press for accepting to publish this book. Last but not least, we appreciate our respective spouses, Hiyam Z. Sarsar and Esther A. Adekunle, for their encouragement and support.

Saliba Sarsar and
Julius O. Adekunle

Introduction

Saliba Sarsar

Democracy is easier to understand than to live. It is not a quick fix, or to be practiced only on election days. It is a generational project that must be anchored in the participation of citizens, accountability of rulers, open economies, and just societies.

Democracy cannot be achieved through manipulated elections or rubber-stamp parliaments. For any country to have democracy, its political structures must be based on a multiparty system without ideological disqualifiers. Its elections must be free, frequent, and fair in order to ensure the consent of the governed. Its judiciary must be independent, and must apply the rule of law in an equitable and impartial manner. Its fundamental individual civil liberties and political rights, such as freedom of expression and assembly, must be protected. Its citizens' human rights, religious freedoms, human development, and economic freedoms must all be guaranteed.

For democracy to work, all major political factions, including opposition groups, must agree to play by the same rules and uphold the same law. The rule of law is essential as a safeguard against those who would limit democracy to its formal trappings by creating to what amounts to a single party system, or those who would seek power with the intention of ultimately disempowering others.

The African Experience

Generally, African countries have had a less than satisfactory democratic record, essentially caused by both external and internal factors. In Egypt, British colonialism usurped the country's resources, and tolerated royal abuses. This eventually led to a revolution in July 1952, and a succession of authoritarian leaders. A popular uprising in early 2011 enhanced the departure of President Hosni Mubarak after almost 30 years in power. This scenario is similar to what occurred in Tunisia, where President Zein El Abidin Ben Ali left power and the country after 23 years of authoritarian rule.

Cameroon is one of the few countries to be colonized by the three European powers of Germany, France, and Great Britain. In addition, it is a multicultural society with more than 250 ethnic groups, giving it the appellation "Africa in miniature." While multiculturalism has, in many respects, been a blessing to the country, it has also served to impede the practice of multiparty democracy.

In Rwanda, there is no evidence that democracy existed before, during, or after colonialism. The many revolutionary and liberation movements did not produce the good governance that encompasses democracy as one of its main features after independence, as occurred in Eritrea. In Nigeria, the evolution of politics reveals a tendency to oscillate between civilian and military rulers.

More often than not, the beneficiaries of democratization have not been its best promoters. Many of those who benefitted from the democratization efforts in the post-1990 period manipulated the electoral system and the constitution making process in their countries to ensure that they retained power. Moreover, in Kenya and South Africa, elections subsequent to the first multiparty elections have not been characterized by higher electoral quality and enhanced democratic consolidation. The worst-case scenarios involve rulers who refuse to step down peacefully when they lose elections, such as that which occurred in the Ivory Coast in 2011, sparking an all-out civil war.

Botswana has had a good track record of healthy multi-party elections, even though a single party has ruled since independence. Benin led the way in 1991 by changing governments peacefully after the ruling party lost the election. Ghana has achieved some success in democracy and development.

While the path of democratization in Africa has to be designed by Africans, democratic nations around the world have an obligation to help Africans help themselves. The dilemma for the United States and other democratic nations is how to move the pace of democratization forward without risking the chances of extreme parties gaining control of their government via electoral victory.

Focus and Organization of the Volume

This book contains specific analyses of the five main African regions in the northern, western, eastern, central, and southern parts of the continent. Each of the ten representative chapters explores the democratic challenge, specifically in Egypt, Morocco, Nigeria, Cameroon, Rwanda, Eritrea, the Insular States, Tanzania, Namibia, and Zambia.

As a background to the political history of Africa, in Chapter 1, Julius O. Adekunle examines the issues of democracy and cultural change before and during the colonial period. He argues that since the pre-colonial times, Africans practiced democracy in one form or another in both centralized and stateless societies. Drawing on examples from different kingdoms to show how Africans conceived and practiced democracy, he asserts that African cultural practices supported political stability. As examined in this book, he also points out that colonialism and modernization were forces of political change, which caused Africans to adopt new forms of democracy.

In Chapter 2, Saliba Sarsar argues that Egypt's successive leaders have been afraid or reluctant to share power and view democracy in broad and generational terms. Egypt's exponential population growth and its incapacity to provide adequately for its citizens on the one hand, and its difficulty to navigate political Islam while engaging in modernization on the other, have made the democratic challenge even more difficult. For Sarsar, democratic reforms are successful to the extent that the regime introduces policies that ensure a separation of powers among the executive, legislative, and judicial branches of government; protect civil liberties and political rights; encourage the development of new political parties and engage the opposition; allow private media outlets to function and prosper; and build confidence among the Egyptian electorate. Improvements in human rights, religious freedom, human development, and economic freedom will complete the picture by enhancing Egyptian wellbeing and prosperity.

In Chapter 3, Raphael Chijioke Njoku analyzes the twists and turns of Moroccan democracy. He assesses the chances for a successful democratic transition in Morocco in light of the implications of the country's ages-long religious and political culture. The possibility of realizing a successful transition from monarchical authority to democratic governance is unlikely, given the king's unwillingness to relinquish his authority and privileges, as well as the fear he and others have that radical Islamist groups might win a popular election in the manner of the National Liberation Front in neighboring Algeria.

Nigerian politics has been oscillating between civilian and military governments since attaining independence in 1960. The first military coup in January 1966 was the first rude interlude on the nascent democratic government. In Chapter 4, Ngozi Kamalu and Fuabeh Fonge critically examine the level of democracy in Nigeria since 1970, when the Nigerian Civil War that began in 1967 came to an end. The Second Republic, that began in 1979, was characterized by a high level of corruption that led to another military intervention.

The Babangida Administration did not provide a safe gateway to democracy. Thus, the struggle to establish true democracy began in 1999, when the country returned to civilian administration.

The Nigerian quest, however, continually gets interrupted by acts of violence that include political assassinations, harassment, and intimidation. In addition, "godfatherism" and political and economic corruption combine to hinder the smooth running of democracy. Human rights have been violated as a result of prevalent insecurity arising from political violence. Hostage taking, especially in the Niger Delta, inflicts negative effects on the nation's economy. Julius O. Adekunle discusses these problems in Chapter 5, concluding that Nigeria has not scored high marks in terms of democracy.

The elusiveness of democracy exists in Cameroon as well. In Chapter 6, Emmanuel M. Mbah explains that while multiculturalism has been a blessing, it has also served to impede democratization. In particular, the unification of former French and British Cameroons, with their various cultural and colonial backgrounds has been a challenge to governance and democratic practice in Cameroon. It has seriously threatened both the *raison d'être* of that union, and the future of Cameroon. Democracy will materialize only when the dictatorship changes and stops relying on intimidation, brutality and human rights abuses, electoral fraud and corruption, patronage politics, and the constant interference in the constitution to suit the powers that be.

In Chapter 7, Julius O. Adekunle analyzes democracy as it relates to political change in Rwanda. He finds no evidence of it before, during, or after colonialism. The regimes before the genocide of 1994 were too ethnically and politically biased. The process of power-sharing, which emanated from the Arusha Peace Accords—a conflict-resolution strategy designed to end the long standing conflict between the Hutu dominated government and the Tutsi guerrilla fighters—could have promoted democracy, but, apparently, the opponents of power-sharing did not embrace them. The plane crash that killed President Juvénal Habyarimana while returning from signing the Accords and the genocide were a clear revelation of the undemocratic political system in Rwanda. While relative peace and political stability have existed since the end of the genocide, there has been no meaningful democracy.

In Chapter 8, Saba Tesfayohaness Kidane analyzes how democracy is understood in present-day Eritrea, and gives a historical overview of the country before it became a sovereign state in 1993. The Eritrean People's Liberation Front, which later transformed itself into the government of the newly born Eritrea, masterminded the political philosophy and direction of the country. It envisioned a state that is far from the modern concept of the ideal democratic state. With active government involvement in the political, economic, social, and cultural lives of the people in Eritrea, top-bottom style of leadership is the rule, rather than the exception.

In Chapter 9, Jose Adrian Garcia-Rojas presents a more hopeful image of democracy in the African insular microstates of Cape Verde, Mauritius, Sao Tome and Principe, and Seychelles and Comoros. In the last fifteen years, for instance, there has been an increase in the stability of their democratic institutions and party systems. This has been expressed by top rankings among African countries in terms of better governance, more freedom, absence of international sanctions on human rights conventions, and clear legal norms and other democratic parameters. Focusing on the similarities and differences between the insular states, Garcia-Rojas explains how Mauritius has had free elections since its independence, how Cape Verde, Sao Tome and Principe, and Seychelles have enjoyed such elections since 1990, and how Comoros has had a hard time consolidating its democratic institutions and party systems.

Shadrack Wanjala Nasong'o focuses on the relationship between political culture and democratization in Tanzania in Chapter 10. Official corruption and economic and political weaknesses remain key obstacles. His main point is that though much has been achieved along the democratization trajectory, there is still a long way to go before the country reaches the democratic Promised Land.

In Chapter 11, M. Fenyo writes about the paradoxes of democracy in Namibia. Although a single political party has dominated the government since independence, Namibia has a rather successful parliamentary democracy. Despite its unevenly distributed wealth, its progressive constitution has provisions regulating the ownership of the means of production, services, education, health, and civil and human rights.

In Chapter 12, Joshua Kivuva examines Zambia's multiparty politics in a single party political culture. He holds that Zambia has moved beyond the initial phase of democratic transition to a more complex process of democratic consolidation and institutionalization. The process, however, has been sidetracked, although not entirely abandoned. The euphoria and optimism that met the first multiparty elections in the country in 1991 has, to a large extent, evaporated. The main argument is that although Zambia has already held four multiparty elections since 1990, this has been attained without any meaningful democratization taking place.

Status of Democracy Index

History, political context, national economy, party systems, ethnic divisions, and external influences—all have played crucial roles in advancing or retarding Africa's democratization processes and practices. Several of the chapter authors have incorporated into their analyses the Status of Democracy Index (SDI), which was developed by Saliba Sarsar to assess the current state and score of democratic life, and how it can be improved in Middle East countries.[1] Since 2008, the SDI has been applied in order to understand the economics of democracy in Muslim countries. There is a special focus on the relationship between order and security on the one hand, and social harmony and economic prosperity on the other.[2]

The SDI is a composite measure that quantifies democratization through consideration of multiple variables: four variables address governance and representative government. These mark how heads of state and members of the legislature are selected, as well as political party development, suffrage, and the maturity of political rights and civil liberties. The annual Freedom House survey provides a fifth variable measuring media freedom. Measurements of religious liberty can be derived from U.S. Department of State reports. A seventh addresses the observance of human rights with the information from Amnesty International, Human Rights Watch, and the U.S. Department of State. The United Nations Development Program's Human Development Index provides a measurement of human development, and finally, the Heritage Foundation's Index of Economic Freedom quantifies economic freedom.

The Status of Democracy Index assigns each of these nine variables 2 points for a total of 18 points. Each score ranges from 0 to 2, with 0 being nonexistent, and 2 being the highest measurement. For example, if the head of state or legislature is not elected, then that country receives a score of 0. Prohibition of political parties would also equate to a 0, while tight controls would merit a 1, and reasonably free functioning would lead to a 2. Media freedom, religious liberty, and respect for human rights are each easy to quantify: 0 for not free, 1 for partly free, and 2 for free. Human development is scored by level: 0 for low, 1 for medium, and 2 for high. Economic freedom, the last variable, is scored on the level of governmental interference in the economy, with 0 for strong, 1 for moderate, and 2 for low interference. It is then possible to convert the totals to a percentage for easy digestion.

Democracy in Africa

Africa

Madeira Islands
(Portugal)

Canary Islands
(Spain)

MOROCCO

TUNISIA

ALGERIA

LIBYA

EGYPT

WESTERN
SAHARA

MAURITANIA

MALI

NIGER

CHAD

SUDAN

ERITREA

CAPE VERDE

SENEGAL

DJIBOUTI

GAMBIA

BURKINA FASO

GUINEA BISSAU

GUINEA

NIGERIA

SOMALIA

SIERRA LEONE

IVORY
COAST

GHANA

ETHIOPIA

SOUTH SUDAN

LIBERIA

TOGO

BENIN

CAMEROON

CENTRAL AFRICAN REPUBLIC

EQUATORIAL GUINEA

UGANDA

KENYA

SAO TOME & PRINCIPE

GABON

REPUBLIC
OF
THE
CONGO

RWANDA

DEMOCRATIC REPUBLIC
OF THE CONGO

BURUNDI

SEYCHELLES

TANZANIA

COMOROS

ANGOLA

ZAMBIA

MALAWI

MADAGASCAR

MOZAMBIQUE

MAURITIUS

ZIMBABWE

REUNION

NAMIBIA

BOTSWANA

SWAZILAND

SOUTH AFRICA

LESOTHO

Chapter 1

Democracy and Political Change in Pre-Colonial Africa

Julius O. Adekunle

Like all societies in the world, African communities have experienced some socio-political changes and vicissitudes due to pertinent factors such as colonialism and modernization. Adopting a historical perspective, this chapter examines the issues of democracy and political changes that took place in the transition of Africa from the pre-colonial to the colonial times. The political structures in pre-colonial Africa, variously referred to as "chiefdoms," "kingdoms," or "empires," existed in a close-knit relationship with the people, and possessed all the apparatus of the modern state arrangement. In the indigenous African political philosophy, the term democracy may not be prominently used, but traces of democracy can be found. This chapter discusses some of the factors that engendered political changes. The impact of colonialism on the African political systems and the concomitant cultural changes are carefully analyzed. Examples from different parts of Africa illustrate cultural and political changes and developments.

Culture, Politics, and Democracy

Before contact with the Europeans, Africans established numerous independent kingdoms and empires. All of them possessed the trappings of the modern state formation, including elements of democracy. From all indications, the formation of states and political institutions in pre-colonial Africa was not an accident of history, but an integral part of the cultural and political philosophy of the African people. The kingdoms comprised of various ethnic groups with similar socio-cultural or historical backgrounds. They controlled the wealth and the trade routes that originated from their regions and those that passed through their borders. There were both secular and theocratic African states, where governments assumed responsibilities such as maintaining law and order, providing economic opportunities, securing of frontiers, and promoting socio-cultural values. The emergence of urbanized, sophisticated, and orderly societies with political consciousness and socio-cultural interaction supported African awareness of the principles of politics and the application of democracy. The early kingdoms of Kush and Axum in the northeast, Ghana, Mali, and Songhay empires in the west, and the numerous Bantu kingdoms, such as the Congo, Luba, Lunda, Lozi, Mwenemutapa, and Rwanda in eastern and southern Africa represented the centralized political arrangements of pre-colonial Africa. Elements of democracy can be gleaned from all of the African political structures.

Democracy deals with governing a society with respect to the fundamental rights of the people. It guarantees and defends people's freedom. While no written constitutions existed in the African indigenous cultural and political setup, various institutions were set in place to respect and protect people's rights and freedom. Variations occurred in the interpretation and practice of democracy because of the differences in political organizations: there were centralized and stateless societies. Each African society, however, operated on a system of government where rules, laws, and traditions were the guiding principles. Although warfare occurred primarily for political and economic reasons, in many cases there was conflict resolution and peaceful coexistence.

Given the prevalent practice of absolutism by the rulers of various African societies, it will be misleading to argue that no form of democracy existed in Africa before the Europeans arrived and imposed their colonial rule based on the Western model of democracy. The colonization of Africa took place between the late nineteenth and early twentieth century, but the political systems in Africa had existed centuries before then. Democracy in Africa in the pre-colonial times should be examined in the context of the cultural, social, and political values of Africans, and not the Western model. Also, Africa did not, and does not, exist as a monolithic society. Hence, the political systems in Africa cannot be treated as a single unit. Variations in socio-political structures make the generalization misleading, but traces of democratic principles and values are discernible. For example, political discussions were openly held, religious practice and social life were not regulated by the government, issues of war and peace constituted part of open discourse, and offenders were given fair trial in the justice system. Women, to a certain extent, also had political influence.

Culturally, Africans accorded their rulers with high respect and honor, believing that their authority to rule was divinely ordained. Because of the hereditary and monarchical system, the king was not elected, but selected by a group of "king makers." While the non-participation of the people in the selection of their ruler is un-democratic in the modern context of democracy, the king was not expected to ignore the wisdom of his advisors and the wishes of his entire people. The success of the king's reign depended largely on his wit, charisma, and ability to work with his council of chiefs. These qualities often helped in leading the people not only politically, but also religiously and in wars. While the king was at the top of the political hierarchical structure, he "did not carry the government upon his shoulders."[1] He delegated powers to his advisory council, officers, and subordinate chiefs. In this respect, the king ruled through the participation and counsel of the chiefs who were representatives of the people. This approach is best represented by the African saying, "a tree does not make a forest." Although culturally invested with extensive political powers, the king could not afford to be autocratic.

In Athens (where the concept of democracy began), not all the citizens participated directly in the political system because equality and franchise were not extended to all the people. While only male adult citizens were allowed direct participation and voted on government policy, women and slaves were denied. Thus, the marginalization of women and slaves limited the application and practice of democracy in Athenian society. Following several criticisms of democracy, the Greeks abandoned it. However, the concept was revisited during the Age of Enlightenment. The argument centered on the equality of all people to have freedom, and a government that is chosen by popular consent. The different definitions and application of democracy make it a fluid political concept. When it is applied to pre-colonial Africa, certain principles of democracy are found in the different political systems.

Political Power and Democracy

Two types of political structures will be examined to underscore how democracy was practiced in the pre-colonial times: the centralized and the stateless. As mentioned above, early African kingdoms included the Kush and Axum in the northeast, the Ghana, Mali, Songhay, Oyo (in western Africa), and the numerous Bantu empires. These were kingdoms where the centralized political system, with the king at the head of the hierarchy, was adopted. Features of centralized governments included a complex system of governance and political institutions with clearly defined functions (no distinct separation of powers existed as in most democratic societies).

In these empires, religion and politics went hand in hand, but institutions were created to protect the rights of the people and to check the arbitrary use of political power and authority. In the Hausa states of Nigeria and Islamic states of northern and eastern Africa, the theocratic system of government came into being with the adoption of Islamic principles. In the Swahili states of eastern Africa, the Shirazi dynasty ruled through Islamic principles until the Portuguese overthrew them. In West Africa, the various nineteenth century jihads brought about cultural and political changes. For example, the Sokoto jihad that began in 1804 was led by Usman dan Fodio, and resulted in the overthrow of the Habe rulers and the establishment of Islamic laws and principles. Similarly, the Massina jihad, led by Seku Ahmadu, and the Tukulor jihad, under the leadership of Al-Hajj Umar, brought about significant political changes in the Massina and Tukulor kingdoms, respectively.

In all of these places, there were traces of democratic principles, even though the political system was autocratic and theocratic in outlook. Rulers often engaged in dialogue with subordinate chiefs and military officials to resolve conflicts and seek peace. There were provisions to check arbitrary rulers and abuse of power.

The Oyo Empire was one of the African centralized political organizations where the king (the alaafin) headed the administration, and theoretically held absolute powers, but ruled with the assistance of two councils: the Ogboni and Oyo Mesi. As Robert Rotberg put it, "The [alaafin] owed his election to provincial councillors and possessed absolutist powers, the secular and supernatural exercise of which was curtailed only in part by an aggregate of institutionalized checks."[2] The Ogboni and Oyo Mesi Councils were the institutionalized agencies of check to provide a balance of political power. The king did not take major decisions unilaterally, but in consultation with the council of chiefs. Theoretically, the alaafin was not bound to take to the counsel of the chiefs but, in practice, he could not afford to ignore them because he relied on them for his peaceful and successful reign as well as for the execution of military campaigns.

There was a religious dimension to the confirmation of the selected candidate for the throne. The Ifa Oracle occupied a conspicuous position in finalizing important decision-making. This religious-political approach, to a large extent, demonstrated that the Oyo people developed a concept of democracy based on decisions, not taken by all the people, but that were for the benefit of all the people. Even before a candidate for the position was selected as a king, the Ifa Oracle would be consulted. Since the king must be chosen from the ruling family, the people did not have any say in the matter. Because of the political structure, the alaafin's subjects simply had to submit to the will of their leader. From this perspective, the Oyo system of government was more of absolutism than of democracy. However, for the unwritten constitution that provided for checks and balances, the system portrays the principles of democracy. It is often said that "power corrupts and absolute power corrupts absolutely,"[3] but this cannot be totally applied to Oyo political situation because of the entrenched limitations to the exercise of the alaafin's power. If the alaafin held absolute powers in theory, he did not in practical terms.

The Oyo Mesi Council checked the political powers of the alaafin. As powerful as the alaafin was, he could not remove the principal members of his cabinet, except in cases of death because they held hereditary posts. Even when disagreements occurred with the alaafin, members of the council retained their positions, but the Ogboni cult intervened. Part of the functions of Ogboni society was the promotion of social harmony, peace, and cooperation on matters that affected the people. Thus, if an alaafin became too arbitrary, he could be opposed, or removed for the good of the people. Indeed, the alaafin could be forced to commit suicide.[4] The process was not that simple. The alaafin held the constitutional right to mention a member of the Oyo Mesi to die with him. Here, the "checks and balances" system becomes ostensible. Essentially, neither the Oyo Mesi nor the Ogboni could dispose of the other without appropriate constraint. Because members of the Oyo Mesi were close to the people, they represented the voice of the nation and "the king must take counsel with them whenever any important matter affecting the state occurs."[5]

Stateless Societies

More has been written on the centralized than on the decentralized states of Africa. One of the main reasons is the abundance of oral traditions from the royal and commoner sources in the centralized states. Since Africa is a continent of diversity, the political system of the stateless societies cannot be ignored. In the non-centralized societies, such as the Bedouin Arabs in northern Africa, the Nuer and Dinka of Sudan, the Masai of East Africa, the pastoral nomadic Somali of northern Somali, and the Igbo and Tiv of Nigeria, there were no formal, complex, or well-defined institutions of government. They also did not have an institutionalized judicial system, yet they maintained strong and orderly societies with relatively peaceful relations. Anthropologists refer to these societies as acephalous, polycephalic, or segmentary. John Middleton and David Tait described these societies as "tribes without rulers," signifying leadership by many clan or lineage heads rather than by kings in an elaborate political system.[6] In the stateless societies, there were no kings, no subordinate rulers, and no official officeholders. Referring to the pastoral Somali, I. M. Lewis pointed out that the people did not have "any administrative hierarchy of officials and no institutionalized positions of leadership to direct their affairs."[7]

Instead, representatives of the different segments or villages composed the political community; usually, they were adult males. All adult men possessed the right to speak on political matters of the community and to belong to councils that had specific assignments. Basically, kinship constituted the hallmark of their political arrangement, and all lineages trace their descent to a common ancestor. While lineage heads were not elected as it occurs in modern day democratic societies, human rights were respected, security was provided, and peaceful co-existence among lineages was promoted. The lineage head indirectly performed judicial, political, and social functions in concert with other people. This shows that in stateless societies, politics were egalitarian and people were involved in the affairs of the community.

According to Middleton and Tait, rather than control from a ruling body, "the relations of local groups to one another are seen as a balance of power, maintained by competition between them."[8] There was a consensus on the rules that guided the behavior of the people. The rules and regulations were maintained not through a government or law enforcement agency, but by control through a group of lineage heads. The Igbo in eastern Nigeria provide a good example of a stateless society. They "developed a complex system in which separate extended family groups balanced political relations within the larger [Igbo] unit."[9] The political system was based on village government. Village councils, elders, and lineage heads performed leadership roles with no investiture of formal political authority. Hence, rather than a king in the centralized states, the village councils functioned as a political unit. Joseph Harris points out that the "village assembly characterized [Igbo] democracy," and he explains further that:

> The elders presented issues to the people, everyone had a right to speak, and decisions had to be unanimous. The village assembly therefore was a body in which the young and old, the rich and poor could be heard. Every citizen's participation was possible and important. Decision-making could often be time-consuming, but the slow procedure itself guaranteed greater individual participation.[10]

Other agencies of political democracy in the Igbo society were the titleholders and age-set organizations. Holding a title was not only prestigious, but also political. A hierarchy of titleholders existed in ascending order, and the ceremony before acquiring the title was accompanied by complex religious rites. Leaders of these numerous organizations ensured that their members maintained law and order, and helped in community development such as the construction of roads and bridges. Age-sets participated in sports competition such as wrestling. They also assisted in maintaining the marketplace, which was the social and political center of the Igbo.

In judicial matters, the first person responsible for settling disputes was the lineage head. The head of the most senior lineage held the staff of authority. According to Daryll Forde and G.I. Jones, the lineage head held the authority to arbitrate in internal disputes, as well as represent his lineage on external matters. He served as an intermediary between the lineage and its ancestors, and he alone was allowed to intercede at the shrine of the founder of the lineage. Wives and members of a lineage, and other co-residents, are subject to the authority of the lineage head, but the heads of their own lineages held the authority to intervene on their behalf.[11]

If the dispute remained un-resolved, it was referred to the elders. In cases pertaining to the declaration of war, adult male members of the community made the decisions. Leadership in wars was not a permanent or hereditary position. Disputes between two villages were often settled through consultation with the oracles. The Igbo people maintained a network of oracles, notably the Agbala of Awku and the Ibibi Ukpabe at Arochukwu. The religious dimension to the judicial system made the people believe in the judgment of the oracles. Harris made an important point that relates well with the democratic nature of the Igbo and indeed the stateless societies. He points out that:

> While the [Igbo] did not evolve a bureaucratic state system of government, they were indeed a dynamic and influential people. Their oracle system, the [Igbo] language, the recognition of ethnic loyalty and mutual obligation contributed to a cohesiveness within which the [Igbo] clearly emerged as a strongly egalitarian and competitive people, believing that all citizens had a right to be heard in their society.[12]

The competition between lineages did not signify chaos or disorder, but unwritten laws and consensus agreement were put into effective use to guide political and social relations. In their study of African stateless societies, Paul Bohanna and Philip Curtin point out that:

> Law in stateless society was almost as effective [as in centralized society] but worked differently. Since there is no monolithic power system in the stateless society, agreement must be reached by consensus, or else by compromise. The two contenders must be brought together in agreement, or at least concurrence, about what is to take place. The principles on which such concurrence is based are usually not as overt as is law in a state society. Although the principles by means of which compromises are concurrence are reached are well known and overt.[13]

Mention can also be made of the Anang, an agricultural ethnic group in southern Nigeria, which was led by a chief (an influential person), elected from the most important lineages. Among the Anang, religion, politics, and social life was regulated, not by political authorities, but by secret societies, particularly the *ekpo*. A council of elders assisted the chief in performing his daily political and religious duties. Justice in the Anang society was the community's responsibility:

> A group of individuals, called the *esop*, meets weekly and is composed of elderly men and women. Although women are present, they may only participate when they testify as witnesses or if they are called upon to advise the court on a proper verdict in the case of another woman. Children are also barred from participation unless they have a specific role to play as witnesses.[14]

Aside from the lineage setting, there was the village group, which served as the highest political unit in some stateless societies. The village group comprised of a cluster of villages with a common meeting place that was used for judicial, political, and social matters. Disputes were usually peacefully resolved, compensations were paid to deserving people, and sanctions were placed on the guilty party. Punishments often included any labor that would benefit the entire community. Thus, in stateless societies there were institutionalized provisions for social justice, especially in resolving disputes or stopping acts of violence. Similarly, among the Bedouin Arabs of northern Africa, kinship and lineage relations were important. Disputes were settled amicably, lineage interests were carefully pursued, and justice and order were regarded as a collective responsibility.[15]

Like other African pastoral people who did not practice the central administrative system, the Abashieni in western Kenya recognized the leadership of Omwami Omukhongo, who was regarded as the "great ruler," even though he did not possess absolute political powers. Omwami Omukhongo's:

> decisions represented an expression of consensus among the heads of the clans or subclans involved in a particular dispute. In other words [he] formulated an opinion only after painstaking consultation with numerous elders. If a case involved many individuals or groups, he would convene a mass assembly in order to assess popular sentiment.[16]

This egalitarian approach to governance, which was characteristic of stateless societies, suggests that power was leveled within, not from above.

Islamic States

With the Arab conquest of North Africa in the seventh century, Islam spread rapidly, and brought about discernible socio-political changes among the Arabs and Berbers. As in the Arabian Peninsula, Islamic principles were adopted, and conversion to Islam was a requirement for obtaining high political offices. Islam became a means of legitimizing political authority. By the nineteenth century, Islam had become a dominant force in the political development of not only northern Africa, but also central, eastern, and western Africa. Rulers played politics of religion and trade, and dealt with Islamic cultural diffusion. Muslim clerics, teachers, and administrators assumed high political positions. Conflicts between traditional worshipers and Muslim fundamentalists became widespread. Caliphates and emirates were established to prevent the contamination of Islam with traditional religion. It was within this framework that the Sokoto, Massina, and Bambara Muslim states evolved during the nineteenth century in West Africa.[17]

The adoption of a theocratic form of administration, using the Shari'a (Islamic Law), means politics and religion are intertwined in Islamic states. For example, in the Sokoto caliphate, the head of the political structure was the caliph on whom all powers and authorities resided. The ruler combined religious leadership and political authority, and received obedience and loyalty from all of his officials and subjects. As the religious leader, the ruler ensured that the tenets of Islam were strictly observed as prescribed in the Qur'an. He also ensured adequate protection of the Muslims. As the political leader, he made sure that the principles of the Shari'a were applied in the justice system. In the administration, there were officials who carried out various functions for the smooth daily running of state affairs. In performing these religious and political duties, the ruler employed the right people; those who were versed in the Qur'an and well trained in the Shari'a. He employed trusted people, and had to always remember to watch over the state affairs in order to keep his officials on the alert in the performance of their duties.

Democracy embraces and promotes secularism and religious toleration, but the relationship between Islam and democracy is complex and requires a careful examination. Since there was no uniformity in the political system of the Islamic states in pre-colonial Africa, it is not appropriate to argue that Islamic states were completely un-democratic because of the adoption of Islamic principles.[18]

Women in African Politics

Politics in the pre-colonial Africa did not exclude women. In many respects, the women played a significant role in the culture and politics of their respective societies. However, each society determined how involved women were, especially in politics. Because men and women participated in politics in different capacities, Audrey Smock contends that, "whatever the system may be, the position of women within it is neither superior nor inferior to that of the men, but simply different and complementary."[19] This suggests that Africans were not only conscious of, but also adopted democratic principles.

Some African women held influential political positions. For example, the Mende of Sierra Leone created positions for female chiefs who were in charge of female affairs. The Queen Mother wielded strong political influence as a kingmaker among the Asante of modern day Ghana.[20] Similarly, the Yoruba of southwestern Nigeria had Royal Mothers. In the Nupe Kingdom, the King's mother, sister, and aunt all enjoyed political powers. The rise of Zaria, as a powerful Hausa state in northern Nigeria in the sixteenth century, has been attributed to Barkwa Turunda, a powerful female political leader. Her daughter, Amina, became the most recognized female political ruler of Zaria. Amina waged several military campaigns against the Nupe and Jukun, whom she defeated. She is remembered as the builder of the spectacular city wall around Zaria. As Robert July pointed out in the Kongo kingdom, "Queen mothers or royal women were important advisors to the crown, acting also sometimes as heads of households or governors of outlying provinces."[21]

Africans are referred to as incurably religious. Religion determined and regulated almost every action of Africa. The existence and recognition of gods and goddesses, as well as priests and priestesses, attest to the gender equality in African religious system. Colonialism did little to change the culture of spirituality of Africans and the religious role of the women. The coming of Islam and the introduction of Christianity did not displace the conspicuous position of women in religion. In post-colonial Africa, women, in particular, played and continue to play significant religious roles in their respective societies. One of the goddesses among the Yoruba is Osun, the goddess of the Osun River. Known for her benevolence, Osun is referred to as the goddess of fertility. Barren women usually sacrifice at the Osun Shrine to request children through her priests and priestesses. Her devotees believe that Osun provides protection from evil occurrences.[22]

Economic Freedom

Economic activities are as old as human existence in Africa. From all indications, the African economy was not stagnant. Instead, it was dynamic — changing, growing, and meeting the needs of the people. From the hunter-gatherer stage, Africans moved to a subsistence economy, to an exchange of goods, and finally to a market economy. Africans adopted a free economic policy whereby people engaged in lawful productive activities—free enterprise. As a result, agriculture thrived, fishing flourished, and commerce expanded because of the unrestricted production, distribution, and consumption of goods. It would appear that geographical environment or vegetation zone, rather than political control, determined the occupational activities and commercial pursuit of the people. For example, the open savanna region in West Africa, with its fertile land, permitted the practice of agriculture, the growth of trade, and the establishment of political organizations. Also, access to the Indian Ocean prompted the growth of trade between the Swahili states and the Arabs, Persians, and Indians in eastern Africa.

The African economy was closely tied to the political system. Kings, believed to own the land and all its resources, controlled the economy. For example, the rulers of the Ghana, Mali, and Songhay empires in West Africa effectively controlled the trans-Saharan trade that developed between North and West Africa where gold (mined in the Wangara region) was exchanged for salt (from Taghaza and Taodeni). Writing on West African trade in the precolonial times, Christopher Fyfe contended that:

> Stages of the gold trade were channelled through a central emporium, a vast market where all the traders had to congregate to meet their customers. From it, the king drew immense wealth. He established the right to own all gold nuggets; others might only trade in gold dust. In this way, he kept control over the value of gold. If the supply of gold nuggets became excessive he would hoard them until the supply was less, or the demand greater, thus preventing inflation. He also levied duties on other export commodities.[23]

The type of political system adopted—centralized or stateless—did not interfere with African economic growth or dynamism. Along with the presence of natural resources, African entrepreneurial skills and styles became vital factors in mobilizing other factors of production, and in facilitating economic growth.

By the nineteenth century, the African economy positively responded to innovative ideas, especially with the use of currency. Hitherto, various things such as salt, cowries, and metals served as the medium of exchange. But, with the abolition of the trans-Atlantic slave trade and the beginning of legitimate trade by the Europeans, new forms of currency were introduced. The imperial powers (such as Great Britain, France, and Portugal) introduced cash crops and wage labor, thereby redirecting African economic orientation. To facilitate the economy, the Europeans constructed roads, bridges, and railroads. They introduced their currencies for the payment of taxation. These changes served as a means of connecting the African economy to the global market. Instead of African rulers, the Europeans dominated the economy because they controlled the global market.

Education

One of the indices of democracy in contemporary times is education. In every society, education is one of the vehicles through which political activities and rights are promoted. Education permits political awareness, as well as an understanding of human rights. However, education in traditional African societies differed in content, methodology, and purpose from Western education. In African traditional societies, education was pragmatic and informal, but freely provided. It was an education provided by society for the benefit of the individual and society. While the society planned the curriculum, parents, elders, and other members of the society served as teachers. The education was designed not only to prepare the youth for the future, but also to empower them to become functional members of society. It was an all-embracing and multi-disciplinary education that taught economics, politics, socialization, and even military service. As indicated elsewhere, "The socio-cultural or political milieu, in most cases, determined the type of education that was transmitted. For example, a child who grew up among the Khoisan of southern Africa learned hunting, a Fulani child learned cattle rearing, an Asante or Yoruba child learned farming, and a Dyula [Wangara] child learned trading."[24] Along this line is the political or administrative education that princes received in the palace. The concept of community and collective responsibility was applied to African education. Hence, the African saying, "it takes a village to raise a child."

While African education was not geared toward office jobs, it prepared the individual for industrial, commercial, and military services. It also prepared the person to take leadership roles within a given society. Because of this all-around education, an African was able to freely participate and meaningfully contribute to political discourse. Although it was provided in an informal setting, the African education was suitable to African needs.

Islamic education came along with the introduction of Islam. Islamic literacy was more narrowly focused than African traditional education, since its primary objective was to teach the doctrines and practices of Islam. Unlike traditional education, Islamic education was formal, but like traditional education, it adopted the memorization method. Students and converts to Islam memorized the Qur'an. Like African education, Islamic education was not directed at securing office jobs. Western education, pioneered by Christian missions and missionaries, came with colonialism, and transformed not only the traditional and Islamic form of education, but also other aspects of African life. Western education has been one of the lasting legacies of colonialism in Africa.

Human Rights

Africans placed a high premium on human existence and fundamental human rights. However, human rights were often lacking in literary analyses in pre-colonial Africa. Vincent Nmehielle points out that the concept of human rights in pre-colonial Africa is controversial. Western scholars, who are skeptical of African socio-political and judicial systems, claim that human rights did not exist in pre-colonial Africa. Nmehielle used Rhoda Howard and Jack Donnelly as examples of Western writers who argued that what existed in Africa was human dignity rather than human rights. This Western stance is an extension of the old argument that Africa did not produce any civilization, or contribute to the development of the world. The argument denies Africans of their ingenuity and sense of law and order. Nmehielle argues on the contrary, by pointing out that:

> The existence of law in pre-colonial Africa was a result of the stage of development of its societies in that era. Thus, in Africa, while one may agree that the predominant socio-economic formations before colonial penetration were communalism, slave-owning societies, and feudalism, laws had to, and did, exist to govern these societies and the relations within them.[25]

It should be emphasized that Africans believed in the right of individuals to exist, own property, associate, and pursue economic activities for their livelihood. Kings neither dictated nor imposed any of these on their subjects.

The trans-Atlantic slave trade between the fifteenth and nineteenth centuries rudely interrupted the social, economic, and political life of Africans. The Europeans violated the economic rights of Africans by turning them (Africans) into commodities. With the brutality that accompanied the slave trade, it was apparent that the Europeans neither recognized nor respected African human rights. The end of the slave trade was the start of legitimate commerce. Although Africans were no longer bought as articles of trade, their economic rights were not restored because the Europeans imposed their economic interests by forcing Africans to produce cash crops that were sold at very cheap prices. Again, Africans lost their political rights with the commencement of colonial rule. Thus, the Europeans infringed on the fundamental rights of Africans with their undemocratic economic, political, and social control.

Colonialism and Political Change

Although some African human and political values were compatible with the principles of democracy, a change occurred with the advent of the Europeans and the subsequent establishment of colonial rule (with its Western political system) at the beginning of the twentieth century. It was a change from the independent kingdoms, with their monarchical forms of government, to the imposed Western political system. The change brought about a political challenge to Africans to adjust to the new form of government. All over Africa, the Europeans consolidated and increased their political power while they limited the political role of African traditional rulers. The Europeans did not give any consideration to the values of the pre-existing political system since they claimed theirs was better. Even with the establishment of colonial rule, it can be argued that democracy was not in full operation because colonialism was imposed on the African people. Africans did not elect the colonial officials, Africans were limited in the administration of their own affairs, and Africans held no freedom in political matters.

For convenience of their administration, the British, French, and Belgians adopted one form of indirect rule or the other. Some African traditional rulers were used to ruling their people, but with instructions from the colonial masters. This meant that the traditional rulers were not allowed to use their own initiatives to govern, but had to comply with the rules and regulations dictated to them by the colonial authorities. Thus, the Native Authority system increased the political advantage of the Europeans. Traditional rulers were saddled with the responsibilities of maintaining law and order and collecting taxes, which went to the Native Treasuries. In this respect, Africans lost the opportunity to develop their erstwhile democratic principles, but were forced to submit to colonial domination.

With colonialism ushering in the Western parliamentary system, emerging African states and their leaders were forced to make political adjustments in order to be in tune with the rest of democratic societies. The change in political practice led Africans in the post-colonial period to vote and elect their leaders in a democratic way. Human rights became more prominent, women became more viaible in politics, and education became an instrument of gaining political positions and power. Women had the right to vote, as well as to run for and hold office. Religious freedom, which had been an integral part of African philosophy, continued. As in the pre-colonial times, Africans continued in their economic interests, but had to pay taxes to the government.

Conclusion

This chapter has examined politics and democracy in pre-colonial Africa, with a focus on two main forms of political structures: centralized and stateless. The place of democracy in the Islamic states has also been discussed. In the different political arrangements, the people conformed to the rules and regulations of their societies. Multiple influences, such as religion, aggressive neighbors, and changing economic patterns, dictated the political philosophy of the African states and their response to situations in pre-colonial times. Numerous political organizations existed as autonomous states, and adopted different political systems.

Whether in the centralized or stateless societies, the concept of democracy in pre-colonial Africa was based on the socio-political values of the community. The diversity in terms of clans, lineages, and villages did not preclude the participation of the people, at different levels or ways, in the political, economic, and social development of their respective communities. Thus, politics were community-centered, and governments were sustained through the collaboration of the rulers and the ruled. This suggests that Africans viewed democracy and politics as a communal and collective duty. While individual responsibilities and accomplishments were recognized, government involved collective participation. In centralized states, the kings provided political leadership, while in the stateless societies, the elders served as heads. Altogether, many people were involved, although not on equal basis, in the political arrangement.

The coming of the Europeans in the second half of the nineteenth century marked the beginning of the loss of power and political change and challenges for African rulers and their subjects. By the turn of the twentieth century, the Europeans consolidated and increased their political power, while they significantly limited the role of African traditional rulers. As the Europeans established their firm economic and political control, they introduced their own form of democracy, while not completely displacing the African concept of democracy.

In the contemporary African political system, the concept of hereditary kingship has become unfashionable. However, in African traditional settings, kings and chiefs still exist, profoundly influencing their people, but with diminished powers and prestige from the government. The shift from the indigenous form of democracy to the modern one is a by-product of colonial rule. This suggests that the main political framework of the political systems of modern Africa was a legacy of European colonialism.

While it is not clearly expressed in Western interpretation and application, Africans conceived and adopted the concept of democracy in their political practice. The elements and indices of democracy, such as economic freedom, religious freedom, fundamental human rights, and freedom of association, were present in one form or another in the pre-colonial African political systems. African societies could be said to be democratic in outlook because of people's participation in politics. In a democratic system, governance is a shared responsibility because different political institutions perform different functions for the good of all. Pre-colonial African political systems were dynamic, and they responded to changes and new challenges, especially with the introduction of colonialism. African cultures infused communal values into their political practices, thus blending with the European interpretation of democracy. Africans experienced serious challenges in the transition from pre-colonial to colonial political systems. They resisted European political domination, but because their resistance failed, they then had to adjust and address the political changes and challenges, ultimately conforming to the Western form of democratic rule.

Egypt

Chapter 2

Egypt: A Long Way to Go before Democracy Succeeds

Saliba Sarsar

Egyptians, with the youth leading the way, finally came out of their political silence. With shouts and tweets, with microphones and placards, with children on their shoulders, with hands interlocked in unity and hope, they took to the streets on January 25, 2011. Inspired by "Tunisia's Revolution" that terminated the presidency of authoritarian leader Zine El Abidine Ben Ali, they advanced toward Cairo's Midan al-Tahrir (Liberation Square). Similar demonstrations occurred in other cities, including Alexandria and Suez. Even though there was intermittent violence, they persisted, with their fellow citizens and the sympathetic media validating their struggle.

A patient, passionate, and tolerant people, the Egyptians exercised their personal and political will to speak out against repression and a weak economy that have beset their country for years. Their voice—not only their viewpoint—rebelled against historic injustices, poverty, and pain, and asserted its rightful place in the collective national journey toward a brighter future.

On February 11, 2011, after eighteen days of street demonstrations, marches, rallies, acts of civil disobedience, labor strikes, and even some violent clashes that resulted in many deaths and injuries, a major change took place. President Hosni Mubarak resigned after almost 30 years in power, leaving Egypt in the care of the Egyptian Supreme Council of the Armed Forces (SCAF) that consists of military officers who control the country's powerful armed forces.

On March 19, 2011, some 18 million Egyptians voted on a referendum on constitutional amendments. While opponents argued that the timeframe was inadequate to enable political parties to organize, over 77 percent were in favor of changes that eliminate restrictions on political rights and allow for parliamentary and presidential elections before the end of 2011. On August 3, 2011, former president Mubarak was put on trial and charged with conspiring to kill over 800 protesters and abusing power to amass wealth by corrupt means. He pleaded "not guilty." If convicted, he faces 15 years in prison, or the death penalty. For abusing power, Mubarak and his two sons—who have been named co-defendants—if convicted, face five to 15-year sentences.

While tomorrow's news has yet to be experienced, what is evident is that more change will be forthcoming. If the revolution of unfulfilled expectations is to lead to the land of promise, then Egyptians will have to choose well as they transition to democratic rule. In addition to walking the arduous road of democratic transformation, they will need to continue practicing leadership and sustaining their commitment in support of good governance and in defense of pluralism. Good governance assures accountability, effectiveness, rule of law, and transparency; pluralism empowers citizens by not only accommodating their differences, but also by embracing them. Citizenship should be the only criterion for inclusion in the national community. Obviously, this best-case scenario might not see the light of day if an exclusionary, theocratic regime (as practiced in Iran), is allowed to take hold in Egypt, or if a strong military continues to dictate daily affairs.

The popular uprising in Egypt is impressive, especially when put in the context of the country's history. Over the years, Egypt has attempted to introduce elements of democratization such as a multi-party system and free elections. However, it remained undemocratic, or what Daniel Brumberg calls a liberalized autocracy, one that moderates authoritarianism with pluralism.[1] Egypt's authoritarian nature was endemic, with reasons ranging from political economy realities[2] to national identity and culture.[3]

Nevertheless, the responsibility for democracy-building ultimately rests with national leaders who are neither afraid nor unwilling to share power and think of democracy in broad and generational terms. Since the overthrow of the monarchy on July 23, 1952, and following a brief rule by General Mohammed Naguib, Egypt has had three strong presidents, a tightly controlled political party system and parliament, few civil and political rights, a restricted media, and limited freedoms and human development. Moreover, Egypt's internal and external relations since the 1952 Revolution were greatly influenced by two superpowers, the Soviet Union from the mid-1950s to the early 1970s, and the United States from the early 1970s until today.

Egypt currently faces many challenges. First among them are its exponential population growth, and its inability to provide adequately for its citizens. Second is Egypt's identity and ability to navigate political Islam on the one hand, and its willingness to engage in modernization and democratization on the other hand, which will be the main focus of this chapter.

Egypt is at the center of three circles: Africa, the Middle East, and the Islamic world. Situated in the extreme northeastern corner of Africa, it borders the

Mediterranean Sea between Libya and the Palestinian Gaza Strip, the Red Sea north of Sudan, and the Sinai Peninsula. Known for the Nile River running northward through it, and for its great civilization and rich culture, it is the third most populous country in Africa (after Nigeria and Ethiopia), and the most populous in the Middle East with over 82 million people. The population lives on 4 percent of the total land area of around 386,000 square miles, mainly along the Nile River. The remaining 96 percent is uninhabitable desert.[4]

Presidents and Presidential Power

Egypt became a British protectorate in 1882. It did not achieve independence until February 28, 1922, and then full sovereignty in 1956, when it nationalized the Suez Canal. Three authoritarian leaders ruled Egypt for over five and a half decades: Gamal Abdel Nasser (1954–1970), with his military-led government, Arab socialist economy, and pan-Arabism; Anwar al-Sadat (1970–1981), with his strong presidential system and open-door policies; and Hosni Mubarak (1981–2011), with his state of emergency that placed restrictions on civil and political liberties amid major socioeconomic problems.

Nasser, who was the eldest son of a village postal clerk and a graduate of the Egyptian Military Academy, led the Free Officers who forced King Farouk to abdicate on July 23, 1952; he formally abolished the constitutional monarchy in 1954. For him, the monarchy represented corruption, feudalism, foreign rule, stagnation, and weakness.

With complete executive and military powers as Egypt's president, prime minister, and head of the Revolutionary Command Council, Nasser "set out to forge an authoritarian state, impose an etatist-populist revolution from above, and challenge Western control of the Middle East."[5] He empowered the masses by giving form to their cultural and historical identity as Arab, African, and Muslim, separate from Western dictation and manipulation. The strength of his charisma and power, however, did not help develop serious political participation and the proper functioning of civil society. A secular political leader, he disagreed with the traditional Muslim philosophy of fusing politics and religion, and persecuted the Muslim Brotherhood that opposed him. Moreover, Nasser had no confidence or trust in political parties. After declaring all such parties illegal, he established the Arab Socialist Union (ASU), a hollow party that left all real power in the hands of Nasser and his fellow Free Officers and advisors. The role of the police and secret services grew as Egyptians sought their internal voice.

Nasser's economic interests and socialist focus, which addressed the equitable distribution of land and wealth, and guaranteed a job to every college graduate, brought him closer to the Soviet Union than the United States. However, this direction resulted in skewed publicly managed projects, and a huge, swollen authoritarian bureaucracy. Although Nasser figured high among the leaders of the "Third World" and the "Nonaligned Movement," his bombastic rhetoric and promises led him toward foreign adventures, including the Yemen War of 1962–66, and the June 1967 War with Israel. Both wars resulted in failure, and cost Egypt dearly in human, psychological, and financial terms.

Nasser's death from a heart attack in September 1970 brought Sadat to the forefront of Egyptian politics. Peasant-born, the son of a civil servant, and a Free Officer, he survived in power longer than anyone expected, doing so through hard work, behind the scenes maneuvering, and friendly relations with the Western world, mainly the United States. Unlike Nasser, he followed an Egyptian rather than an Arab foreign policy. He moved away from the Soviet Union and sought to recapture Egypt's honor as a result of the Arab defeat by Israel in the June 1967 War through the October 1973 War. This was followed by a political solution to the Arab-Israeli conflict, which resulted in Sadat's surprise visit to Israel in November 1977, the Camp David Accords in 1978, and the Egypt-Israel Peace Treaty of March 1979. His accommodation policies toward Israel brought him the alienation of most in the Arab world, and probably hastened his assassination in October 1981.

The severe economic problems—a population that was nearing 35 million in the mid-1970s, few natural resources and basic raw materials, limited available land, a shortage of investment funds, a rising level of foreign debt, bureaucracies swollen with unproductive workers, rising unemployment, and inflation—caused serious political discontent. These problems moved Sadat to open up Egypt's economy through less import substitution and more exports, thus distancing himself from Nasser's state-run socialist system and liberalizing its political system. Although he enhanced the inner workings of bureaucratic and technological institutions, and allowed political parties to grow as he abolished the ASU, the overall evolution of democratic rule was weak. Sadat kept strict control over political parties, as well as what he perceived to be radicals, Muslim and otherwise. As Raymond A. Hinnebusch explains, "Sadat, it appears, wanted to have democracy and yet keep his power free from challenges; when he was forced to choose he invariably opted for authority over democracy."[6]

Mubarak came to power in October 1981, following Sadat's assassination at the hands of Muslim fundamentalists within the Egyptian military, who belonged to Al Takfir Wal Hijra ("Repentance and Flight from Sin"). They accused Sadat of being unjust, and a traitor for aligning himself with both Western imperialism and Israel, or Zionism. Mubarak, a former Air Force commander and Vice President, maintained Egypt's close ties with the United States and peace with

Israel, thus reestablished his country's relations with the Arab and Muslim worlds. He backed Iraq's Saddam Hussein's war against Iran in the 1980s, but broke ties with Hussein when Iraq invaded Kuwait in 1990. He also committed some 35,000 Egyptian troops to serve with the UN-U.S. coalition during the Gulf War. Following the U.S.'s invasion of Iraq in 2003, which he did not fully support, he joined the U.S. as a strong ally against the war on terror.

The Military Role

The military has played important roles in preserving Egypt's authoritarianism; the stability, power, and continuity of its elite; and the unity of the country. Nasser, Sadat, and Mubarak have all come from the military, and the link between the military establishment and the government has always been strong.[7] More often than not, the military has been used, along with the national police and the Central Security Forces (CSF), to suppress enemies of the regime. It was also used to establish order after the 1977 food riots, and the 1986 mutiny over terms of service by CSF personnel. However, the army has also been used to put out fires in more ways than one. "When bread shortages swept in Egypt in 2008, the government didn't rely on the free market or its own warehouses, but turned instead to army bakeries to churn out millions of flat loaves to calm the angry masses. A few months later, as fire raced through the upper house of parliament, soldiers helped put out the flames."[8]

For military officers, protecting the regime carries professional and personal benefits. As Steven A. Cook argues, "senior officer corps positioned themselves at the nexus of state and private sectors in order to reap the benefits of both."[9] The military has received more than $1.2 billion in aid from the U.S. In 2005, Egypt spent an estimated 3.4 percent of its Gross Domestic Product on military expenditures.[10] Its democracy index remained at the 50th percentile.[11]

A fear some have is what happens to stability and the future of democracy if the military were to switch sides from authoritarian leaders to Islamists? Expressing this fear, David Bukay writes, "The new Islamic wave could undercut not only the stability of traditional military regimes, but also meaningful reform and liberal opposition."[12]

In addressing the popular uprising of January–February 2011, Mubarak elevated three military leaders to positions of political importance: Lieutenant General Omar Soliman from Intelligence Chief to Vice President, Air Marshal Ahmed Mohamed Shafik from the former Head of the Air Force to Prime Minister, and Field Marshall Mohamed Hussein Tantawi from Defense Minister to Deputy Prime Minister. When he stepped down as President, he assigned the Egyptian

Supreme Council of the Armed Forces (SCAF), headed by Tantawi, to lead and transition the country to the next elections. Whatever evolves in Egypt, the military will remain the backbone of the regime, calling the shots when the need arises.

The Judiciary

Historically, the judiciary's voice ebbed and flowed with the dictates of the ruler and ruling elite. From being the most respected and trusted branch of government prior to the 1952 revolution, it became more neutral, or rather it was neutralized by the government since then. Occasional calls by the Judges Club in Cairo for law reform and judicial independence were suppressed, such as Nasser's "massacre of the judiciary" when he fired over 100 senior judges in 1969 and the 1972 law under Sadat, which gave the Executive Branch dominance over the judiciary. There is also the stripping of immunity from fifteen judges from the Judges Club election committee under the Mubarak regime in 2005 for their refusal to cover up for the government's behavior, ranging from the Emergency Law to election fraud.

Generally speaking, however, the judiciary became more vocal and independent. In fact, it experienced a renaissance during the Mubarak regime. For instance, there was only one Supreme Constitutional Court (SCC) ruling in 1980 which upheld the government decree, while there were over thirty rulings from 1980 to 2000. Of those, two-thirds of the rulings determined that the government's actions were unconstitutional. As Mona El-Ghobashy explained, judicial independence was best reflected in the 2000 SCC's ruling "requiring full judicial supervision of parliamentary elections for the first time in Egyptian history."[13] Judicial independence is essential for the strengthening of civil and political rights, and the protection of human rights.[14]

Following Mubarak's resignation, the Egyptian SCAF suspended the Constitution, and appointed an Islamist judge to head the committee that was drawing up a new constitution. A Coptic judge also served on the committee. Whether or not the new rulers of Egypt will accept the judiciary as an independent authority remains to be seen.

Parliament, Political Parties, and Elections

When the Egyptian SCAF took the reins of power, it dissolved the parliament. Prior to this time, Egypt's parliament was bicameral. The upper house, Majlis al-Shura (in Arabic for Consultative Council), had 264 members, with

88 of them being appointed by the president. The rest were elected to six-year terms, with half of them coming up for election every three years. The lower house was the People's Assembly (Majlis al-Sha'b in Arabic), which had 454 members serving five-year terms, with ten of them appointed by the president.

Prior to September 2005, the People's Assembly nominated Egypt's presidential candidate; the nomination was then validated by a national, popular referendum. Starting in 2005, the presidential campaign had more than one candidate, and the president was elected by popular vote for a six-year term. There were no term limits.

The Arab Socialist Union (ASU) dominated Egyptian politics from 1962 to 1978. Founded by Nasser, its platform mirrored his national agenda of nationalization, agrarian program, and constitutional reform. When Sadat initiated political reform in 1976, he permitted the establishment of three wings—left, center, and right—within the ASU, which eventually developed into independent parties after the demise of the ASU. The creation of the National Democratic Party (NDP) (al-hizb al-watanni al-dimuqrati, in Arabic) was led by Mubarak, with his youngest son Gamal as the deputy secretary general. As its website indicated, the NDP stands for progressive values and advocates for inclusion, Egyptian national identity, religious tolerance, positive moderation, and democracy. Specifically, it "highlight[ed] the importance of continuing the drive toward democracy through bumping up respect for the constitution, the supremacy of law, public freedoms, and also underlining the importance of transparency, accountability, and the freedom of the press. It condone[d] all forms of participation, and the preservation of the political rights of laborers and farmers."[15]

Other main parties, which required approval by the government, included the National Progressive Unionist Grouping (*Tagammu* in Arabic), the New Wafd Party, and the al-Gahd (Arabic for Tomorrow) Party. Political pressure groups existed, but also needed sanctioning by the government. These groups included the Muslim Brotherhood (which was banned from organizing as a political party because of its religious-based ideology and work, but which had run candidates as independents and controlled 88 seats in the People's Assembly), trade unions, professional associations, and Internet groups.

Mubarak abandoned Sadat's open-door policies and eliminated some of the corruption that resulted from them. He allowed free multiparty national elections in 1984, the first since the 1952 Revolution. The elections were unfair because the law requiring political parties to garner a minimum of 8 percent of the popular vote restricted voter and party involvement. Mubarak, being the sole candidate, won for a six-year term, and his NDP secured a majority of the seats in the Assembly.

Three years later, the parliamentary elections had four approved political parties compete with the NDP; they won 17 percent of the vote. The Muslim Brotherhood, prohibited from operating as a political party, ran candidates as independents and achieved important gains.

The 1990 parliamentary elections maintained the NDP's dominance; the key opposition parties boycotted the elections because of the state of emergency. In the 1995 parliamentary elections, little gains for the opposition parties were scored, but the election environment gave opposition candidates—Nooman Gomaa of the liberal Wafd Party and Ayman Nour of the al-Gahd Party—a real opportunity to address large-scale rallies. It also gave rise to the Centrist Party (hizb al-wasat, in Arabic), which stands for civil liberties, women's rights, human rights, national unity, and democracy, and includes the extension of membership to the Coptic Christian community while using Islamic values as a common denominator.[16]

This contrasts sharply with the October–November 2000 parliamentary elections in which the judiciary played a supervisory role; the Muslim Brotherhood and the Wafd won 17 seats, "despite a huge campaign of harassment by police to keep Islamists out of parliament—the only blemish on what has been hailed in Egypt as an unprecedented clean vote."[17]

Governance was far from good, and remained centrally controlled by the Executive Branch. Political reforms occurred in 2004 when Mubarak shuffled his cabinet, bringing into it younger technocrats. The opposition, consisting of leftists, liberals, and Islamists, felt the reforms were superficial as they did not address direct, multicandidate presidential elections; the abrogation of emergency law; full judicial supervision of elections; the lifting of restrictions on the formation of political parties; and an end to government interference in the operation of nongovernmental organizations.[18]

Despite a government crackdown in the third round of the 2005 parliamentary elections, the opposition achieved important gains, with the Muslim Brotherhood winning 88 seats as independents, which was around 20 percent of the total. In the same year, multicandidate presidential elections gave Mubarak 88.6 percent of the vote. Judicial supervision of the elections was inadequate, and the ruling NDP kept its dominance, whilst there was a strong showing by Muslim Brotherhood parliamentary candidates. Opponents were muzzled, as in the case of Ayman Nour, the Al-Ghad Party head, who was sentenced to five years in prison in December 2005 for allegedly forging signatures required for registering his political party. In 2008, his party headquarters was burnt down, and soon after his release in 2009, he was partially burnt when someone threw a chemical product on his face.

The April 8, 2008, local elections brought about tough times for Egyptian governance as social unrest, authoritarian practices, and opposition party divisions increased. As Mohammed Herzallah and Amr Hamzawy explain, the elections were "plagued by social unrest and political discord. In the weeks prior to the elections, labor protests escalated, precipitating a harsh crackdown that resulted in at least two fatalities and many injuries."[19] As a result of this discord, the Muslim Brotherhood boycotted the elections, and with a voter turnout not exceeding 5 percent, the ruling NDP had a free hand to win by some 95 percent of the seats at stake.

The democratic progress underway has resulted in abolishing the Ministry of Information and appointing new cabinet ministers from several opposition parties or groups, including the Liberal Wafd Party and the Tagammu Party. The Centrist Party was allowed to register as a political party after 15 years of trying. Concerns remain as to the upcoming elections, mainly pertaining to the arbitrary controls on the registration and operation of political parties built in the law, and the time needed for liberal political factions or political parties to organize and compete effectively vis-à-vis well-organized groups such as the Muslim Brotherhood.

Political Rights and Civil Liberties

Prior to January 25, 2011, political tolerance among officials was very low, at a time when it was high among citizens. This is illustrated in Table 1. All citizens had political rights and civil liberties, as exemplified by the right to form political parties, membership in political parties, running for elective office, and voting. These rights, however, were restricted by law, such as establishing parties based on religion, gender, or ethnicity. Freedom of speech was limited by "vaguely worded statutes criminalizing direct criticism of the president, the military, and foreign heads of state, as well as speech that is un-Islamic, libelous, harmful to the country's reputation, or disruptive to sectarian coexistence."[20]

There was apathy, which was generated by Egypt's Emergency Law and other political realities. Independent liberal writers and intellectuals, such as Ayman Nour, the head of Al-Ghad Party, were often silenced. Moreover, as a series of focus groups on women's rights conducted with citizens found, "Many Egyptians see formal politics as an elite game and view debates among political leaders as irrelevant to their lives and concerns. Few Egyptians say that they have ever voted in elections. Reasons ... include not seeing a direct impact on their lives, perceptions of electoral fraud and cheating, and bureaucratic efficiencies making it difficult to obtain voter identification cards."[21]

Since January 25, 2011, Egyptians have been most vocal about their rights. They have been persistent about demanding real change in the constitution and the governing structure, and ending the emergency law in place since Sadat's assassination in October 1981. Nevertheless, military tribunals have tried more than 5,000 civilians, many of whom are peaceful protestors, since the SCAF took control on February 13, 2011. At the same time, former senior officials are being tried before civilian courts on charges of corruption and using lethal force against protesters. It is hoped that the approval of the landmark referendum on constitutional amendments will open the door for more political rights and civil liberties.[22]

Table 1. Egypt and Opinions on Political Tolerance (in Percent)

	Very Important	Somewhat Important	Not Very Important	Not at All Important
Expressing Unpopular Political Views	67	29	3	1
Importance of Democracy	75	24	2	0
	Completely Free	Somewhat Free	Not Very Free	
Status of Free Expression	27	38	35	
	Most of the Time	Only Sometimes	Rarely	
Fairness for Opposition Parties	31	44	25	
Legislators Differing From Party	29	43	28	
	Are Fairly Represented	Are Not Fairly Represented		
Representation of Women	54	42		
Representation of Minorities	45	51		

Source: Based on WorldPublicOpinion.org poll of 21,285 respondents in 24 nations that comprise 64 percent of the world's population. The margins of error range from +/-2 to 4 percentage points. The surveys were conducted across the different nations between April 4 and June 30, 2009. See World Public Opinion.org., World Public Opinion on Political Tolerance: A Study of 24 Nations, Sponsored by the Inter-Parliamentary Union, International Day of Democracy, September 15, 2009 at http://www.worldpublicopinion.org/pipa/articles/governance_bt/638.php?nid=&id=&pnt=638&lb=.

Media Freedom

Media is the modern source of democracy, as it generates increased public awareness and attitude changes among people. In Egypt, much of the information was, and is, filtered through government sources. Egyptians are heavily engaged in socio-political discourse and their press has high national and regional appeal, hence a strong following in the Arab world and North Africa. Yet, the government harassed, repressed, and imprisoned journalists when it felt they had crossed the "red line." Constitutional guarantees amounted to little when the government was "offended." "Even after the 2006 amendments to the Press Law, dissemination of 'false news,' criticism of the president and foreign leaders, and publication of material that constitute[d] 'an attack against the dignity and honor of individuals' or an 'outrage of the reputation of families' remain[ed] criminal offenses that [were] prosecuted opportunistically by the authorities."[23]

The government owned media outlets, and controlled the three leading newspapers whose editors were appointed by the president. To avoid problems, journalists had resorted to self-censorship, particularly on issues surrounding the president and human rights abuses. All those who deviated from this rule faced arrest and imprisonment. A prime example includes the conviction and imprisonment of four leading editors in fall 2007 for allegedly "insulting the president," based on their criticism of his views of Hezbollah in Lebanon, and of leading members of the ruling NDP.

The government also controlled radio, television, and satellite stations: programs were subject to state monitoring. The Internet, which had become part of daily life for around 15 percent of all Egyptians, had also come under government scrutiny. Web publications were subject to the same statutes governing the regular press. In 2006, blogger Abdel Kareem Nabil Suleiman, known by his pen name as Karim Amer, was given a four-year prison sentence for his writings, mainly for insulting Islam and the president. In 2007, blogger Abdul Monem Mahmoud spent one and a half months in prison for belonging to the Muslim Brotherhood, and for defaming the government. Books, films, and plays were subject to censorship as well. According to Freedom House, the Egyptians pursued a media crackdown throughout 2010, "closing independent outlets."[24] In the days leading to Mubarak's departure, Wael Ghonim, the Google executive, was jailed for his role in helping to organize the protests in Egypt. On April 10, 2011, a secretive military court sentenced liberal blogger Maikel Nabil to three years in jail for criticizing the army for abuses against protesters and for conducting forced virginity tests on female detainees. However, it is expected that media freedom will increase, as the political and legal changes underway provide for more independence.

Religious Freedom

Egyptians are approximately 90 percent Sunni Muslim, with a very small community of Shia Muslims. The remaining 10 percent is split between Copts (9%) and other Christians (1%). The Jewish community is almost nonexistent, with only about 200 people. Islam is the official state religion, and Shari'a (Arabic for Islamic law), is the primary source of legislation. Although the Egyptian Constitution called for religious freedom, the Egyptian government restricted these rights in practice. Non-Muslim religious communities that were officially recognized by the government usually worshiped without harassment, and kept contact with coreligionists in other countries. Among them are the Copts, representing the largest Christian community in the Middle East. Some of them felt discriminated against, harassed, or disempowered. Often, the issue is not religious but political and social. In appeasing the Muslim Brotherhood opposition, the government made it harder for the Copts. Also, social distancing is a factor.

> Because Copts tend to live in their own neighborhoods or villages there has developed a social line of separation between them and broader Egyptian society. When the local community is economically comfortable, communal tension is minimal. When there is widespread poverty and misguided local leadership, inter-communal trouble can be expected. The role of community leaders—the Christian bishops and the Muslim clerics—is crucial for prevention of tension.[25]

Those who were not recognized by the Government (e.g., Baha'is, Jehovah's Witnesses, and Mormons), or those who converted from Islam to other religions face discrimination. As the International Religious Freedom Report 2008 stated:

> A lower court ruling interpreted the Constitution's guarantee of religious freedom as inapplicable to Muslim citizens who wish to convert to another religion. The ruling is under appeal. Separate court rulings provided for 13 Christian-born converts to Islam to obtain identity documents indicating their conversion back to Christianity and allowed some Baha'is to obtain civil documents. However, the courts included requirements effectively identifying the Christian converts and Baha'is as apostates, potentially exposing them, if implemented, to risk of significant discrimination by both government and societal agents. In addition, a lower court held that the Constitutions guarantee of freedom of religion does not apply to Baha'is.[26]

Identity papers were essential in Egypt, as in most other countries. Without them, people cannot secure a driving license, open a bank account, secure a public loan, own a house, or register their children in school. In addition, Apostates did not only encounter social difficulties, but many risked their livelihoods and lives as well.

In addition to the issue of religious freedom or its lack thereof, there had been an increase in conservative religious fervor and a steady rise of Islamic political forces in Egypt which brought forth nuanced responses from the government. The main attention was placed on the Muslim Brotherhood, founded by Hasan al-Banna in 1928. Members were drawn from the professional and working classes, and had much influence through activities in charities, education, mosques, and trade unions. After being banned and persecuted under the Nasser regime, members of the Muslim Brotherhood were rehabilitated under Sadat's rule to be a counterweight to the forces of the Left. They were engaged in a struggle for power, as well as a balancing act with the Mubarak government that acknowledged their existence, but also regarded them as a threat.

As a Cairo-based journalist argued, there was an "ominous competition for moral authority between the government and political Islam. The government change[d] its moral tone not only to please the people, but also to placate those calling for democratic reform, and so the warp and weft of contradiction and compromise continue[d] to hold the country together—in religion, culture, and politics."[27] A study published in the Cairo-based Coptic weekly *Watani* showed how the government had Islamized the elementary school curriculum, perhaps as a way to placate the Islamic base.[28] Dr. Hala Mustafa, the Editor-in-Chief of *Al-Ahram*'s political quarterly, *Democratic Review*, believed the government had played a complicit role in the rising tide of Egyptian Islamism. She wrote:

> In particular, legislation restricting the establishment of political parties and the weakness of officially recognized political parties resulted in a situation where, for nearly five decades, the mosque ha[d] been the only available venue for expressing political opinion and opposition to the regime. But the conflict between the regime and the Islamists [was] driven less by ideological differences than simple power politics.[29]

Khairi Abaza went further to explain the Egyptian regime's strategy by presenting the thesis that "if the only well-organized opposition [was] from Islamists, the regime will [have received] support internationally and from many at home to maintain the status quo. Therefore, the most significant threat to the ... political system in Egypt [will have been] a strong liberal opposition, which could [have pressured] the regime for more reforms."[30]

With democratic processes evolving in Egypt, there is a new opportunity for the kind of changes necessary to address religious discrimination there. Egyptians should pursue a pluralistic mode of existence where citizenship is the only basis for inclusion in the national community. While everyone has an important role to play, religious leaders must take an active role in promoting coexistence between different faith communities, and coming down strongly against religiously motivated violence.[31]

Human Rights

The 2008 report of Amnesty International failed Egypt on its human rights laws and practices. Constitutional amendments that passed through parliament on March 19, 2008 "cemented the sweeping arrest powers of the police, gave broad authority for state agents to eavesdrop on private communications, authorized the president to bypass ordinary courts, and paved the way for new anti-terrorism legislation expected to further erode human rights protection." Other amendments related directly to campaigns and elections, specifically restricting the roles of judges in supervising elections and referenda, as well as banning religion-based political parties. The latter related to the outlawing of the Muslim Brotherhood as a political party and in reaction to its 2005 electoral success.[32]

The 2008 report also indicated "the degrading and inhumane conditions" to which around 18,000 administrative detainees were subjected, some of who had been held for over a decade. Torture and ill treatment, such as electric shocks, solitary confinement, sexual abuse, rape, and threats of death were common. Trade unionists and nongovernmental organization (NGO) activists were also repressed as public and private sector workers went on strike to protest rising inflation and increased poverty, the most intense in decades. Some newspaper editors, journalists, and bloggers faced the same fate as they were accused of disturbing the public order and hurting the country's image.[33]

Women continued to be harassed, professionally and sexually. The 2008 report added that "the Egyptian Center for Women's Rights said sexual harassment was on the rise, and that two women were being raped every hour in Egypt." Moreover, the report stated that "the African Commission on Human and Peoples' Rights said it would consider … a case filed by 33 human rights organizations against the Egyptian government's failure to prevent and prosecute physical and sexual assaults targeted at women journalists and demonstrators during a protest in May 2005."[34] Overall, women were prevented from succeeding both in political society and civil society. Their voice was dependent on men and not fully developed in Egyptian life. As Michaelle L. Browers argued, " … whereas women in the informal sector [were] rendered invisible by their dependence on household economic units, women in the formal sector remain[ed] dependent on the family connections and educational privileges that enabled their gains. The neglect of informal institutional arrangements in favor of more organized civil society groups help[ed] to reinforce women's marginalization from formal social policies and maintains their subjugation to men."[35]

Human rights abuses must end. Through their joint heroic efforts, Egyptian men and women have shown their serious commitment to generate positive change in their political and social lives. The way forward must be enshrined in laws and due process, and anchored in civility, inclusivity, and respect for the other.

Human Development and Human Poverty

The Gross Domestic Product (GNP) per capita in Egypt is estimated at $6,200. Human development goes beyond income to include a deeper reflection and understanding of human wellbeing. The Human Development Index (HDI), which ranks countries on a scale from zero to one, is composed of three dimensions of human development: living a long and healthy life (measured by life expectancy), being educated (measured by adult literacy and enrollment at the primary, secondary, and tertiary levels), and having a decent standard of living measured by purchasing power parity (PPP) income. Between 1980 and 2010, Egypt's HDI rose by 1.5% annually, from 0.393 to 0.620, which gave it a rank of 101 out of 169 countries with comparable data.[36]

The level of human development is related to that of human poverty, which is measured by the Human Development Index (HPI-1). This index focuses on the proportion of people below a threshold level in the same dimensions of human development, which represents an alternative to the $1.25 a day (PPP US$) poverty measure. For Egypt, the HPI-1 value is 20 percent, which ranks it 48th among 108 developing countries.[37]

Economic Freedoms

Most of Egypt's economic activities take place around the highly fertile Nile valley. While such activities were centrally controlled during the Nasser regime, Sadat and Mubarak opened them up substantially. This was done through foreign investment flow and growth in the Gross Domestic Product (GDP).

The 2010 estimate puts Egypt's GDP (using the official exchange rate) at $216.8 billion, with agriculture contributing 13.5 percent, industry 37.9 percent, and services 48.6 percent. Egypt's inflation rate stands at 12.8 percent, and its unemployment rate at 9.7 percent. Egypt's exports, which stand at $25.34 billion (2010 est.), include crude oil and petroleum products, cotton, textiles, metal products, and chemicals. Its imports, which stand at $46.52 billion (2010 est.), include machinery and equipment, foodstuffs, chemicals, wood products, and fuels. Egypt's external debt is over $30 billion (December 31, 2010 est.), which ranks it 65th in comparison to other countries, and keeps it beholden to its trade partners, particularly the United States, China, Italy, and Germany.[38]

According to the Heritage Foundation/Wall Street Journal 2011 Index of Economic Freedom, Egypt's economy ranks as the 96th freest in the world out of 183 countries, with its overall score just below the world and regional averages. It made "significant gains in investment freedom offset by worsened scores for government spending and monetary freedom,"[39] as indicated in Table 2. Moreover, Egypt has low personal income and corporate tax rates at a time when it has high inflation. Its employment opportunities and productivity growth are hampered by rigid employment regulations.

The Egyptian government is large, with its spending consuming over 33.5 percent of the GDP. The informal economic sector, which represents some 35

Table 2. Economic Freedoms of Egypt

Economic Freedoms		Score	Average
Business Freedom	↓	64.5	64.3
Trade Freedom	–	74.0	74.8
Fiscal Freedom	↓	89.6	76.3
Government Size	↓	65.3	63.9
Monetary Freedom	↓	60.8	73.4
Investment Freedom	↑	65.0	50.2
Financial Freedom	–	50.0	48.5
Property Rights	–	40.0	43.6
Freedom from Corruption	–	28.0	40.5
Labor Freedom	↓	53.6	61.3

Source: Egypt, Information on Economic Freedom, Heritage Foundation at http://www.heritage.org/Index/County/Egypt.

percent of GDP, continues to grow and is considered counterproductive to future economic growth and reform.

In Egypt, corruption in society and public affairs is extensive and persistent. Without *wasta* (which implies mediation, influence, or pull in Arabic), or a facilitation fee, little can get done. High-ranking officials use the law to their advantage, selling public companies at undervalued prices and not getting into trouble unless they fall out of favor with the established authority. Bribery, crony-ism, nepotism, and patronage are part of daily life. This corruption climate serves neither Egypt's business relations and human development, nor its na-tional ethos and image. A 249-page report by the opposition movement Kifaya, titled *Corruption in Egypt: A Black Cloud That Never Passes*, details corruption in several governmental ministries, including Agriculture, Antiquities, Finance, Health, and Petroleum, and provides a section on the interference of security forces in public life. With information compiled from local and international reports, such as Egyptian court and legal records, media sources, UNDP, and Transparency International, the report argues for regime change as the only way to end corruption.[40] It is no surprise that Egypt ranks 98th out of 178 countries in Transparency International's Corruption Perceptions Index for 2010. The gov-ernment's attempt to stem the tide of corruption has been ineffective thus far.

Deeper institutional reforms are necessary "to sustain long-term economic growth and development. Those reforms include strengthening the judicial system, better property protection rights, and effectively eradicating corrup-tion, which is perceived to be widespread."[41] Mubarak's departure is expected to usher in a new dawn for Egypt.

Status of Democracy Index (SDI) and the Challenges Ahead

Considering its experience, or its lack thereof with democracy, it can be stated that Egypt has a long way to go before it can shed its authoritarian na-ture. Its overall SDI score for 2010–2011 is 9.5 out of 18, or 52.7 percent, which is a modest improvement over its 2008–2009 score, as is shown in Table 3. The popular uprising of January–February 2011 is having an impact on Egypt's democratic progress, especially in the areas of civil and political liberties, press freedom, and human rights.

Egypt has to overcome many challenges before it can be considered demo-cratic. Although Egypt has a rich set of trade unions, professional associations, community organizations, and interest groups that mediate between private and public space, these need to be better integrated into public life. As Egyptian Amer-ican sociologist Saad Eddin Ibrahim, who is a leading human rights and democ-racy activist argues, "Normatively, 'civil society' implies values and behavioral codes of tolerating—if not accepting—others and a tacit or explicit commit-ment to the peaceful management of differences among individuals and col-lectivities sharing the same 'public space'—that is, the polity."[42] As Khairi

Abaza also suggests, "Only the hope of reform and the creation of a viable opposition will encourage Egyptians to participate in their government and lead to the democratization that Egypt so badly needs."[43]

Table 3. Egypt—Status of Democracy Index

	2008–2009	2010–2011
Free Election Head of State	1.0	1.0
Free Election Legislature	1.5	1.0
Civil Rights/Political Parties	1.0	1.5
Suffrage	2.0	2.0
Press Freedom	0	0.5
Religious Freedom	1.0	1.0
Human Rights	0.5	1.0
Human Development	1.0	1.0
Economic Freedom	0.5	0.5
Total SDI Score	8.5/18	9.5/18
Percentage SDI	47.2	52.7

Legend:
Free Election Head of State: 0 = no; 1 = indirect or partially; 2 = yes
Free Election Legislature: 0 = no; 1 = indirect or limited; 2 = yes
Political Rights/Civil Liberties/Political Parties: 0 = prohibited or nonexistent;
    1 = controlled by government approval; 2 = reasonably free
Suffrage: 0 = none; 1 = some; 2 = yes
Press Freedom: 0 = not free; 1 = partly free; 2 = free
Religious Freedom: 0 = none; 1 = some; 2 = yes
Human Rights: 0 = not observed; 1= partly observed; 2 = fully observed
Human Development: 0 = love human development; 1 = medium human development;
    2 = high human development
Economic Freedom: 0 = repressed; 0.5 = mostly not free; 1 = moderately free;
    1.5 = mostly free; 2 = free

The road to democratic reform starts when those in power introduce true policies that ensure a separation of powers among the executive, legislative, and judicial branches of government; protect civil and political rights; encourage the development of new political parties and engage the opposition; allow private media outlets to function and prosper; and build confidence among the Egyptian electorate. Improvements in human rights, religious freedom, human development, and economic freedom will complete the picture by enhancing Egyptian well-being and prosperity.

Morocco

Chapter 3

Morocco: Democracy in an Islamic Kingdom

Raphael Chijioke Njoku

This chapter examines the progress of democratization in the Islamic kingdom of Morocco. The Status of Democracy Index (SDI) was utilized as a yardstick for measuring the commitment of the ruling elite in bringing about a more liberal and representative government. The quest for democracy in Morocco is important for obvious reasons. First, it directly conflicts with monarchical authority. At best, advocates of democracy are negotiating for more citizen participation in the decision-making process of their country. Second, Morocco, along with Jordan and Egypt, are among a small number of Arab countries that the United States Congress has embraced as partners in the fight against fundamentalist violence. The dilemma for the U.S. is moving the pace of democratization forward in countries such as Morocco. This must be accomplished without extremist parties such as Hamas gaining seats of power via electoral victory in the 2006 legislative elections in Palestine.[1]

Morocco's recent liberalization program gained momentum with the ascension to power of young Mohammed VI after the death of his father in 1999. Early on, his father, King Hassan (r. 1961–1999), had launched the transition program in response to the global movement towards democracy of the 1980s. In his first broadcast to the people in 1999, Mohammed VI had promised to "strongly adhere to the system of constitutional monarchy, political pluralism, economic liberalism, regional and decentralized policy, the establishment of the state of rights and law, preserving human rights and individual and collective liberties, protecting security and stability for everyone."[2] These and other broadminded promises endeared the new king in the hearts of his people. Today, the pressure for democratization has increased, revealing the dilemma faced by a conservative theocratic system that seeks an identity with the process of change, but is reluctant to degrade the age-honored theocratic monarchy that still stands as a symbol of national unity.[3]

The Historical Context

Morocco's march towards democracy is surrounded by a unique but familiar form of ambiguity common to most of the modern countries in the Middle East. This peculiarity is a product of Morocco's cultural heritage as well as its colonial experience. Several centuries prior to colonialism, Morocco had passed through different brands of dynasties that had been established on Islamic ideals. Beginning in 1666, from the foremost Muslim dynasty of 789–987 AD, to the era of the present ruling dynasty of the Alawis or (Alouites), the political rights of citizens before the leader were understood to be the same as the relationship between the believer and his maker (Allah). Since the Alawis claim descent from the Holy Prophet of Islam, it is only Allah — the all-powerful and the merciful — who both chooses and sustains the leader of his community of believers (*ummah*). This common belief was tested under French colonial rule as the colonial state expanded its authority and interests. In the first two decades of colonialism, the Berbers primarily championed indigenous resistance to colonial authority, while French-Arab collaboration endured. It was only in the 1930s that the emergent Arab educated nationalists began to fight against colonial injustice. They also found in the young King Mohammad ben Yusuf (popularly known as Mohammed V) a potential ally in the movement to overcome colonial domination.

Unlike Algeria, where the emergent nationalists broke links with the traditional (*Beys*) rulers, in the late 1940s and 1950s Moroccan nationalists forged a strong bond with a monarchy that was eventually marginalized by French officials. The nationalists cashed in on this alliance with the monarchy to gain wider popularity. Mohammad ben Yusuf rode roughshod on the nationalist cause, reinventing himself as the voice and symbol of freedom. Central to understanding Moroccan politics and society today is the monarchy's role in the context of decolonization, which structured a peculiar form of political culture that has positioned the traditional institution as a legitimate claimant to the postcolonial state.[4]

Usually, monarchies and radicals are strange bedfellows. It was no surprise then that the radical forms of political activism that served the needs of the colonial times came under censorship after independence in 1956. C. R. Pennell has identified some of the most radical movements that relentlessly attacked the king of Morocco in the early 1980s, including Abd al-Karim Muti's Islamic Youth (*al-Shabiba al-Islamiyya*) movement. In a daring show of contempt, the leader of the movement sent an open letter to the king saying, "We say to you: Fear God in his religion and the religion of the Prophet before he turns you into a monkey, after having changed you into a drunkard and an opium addict."[5]

Although critics believed the common idea that the monarchy employs violence to silence its opponents, it is noteworthy that the piecemeal programs of decentralization in Morocco were informed by fear of the unknown. A good example is the 1976 Communal Charter that was aimed at strengthening local councils' administration and creating alternative centers of autonomy and political expressions. In the end, the program came short of providing enough sphere of autonomy for the regional council leaders. The expected legal structure within which civilian groups could experiment and adopt institutionalized forms of participation was denied. It was only in the 1999 constitutional amendments, following the popular referendum of that year, that the various regions in Morocco were officially recognized as local councils with the prerogative to deal with matters related to each region's affairs. This concession from the monarchy must be understood as part of its policy response to the broader and more complex nature of the emergent global economy defined by an increasing relevance of non-stateside actors in economic development—a reality that has called into question the continued role of the patriarchal state as the appropriate manager of national economy and initiator of its development programs.[6] The relevant question then becomes whether the monarchy would be willing to supervise a democratically elected head of state, and allow its privileges and authority to be degraded into a ceremonial position similar to the monarchies of Great Britain, Spain, and Sweden.

Free Election of Head of State

In the established literature on democratization, free election of the head of the government of a country has long been viewed as one of the crucial indicators of a democratic system.[7] This ideal is based on the premise that dictatorship regimes and personal rulers cannot be sustained with an electoral process that is free and fair. Samuel Huntington has presented a unique discussion on common trends peculiar to democratic transitions in Third World countries since the 1970s, which may help elucidate understanding on how free elections defeat undemocratic regimes. Huntington observes that outcomes of democratic transitions were subject to the choices made between authoritarian reactionaries, moderate reformers, and radical revolutionaries in a given political context.[8] In a study of histories of regime changes in those countries that did democratize between 1974 and 1990 (including Brazil, Bolivia, Ecuador, Chile, Nicaragua, Peru, and Turkey), among others, Huntington found that these countries oscillated between democratic order and more conservative military regimes as a result of incidences of radicalism, corrup-

tion, and disorder. Other reasons identified for non-consolidation of democratic gains include persistent economic problems, extremist policies by newly
democratic governments, drastic reactions by former dictatorships, unchecked
polarization of the polity, and decolonization hangovers.[9] These issues set in
motion a rapid state of waning legitimacy and performance dilemma, and
thus, tend to bring negative consequences on the democratic destination.[10]

Huntington's model is important in understanding Morocco because it focuses on avenues through which political leaders and the public ended authoritarian systems and created democratic ones.[11] Although the routes to
changes differed from country to country, a common understanding on the
processes could be established. According to Pinkney, who has synthesized
Huntington's thesis, a discovery was made on the decisive influences of such
variables as specific political structures, government-opposition, elite's behavior, and masses' reactions. Other variables include the specific groups in
society; the influences exerted by external powers and groups; the ability of
some groups to persuade or coerce others; the extent of conflict/consensus
order; the nature and extent of changes sought or achieved; and the speed of
change. A combination of these factors are obviously present in Morocco, and
they can make or break the democratic transition in that country. Given that
the struggle for democratization involves the daunting task of overcoming non-
democratic regimes, Huntington's study focused on the seeds of challenge to
authoritarianism; the configuration of interests; the resolution of conflicts; the
opportunities and limitations presented by different forms of authoritarianism; the genuineness of the transitions to democracy; and the particular transactions and achievement of distinct results.[12]

Huntington identifies a four-fold typology of authoritarian regimes: one-
party, personal, military, and racial oligarchy, with apartheid South Africa as
an example of the last. While most countries in Africa had experienced one-
party dictatorships, Morocco's experience has been with personal rule of a
theocratic nature. This presents a peculiar problem because it is not like a military dictatorship, which Huntington sees as most capable and willing to relinquish
power so far as personal safety of the ruling group are guaranteed as a whole.[13]
Like one-party systems, personal rulers normally present greater institutional
and ideological barriers to democratization, and are even more reluctant to
retire than military or party dictatorships unless their exit is eventually brought
about by death. Generally, success in most of the recent transitions tends to come
easier when the transition moved in a gradual sequence, with hard-liners, soft-
liners, and moderates finding common understanding. This scenario fits the
description of the unfolding democratic movement in Morocco. In other words,
the co-option of all opponents in the political process is important to ensure

stability.[14] The principal lesson, therefore, is that gradual, moderate, and consensual decisions often yield more significant and long-lasting results than non-compromising and radical antagonism.[15]

The crucial question remains: why should the monarch in Morocco agree to negotiate for democratic governance? Two obvious reasons include the desire for legitimacy, and the prospects of achieving a regularized system of decision-making. This becomes more critical following the recent wave of political protestations that have pulled down autocratic regimes in Algeria on January 14, and in Egypt on February 11, 2011. But the truth is that the Moroccan monarch, especially under Mohammed VI, still enjoys the respect of the majority and, therefore, some degree of legitimacy. Also, the king has been busy setting up and regularizing parliamentary structures of decision making. Given these initiatives, it could hardly be expected that the monarchy will in the end concede to a loss of all monarchical privileges to secular politicians in the near future. As Pinkney pointed out, the problem in focusing on the structural form of authoritarian government is to assume that it is an independent variable.[16] The plausibility of a stable, long-term democracy emerging in Morocco may not depend on the King allowing a free and fair election in which he would serve only as an umpire. As a Moroccan citizen opinioned, "Mohammed VI will defeat any of the current opponents in a free and fair election, however, it is encouraging to know that there are underlying conditions favorable for cooperation and consensus."[17] These assets cannot be dismissed until the political process is better prepared and ready for democratic governance.[18] Indeed, a bold step towards this readiness was initiated with the free election of a legislature and national council in 1999.

Free Election of Legislature and National Council

The recent effort at constituting an elected legislature actually goes back to the 1980s reign of King Hassan (r. 1961–1999), and was wisely conceived to placate a broad spectrum of demands brought upon the monarchy by a rainbow coalition of interest groups—comprising of civil, military, and religious groups. Particularly in the 1970s and 1980s, when royal houses in Libya, Yemen, Iraq, and Tunisia were swept away by military coups and revolutionary leaders, King Hassan survived through a combination of constitutional maneuvers and political promises.[19] He voted into law a program of decentralization in 1973, and followed this up with constitutional reforms in 1986, 1992, and 1996. The 1996 reform was a watershed because it created a bicameral legislature—namely a Lower House, "House of Representatives" (Majliss-annouwab) to be chosen entirely by universal adult suffrage and an Upper House "House of Counselors"

(Majlis al-Mustacharin) representing the active forces of the nation elected by indirect suffrage. While the program was still unfolding before his death on July 23, 1999, King Hassan retained power and respect by mobilizing the support of influential traditional and international networks, including local chiefs, rural notables, Sufi orders, prominent urban families, and Western countries. They viewed him as a crucial ally in Middle East politics, thus offsetting the pressures from nationalist parties.[20]

The positive impact of the 1980s program of decentralization perhaps influenced Hassan's successor, Mohammed VI, to quickly declare his commitment to the political process initiated by his father as soon as he stepped into power in 1999. The new king has demonstrated his readiness to go beyond the original intentions of his father. On October 2, 2002, Mohammed VI appointed Driss Jettou as Prime Minister and also chose a Council of Ministers to run the nation's ministries and everyday business. Since the people did not properly elect these officers, Jettou and other appointees have remained under the monarchical authority. The Constitution states unequivocally that the positions of the Prime Minister and other members of the government are subject to termination on "His own initiative or by the fact of the resignation of the Government."[21]

The parliamentary elections of September 2007 were aimed at giving the decentralization process a big boost, and more semblance of legitimacy. In the election, 33 political parties contested, and dozens of independent candidates hoped to secure seats in the assembly. At the end of the elections, 325 members of the House of Representatives were chosen by direct election, and a 270-member House of Counselors (Advisers) was chosen by indirect election. Perhaps the most interesting aspect of the elections is that 10 percent of the elective positions were reserved for women. In other words, 32 women are now serving in the newly constituted House of Representatives. That puts Morocco first among countries in the Arab world that are favorably disposed to empowering women and bringing them into leadership positions. Overall, the outcome of the parliamentary elections, which involved a record number of political parties, leads to the conclusion that the monarchy has rightfully recognized the place of political parties and the freedom of citizens to ascribe memberships into their parties of choice as an important aspect of building a solid foundation for democratic politics in the country.

Formation/Freedom of Political Parties

As previous studies on the state of democratization in Morocco attest, freedom of party politics and formation of political parties is one of the areas for which the government has been highly praised. It is worthy to note that colonial political associations like the Istiqlal provided the institutional support under which nationalist ideals were first articulated and expressed on the road to independence in 1956. Multiparty politics has been a unique part of Morocco, although monarchical authorities have limited their spheres of activities. Out of 33 viable political parties in Morocco today, the three most popular are the Socialist Union of Popular Forces (SUPF), the Independence Party—best known as Istiqlal—and the Justice and Development Party (PJD). Although all the parties are pro-Islam, the PJD espouses more strict Islamic principles, and enjoys strong support from the monarchy because it shares some common ideals with the powers that be, especially in regards to fighting corruption and protecting religious ideals.

The model of explanation on democratization from the perspective that places "priority to conjectural factors and strategic choices—and more clearly political determinants," is genetic, as opposed to the functionalist view, which is concerned with the long term or macro socioeconomic determinants.[22] While Morocco had a tradition of a multiparty systems since the 1960s, this hardly translates to any special gains along democratic lines.[23] The unparalleled participation of more than 26 political parties in the elections of 2002, and 33 in the 2007 elections remains a credit on the side the government to get the people involved in the political process. All the same, the increase in the number of parties vying for elective positions in the 2007 parliamentary elections reflects the desire of citizens to exercise more rights in the decision-making process of their country.

According to Seymour Lipset and others, political parties ought to be conceived as the most important mediating institutions between the state and the citizenry.[24] In this concern, it is crucial that parties exist with a permanent significant base of support as a condition for democratic stability. The ability of political systems to moderate and manage conflict, without being driven to authoritarianism or chaos, leads to the logical consideration of the role of political institutions on the survival of democracy. Hence, Geoffrey Pridham and Paul Lewis argue that political parties are strategically penitent to both the genetic and functionalist theories for two major reasons: they provide the most powerful political actors and are usually seen as strategic vehicles, and they present an important linkage with channel for impact of socio-economic determinants on political change. Where previous studies identified political parties as playing significant roles in the process of transition, the authors place it "at the forefront of transition tasks such as managing free elections, and drawing up constitutions and government policy making, not to mention establishing elite loyalties to the new democracy, promoting democratic values through practice or rhetoric and thus contributing to system legitimation."[25]

Strong political parties make democratic compromise easier, as witnessed in Spain after the end of Franco's four decades of authoritarian regime.[26] Spain in the 1970s and Brazil in the 1980s demonstrated that when authoritarian rulers gave up power, strong political institutions were able to exercise firm control over the process of transition to democracy.[27] The emphasis here is on the underlying strength and adaptability of institutions, rather than on the characteristics of political culture. Martin Heper and Ahmet Evin, in their study of *State, Democracy and the Military in Turkey*, express concern that over-powerful institutions can be as damaging to democracy as weak ones. In the case of Turkey, the state was re-consolidated along [over-powerful] bureaucratic lines, which remained isolated from society.[28] As a result, the political sub-system suffered repression, and the sort of autonomous political engagements accepted as healthy in most Western democracies were seen as a threat to public interest.

One of the strengths of the political party approach to building democracy is that democratic evolution is seen in the broad historical perspective, instead of being explored from the starting point of conflict within the previous authoritarian regime.[29] There is also the advantage of focusing more on the "political." On this premise, material wealth, democratic attitudes, and an interdependent relationship between social groups will be of relevance in aiding democracy unless institutions evolve that can translate political choices, demands and decisions into actual decision "outputs." This is achievable through institutions such as parties, pressure groups, legislatures, and bureaucracies whose roles and existence have mass followership.[30]

As E.H. Stephens' study on Latin America further illustrates, strong political institutions help to stabilize political systems.[31] For Morocco, therefore, it is obvious that the government has allowed significant progress in this area of institutional support. The existing political parties are supported by such civil and political associations as the Democratic Confederation of Labor or *Confédération démocratique de travail* (CDT), General Union of Moroccan Workers or *Union Général des ouvriers marocains* (UGTM), Moroccan Employers Association or *Association Marocaine D'Employeurs* (CGEM), National Labor Union of Morocco or *Syndicat national du Maroc* (UNMT), and the Union of Moroccan Workers or *Union des ouvriers marocains* (UMT). Apparently, these groups will continue to prompt the monarchical authorities to continue the march towards a full-blown democracy. Obviously, it is in recognition of the parties and associations as power rivals that the political elite has tried to influence through co-option. In Morocco, there are few examples of partnership between elected politicians and NGOs that seem to respect the need for independent pursuit of their goals. Rather, the political elite aims to run these associations, and as a result, it is difficult to distinguish a true NGO from the various political parties that are inching their ways into the law-making process.[32] In her book, *Dangerous Alliances: Civil Society, the Media and Democratic Transition in North Africa,* Lise Garon criticized this form of politics common to North Africa.[33]

In broad terms, three major components of political associations are gradually gaining some measure of influence on the public decision-making process. These are the association of entrepreneurs, labor unions, and political parties. For analytical convenience, one may, after Dris Ben Ali, divide the unionist movements in Morocco into two main groups. The first class of unionist movements, linked to the central authority, is strictly limited to professional issues, and it is more or less apolitical. In fact, the Moroccan Workers Union (MWU) embodies this category of associations, and it enjoys a wider support as the first historical union movement in postcolonial Morocco. In the 1960s, members of the MWU were closely linked to the National Union of Popular Forces (NUPF). As an umbrella organization for wage earners, the MWU today commands a strong membership, as well as financial means. As a force at the parliamentary level, it is well represented at the Upper House or the Chamber of Counselors. Various regional, local, and professional councils elect members to the Upper House.[34]

The second group is comprised of those unions that were created by political parties. This refers to the General Union of Moroccan Workers (GUMW), linked to the *Istiqlal* Party, and the WDC (Workers Democratic Confederation), linked to the Socialist Union of Popular Forces (SUPF). Before now, the two groups were close allies, but since the past decade, the WDC has pulled aside as an independent party. The two groups recruit the majority of their members from among government employees and wage earners in the public sector of services. Meanwhile, their close affiliation with political parties has led them to politicize their action and to give to their demands a dimension other than purely professional unionist demands. Like the MWU, these unions have also secured strong representation in the Upper House (the Chamber of Counselors), and they take part in major policy debates, including budget planning and labor-related policies.[35] In light of this reality, it becomes even more crucial that universal adult suffrage is now a defining attribute of democratization in Morocco.

Suffrage

One of the most distinguishing attributes of liberal democracy, as exemplified by the U.S. system and other advanced Western democracies, is the right of citizens to both participate in the choice of their leaders as well as the right to vie for elective positions in their country. The Transition School in political science theorem has argued that the historical processes surrounding the evolution of a society offer a parallel explanation to democratization and institutional consolidation. According to D.A. Rustow, there are three phases in the process of transition to democracy: the preparatory, the decision, and the habituation phases. "These involved respectively a struggle by rival groups which sort out their conflicts through accommodation, a decision to accept diversity and to institutionalize democratic procedures, and a phase when political elites and public begin to operationalize democratic methods and become used (or reconciled) to them."[36] Similarly, Robert Dahl argues that ideal liberal democracy fared best if political competition preceded "inclusiveness."[37] Historically, Western democracies in their evolutionary circles first enjoyed the advantage of a long period of competition for power based on a limited franchise, during which the main rules and conventions of political decision making were able to evolve. In other words, the long period of power struggle, and "exclusiveness" at the early stages made precious the privilege derivable from eventual extension of political rights, especially suffrage, to the rest of the population. This practice guaranteed the West a safeguard for conformity and a clear understanding that newcomers were to abide by the existing rules. Added to this is the understanding that avenues for change have a prescribed process that must follow certain accepted ways, thus ensuring stability and continuity.

Perhaps the post-apartheid era in South Africa, where conformity to the rules of the game have been maintained, may buttress the fact. Prior to 1990, when black people were completely enfranchised following the end of the apartheid system, the white oligarchy constituted themselves into an elite with exclusivist privileges. In the rest of the continent, the postcolonial states, including Morocco, began their independent politics with universal suffrage and with party and pressure group leaders bearing theoretical (not practical) knowledge of the ways in which participation through lobbying and the ballot box had advanced the claims of diverse groups in the Western world. Consequently, high expectations brought over-bearing pressure on the political system at a time when the system had barely become institutionalized, and when the resources available to meet mass demands were lacking.[38] The situation thus constituted a formidable disadvantage in the sequences of political development and democratic consolidation in the emergent states.

Nevertheless, it is difficult to judge whether the cost of disfranchisement would have been lower than the cost of enfranchisement, especially after the colonial experience in Africa. More precisely, the problem of political membership might be slated as between the culturally and psychologically determined sense of personal-group identity and the political definition of the community.[39] Suffrage also connects with citizenship. In the paradigm of modernization, penetration of political rights involves equality—the equalization of obligation and duties and individualization of citizenship.[40] This view is strongly supported by Geraldo L. Munk, who argued that political actors make choices, but not in circumstances of their own choosing. According to Munk, the segregation of structure and process in explanations on the origins of transitions and, to a great extent, the prospects of democratic consolidation leads to what he qualifies as "a loose conceptual framework."[41] Also, exiting historical and cultural elements could equally present inhibitions and encourage authoritarianism. Hence, press freedom is rightly identified as one of the preconditions for liberal democracy.

Media Freedom

Media freedom is one of the sacrosanct attributes of democratic practice. In the United States, for instance, the media plays the role of watchdog of politicians, and more importantly, acts as a pressure group and mediator between the people and the government. The common expectation, therefore, is that developing democracy in developing countries must go hand-in-hand with press freedom. The Moroccan modern press that dates back to the beginning of the colonial era, serving to consolidate French colonial rule, had gradually evolved in phases and periods in response to both international events and nationalist goals. Press ownership has also transformed in phases from a mouthpiece of colonial administration, to a supporter of monarchical authority since gaining independence in 1956. The latest development is the gradual emergence of private ownership of newspapers and magazines.

Generally, monarchical authority has created problems of freedom for the media in Morocco. The major government-owned newspapers include the *Al Anbaa*, *Le Matin* (*The Morning*), and *Assahra*, all of which are published daily. The government controls newspapers through bureaucratic supervision of news broadcasts and appointment of trusted managers of the media houses. Such governmental censorships have attracted both local and foreign condemnations. In 2003, for instance, a media rights organization *Reporters without Borders (or Reporters Sans Frontières)* based in Paris, strongly condemned the habitual prying in the press by the intelligence services. It attacked Morocco's press law, which stipulates various prison terms for writings that question the relevance of Islam in society, continued monarchical authority amidst the new global quest for democratic institutions, or the legitimacy of Morocco's territorial claims over the Western Sahara.

In spite of government censorship, it is important to appreciate the recent strides that have been recorded in the continuing expansion of the print media. Recent legislative openings have resulted in increases in the number of daily, weekly, and monthly newspaper houses in Morocco. In 2000, there were about 1,780 local and foreign newspapers in circulation. These newspapers and magazines cover a wide spectrum of interests—politics, religion, medicine, economy, sports, women, computers, arts, decoration, youth, education, and so on. They carry news items, editorials, advertisements, and columns reflecting the gradual response of the sociopolitical space to the globalizing world order with the monarchy demonstrating more tolerance to criticism and divergent views. A state statute of August 2, 1995, allows for expression of political ideas and socio-cultural opinions within a defined press code, which empowers the Minister of Interior to censor any publication that is considered offensive to government. As in all Islamic states, most Moroccan newspapers devote a front section to Islamic sermons. Low literacy levels limit newspaper readership, and competition among publishers for advertising is intense. Since 1999, Morocco's private press had been gradually engaging in free debate on a number of previously tabooed issues, including social problems.

Radio and Television

Like the print media, local radio broadcasting began in Morocco in 1924 under the French colonial administration. After World War II, the government granted nationalists the freedom to establish radio broadcasting. Shortly before its independence, the French colonial authorities also established the first television station in Morocco in 1954. This was indeed the first in the entire Arab world. In November 1958, the late King Mohammed V established the Maghrib Arab Press Agency or *Maghrib abd Arabe Presse* (MAP), with the motto "News is sacred, comment is freedom." The MAP has wide local and international outreach and is a leader in international news broadcasting in Morocco. Radio and TV broadcasting, like print media, serve to educate, inform, and entertain the people. The expansion of the economy since the end of colonialism has made more radio and television sets available to the people, and the number of stations has increased.

Nation-wide television network began broadcasting in 1962. Similar to the fate of the print media, the television stations are also under governmental control. All materials shown on television usually pass through strictly bureaucratic surveillance. In the beginning, televisions relied on foreign programs and films. The Center for Moroccan Cinema, or *Centre for Cinématographique Marocain*

(CCM), founded in 1944, influenced TV programs until independence in 1956 when the organization was turned over to the new government. The government uses television as a medium to propagate religious morality and encourage civic engagements. As a vehicle for transmitting education and culture, the stations also maintain school programs. A recent study has noted that television "generally thought of as placing few literary requirements on the viewer, now reaches the homes of Moroccans of all socioeconomic levels."[42] The Moroccan television industry continues to grow and to seek the means to adapt to its local milieu.

The focus of improvement in this sector has been on adaptation to new global technological advances. Today, the electronic media covers nearly all parts of the country. The government-owned Moroccan Broadcasting Network, *Radio-Television Marocaine* (RTM), covers a wide-range of audiences in Arabic, French, English, Spanish, and the three major Berber dialects— Tamazight, Tachelhit, and Tarifit. The government also retains substantial control of the Medi 1 (Radio Méditerranée International) based in Tangier. The Medi 1 broadcasts programs in Arabic and French. The number of household ownership of radios and televisions has increased substantially in the past two decades.[43] Also, the moderate cost of satellite dishes has enabled about 1.2 million viewers to gain access to a wide variety of foreign programs.

The government owns the two major television networks, the RTM and 2M-TV based in Casablanca. Meanwhile, the government has expressed the intention to liberalize and privatize these state-owned media houses, but the plan may be a long way off because the monarchy is mindful of the likely political costs of losing control of the media. Altogether, there are about 35 television stations operating in Morocco. This includes the Western Sahara, where the National Radio (NR) and Saharan Arab Democratic Republic (SADR) were launched in the 1970s. They both continue to serve the independent struggle of the Polisario Front, and transmit the news in both Arabic and Spanish.

Internet

Despite a lack of consistent government policy for development, Moroccans have boldly taken on the emerging trend in Internet access. With the exception of South Africa and Nigeria, Morocco has one of the largest telecom sectors in Africa. There are about half a million Internet users in the country, and the government can censor any Internet site, particularly those hostile to its policies on Western Sahara. Web users in Morocco can access information from offices and private homes.

Overall, an assessment of media freedom in Morocco in the twenty-first century reveals that this sector has grown stronger in the past two decades. There is still plenty of room for improvement, for this deficiency also has implications for freedom of expression in other matters, including religion.

Religious Freedom

Islam disapproves the rule of non-Muslims over the community of believers (or *umma*). In Morocco, as in other Islamic states, the political leader must also be able to lead the faithful. The Quran prescribes the unity of the individual, state, and society under the all-powerful will of God. Islamic rulers exercised both temporal and religious authority; to them the Western idea of separation of church and state appears irrational. Islamic countries like Morocco are theoretically divided into three domains. All Muslims collectively formed the abode of Islam (*Dar al Islam*). The People of the Book, that is the adherents of other revealed monotheistic religions—Judaism and Christianity—are allowed to practice their religion as "protected people" (or *dhimmis*). Polytheists are consigned as people in darkness that are in need of salvation. Accordingly, the people are designated as either citizens, as in the case of Muslims, or subjects comprising of all others who do not practice the faith. These designations come with all the accoutrements of power and privileges.

To obtain legitimacy, the leader of the Islamic community must demonstrate attributes of holiness and charisma. The leader is believed to impart some of this blessedness to the people and objects with which they come in contact. It is commonly accepted that the predisposition to have special holiness or blessings runs in families, hence monarchical governments rule most Islamic countries. Expectedly, Prophet Mohammed is believed to have the most charisma and holiness. Therefore, his descendents (the *Shaifa*) are highly respected because they are believed to have inherited an abundance of divine blessings from the great Prophet of Islam.

In this understanding, it is crucial to reiterate that no society is without a tradition of civil society, including those under the sphere of Islam. The non-Western societies are also not anti-democracy. What religion brought upon the politics of most states under the sphere of Islam is an ideological pretext for the ruling classes to appropriate absolute powers and privileges that are often legitimized with claims to holy ancestry (*Shaifa*) with Mohammad (the Holy Prophet of Islam). With the king of Morocco enjoying this claim, as Dris Ben Ali aptly observes, his authority "became present everywhere, intervening into everything, and invading nearly every social and political space."[44] Indeed, since independence in 1956, the succeeding kings of Morocco have not only acted as the guardians of citizens, but also as the self-appointed managers of national resources. Monarchical authority demands that citizens offer complete allegiance and cooperation to the Islamic state. Any voice of opposition is generally interpreted as a heresy, an opposition to Islam and the Prophet Mohammed. It is within this implicit understanding of politics going back to the pre-colonial era that the succeeding rulers of Morocco have attempted, with mixed results, to appropriate forms of patriarchal authority. This often alienates, but sometimes encourages partnership and dialogue with the civil populace. The quest for liberalization in Morocco must, however, respect human rights.

Human Rights and Women's Rights

For the ongoing transition to progress, more guarantees on freedom and human rights are required from the government as the new generation looks forward to a democracy in their country. Under Mohammed VI, the government has also attempted to improve upon its human rights records and pursue a program of economic liberalization that is envisaged to introduce greater private sector participation and control. In the past, many political opponents were prisoners who experienced tortures in detention. The unlucky ones died in detention. In his first national address shortly after his father's death, Mohammed VI reiterated his commitment to constitutional monarchy and political pluralism.

The emerging order, which promises to empower social actors and forces previously kept on the margins, also highlights issues related to women, young people, Berbers, economic aids and economic development issues, human rights and civil liberties, and campaigns against corruption. As elucidated by an expert on North African societies, the attitude and role of women in society is largely informed by the people's worldview and customs, including prevalent economic, demographic, and political culture.[45] In general, men enjoy a position of higher social status, and appear to dominate women in certain aspects of life. A stereotypical notion of a woman's role is to provide maternal care for her children and the household. It is her responsibility to shop, cook, feed, and educate the children while the man is at work. Moroccan women maintain sanitary conditions in the house, and during their leisure time, they may visit family members, friends, or attend prayers at the neighborhood shrines or mosques. Even in the countryside, where Berber women share the agricultural duties with their husbands and do not wear restrictive veils, they are still obligated to conform to their primary responsibilities of childcare and food preparation. Muslim women rarely accompany their husbands to social events outside of the household, especially since they have so many responsibilities in the house to occupy their day. While men live a much more unstructured life, women are still expected, but not forced, to adhere to certain codes of behavior, especially before marriage. For instance, it is considered crude for young women to marry outside their race or faith, travel abroad without obtaining parental consent, or to be unaccompanied during late hours. In Morocco, it is forbidden for the predominantly Berber-Arab women to be married to French, Spanish, or Jewish men, but their men are free to marry outsiders. Unlike men, women are scolded for smoking in public. When a woman errs, it is also part of the culture for a man to beat his wife—an act that is considered an "abuse" in Western societies.

However, the notion of male domination is neither as simplistically assumed by outsiders nor uniformly practiced. As a study notes, "a closer examination of the structure and operation of the household reveals the presence of a considerable measure of 'unassigned power' which women compete for and utilize to further their own needs and wishes."[46] For instance, a woman's age and status within the household play an important role in her influence and decision making in society. Older women are highly respected, and often enjoy the support of their children. They are honored and revered as wise, responsible, and trustworthy. Also, while Berber women may have more freedom in the countryside, some educated urban women also enjoy relative respect and freedom than their less educated cohorts. Similarly, uneducated men perform more traditional forms of labor than their educated counterparts. A 1997 study by the International Food and Agricultural Development (IFAD) in the Taforalt-Taourist region of the Oujda province of Eastern Morocco has shown that while women generally aspired to the lifestyle of a "rich woman" (which implies not having to perform menial tasks such as weaving, water collection, and animal husbandry), men and women from the poorer households compromise on these issues in the happiness of their families.[47]

In the past, the public spheres of government, law, warfare, and trade used to be the exclusive domain of men. Today, government involves the active participation of women who are serving as political delegates, ambassadors, airline pilots, company directors, and royal advisors. More evidence of these open policies was the march of 40,000 women in 2000 for support of increased rights for women. Through personal achievements, some women have established themselves as eminent scholars, world athletes, writers, publishers, journalists, and activists. Overall, gender discrimination is no longer practiced. Women are now free to pursue university education, and their career prospects have continued to expand. Similarities and dissimilarities exist between the Western and Islamic social organizations and in gender relations. While patriarchal authority still dominates the social order in Morocco, many Western societies have instituted laws aimed to protect women's rights. All patriarchal societies, including the United States, have either now or in the past operated social systems that privileged men over women. However, some countries have recently taken steps towards realizing a freer society by passing legislative acts aimed at achieving equality of the sexes.

Human Development

As witnessed across Africa, the early 1980s marked a crucial turning point in the economic, social, and political life of Morocco. Confronted with budget deficits, high levels of unemployment, widespread civil unrests, and rumors of coups and assassinations plots, King Hassan commenced a program of reforms that saw the first official opposition party led by Abderrahmare Youssoufi in 1998.[48] Mohammed's ascension to power in 1999 witnessed a commitment to improve human development through economic liberalism. The king promised to tackle poverty and corruption, and also to create more jobs for the army of unemployed graduates. These promises initially suggested that the new king was serious about his liberalization program. In a move that was widely viewed as "the dawn of a new era" of accountability, Mohammed VI attempted to distance himself from the allures of his father's numerous royal palaces, and disposed of a number of the royal limousines. While these moves endeared the new king into the hearts of his countrymen, especially young people, his opponents continued to express doubts about the seriousness of his liberal pretensions, arguing that the new king lacked both the experience and commitment to uphold human rights and free speech.[49] This view, also shared by some business groups and Non-Governmental Organizations (NGOs), is better understood in the light of the political economy of the state.

Seymour Martin Lipset, in a pioneer study *Political Man: The Social Basis of Politics*, found a strong correlation between democracy and a country's level of economic development or modernization.[50] According to Leroy Vail, modernization theorists suppose that with "greater access to education, improved communications, and the shifting of people from the slumbering 'traditional' rural sector economy to the vibrant 'modern' industrial sector,"[51] ethnic consciousness will give way to national consciousness. Therefore, the strengthening of the state, the expansion of economic output, and the integration of new peoples as full and useful participants in the institutional, social, political, and cultural patterns of the modern world hold the key to solving socioeconomic and political issues.[52]

Thus, educational reforms in Morocco should reflect upon the lessons from the country's past and how to use this history in order to build a better and articulate sociopolitical order. In recognition of this function, the government has put in place a universal education program that is free and compulsory from ages 7 to 13. The 2004 literacy level is 51.7 percent of the population, which is comprised of those 15 years and above. The male-female literacy ratio is 64.1 to 39.4 percent. Although some families are strongly committed to the education of their female members, girls tend to spend less time in school because their families often need them to assist the older women in their domestic tasks. Schools teach in Arabic until the third grade, after which bilingual education starts in both Arabic and French. After secondary school education, the ratio of female-male enrollment drops sharply, often standing at 3:5. While university education is highly valued because it holds the promise of raising individual social status and standards of living, the wealthy have a privileged access to higher education. The percentage of school enrollment for Moroccans has been on the increase over the past two decades. Among the most popular universities in Morocco are the University of Rabat and the Islamic Karouine University. Invariably, improvements in education have resulted in creating more economic opportunities, especially for the young people flocking to the cities.

Overall, human development holds a crucial promise on the journey to democratization and liberalization. As Lipset has argued, with increased wealth, most powerful groups, as well as poorer ones, could secure some redistribution of wealth without much inter-group antagonism. In such a circumstance, the richer group is independent of state control on one hand, and on the other it has no great obligation or commitment to cater for the poorer group. Such a scenario relieves the pressure from the state, which can then govern with ease. In their cross-national study of 224 regimes, Adam Przeworski et al. concluded that the risk of a democratic breakdown falls as annual per capita income increases. Beyond the $6000 mark, "democracies are impregnable and can be expected to live forever."[53] In this regard, Lipset saw such variables as urbanization, industrialization, per capita income, and the level of education as harbingers of democracy.[54] In his calculations, the 'lower class' is more likely to be integrated within the polity in an economically viable state. With proper integration, there are slim chances for them to turn to opposition or counter ideologies. Again, since wealth is independently redistributed, the private sectors are likely to make sacrifices to expand education

and social welfare, or permit trade unions to pursue demands for better working conditions.[55] In addition, the middle-class in a country can be reinforced
by socioeconomic development, which is good for democracy because it "tem-
pers conflict by rewarding moderate and democratic parties and penalizes extremist groups."[56] Lipset further argues that a legitimacy crisis may arise if
rising social groups were denied political access or if new class divisions reinforced older divisions based on ethnicity and confessional affiliations.[57] He
advocates that, "to attain legitimacy, what new democracies need above all is
efficacy, particularly in the economic arena, but also in the polity. If they can
take the high road to economic development, they can keep their political
houses in order."[58]

Similarly, Samuel P. Huntington authoritatively asserts that "In short, if you
wish to produce democracy, promote economic growth."[59] According to Huntington, there are several reasons for this relationship.

> Economic development involves higher levels of urbanization, liter-
> acy, and education. It also involves a shift in occupational structure,
> with a decline in the size and importance of the peasantry and the
> development of a middle class and an urban working class. The lat-
> ter groups increasingly want a voice in and influence over policies
> that affect them. With higher levels of education, they are able to
> organize trade unions, political parties, and civic associations to pro-
> mote their interest. Second, economic development produces more
> resources, public and private, for distribution among groups in so-
> ciety. Politics becomes less of a zero-sum game, and hence compro-
> mise and toleration are encouraged. Third, economic growth produces
> a more complex economy that becomes increasingly difficult for the
> state to control; as we have seen in the case of the command
> economies, state control can only be maintained at the price of eco-
> nomic stagnation. Fourth, the easing of state control of the econ-
> omy leads to the creation and growth of independent centres of
> power, based on private control of capital, technology, and com-
> munications. The bourgeoisie who hold these assets want a political
> system in which they can exercise influence, one that is not dominated
> by a military junta, a politburo, or a dictator and his cronies. Fi-
> nally, while in the short term rapid economic growth often exacer-
> bates income inequalities, in the longer term it produces greater
> equality in income distribution.[60]

In this light, about four decades ago, Barrington Moore concluded "No
bourgeoisie, no democracy."[61]

Economic Freedom

Human development is synonymous with economic freedom. However, there is a difference as to how this relates to democratization and liberalization in the sense that there can be human development without economic freedom, as seen with communist countries like China and Cuba. So far, the Moroccan state is working hard to advance human security through human development and some measure of economic freedom. Following the recent political openings, the emergent class of entrepreneurs is perhaps the most visible outcome of the ongoing depolitization process in Morocco. Prior to the 1990s, entrepreneurs were merely rent-seekers who jostled for favor in the familiar "prebendal" postcolonial political culture of reward and punishment under the direction of the state.[62] Consequently, the impoverished and marginalized masses largely viewed the emergent entrepreneur class as parasites and held them in contempt. With liberalization and privatization programs, which saw the relative easing of state hold on the economy, successful entrepreneurs started to acquire a new respectable status as public actors. Yet, a careful understanding of the process will best describe this development as mere elite cooption in a well-oiled clientage network, linking political "good boys" with rewards originating from the king's palace down a chain of commands under royal loyalists.

As a group, the new entrepreneur class has solidified their newly found social relevance under the General Confederation of Morocco's Enterprises or *Association Marocaine D'Employeurs* (CGEM). The CGEM secured the formal recognition of the state in July 1996 under an agreement signed by the Minister of the Interior. Of course, this recognition was relatively easy after the government had received assurances that it could count on their continued loyalty as partners in progress. With this recognition, the CGEM has become a loyal partner with the state in the depolitization and liberalization program. At best, it acts as a go-between for the state and the ordinary people. In the ongoing process of economic reforms, the CGEM positions itself as a defender of the masses' interests, and it often comes out publicly with populist statements. Nonetheless, how many of these statements are originating from the king is difficult to ascertain.[63]

Through its deregulation program, the Moroccan state rewards its supporters by selling state companies such as banks, construction, tourism, and agro-allied concerns to the king's associates at nominal prices.[64] The continued practice of institutionalized client-patron redistributive culture has proved detrimental to the full realization of the high expectations of the recent liberalization movement. This has prompted a weary observer like Addeslam

Maghraoui to contend that, "although favorable to democracy on the surface, Morocco's liberal reforms have actually worked against it by *depoliticizing* the public sphere." By "depoliticization," Maghraoui means "the marginalization of questions of legitimacy or sovereignty and—in the Moroccan case especially—the concomitant political primacy given to economic issues."[65] As clientelism engenders practice of unfair redistribution, the increasing exclusion of young people from economic and political life has the potential to engender a more radical and violent backlash. Elaborating on the necessity for the ongoing economic and political transition to be pursued in a manner that will enable equal opportunities for all classes of citizens, Ali argues that:

> A political game limited to the notables and docile elites has not been able to accommodate the presence of a middle class in full expansion. Finally, the opening up of the world market and the economic liberalization started by the government since more than two decades has given birth to new types of practice, where autonomy and responsibility are claimed as rights.[66]

The king may adopt a consensus and compromise approach when cohesion is required among various parties. This process provides civil society with the opportunity for direct participation in decisions that concern their immediate constituencies. This was clearly the case in the enactment of the labor code approved by both Houses of the Parliament in July 2003. Yet, the king may exercise his "rights of the sovereignty" when dealing with national security, Islamic principles, and important economic or social issues. In fact, the decision to embark on economic reforms or Structural Adjustment Programs (SAP) was exclusively the king's call. Of particular interest is the careful manner followed by the king to explain to the people why such a crucial program of survival was unavoidable. On other occasions, the king has considered public appearances or speeches to Parliament necessary as a forum to outline specific policy directions or projects that are in the pipeline. Additionally, the king also employs a sort of arbitrage as a form of interaction with civil society. Through personal intervention, this strategy allows the king to act as an intermediary between divergent interests.[67]

Conclusion

This chapter focused on the status of democratization in the Islamic kingdom of Morocco. To gauge the degree of success attained so far on the road to democratization, the Status of Democracy index (SDI) was adopted measuring (1) free election of heads of state, (2) free election of members of the leg-islature, (3) political party development, (4) suffrage and the maturity of po-litical rights, (5) media freedom, (6) religious liberty, (7) respect for human rights/women's freedom, (8) human development as articulated by the United Nations Development Program (UNDP), and (9) economic freedom. The re-sults show that even with its piecemeal approach to liberalization and democ-ratization, Morocco ranks first among the very few countries trying to enthrone a more open and popular political order in the entire Middle East and North-ern Africa. The truth of the matter is that the 2011 wave of mass protests going on in the Arab world (particularly in North Africa) have the potential to top-ple the entrenched political systems of the region in favor of a more demo-cratic space. This is more likely in countries with serious economic problems. For Morocco, the saving grace for the monarchy may be there if the king moves quickly to make more concessions and compromises in line with the common expectations of the people. There is also the crucial economic factor on which scholars could predict the chances of either stabilization or breakdown of North African politics in the next few years.

Nigeria

NIGER

CHAD

R. NIGER

Sokoto

Katsina

Nguru Gashua

Birnin Kebbi

Kaura Namoda

Jega   Gummi

Maiduguri

Malumfashi   Karaye Kura

Bama

Bebeji   Rano Takai Jamaare

Azare   Potiskum

Birnin Kudu

Zaria   Buruimburum Santamiya Misau   Fika

Bin Yauri

Gwaram Gabarin

Gurai

Mubi

Kaduna

BENIN

Bauchi   Gombe

Kachia   Jos

NIGERIA

Abuja

Jalingo

Keffi

Oshogbo

Makurdi

Gbongan   Ilesha

Oturkpo Gboko

Ibadan   Ife   Akure

Abeokuta   Ondo   Owo

Nsukka

Enugu

Awka   Abakaliki

Benin City

Lagos   Onitsha

Sapele

CAMEROON

Warri

Ikot-ekpene   Calabar

Port Harcourt

ATLANTIC OCEAN

Chapter 4

Nigeria: The Quest for a Lasting Democracy in the Post-Civil War Era

Ngozi Caleb Kamalu and Fuabeh P. Fonge

The evolution of Nigerian politics since independence has revealed a tendency to vacillate between the civilian and the military rules. Since its attainment of independence in 1960, the nation has experimented with three civilian regimes; first, under Dr. Nnamdi Azikiwe, its first President (1960–1966) and later from 1979 to 1983 under the tutelage of Alhaji Shehu Shagari. Olusegun Obasanjo, a former military leader, was also elected as civilian head of state and governed through two successful terms amounting to eight years in office before he handed over the reign of government to Alhaji Umaru Musa Yar'Adua, a non-military man who won the bitterly contested and controversial April 2007 presidential election. Although he came from a political dynasty, Yar'Adua rose from obscurity to become the Nigerian head of state. His late father was a federal minister, but Umaru Yar'Adua's political activities were largely overshadowed by that of his late brother, Major-General Shehu Musa Yar'Adua who served as Obasanjo's deputy during his first term as military head of state. Shehu Musa Yar'Adua later died in prison during the rough turbulent days of Abacha's regime. Umaru Musa Yar'Adua was also the first president of Nigeria since Nnamdi Azikiwe with full university education. Umaru Musa Yar'Adua, the 13th president of Nigeria did not complete his first term of office. He ruled May 29, 2007 to May 5, 2010, when he died in office of natural causes and the mantle of power was shifted to yet another civilian head of state, President Goodluck Ebele Azikiwe Jonathan. At the time of this writing, the incumbent president Jonathan has been in power since May 6, 2010.

This chapter is aimed at examining Nigeria's post-1970 civilian regimes, including the progress made toward the establishment of the Third Republic. In this regard, this chapter will explore the nature of institutions on which the

Shagari regime (Second Republic) was founded. This includes the prevailing political culture and political events that took place in order to understand some of the reasons that necessitated a military intervention.

Furthermore, this study will explore various actions taken by the Babangida regime to facilitate a smooth transition to a civilian regime in the Third Republic. Special emphasis will be placed on the institutional arrangements made toward the attainment of such goal, in terms of party formation, ideology, political campaigns and constitutional provisions. The goal is to assess these mechanisms in the context of preceding democratic regimes to see whether old mistakes can be corrected, and measure the probability of this experience succeeding, given Nigeria's complex social and political milieu.

Another arduous task of this probe is to test the "changing guard doctrine" used by many students of military politics to charge that coups and counter coups in Africa are not intended to introduce the vital "reform ethic" into government, but rather a strategy to deceive the gullible, naïve, and negligent public and hold on to power. Hence, this investigation is committed to establishing whether or not the actions and strategies adopted by the Babangida military government toward a democratic transition was an attempt by the military through threat, deceit, or other forms of political mechanism and maneuver to manipulate the popular will and cling on to power. The chapter is also intended to evaluate the prospect of a peaceful and enduring democratic rule in Nigeria's Third Republic.

An important thesis of this study is that Nigeria's post-civil war Second Republic relied on parochial institutional structures that promoted national disunity due to ethnic and religious sentiments. While voting patterns followed ethnic, religious, and regional lines, the elite individual culture fostered unrestrained corruption, indiscipline, and class divisions. This was combined with the centrifugal effects of labor unrest, ethnic and religious strife, student protests, and how the unpopularity of the Shagari regime provided a rationale for military intervention.

Moreover, there was a significant public unease and suspicion resulting from the belief that the Babangida regime was not fully committed to handing over power to a democratically elected government in 1993. A case in point was his abrupt change of the targeted handover date from October 1, 1992 to January 2, 1993. Also, in support of this notion was the campaign by alleged proxies that he never publicly denounced, calling for a diarchy. The group was sternly denounced and bitterly challenged by pro-democracy movements.

The authors express skepticism over the proposed democratic transition, given the fact that political and military power in Nigeria was skewed in favor of the northern sector of the country. As a result, power tends to be consolidated in the hands of northern elite, based on religion, ethnicity, and geographic origin. Hence, the primary hidden and possibly unintended role of the army was to guarantee that power be retained by the northerners on a permanent basis and to defend it. The decentralization of military control is the answer to ethnic and regional political imbalance; but it must be noted that this approach has been unproductive owing to resistance by the northerners. Since reliance on democratic rules works against group monopoly of power, an attempt to institute a system of government where power shift is a reality seems to have been doomed in Nigeria. The unexpected death of Umaru Musa Yar'Adua on May 5, 2010, suddenly changed the dynamics of power accumulation and provided an opportunity for a non-Northerner, Goodluck Jonathan, to become the next president of the country. It is too early to judge, but the impending presidential election would either establish or refute Jonathan's authenticity in power.

Nigeria: Location, Demography, and Pre-War Politics

Oil-rich Nigeria and the most populous African nation was a British colony until October 1, 1960, when it regained its independence from Britain. With the current estimated population of about 152 million, the nation has witnessed a significant population increase from its 1966 figures of 55.66 million that was paradoxically a decline from the 120.5 million projection based on the 1963 data.

According to the *Nigerian New Digest*, this makes Nigeria not only Africa's most populous country, but also the 11th most populous nation in the world with growth rate of 2.1 percent, a rate that is 1.2 percent short of the figures estimated by international organizations.[1] Nigeria, as a geographic entity, is bounded in the north by the African nations of Niger and Chad; in the west by the Republic of Benin; in the east by Cameroon, and in the south by the Atlantic Ocean. Within the Nigerian federation are 30 states and the federal city territory of Abuja, which replaced Lagos as the new capital.

At independence, and prior to the civil war, the country experienced a short-lived civilian administration with Dr. Nnamdi Azikiwe as President and Alhaji Abubakar Tafawa Balewa as Prime Minister. The first military coup d'état that took place in January 1966 brought to power the short-lived administration of Major General Aguiyi Ironsi that collapsed in July of the same year as the result of a counter coup engineered by the then Lieutenant Colonel Yakubu Gowon. The political turbulence that ensued led to a secession attempt when the Igbo-dominated Eastern Region declared itself the independent Republic of Biafra. A civil war ensued following attempts by the federal authority to bring its rebellious region back to the national fold. The war lasted from 1967 to 1970 when the last vestiges of the Biafran Armed Force were crushed by federal troops.

The Shagari Regime: Political Institutions and Cultural Underpinnings

The end of the civil war rehabilitation and resettlement activities took place under the Yakubu Gowon regime that was later overthrown in 1975 in yet another military coup d'état orchestrated by General Murtala Muhammed who, in turn, was killed in an abortive Dimka Coup. Muhammed was succeeded by General Olusugun Obasanjo who continued with his predecessor's administration's plan to hand over power to a democratically elected civilian regime. In October 1979, the national mantle was handed over to President Shehu Shagari.

But, this experiment was short-lived because the house of the nation appeared to be built on shaky political ground. Hence, the national ideology, party formation, and political attitudes did not prove suitable for political integration and national consolidation.

Party Formation and Voting Behavior

The roles played by selected centrifugal forces that have marred the national unity in Nigerian politics predating this time have been of concern to its nationalist leaders. These centrifugal factors include ethnicity, regionalism, class, leadership personalities, religion, language, and national ideologies. Hence, the urge persisted for the establishment of nationally based political parties with broad-based appeals. Also, at-large statewide constituencies in national elections were emphasized to ensure that elected officials were committed to the general welfare as opposed to narrow or parochial constituent interests. As Jon Kraus observed, "an independent Federal Electoral Commission (FEDECO) was established to enforce the regulations that enhanced this goal. Its main objective was to register only parties with national appeal and representation."[2]

Based on the above criteria, five political parties were registered to compete within the 19 states of the federation. The parties were the Unity Party of Nigeria (UPN), National Party of Nigeria (NPN), Northern People's Party (NPP), Great Nigerian People's Party (GNPP), and People's Redemption Party (PRP). However, the party formation arrangements virtually mirrored ethnic and regional identities. For example, the NPP was formed and headed by Dr.

Nnamdi Azikiwe, the first President of Nigeria, who was of an Igbo ethnicity and extraction.

The party's stronghold was among the Igbos in the present Anambra and Imo States, but with considerable support among the people of Benue and Plateau States as a result of coalitions and alliances built. It should also be noted that these are constituencies that have strong cultural affiliation in terms of geography and education with the Igbos. It was no surprise that Azikiwe's NPP did not fare well among the ethnic inhabitants of Cross River State perhaps because of the widely held negative perception about Dr. "Zik" by the Efik who remember vividly his unfair treatment of their ethnic symbol Professor Eyo Ata in the First Republic. According to Chinua Achebe, when Dr. Azikiwe won the first general election to the Western House of Assembly in the heart of Yoruba land, Obafemi Awolowo "stole" the government from him in broad daylight.

Rather than staying in the Western House as the leader of the opposition party on principle, Zik compromised his right to ethnic pressure from his main rival Awolowo and fled to Enugu, the then capital of Eastern Nigeria, to dethrone Eyo Ata. Thus, as stated by Achebe in *The Trouble with Nigeria*, "the brutal treatment offered Eyo Ata, an Efik, in Enugu did not go unnoticed in Calabar. It contributed in no small measure to the suspicion of majority Igbo by their minority neighbors in Eastern Nigeria."[3]

The NPN, a mainly Hausa-Fulani based party, appeared to have appealed the most to the Efiks. The party also enjoyed strong support in both the Middle Belt and Southeastern states. The head of the ticket was a former Hausa school teacher, businessman, and former federal commissioner, Alhaji Shehu Shagari, who picked an Igbo millionaire and architect, Alex Ekwueme, as his running mate. Perhaps the choice of Alex Ekwueme as the Vice Presidential candidate was intended to mask the depth of natural dissatisfaction harbored by Ibos toward Shagari. The difference between the party identification of NPN vis-à-vis UPN in the Igbo heartland may be attributed to Achebe's observation that:

> Chief Awolowo had a well-deserved reputation for anti-Igbo politics which, over a period of years, had permeated every stratum of Igbo society. And although Shagari did not inspire similar personal antipathy he did inherit the odium of the 1966 massacres in the North and the later federal government discrimination against Igbo areas during the military administration in which he, even more than Awolowo, had participated.[4]

The UPN was Yoruba based, with an overwhelming lock on the Western allegiance. The Late Chief Obafemi Awolowo, the former leader of the Action Group in the 1960s, headed it. A self-made millionaire, lawyer, and feudal landholder, he had embraced the socialist political philosophy. The party's support outside the Yoruba ethnic group was almost nonexistent. Among the Igbos in the South, he had cultivated a wide-ranging distrust mainly because he wanted the Igbos of Biafra punished in revenge after the civil war, which ended in January 1970. This sentiment was reflected in his policies toward the Igbos. As Achebe again noted:

> There were hard-liners in Gowon's cabinet who wanted their pound of flesh, the most powerful among them being Chief Obafemi Awolowo, Federal Commissioner for Finance. Under his guidance a banking policy was evolved which nullified any bank account which had been operated during the civil war. This had the immediate result of pauperizing the Igbo middle class and earning a profit of 4 million pounds for the federal government treasury.[5]

Waziri Ibrahim who was once affiliated with the NPP led a splinter Great Nigerian People's Party (GNPP) after his attempts to steer the party to a new direction failed. The GNPP drew the bulk of its support from the Kanuris ethnicity in the Bornu and Gongola States. Although it is a northern-based party, it still remained a minority party in both the northern and southern regions of Nigeria.

Alhaji Aminu Kano headed the People's Redemption Party (PRP). It had wide support among the Hausa in the North, especially with strong footholds in Kano and Kaduna states. Although it held populist views, it nonetheless commanded great support among the nationalist intelligentsias. As Achebe testifies, Kano was "selflessly committed to the common people of our land whom we daily deprive and dispossess and whose plight we treat so callously and frivolously."[6] He goes on to praise Kano as a man of great intelligence and foresight who traded his personal and class privileges to identify with the downtrodden. In his tribute, Achebe concludes: "After his example, no one who reduces the high purpose of politics which he exemplified down to a swinish scramble can hope to do so without bringing a terrible judgment on himself. Nigeria cannot be the same again because Aminu Kano lived here."[7]

Data Analysis and Voting Patterns among Ethnic Groups

Looking at the pattern of voting among the groups, for the five political parties that contested the 1979 presidential elections, we find that the Igbos overwhelmingly voted for the NPP. Around 85 percent of the Igbo vote went to the NPP. The Igbo vote for NPN was second, with 11 percent of the votes. The Igbo votes that went to the GNPP and PRP were very minimal, representing barely 1 percent to 2 percent of the votes cast. The NPP was a home-based party of the Igbos, and was presided over by an Igbo native son, Dr. Nnamdi Azikiwe. This might have accounted for the massive thrust of the Igbo votes toward NPP. This phenomenon was, however, predictable. The NPN, which received the second largest percentage or share of Igbo vote of 11.2 percent, was a non-Igbo ethnic based party. But, it had an Igbo "native son," Alex Ekwueme, as its Vice President. This selection could suggest why it might have drawn a substantial number of ethnic Igbo votes. A very meager percentage of votes went to the other minority parties, namely GNPP and PRP probably because they were not perceived as having the chance to win, primarily because they lacked the necessary resources to effect and run a credible campaign or because they did not run on a persuasive or popular platform.

Table 1. Presidential Election Results, 1979

Ethnic Group	(in millions)	Votes Cast for Political Parties				
		UPN	NPN	NPP	GNPP	PRP
Igbo	2.4	.02	.26	2.0	.05	.02
Hausa	4.0	.14	1.7	.09	.57	1.42
Yoruba	4.7	4.0	.53	.10	.04	.02

Source: *Africa Research Bulletin*, Aug.1–31 (1983), 6936. See also, Oyeleye Oyediran, *The Nigerian 1979 Elections* (Macmillan Nigerian Publishers Ltd., Lagos, 1981). Any discrepancy may be due to rounding.

This same trend is also observed among ethnic Hausa voters. The NPN, which received the largest share of up to 44.3 percent of the ethnic Hausa vote, was home-based and headed by an ethnic figure. The paradoxical discovery is that even though GNPP was Hausa-based, just like NPN, and also headed by an ethnic candidate, it nonetheless captured only 14.5 percent of Hausa votes, as opposed to 44 percent won by NPN. This development was contrary to popular expectation and prediction. Voters' preferences in choosing NPN over GNPP might have been precipitated by the marginality of the utility associated with the choice of one political party over the other. These choice criteria conceivably were based on which political party had more resources, better goals and objectives, more appealing candidates, and greater probability for success, or had won the voters' allegiance.

UPN was the only viable party in existence in the Western Region and was also headed by its native son, Obafemi Awolowo. It was not a surprise that it won the highest percentage of Yoruba ethnic votes—close to 85 percent. Other contesting parties received a meager ratio, perhaps because of the limited knowledge of the voters about other parties due to inadequate campaigns that they conducted among other ethnic groups, poor strategy, and a measure of distrust for non-indigenous ethnically based polity.

Table 2. Percentage of Presidential Election Results, 1979

Ethnic Groups	Votes Cast (in millions)	% Votes for Political Parties				
		UPN	NPN	NPP	GNPP	PRP
Igbo	2.4	.70	11.2	84.7	2.3	1.0
Hausa	3.91	3.6	44.3	2.3	14.5	36.1
Yoruba	4.71	85	11.3	2.2	.80	.30

Source: Data adapted from African Research Bulletin, August 1–3 (1983), 6936.

Shagari Declared Winner in Spite of All That Transpired

Despite winning more votes than other competing parties, Shagari's NPN did not win a clear majority in accordance with the rules set by the Federal Electoral Commission, FEDECO. However, FEDECO went ahead and declared Shagari the winner. If this had been a local or limited small-scale election, a run-off election would have been ordered. Instead, Awolowo, the runner up, contested in the Supreme Court the legitimacy of Shagari being declared president. As Jean Herskovits noted, the court affirmed the FEDECO ruling of September 26, five days before Shagari's inauguration, thereby resolving a critical electoral dilemma.[8] Specifically, in the words of Jon Kraus, "despite the fact that NPN's Shagari won 33.8% of the presidential vote but merely one-fourth of the vote in only 12 of the 19 states, thus scoring less than the prescribed two-thirds, both FEDECO and the court decided that two-thirds of the 19 states could be achieved by Shagari."[9] Although the court exercised its power of "judicial review," it nonetheless did not settle the suspicion among the warring parties. The consequence was that the Supreme Court ruling failed to heal the wounds. Hence, Awolowo and the UPN registered their disapproval by declining to recognize Shagari as president.

Larry Diamond captured the timely danger posed to Nigerian politics at this juncture when he observed that there was little doubt to the fact that the temperature of Nigerian body politics was rising. Political conflict became more heated and so polarized that mutual trust between the parties deteriorated to the point where Chief Obafemi Awolowo threatened that if voting machines were adopted in the subsequent election due in 1983, he would instruct his supporters of UPN to demolish them in order to thwart the possibility that the NPN might use them to rig the election.[10]

As a strategy to establish a working majority in the National Assembly, the UPN entered into a coalition accord with Nnamdi Azikiwe's NPP. This alliance immediately forced Shagari to reposition his party platform on domestic policy. The focus of his administration was to promote indigenous production of food as a way to conserve skyrocketing expenditure on imported consumer goods. The aim was to save foreign exchange earnings and inevitably channel the income into national development programs. Also, this move was intended to decrease Nigerian dependence on oil exports. To illustrate Nigeria's financial position and the need to control imported products, an IMF report in 1985 showing trends in Nigeria's aggregate exports, import expenditures, and foreign exchange reserves showed a gloomy picture in its financial position between 1980 and 1984. According to a report by the International Monetary Fund (1985), Nigeria's export earnings declined, almost by half, from $25.7 billion in 1980 to $11.9 billion in 1984. With respect to foreign exchange reserve, Nigeria's foreign exchange savings shrank drastically from $10.2 billion in 1980 to a meager $1.5 billion in 1984. Overall, its declining earning, and insolvency manifested so much in the amount of imported goods it was able to pay for. For example, Nigeria's imports in goods declined by almost 50 percent, from a whopping $21.9 billion in 1980 to a minuscule amount of $11.5 billion in 1984.[11]

In pursuit of the "Green Revolution," the Shagari administration poured huge sums of money into agriculture and related areas to stimulate and sustain local production. As such, agro-industrial projects and financial institutions that could provide financial and loan services to small peasant farmers were supported. But, as Okello noted, these small scale farmers whose access to improved technologies, seeds, and fertilizers were essential for raising food production were totally ignored because government officials were reluctant to implement small farmer projects even when credits were provided.[12]

Class Formation, Ethnic Pluralism, and Political Culture

While the standard of living of many Nigerians had declined, partially because of skewed development strategies and patterns of development that tended to promote more investment in industry, transport, and communication—capital intensive rather than labor intensive projects—a new class of capitalists and middlemen was cultivated. These people had embraced what Daniel J. Elazar identified as "individualistic" political subculture.[13] In other words, there was emphasis on politics as a means of promoting and advancing the social and economic interests of groups or the individual.

Materialism and the parade of the spoils of office became the rallying cry. Politics became rooted in group obligations and personal relationships or patronage. The smuggling of rice, flour, clothes, and jewelry that were banned in 1979, generated enormous profit. Even new, government regulations to control smuggling exacerbated the situation. The motivation to undermine government policies is not far-fetched. According to Bill Freund, Nigerian businessmen entered into deals in such areas like commerce, real estate, or transportation where turnovers and profits remained relatively high. Hence, they shied away from manufacturing and agriculture where long-term investments were imminent.[14] Sayre P. Schatz has likened this economic and political evolution of Nigeria to a transition "from nurture to pirate capitalism." According to his conjecture, pirate capitalism was the consequence of the oil transition since the 1970s.

Government coffers have become a source of enrichment for those who want to live above the average Nigerian standard. But for the moralists, the military, the civil servants, or politicians, the pursuit of productive and honest economic activity as a way of getting ahead or generating surplus has become an illusion or myth. Thus, he continued: "Manipulation has taken the place of monopoly as the inimical alternative. Manipulation of government, the most attractive route to fortune, has diverted effort into unproductive channels. The predominance of such widespread manipulation signifies pirate capitalism, and is a major factor in the emergence of the inert economy."[15]

Among the documentation of a number of extreme corruption cases in government is Karin Barber's revelation that the then Governor Awwal Ibrahim of Niger State was found to be carrying three million Naira on a visit to London.[16] Shagari regime was plagued by many other problems that undermined its stability, sowed the seeds of popular discontent, and finally laid the foundation for its eventual collapse. First, the regime was racked by prolonged labor disputes. In 1976, the military government froze all government wage increases, but increased wage demands continued, and resulted in the establishment of a movement known as the Nigerian Labor Congress (NLC) that, with its 42-member affiliate, fought for the restoration of civil service privileges like basic allowances and car loans. Also, using ultimatum and deadlines, the NLC demanded minimum wage increases from 60 Naira to 300 Naira per month. These demands either fell on deaf ears or were overlooked by Shagari. But, he worked out a compromise through the National Assembly to approve an increase to 125 Naira, or about 150 Naira including allowance.

This compromise did not put to rest all outstanding labor disputes, especially since a precedent had been established. In December 1980, the Senior Staff Association of NEPA (National Electric Power Authority) walked out of their jobs demanding salary increases of 133 percent, which eventually resulted in a three-day total blackout in Nigerian major cities. This threat to national stability did not go unchecked. In order to undermine the solidarity of the unions, the government chose to prop up a new union ideology. It supported the emergence of a new competing labor federation and backed changing union binding clauses including a "check off law" from choice of opting out to voluntary participation. Before this time, the cost of labor unrest to national unity and consolidation had been irreparable. The Shagari Administration was further dogged by a series of religious riots in the North. The most striking event that occurred in December 1980 appeared to be a struggle for authority between traditionalism and modernity.

A small Islamic sect, the Maitatsine, which opposes the programs and values of a modern state and instead embraces populist traditional goals committed to reducing class privileges, materialism, and other institutional inequality had dramatized its existence in the riots that led to the death of about 5,000 people. Also, in 1981, a query to the Emir of Kano from Governor Abubakar Rimi charging the former of deliberate disrespect of the state government fuelled bitter anger that erupted from supporters of the Emir on a massive scale on July 10, 1981. They frowned at the governor's challenge of the traditional authority of the Emir.

The letter from the governor who had been resented by the traditional religious leaders as an enemy of traditional institutions incited a violent protests that resulted in the burning down of the State Government Secretariat, the Radio Kano facilities, the State House of Assembly, and the death of Governor Rimi's chief political adviser, Dr. Bala Mohammed. Not only was the Governor accused of treating the Emir as a symbol of feudal institution, but his letter to the Emir was described as "most disrespectful and although suitable for admonishing a clerk, was most unsuitable for addressing a venerated traditional and religious leader." When the *New Nigeria* reported the circumstances of the letter and suggested the possibility of dethroning the Emir, the newspaper "called on people of goodwill to take every constitutional measure to defend their traditional institutions."[17] It was, therefore, not a surprise when on December 31, 1983, an official announcement reported of a coup conducted by Major-General Muhammadu Buhari and his Deputy Tunde Idiagbon. A new page in Nigerian post-civil war politics was turned. However, the Buhari-Idiagbon regime was short-lived.

On August 27, 1985, the Buhari-Idiagbon regime was succeeded by the government of General Ibrahim Babangida that later promised to conduct a peaceful political transition from military to civilian government by the end of December 1992. Having survived two military coups, one by Major-General Mamman Vatsa, the Minister of Defense in March 1986, and later by Major Orka, the Babangida regime appeared committed to a handover to an elected regime.

Political Foundation for the Third Republic

The historical characterization of Nigerian political institutions had mirrored what Oyeleye Oyediran and Adigun Agbaje see to be "virtually in the worst forms of an unstable democracy." Describing the political situation in Nigeria, Oyediran and Agbaje stated: "most parties are narrowly based, tied to some great and unassailable leader who tends to stamp the organization not with any grand ideological vision but his personal biases. Besides, each is ethnically based, mass mobilizing and confrontational in orientation."[18]

The military government of Ibrahim Babangida tried to reorient Nigerians from personality to policy-oriented politics. In trying to achieve this goal, the administration, in 1986, created the Political Bureau whose main task was to conduct a one-year study and recommend a national consensus on the constitutional future of the country. The report recommended that given the nation's past and present dynamics, a two-party system with some degree of control would be more appropriate.[19]

In support of the recommendations of the Political Bureau's Report, President Babangida, in a national broadcast on October 7, 1989, said that the concurrence of the National Electoral Commission (NEC) to consider two parties was not "flattering in any way as they had firm roots in the past whose burden must be shed if the country is to move forward."[20] In fact, many political observers and analysts have dubbed the choice of forcing a two-party system on the Nigerian populace "guided democracy."

The extent to which the Babangida administration exerted political control has been severely resented, especially in its extreme regulation of democratic behaviors in order to achieve what Oyediran and Agbaje referred to as "legit-imate politics" when they noted that:

> The state has attempted to co-opt or even coerce political groups into submission or eliminate them. It has tolerated popular will and demo-cratic principles when they have not defied the will of the ruling class. Rather than encourage popular democracy to flourish, the state has de-liberately constrained popular political mobilization and participation.[21]

The military government received and accepted the report. It followed suit by setting up a panel to review the 1979 constitution that formed the legal basis of the Second Republic under Shehu Shagari. Even, President Babangida also used the opportunity presented by the report to uphold his fears that a two-party system would undermine Nigerian democracy. However, he observed that any deficiencies in institutional arrangements could be offset with ade-quate electoral and constitutional safeguards.[22]

Henceforth, selected elements in the constitution dealing with the number of party rules, campaign financing, goals, and registration procedures were consolidated in the decree promulgated by the military government in May 1989. The nucleus of this fiat was contained in sections 219 to 227. For ex-ample, section 219 states that: "No association other than a political party rec-ognized and registered under this constitution shall canvass for votes for any candidate at any election or contribute to the funds of any political party or to the election expenses of any candidate at an election."[23] Section 220 of the con-stitution contains the following provisions:

1. Only two political parties shall exist in the federation.
2. Each party's constitution and officials must register with the National Electoral Commission (NEC).
3. The membership of each party must be open to all.
4. The headquarters of each party must be located at the new federal capital, Abuja.
5. The party symbols must not project or convey any religious, regional or ethnic sentiments.[24]

As a consequence of the above safeguards, enforcement of the six-year-old ban on party politics was revoked on May 3, 1989. As a prelude to the elections, the Babangida administration foresaw the need for a massive public education to cultivate appropriate political culture conducive to Nigerian political milieu.

In 1987, the Directorate for Social Mobility was created to carry out a na-tion-wide political education that could guarantee an orderly transition in governance, political discipline, and an informed and disciplined electorate.

The ancillary to the Directorate for Social Mobilization was the Center of Democratic Studies that provided political training and education for politicians and interested party candidates in the form of workshops and lecture series.

The next action taken by the Babangida administration was to evoke Decree No. 25 of 1987, which prohibited any organized political participation by former and current public office holders. This naïve ban of old politicians was ingrained in the philosophy of embracing the incorruptible and untainted, thus, injecting new political attitudes into the body politics. Moreover, it was intended to groom and cultivate a new cadre of leadership. This, nonetheless, defied the general notion that people are a product of their political ecology. The controversy generated by the drive to embrace the "unspoiled" and "new blood" candidates resonated in Obinna Anyadike's column when he wrote:

> President Babangida's new brand of politics for the transition from military to civilian rule depends on drawing in a "new breed" of Nigerian politicians from the grassroots, while excluding the old breed of wealthy and ambitious businessmen. But to cynical Nigerians, the new breed looks suspiciously like the old dressed up in new clothes.[25]

In a similar comment on this matter, Achebe was very critical of the exclusion of old politicians like Dr. Nnamdi Azikiwe from active political life. He maintained that bans constitute an admission of guilt. He felt that such exclusions were without any constitutional basis, and criticized the age limit, for example, as being "unjust." However, he viewed the prevailing Nigerian political calamity as a product of the NEC report and recommendations, and blamed the politics of unenlightened electorate whose votes are being taken for granted. He observed that the so called "new breed" politicians were no different from the corrupt and crooked "old guards" who have voluntarily chosen avenues that will guarantee them immediate gratification to the detriment of building a new political consciousness and social order out of our tragic experiences.[26]

Before the July 19, 1989, deadline set by the National Electoral Commission for registration purposes, 49 prospective parties had emerged. From October 1989 to December 1992, the Babangida regime was committed to providing funds for two parties, namely National Republican Convention (NRC) chaired by Tom Ikimi and the Social Democratic Party (SDP) led by Baba Gana Kingibe, to prevent people from gaining undue influence on both the candidates and political parties. Already, among the 30 states of the federation, the NRC had won governorship elections in 17 states while SDP bagged 13 gubernatorial seats. To no surprise, President Babangida in compliance with the recommendations of the NEC declared NRC and SDP official political parties.

The May Disturbance: A Staged Threat?

According to reports by the *National Concord,* reproduced by the *Nigerian News (USA)* of April 24, 1992, elected civilians had already assumed power on the basis of the December 8, 1990, elections in the local government council level. Consequently, civilian governors had been sworn at the state level. The primaries for the National Assembly were held on May 16, 1992, while the general elections took place on July 4, 1992. The presidential primaries originally scheduled for May 2, 1992, were postponed to August 1, 1992.[27]

In a paid advertisement titled "The Quest for Democracy in Nigeria: An agenda for Political, Democratic, and Economic Stability," the Campaign for Democracy (CD)—an association credited as having strong ties with the Babangida regime and in most cases propagating its official policy—asserted that the military government was scheduled, in accordance with the Transition to Civil Rule program to completely hand power over to a civilians government on January 2, 1993. This overrode the October 1, 1992, initial target date for an official handover—a date that corresponded with the month Nigeria gained its political independence from Britain.

According to the CD, this political arrangement exposed the nation to a "diarchy" or short transitional period between the swearing of public leaders in state and local government level and a joint military rule at the Federal level pending the completion of general elections. But, Keith Atkins, author of the announcement, appeared to justify the general public's acceptability of a diarchy as a permanent feature of Nigerian politics.[28]

The publication raised eyebrows among the populace, especially the proponents of a democratically elected government. It should be recalled that the CD was subsequently suspected of being the mouthpiece and public relations agent of the Babangida regime on the issue of rationalizing the need for the military to cling to power indefinitely, an unpopular subject capable of instigating the wrath of the public. A shocking revelation was the group's judgment that a diarchical system (a model where the military and civilians jointly rule) was plausible because, as it predicted:

> the clamor for a complete handover to the civilians is abating as recent
> events and developments gradually dampen Nigerian's spirits and cast
> shadow of doubts on whether in fact a solid foundation has been laid

> for the Third Republic and as to how long the republic will last. The
> optimistic days for a peaceful handover seem long gone. The forces
> of disintegration are prevailing in all spheres: political, economic and
> military. The transition program now looks no more than a staging
> post on the road into abyss. Indeed, there is a feeling in many quar-
> ters at the present time that the Third Republic will be dead before it
> is born. That it will be still born. It will collapse in a matter of months
> if not weeks.[29]

For sure, those "recent events and development" were subtle reminders of the nation-wide civil disturbances that began on May 13, 1992. This sober po-litical requiem for the Third Republic deserved rebuttal and a pro-democratic body wasted no time in responding to the call.

The CD lambasted the call for a diarchy that was proposed by Keith Atkins, and accused the Association for Better Nigeria of conspiring with the Babangida regime to sabotage an orderly transition to a civilian government. It believed that the Babangida regime's political transition program was a fraud; and the imposition of a two-party system was viewed as a symbol of dictatorship. More-over, the CD called Babangida's national programs, including Structural Ad-justment Program (SAP), a monumental failure and appealed to the nation to do whatever was constitutionally possible to thwart his absolute rule.[30] The May riot was triggered by shortage of gasoline in the midst of economic hard-ship initiated through government austerity measures.

The persistent shortage of gasoline was attributed to the idling of three of Nigeria's four refineries. Public transportation costs skyrocketed to about 400 percent. The specter of three out of the nation's four refineries being shut down at the same time convinced the masses, more than anything else, that the prob-lem was the result of corruption and possibly government conspiracy to insti-gate violent public reaction that would trigger government clamp down, and create a sort of climate that the military could use to justify suspending the transition plan to a civil government.

But, the government's story was that the shortage was caused by lack of spare parts, poor maintenance, and the activities of smugglers who hoarded gasoline bought on government subsidized prices. It was reported that the hoarders' profits were ten-fold their Nigerian price of gasoline when sold across the borders in neighboring Chad, Benin, or Cameroon. To save face and es-cape public embarrassment, the Babangida government announced the clo-sure of all gas stations within 16 miles of Nigerian borders with its neighbors. No longer able to contain their anger, the masses released their frustration by sporadic looting of offices, banks, and shops, especially in downtown Lagos and beyond. The disturbances soon spread to university towns in the eastern sector of the nation. During this time, riot erupted on various university campuses throughout the country, including the Universities of Benin and Lagos. The call by rioters for Babangida's resignation that filled the air fell on deaf ears. As a consequence, the two universities were closed. But, according to Francis Emelifeonwu, a correspondent for the Associated Press, at least six Nigerian universities were closed in 1992 as the result of protests against the government that had placed hard economic conditions on the populace conditions encouraged by Western financial donors and the International Monetary Fund (IMF) as a prerequisite of economic assistance and debt relief.[31]

The scope and threat that the disturbances posed for the nation could not be underestimated. While the protesters battled with the police, they built barricades of bricks and burning tires to enforce a two-day general strike called by the Nigerian Labor Congress in support of the protesters. While doubts existed as to whether or not the military government of Ibrahim Babangida harbored plans to hand over power to an elected civilian government, it is true that this gesture of solidarity shown by organized labor in a period of crisis that paralyzed businesses served as a reminder that all things were not well in Nigeria.

Conclusion

Since independence, Nigeria—a multi-ethnic, multi-religious, and multi-linguistic entity has experienced political instability, emanating from constant military interventions and a three-year civil war that ended in 1970. After the war, the stage was set for the institution of an enduring democratic rule in the nation's post-war history. The Shagari administration, alternatively called the "Second Republic," which was voted to power in October 1979 became a symbol of this experiment. Also, the dashed hope that the military would be sent to the barracks for good was raised once again. Unfortunately, the institutional arrangements on which this model political experiment was built mirrored parochial interests incapable of nurturing, sustaining, and promoting national integration and consolidation. Party formation and voting behavior emanating from the new arrangements were exemplary showcases. Even, the depth of confrontation among party candidates denied the Shagari regime the popular mandate necessary for legitimate governance.

The individualistic political subculture embraced by the elite that promoted self-interest over that of public welfare, and their resultant corrupting influences poisoned the moral fabric of the Nigerian nation. As such, the nation was subjected to the sort of excessive consumerism that resulted in massive corruption, embezzlement by government officials, and the depletion of the nation's foreign exchange reserves, all at a time of declining standard of living among the masses.

As expected, the national consensus was further threatened by endemic labor strikes and religious conflicts that gave impetus to Mohammed Buhari's military intervention in December 1983. When Ibrahim Babangida came to power on August 27, 1985, he promised to give a third democratic experience a try. In support of this goal his regime, by decree, created two political parties, banned individual campaign contributions, prohibited the active participation of seasoned politicians, and barred third-party candidacy.

These actions clearly violated the spirit of democracy that encourages unregulated and inclusive political participation. However, under certain circumstances, restrained political action and control are necessary because of the social and political complexity of the society. These violations, nonetheless, raised a haunting issue that questioned the constitutionality and legitimacy of a non-elected government designing and regulating the transitional stages of this "third republic," especially and in view of the fact that civilian governments had previously been elected in local and state levels. The presidential elections were aimed at completing the "three tier" plan for an eventual hand over to elected civilian government by October 1, 1992. But, certain events raised suspicion of Babangida's intentions. First, he extended the targeted handover date to January 2, 1993. Furthermore, his supporters, through media campaigns, were canvassing for a "diarchy"—model of governance in which he was to remain in power and rule with civilian governors, local government counselors, and national legislators who had already been installed. Due to the fact that he did not clarify these lingering doubts, people viewed him as a "conspirator by silence." This action further reinforced the charge of duplicity of the Babangida regime and its unwillingness to hand over power. Another factor that negated a smooth transition of power was the acute shortage of gasoline in 1992 due to the grounding of three of the nation's four refineries, consequently leading to mass riots and student protests.

Many people could not understand why 75 percent of Nigeria's refineries were shut down by the regime without a mandate from the nation's legislative bodies. Popular chants of "Babangida must go!" that echoed and resonated in the streets attest to the depth of ill-feeling toward the regime's performance. Everything considered, the Babangida regime might have had a genuine intention to hand over power to an elected civilian government according to his supporters. Otherwise, he would not have invested so much time, effort, and money toward this objective. But, the dynamic of Nigerian politics, in terms of regional, ethnic, and religious influences was what eventually determined who the president of the Third Republic was going to be. The evolution of Nigerian politics has shown that power, especially since after the civil war, has remained and revolved mainly in the hands of ethnic northerners. To a large extent, the power was sustained with their control of the military establishment that consolidated control of the power over the years. In fact, the military in Nigerian politics has proved to be nothing more than a sponsor of this power consolidation in the hands of the Northern elites/oligarchy.

Since independence in 1960, Nigeria has experience a continuous swing of power between civilian and military governments. First was the 1966 coup d'é-tat initiated by Chukwuma Kaduna Nzeogwu, which overthrew the civilian government of President Nnamdi Azikiwe and Prime Minister Abubakar Tafawa Balewa and enabled Lt. General J.T.U. Aguiyi Ironsi to become the country's first military head of state. Following the assassination of Ironsi in a counter coup that same year, the military government of Yakubu Gowon took over power and ruled till 1976 when Murtala Muhammad took over power in yet another military coup d'état. Following Muhammad's murder in another attempted coup, his Deputy, Olesegun Obasanjo completed his predecessor's term, and in 1979 handed over power to the civilian regime of Shehu Shagari. Shagari ruled from 1979 to 1983 when his regime was toppled in yet another military coup staged by Muhamaddu Buhari who governed from 1984 to 1985. In 1985, Ibrahim Babangida took over power in yet another military coup and governed until 1993, before handing over power to a civilian transitional/provisional government of Ernest Shonekan. That same year, Sani Abacha's government took over power in a military coup and ruled until 1998 when it was succeeded by the military government of Abdulsalami Abubakar, following Abacha's death. Abubakar then ruled Nigeria from 1998 to 1999 when he handed over power to the elected civilian government of Olusegun Obasanjo. Obasanjo, in turn, ruled Nigeria as a civilian head of state from 1999 to 2007 when, upon the completion of his second and last term in office, he handed over power to the civilian government of Umaru Yar'Adua.

Following the controversy surrounding the election of Umaru Yar'Adua of the People's Democratic Party (PDP), his mandate to govern was marred by court challenges by his rival candidates, such as Atiku Abubakar of Actions Congress (AC) and Muhammed Buhari of All Nigeria People's Party (ANPP). Atiku's challenge of Yar'Adua's election was based primarily on the ground that the Independent National Election Commission (INEC) had barred him from running because of some unsubstantiated and fictitious charges of fraud. Although the courts later cleared him and reinstated his candidacy, it was too late for him to run a credible national campaign thereafter.

The other candidate, Muhammed Buhari of the ANPP challenged INEC's declaration that Yar'Adua won the presidential election with 70 percent of the vote, on the basis that the election was rigged with electoral malpractices, fraud, and intimidation. It should be recalled that international observers such as the European Union had declared that the election was below accepted international standards. Even the Associated Press had reported several incidents of electoral malpractices, including intimidation, ballot stuffing, and outright violence designed to interrupt voting and, therefore, undermine or sabotage the electoral process. It was not until December 12, 2008, that the Nigerian Supreme Court ruled in favor of Umaru Yar'Adua. In its ruling, the court acknowledged that there were flaws in the election, but maintained that the plaintiffs could not prove that the problems associated with the electoral process were so widespread to the extent that they could nullify the results of the election. Having sidelined opponents of the regime in power at the time, many observers believe that the rationale of the Supreme Court ruling rested heavily on considerations of national interest—Nigerian stability rather than the merit of the ballot exercise. Nevertheless, President Yar'Adua's health remained a national concern and preoccupation. Rumors of his taking leaves of absence and actually traveling to foreign countries for medical treatment filled the air and eventually dominated public discussion, especially in drinking and entertainment parlors.

It should be recalled that Yar'Adua collapsed due to an undisclosed ailment in 2007 on his campaign trail and was airlifted and rushed into a German hospital. Also, in April 2008, he returned to Europe for further treatment of what the Nigerian media described as an "allergic reaction." Many hoped and prayed for the Yar'Adua regime to mark the end of Nigeria's government spectacle of epileptic-style regimes, where numerous administrations and leaders easily come and go. Those prayers were not answered, as Yar'Adua never recovered from his infirmity. Oluwarotimi Odunaya Akeredolu, president of the Nigerian Bar Association (NBA), had stated in December 2009, that Yar'Adua should have handed over power to Vice President Goodluck Jonathan in an acting capacity during his illness and the statement was backed up by the NBA national executive committee.[32] The heated argument generated by this legal interpretation of the National Constitution prompted the Supreme Court of Nigeria to rule on January 22, 2010, that the Federal Executive Council (FEC) had 14 days to decide on a resolution about whether Umaru Yar'Adua "is incapable of discharging the functions of his office." The ruling also stated that the Federal Executive Council should hear testimony of five doctors, one of whom should be Yar'Adua's personal physician.[33] Following this ruling, the Senate on February 9, 2010, determined that presidential power be transferred to Vice President Jonathan, and that he would serve as Acting President, with all the accompanied powers, until Yar'Adua returned to full health.

Although Yar'Adua returned to Abuja on February 24, 2010, his state of health was unclear, and to refute popular speculation that he was dead, various political and religious figures in Nigeria visited him during his illness saying that he would make a recovery. He did not. On May 5, 2010, Yar'Adua died in the Aso Rock presidential villa. Jonathan was sworn in as Yar'Adua's replacement on May 6, 2010, becoming Nigeria's 14th Head of State. At the time of writing, President Jonathan had already won the ruling party's primary election on January 14, 2011, after fending off a challenge from the mainly Muslim north, setting him up as the favorite in April's landmark elections. Some view the April 2010 ballot as one of the most important political events in the history of Africa's most populous nation, especially as it is coming amid unrest in various regions and rifts between the mainly Muslim north and predominately Christian south. A chronological summary of the leadership and regime changes in Nigeria is reflected in Table 3.

It is most likely that in the future, Nigeria will continue to experience peaceful civilian government transitions and successions. But, for how long it will survive thereafter, is a legitimate question. The army people have tasted power and they appear to like it; and will do whatever necessary to protect and preserve this power privilege even to the detriment of national stability. What has happened is that handovers to civilian governments serve the strategic interests of military men by extricating them from blame and thereby saving their heads from public anger or those of their colleagues. Hence, the doctrine of the "old guard" is bound to live with us for a long time. The only way to guarantee a durable democracy in the Third Republic is to regionally and ethnically neutralize the national army. This can be done through mass demobilization or decentralization through the creation of a rival force, like the National Guard in the United States or the military versus the gendarmerie in francophone Africa. What Nigeria needs is a new army that is hierarchically multiethnic and able to serve as checks and balances to the monopoly of violence by the current ethnically-based and regionally-biased national army.

However, the implication of this option is that political power may be redistributed among groups and regions and this may face steep resistance from those benefiting from the current situation. This proposition may not even be a viable option because it is most likely to plunge the nation into unwanted crisis or possibly a civil war. But, our hope for a lasting democracy in Nigeria will continue to be dashed as long as the prevailing power relationships are maintained.

Table 3. Nigerian Leaders Since 1914

Nigerian Leaders in History	Administration	Date of Leadership	Designation
Sir Lord Frederick Lugard	Colonial	1914–1919	Governor General
Sir Bernard Bourdillon	Colonial	1635–1943	Governor General
Sir John Macpherson	Colonial	1948–1955	Governor General
Sir James Roberson	Colonial	1955–1960	Governor General
Benjamin Nnamdi Azikiwe	Civilian	1 Oct 1960–16 Jan 1963	President of the Republic
Alhaji Abubakar Tafawa Balewa	Civilian	30 Aug 1960–15 Jan 1966	Prime Minister
Johnson Thomas Umurakwe Aguiyi-Ironsi	Military	16 Jan 1966–29 Jul 1966	Head, Military Government
Yakubu Gowon	Military	1 Aug 1966–29 Jul 1975	Head, Military Government
Murtala Ramat Muhammed	Military	29 Jul 1975–13 Feb 1976	Head, Military Government
Olusegun Obasanjo	Military	14 Feb 1976–1 Oct 1979	Head, Military Government
Alhaji Shehu Usman Aliyu Shagari	Civilian	1 Oct 1979–31 Dec 1983	President of the Republic
Muhammadu Buhari	Military	31 Dec 1983–27 Aug 1985	Head, Military Government
Ibrahim Badamasi Babangida	Military	27 Aug 1985–4 Jan 1993	Chairman, Armed Forces Ruling Council Chairman, National Defense and Security Council
Ernest Adekunle Oladeinde Shonekan	Civilian	26 Aug 1993–17 Nov 1993	Head, Interim National Government
Sani Abacha	Military	17 Nov 1993–8 Jun 1998	Chairman, Provisional Ruling Council
Abdulsalam Abubakar	Military	9 Jun 1998–29 May 1999	Chairman, Provisional Ruling Council
Olusegun Obasanjo	Civilian	29 May 1999	President of the Republic
Umaru Musa Yar'Adua	Civilian	29 May 2007–5 May 2010	President of the Republic
Goodluck Ebele Azikiwe Jonathan	Civilian	6 May 2010-Present	President of the Republic

Sources: *http://www.onlinenigeria.com/leaders.asp* and *http://en.wikipedia.org/wiki/Goodluck_Jonathan*. The section on Goodluck Jonathan was added by the authors.

Nigeria

Chapter 5

Political Violence, Democracy, and the Nigerian Economy

Julius O. Adekunle

Politics and violence have become synonymous in Nigeria, and correlate with a negative effect on the economy. Political violence has pierced the peace and stability of the country, creating a climate of fear which is inflicting significant damage to the democratic process. Since 1999, when the country returned to democratic rule, ethnic, religious, and political violence have proliferated. Although political violence has a long presence in Nigerian history, the pervasiveness of violence and degree of the damage to the peace, stability, and economy of the country have been very disturbing. Admittedly, violence is an enduring feature of human existence. It is one of the mechanisms through which both negative and positive changes have occurred. In pre-colonial times, the numerous kingdoms that now constitute Nigeria fought several internecine and imperialist wars; the violence and political strife continue in modern day Nigeria.

By the end of the nineteenth century, there were continuing acts of violence during the period of Europe's imperialistic involvement in Africa. In Nigeria, many kings, especially in the Niger Delta, resisted European economic and political domination. These resistance movements were crushed, and the rulers were sent into exile. Thereafter, colonialism was instituted through the instrumentality of violence.[1] During the colonial period, violence was not eliminated because the British adopted a "divide and rule" policy that pitched one group against another. To this very day, ethnic conflicts, religious violence, and incessant clashes over the control of economic resources have significantly weakened the unity, peace, political sustainability, and democratic system of Nigeria. The more Nigeria strives to unite, the more acts of violence tear the country apart. Nigeria has become a country under siege. Nigerians are living under a fearful atmosphere as a result of political violence, which leaves in its wake significant and lasting socioeconomic concerns.

The period between 1999 and 2007 was one of the most violent eras in Nigerian history. Not only did violence occur in every part of the country for different reasons, but it became even more prevalent and more deadly. For Nigerians, violence has become the most acceptable means of response to even trivial issues. Approximately 10,000 people have been killed and 500,000 have been displaced in the wake of a series of devastating ethnic, religious, and sociopolitical conflicts in the country.[2] The Niger Delta, which is the main source of the country's wealth, has become a problematic area for the government and for the economy of the country. Hostage taking has become a business for some people, and it is significantly damaging the country's economy. How can Nigeria overcome the seemingly unstoppable acts of violence and pursue peace and a sustainable economy? This chapter examines some acts of violence and their implications on the democracy and political economy of Nigeria.

Politics of Violence

Violence is part of human nature, and sadly, it is a common phenomenon. During the colonial period, there was a series of violent acts between the British and Nigerian traditional rulers for economic reasons. The resistance of the Aba women on tax assessment in 1929 was a major act of political and economic violence. While Nigeria did not go through political violence in the magnitude of the Mau Mau rebellion (1952–1955) in Kenya, numerous anti-colonial riots marked the decolonization process between 1945 and 1960. Clearly, violence does not have only political dimension; it is multidimensional. As argued elsewhere, violence "occurs in almost every facet of life and has the potential to disrupt and polarize a nation's socio-political system."[3]

Facts of history indicate that hooliganism and intimidation are not a new phenomenon in the Nigerian political system. Since the formation of political parties after World War II and up to the immediate years of independence, violence has been ushered in through the employment of political thugs. Politicians hired cutthroat types to carry out acts of violence and intimidation on opponents. In the First Republic (1960–1966), campaigns were conducted under fearful conditions because thugs would scare away the supporters of opposing parties. Elections were conducted under a tense environment because hooligans manned polling booths. Thuggery became an integral part of politics; indeed, it was a profession for the jobless and uneducated youths who thronged to politicians for money, favors, or jobs. Thuggery became a means to secure and maintain power for politicians. It is a threat to sustainable democracy and a mechanism of perpetuating political corruption.

Thugs, who are also called "area boys," add more to the level of insecurity by being involved in political assassinations. The political atmosphere in contemporary Nigeria is so tense that violence has become the order of the day. There have been several inter-party as well as intra-party acts of violence with opponents being killed, kidnapped, maimed, or harassed. Everywhere has become a potential arena for political disaster, and everyone is susceptible to attack and humiliation. High profile political assassinations are not a new phenomenon in Nigeria, but in recent times, the rate of assassinations has become very disturbing. Hired assassins run rampant, unleashing fear and terror on the opposition. Critics of governments and journalists have not been spared the violence as they also are arrested, imprisoned, or killed.

On October 19, 1986, Dele Giwa, the founder and editor-in-chief of *Newswatch* magazine, was killed in a letter bomb in what was believed to be a political assassination. This was the first time this unique technique of terminating a person's life was used in Nigeria. Giwa, a fearless journalist, was reportedly planning to reveal a high profile corruption case when he was brutally murdered. In spite of the investigation that followed, no one claimed responsibility, and Giwa's killers were not found. Not finding Giwa's murderers was a reflection on the ill-equipped and inefficient Nigerian police, in addition to the indifference in the resolve of the Ibrahim Babangida military administration to find the culprits. The last of Babangida's mischievous acts before leaving office was the cancellation of the June 12, 1993 presidential election results. In Nigerian political history, international observers and political analysts have declared that election as the most credible, free, and fair. Chief M. K. O. Abiola, a successful businessman and a Yoruba Muslim, convincingly won the election against Alhaji Bashir Tofa, a northern Muslim and industrialist. Without any acceptable explanation to the electorate, Babangida annulled the results. The annulment, therefore, prolonged the return to a democratic rule and indeed threatened the unity and political stability of the country. To placate the angry Yoruba people who believed they have been disrespected and marginalized, Babangida handpicked Chief Ernest Shonekan to lead an Interim Government, which was supposed to organize a fresh election to usher in a civilian rule.

The Interim Government was short-lived, lasting only three months. Sani Abacha (1993–98) seized power, arrested, and then-imprisoned Abiola. He denied Abiola the leadership of the country according to the people's mandate, and disallowed Nigerians the long-awaited democratic rule. Abacha's seizure of power is an indication that Babangida and Abacha stage-managed the handing over to an Interim Government with a Yoruba leader in order to create the impression that the Yoruba people were in political control. As Abacha's plans and his thirst for power unfolded, the Yoruba people became victims of his political machinations. Abiola's insistence of his electoral mandate and Abacha's abuse of power created so much ethnic and political tension that Nigeria was on the brink of breaking apart. While in prison, Abiola's wife, Kudirat Abiola, was murdered in what was an apparent political assassination. She was presumably murdered to silence Abiola, who constituted a political threat to Abacha.

Similarly, there is the case of Alfred Rewane, an Itsekiri entrepreneur and a strong pillar of the pro-democracy movement. Rewane also was murdered under strange and suspicious circumstances, and his killers were never found. In 1995, Abacha alleged that a coup was planned to oust his government. Among the plotters were many Yoruba people, including General Diya Oladipo (second in rank to Abacha), Gen. Shehu Musa Yar'Adua, and General Obasanjo (rtd). These three, along with the other supposed coup plotters, were sentenced to 25 years of imprisonment. The most outrageous act of Abacha's regime was the killing of Ken Saro-Wiwa and eight other Ogoni political activists who were protesting against the Shell Oil Company for the destruction of their land and the failure to receive compensation in turn.[4] No government has committed more human rights violations than that of Abacha. As a military leader, Abacha did not respect democratic principles, and his government seemed to endorse and promote violence. No administration has jettisoned freedom of speech and freedom of association more than that of Abacha. Nigerian citizens of every category—politicians, journalists, and commoners all lived in fear. Frontline politicians, social activists, and advocates of democracy were harassed, arrested, and imprisoned while some, including Professor Wole Soyinka, left the country to live in exile. In 1998, the European Union (EU) was alarmed by the rate of political violence and Abacha's wanton violation of Human Rights. The EU also condemned Abaha's foot-dragging over transition plans to restore democracy. Abacha even refused to yield to the EU's demand to release political prisoners. His administration was indeed a "reign of terror." Only Abacha's sudden death and that of Abiola in prison raised the beam of hope for democracy. General Abdul-Salami, who succeeded Abacha, was amenable to change and to transiting to a democratic rule.

Although Nigeria returned to democracy in 1999 with Olusegun Obasanjo as the President, peace, security, and unity were not restored. The unwarranted annulment of the June 12, 1993, elections, and the sudden death of Abiola in prison continued to shake the foundations of Nigerian unity. The Yoruba were embittered in the wake of Abiola's denial of political leadership and his consequent death in prison in 1998. To add more to their predicament, Bola Ige, the Federal Minister of Justice, was murdered in his own home on December 23, 2001. No one has been indicted for the killing. A series of political assassinations followed in different parts of the country between 2002 and 2006. As politicians were gearing up for the 2007 elections, Funso Williams, an engineer and popular gubernatorial candidate in Lagos State, who was an advocate of non-violent politics, was reportedly strangled and stabbed to death in his bedroom in July 2006. Of Funso Williams, Sonnie Ekwowusi of *ThisDay* newspapers wrote: "It is indeed a great irony that an apostle of no bitterness and non-violence in Nigerian politics was visited with the most cruel violence and barbaric murder."[5] A month later, unidentified assassins murdered Dr. Ayodele Daramola, a World Bank consultant and gubernatorial candidate in Ekiti State in his home. Inordinately ambitious politicians often engage the services of hired assassins who employ very sophisticated methods of killing prominent and promising politicians.

Politics has become a war in which a variety of weapons are used to defeat the opponent; politicians see each other as deadly enemies. Shehu Sani, Literary Editor of *New Nigerian* Newspapers, sums up the motives for the murders as: "greed, desperation for power, allergy to healthy political rivalry and intolerance of dissenting opinions."[6] Also exacerbating the situation is the level of social inequality and the high rate of unemployment in Nigeria, which permits the youth and unemployed to become instruments of violent and destructive acts. While politicians flaunt their wealth, many people live in abject poverty. As a result of frequent and unwarranted political killings, A. A. Igbafe and O. J. Offiong show in their study that approximately 53 percent of the political assassinations took place between 1991 and 2000.[7] Almost the same figure can be mentioned for the period between 2001 and 2006. These disturbing figures point to the unstable political and economic state of Nigeria. Table 1 on the following page shows the extent of political violence between 2002 and 2006.

This list only shows the nationally prominent politicians. Many more people have been killed in local areas for political and electoral-related reasons; the assassination of innocent people is not restricted to politicians. Journalists such as Abayomi Ogundeji, Omololu Falobi, Godwin Agbroko, Bayo Ohu, Dipo Dina, and Edo Ugbagwu have been brutally gunned down for no apparent motive. While these wanton killings may not be purely politically motivated, they are testaments to the level of insecurity in every part of the country. Sonnie Ekwowusi rightly describes the extent of fear that exists in Nigeria: "In Nigeria our lives are ruled by fear; fear of the police; fear of market touts in uniform; fear of the unknown; fear of street urchins and street gangsters; fear of next door neighbors and fear of armed robbers."[8] Without a doubt, Nigerians want to live in a peaceful, democratic, and secure environment. More than anything, they want freedom from fear.

Table 1. A Selected List of Political Assassinations

S. Ade Awonusi	January 7, 2002
Barnabas and Abigail Igwe	September 22, 2002
Ogbonnaya Uche	February 7, 2003
Theodore Agwatu	February 22, 2003
Marshall Harry	March 5, 2003
Rasak Ibrahim	March 20, 2003
Anthony Nwodu	March 21, 2003
Ikkena Ibor	March 27, 2003
Onyewuchi Iwuchukwa	April 19, 2003
Toni Dimegwu	April 20, 2003
Ajibola Olanipekun	June 20, 2003
A. K. Dikibo	February 14, 2004
Luke Shingaba	March 4, 2004
Philip Olorunipa	March 7, 2004
Sunday Atte	February 5, 2005
Alibi Olajoku	March 15, 2005
Patrick Origbe	June 3, 2005
Lateef Olaniyan	July 16, 2005
Anthony Ozioko	July 27, 2005
Jesse Arukwu	July 2, 2006
Funso Williams	July 27, 2006
Ayodele Daramola	August 14, 2006

Because of the lack of security and the inability of the ill-equipped police to cope with the frequent and high profile killings, some Nigerians find solace in religion. A Nigerian declared, "Our lives are in the hands of God."[9] Respect for human life has lost its meaning because politics is filled with bitterness. The political slogan seems to be "politics with bitterness." In colleges and universities, cultism has instilled fear in innocent and law-abiding students. The outbreak of religious riots does not lend support for the search for peace. Everywhere that Nigerians turn, they are met with fear. No one is safe. Killers get away primarily because of the weak and ineffective methods of investigations. It has become almost impossible "to track down high profile people and assassins involved in high profile murder."[10]

Nigeria receives pressure from the greater world community only when violence erupts in the oil regions or when foreigners are taken as hostages. Although the international community respects the integrity of domestic policies in each country, the issue of political violence and its impact on international trade warrants the attention and action of human rights organizations and world communities. Nigerian economic allies such as the United Kingdom and the United States must assist in providing the necessary infrastructure, which will stabilize the political system and facilitate economic growth. Continuing violence often results in a ripple effect on the society and its relations with the outside world. Western countries often warn their citizens not to go to Nigeria simply because of the acts of violence and the high level of insecurity.

"Godfatherism"

"Godfatherism" is not a new concept in either politics or in other areas of life, but it has become an integral part of Nigerian politics. It is common to have a "godfather" who helps to put his "godson" in a position of political power and influence. Godfathers are powerful politicians who have political connections and are able to sway the electorate in favor of their godsons in elections. They function as the political weight and financier of their godsons. They not only nominate, but also strategize to ensure that their candidates are installed in power. The godfather himself does not assume power, but works through a surrogate who returns the favor with loyalty and financial commitment. Trouble often erupts between the godfather and the godson if any or both conditions are not met. Godfatherism is not only a political occurrence, as it exists in other sectors of life, including the religious, social, economic, and academic. Godfathers go beyond being mentors because of their controlling power over their surrogates. According to Israel Okoye, godfatherism:

> is as old as competitive struggle for power and governance is in all polities. However, it has different names in different political cultures. Differences also abound in terms of its characteristics and implications in society.... It has, however, gained prominence in Nigeria's political lexicon as a result of the fact that the phenomenon it refers to has become a dominant feature of electoral politics and governance in the country.[11]

Historically, godfatherism evolved with the core of politicians who led Nigeria to independence in 1960. Since then, it has been a continuing practice. From one civilian administration to the next, it has become fashionable for younger politicians to ensure the backing of a godfather, an experienced politician. Obafemi Awolowo, Nnamdi Azikiwe, Ahmadu Bello, and Aminu Kano are all first-generation politicians who served as both ethnic and regional god-fathers. The Awolowo-Akintola conflict, which led to a major crisis in the Western Region, and which partly contributed to the outbreak of the Nigerian Civil War (1967–1970), is a case in point. In this circumstance, it was a breach of loyalty that led to the rift. There is credibility in Akinola Adeoye's argument that the failure of Awolowo, Azikiwe, and Aminu "to live above ethnic politics aided the ascendancy of Shehu Shagari as Nigeria's president in 1979."[12] Nnamdi Azikiwe himself benefited from the godfatherism of Sir Louis Phillippe Odumegwu Ojukwu who was a businessman in transportation and the father of Odumegwu Ojukwu (Ikemba Nnewi).

Many politicians in the southwestern part of Nigeria, such as Bola Ige (former governor of Oyo State), Lateef Jakande (former governor of Lagos State), and Ebenezer Babatope (former director of organization for the Unity Party of Nigeria (UPN)), were godsons to Awolowo. Generally known as "Awoists," these politicians benefited significantly not only from Awolowo's mentorship, but also from his political philosophy and programs, which were oriented to appeal to the masses. Similarly, Azikiwe's godsons were called "Zikists," and they formed what was known as the Zikist movement.[13]

In Anambra State, Chris Ubah declared himself "the greatest godfather in Nigeria because this is the first time an individual single-handedly put in position every politician in the state."[14] He was the godfather of Chris Ngige who became the governor of the state in 2003, and soon after he and his godfather fell apart, culminating in Ngige's removal as governor in 2006. The Ubah-Ngige saga is a clear example of the influence and the destructive element of godfatherism.

A similar situation arose in Oyo State between Lamidi Adedibu and Rasheed Ladoja. Adedibu, a well-known political kingpin and power broker in Oyo State, was instrumental to Ladoja's election as Oyo State governor in 2003. A serious impasse arose between them because Ladoja failed to take instructions from his godfather and refused to give financial support. Adedibu employed his political arsenal and maneuver to organize Ladoja's impeachment in January 2006. Although Ladoja was reinstated after eleven months, the godfa-ther-godson relationship had become irretrievable. Alao-Akala, the deputy governor, assumed governorship roles and adopted Adedibu as his godfather. Until Adedibu's death in June 2008, Alao-Akala remained loyal to him.

In Lagos State, the squabble between the governor, Babatunde Fashola, and his predecessor, Bola Ahmed Tinubu, is associated with godfatherism. While the power to influence the electorate remains with the godfather, the author-ity to exercise political power resides in the hands of the godson. When the two clash, it is usually over self-interest issues, and the godfather often initiates the removal of the godson from power. Among the current governors in Nigeria, Fashola is regarded as a performer and an achiever. He tried to bring significant socio-\economic development to Lagos and sanity to politics. Surprisingly, attempts were being made to impeach him. Why would such a successful governor be removed from office? The main reason is the fall out between him and Tinubu, his godfather.

The godfathers who felt disappointed in their godsons have adopted various mechanisms of intimidation, violence, and impeachment to disturb the administration of their respective states. An African proverb states that "when two elephants fight, the grass suffers." In this situation, the people of the states suffer from the machinations of the politicians and from bad governance. Greed and abuse of power are partly the driving forces behind the godfather-godson conflicts. The instigation of impeachment by godfathers is anti-democratic, and it is an attempt to promote political disturbances. Hooligans, motor touts, and jobless youths are being deployed to foment trouble and disturb political peace in different parts of the country.

Insecurity caused by the rift between godfathers and their political godchildren indirectly links up with the fear that foreign investors have, and why they are not comfortable investing in an environment where there is political instability. There have been cases of insecurity in states where godfatherism takes political center-stage. Clearly, godfatherism encourages political corruption and it is a means of denying competent, qualified, and legitimate candidates of securing political positions. The language of godfatherism is "who you know and not who you are." It is a hindrance to political growth, a stumbling stone to sustainable democracy, and a retrogression to economic development. Akinola Adeoye claims that godfatherism "has become a menace pulling down the foundations of masses-driven governance, denying Nigerians the much-deserved dividends of democracy." He likens the relationship to patron-client politics, which "does not have a universal meaning in world politics."[15]

Extension of Term

The political attitude of African leaders wanting to remain in office for the duration of their lifetime manifested in Nigeria when Obasanjo wanted to elongate his term. As his second term was winding down, Obasanjo began the political maneuver that would keep him in office for a third term. His inordinate political ambition almost tore the country apart. Obasanjo represented the undemocratic attitude of African "die-in-office" political leaders. Examples from many countries indicate that measures taken to change their constitutions to suit the personal agendas of their political leaders have become an integral part of the political schemes of African heads of state. Muammar Gaddafi, Africa's longest serving leader, ruled Libya for over 40 years. Hosni Mubarak of Egypt was forced to resign after 30 years of dictatorial leadership. Robert Mugabe of Zimbabwe was elected as the Prime Minister in 1980, and president in 1987. He is still in power. Given his elongated time in office, it is apparent that Mugabe no longer possesses new political and progressive ideas to move the country forward. In spite of the mounting political, economic, and social problems facing Zimbabwe, Mugabe has bluntly refused to honorably step down. President Mathieu Kerekou led Benin for nineteen years (1972–1991), and in Gabon, Omar Bongo was in power for forty-two years (1967–2009), dying in office. Paul Biya of Cameroon has remained in power since 1982. The recent successful political revolutions in Tunisia and Egypt and the forced change in Libya epitomize the hunger of the masses for democracy. Because of their obsession for power, these political leaders manipulate the constitution, and diplomatically surround themselves with loyalists in order to keep themselves in power.

The third-term agenda caused chaos among politicians, including the rift between Obasanjo and Atiku Abubakar, the vice president. Obasanjo loved power and planned to retain it. His schemes included edging out Atiku, who was aspiring to the presidency. The move to change the constitution in favor of Obasanjo's political ambition was a flagrant violation of democratic principles. In countries such as the United States of America, no president has been allowed to run three times since 1945, when Franklin D. Roosevelt, a four-time president, died. The provisions of the constitution and democratic process have to be recognized and respected. The third-term attempt unleashed turmoil and conflict in a country already overwhelmed with division and violence. Any attempt to amend the constitution for a personal agenda is a threat to political stability and the sustainability of democracy. Political thinkers and world communities believed that a third-term rule for Obasanjo would be uncharacteristic of a man who handed over power to a civilian elected government in 1979, and who claimed to operate on the principles of democracy.

Obasanjo failed to achieve his ambition because of the stiff opposition that accompanied the idea. Given Nigeria's past experience of military dictatorships and the economic hardship that resulted from political instability, the thought to amend the constitution to allow the president a third term generated much uneasiness and anxiety that the peace of the country would be disrupted. Condemning the third-term ambition, Chief Sunday Awoniyi, chairman of the Arewa Consultative Forum (ACF) and former national chairman of the Peoples Democratic Party (PDP), wrote a personal letter to President Obasanjo, urging him to leave office in accordance with the constitutional stipulation. Chief Awoniyi was of the opinion that the president's plans were "in complete contradiction to [his] administration's sermons on integrity, transparency, and accountability. They are immoral. They are irreligious."[16] They were also not politically prudent.

The former United Nations Secretary-General, Kofi Annan, advised African leaders to play by the transparent rules of democracy by accepting their respective constitutions.[17] Tampering with a constitution to perpetuate personal interest would be inviting chaos. Many African leaders have done so in order to retain power. Obasanjo's quest for a third term caused more than political problems; it indirectly created economic woes as well. Many foreign countries, especially the industrialized ones with strong economic ties to Nigeria, opposed the move. For example, the United States of America did not support it because it contravenes the constitution and violates democratic principle.

Obasanjo was not the only politician who wanted to see changes to term limits for political offices. Fearing the loss of power and in view of the rampant political violence, some politicians tried to strategically position themselves by suggesting a single six-year term for elected officials. For example, in 2001, the presidential committee on the review of the constitution argued that a staggered two-term system left public officials desperate to return to power after the first term. The committee, therefore, recommended a single term of six years. Not surprisingly, many public officials, including Chinwoke Mbadinuju, the governor of Anambra State, strongly supported the compelling and practicable recommendation.[18] His premise was that "the temperature of the system which appears overheated now will immediately drop to normal because the tempo to get re-elected and the tempo for the opposition to upstage the incumbent is so much."[19]

The collapse of the third-term agenda and the fall out between Obasanjo and Abubakar Atiku, the vice president, led to the struggle of finding a credible and suitable presidential candidate for the PDP. Hence, Obasanjo became a godfather by single handedly picking Shehu Yar'Adua, the then governor of Katsina State. Two reasons can be advanced for Obasanjo's choice. First, Musa Yar'Adua (Shehu's older brother), was Obasanjo's military colleague and close friend (Musa Yar'Adua died in prison). Second, Obasanjo tried to mollify the northerners who had strongly supported him. Obasanjo campaigned for Yar'Adua and ensured that he won the election; he was installed in power in 2007. Because of how things panned out, it was generally believed that Yar'Adua's presidency would be an elongation of Obasanjo's. Indeed, Yar'Adua continued with some of Obasanjo's policies, especially the war against corruption. Hence, he was criticized for being Obasanjo's stooge. However, Obasanjo's role as a godfather did not seem to last. This became apparent when Yar'Adua fell ill and was unable to perform his presidential functions. Obasanjo was one of those who quickly called for his replacement.

Corruption as a Roadblock to Democracy

There is corruption in every society, but the difference is the level at which it exists and the degree of havoc it inflicts on politics. In the early years of Nigeria as an independent nation, politicians were accused of enriching themselves at the expense of the people. There have been cases of embezzlement, misappropriation of funds, and lack of accountability. Investigations into bribery and corruption cases occurred from the Azikiwe-Balewa period to Olusegun Obasanjo's second term. Politics became a source of wealth rather than a means of serving the people. Contracts were inflated, while the jobs did not get done. Bribery became part of the political game as the idea of giving back ten percent of the contract led to contractors inflating the cost. The language of corruption was "everybody does it." Does it mean that corruption and greed are acceptable cultural practices? Has gift giving encouraged corruption? Historical evidence indicates that corruption is not an integral part of African culture. In the affairs of the nation, bribery, corruption, graft, fraud, and nepotism are roadblocks to economic growth and political progress at both the local and national levels.

The rate at which politicians and public officers engage in corruption rose dramatically since the return to democratic rule in 1999. Since then, corruption has become more or less institutionalized. Prominent among the corrupt institutions are the local governments, police, national and state assemblies, and executives of federal and state establishments. What caused the sudden rise is uncertain. Could it be that politicians and public officers have easy access to public fund? It is not uncommon to find state governors and politicians flaunting their wealth. While the common people are languishing in poverty, the privileged ones are living a life of opulence. This is an indication that national wealth has not been fairly or equally distributed.

For many years, International Transparency rated Nigeria as one of the most corrupt countries in the world. During his first term in office, Obasanjo's administration made efforts to wipe out or at least reduce the level of corruption by establishing the Economic and Financial Crimes Commission (EFCC) with Nuhu Ribadu as its Chairman. This was and remains a laudable program given the rate and manner by which politicians enriched themselves. The setting up of EFCC created fear in some people, especially the politicians who have access to public funds. Many politicians are adopting different strategies to secure and preserve their power, position, and wealth. Ribadu once declared that Ibrahim Babangida, Sani Abacha, and Abdulsalami Abubakar (the past military rulers), were responsible for the escalation of corruption because they made it part of their guiding principle in governing Nigeria. Ribadu stated that, "The trouble with Nigeria is that we have allowed its influence to rule every aspect of our national life, to the extent that it has in fact become the way of life for most of our countrymen."[20]

Clearly, corrupt and rapacious people dominate the politics of Nigeria, while innocent taxpayers are losing the battle for economic and political sanity. Politicians use their influence to legitimize their ill-gotten wealth and to hire hoodlums who carry out acts of violence. The commoners could only look unto the heavily criticized EFCC as their savior to recover the huge amounts of money that have been embezzled and hoarded. According to Alex Last, a BBC correspondent in Nigeria:

> Nigeria is ranked as one of the most corrupt countries in the world. Daily, low-level corruption is visible on the street; policeman extorting money from motorists to supplement their meager wages. But it is in the world of politics and government, where corruption has been most damaging. For decades the government has accrued huge oil revenues, yet the country suffers from a lack of basic infrastructure, and tens of millions live in poverty. At the same time, some politicians and their business associates have amassed personal fortunes.[21]

The first public officer to be accused of and arrested for corruption by the EFCC in 2005 was Tafa Balogun, former Inspector General of Police. Two Nigerian governors were charged with the crime of money laundering in London, with one of them being impeached from office. The EFCC investigated some state governors for misappropriation of public funds.[22] At the upper and lower levels of power, the culture of corruption seems to be pervasive. This poses a threat to the politico-economic stability and unity of the country. By 2007, the EFCC had investigated 30 politicians, with only four being convicted. Nigerians believe that the EFCC has not been an effective agency because corruption remains rampant in the country. Many politicians and top government officials live on wealth that has been obtained illegally. It seems that Nigerians celebrate corruption rather than condemn it. The idea that is conveyed to the world is that greed is good, and corruption is acceptable. For example, Chief Bode George, the former Nigeria Ports Authority (NPA) Board Chairman, and a top member of the ruling People's Democratic Party (PDP), was charged for inflation of contracts and contract splitting. He was sentenced to two years imprisonment without the option of a fine. When released from prison, Bode George organized a church thanksgiving service. Obasanjo, the former President, and a delegate from PDP, attended the service. Corruption is indeed a hindrance to sustainable democracy. For how long can the common people tolerate bad governance and corrupt leadership? For how long will Nigeria survive this wanton disregard for democracy? For how long will Nigerians tolerate the politics of greed?

Intermixing Violence: Religion and Politics

Historically, the religion and politics of Nigeria have intermixed extensively. In the pre-colonial political systems of the various Nigerian societies, it was difficult to separate religion from politics. For example, the Yoruba people believed that religion was the foundation of political authority, as well as a source of political empowerment. The king not only provided political leadership, he also led his people in religious matters. The Igbo recognized oracles that were consulted before embarking on warfare. In the Islamic culture, religion was not separate from politics. However, the struggle for political power often resulted in violence, or people employed religion to achieve their political ambition.

The issue of the Shari'a (Islamic law) destabilized political, ethnic, and religious relations, especially in the northern states where the Shari'a was introduced in 2002. Christians, under the auspices of the Christian Association of Nigeria (CAN), opposed the implementation of the Shari'a because it does not fall within their religious beliefs and practices. In northern Nigeria, youths unleashed terror on the people to ensure that the Shari'a was instituted. In cities and universities, people went on rampages, killing people, burning cars, properties, churches, and mosques, and destroying private businesses. In many cases, religious differences have merged with ethnic rivalries as they occurred at different times in Lagos, Sagamu, Aba, Kaduna, Kano, and Jos. Existing rivalries from the past military regimes have resurfaced. With its newfound freedom associated with democracy, Nigeria is going through a revolution with the expectation that those people who were wronged in the past would fight back.

The argument has been made that politicians use religion to achieve their political ambitions or enhance their political positions. It was also argued that the northern Muslim governors who adopted the Shari'a did so to discredit Obasanjo, a southern Christian president. The supporters of the Shari'a vigorously denied this claim. The federal government was unable to stop twelve states from implementing the Shari'a. The point to note is that religion should be used as a constructive, not as a destructive element. It should be used as a unifier, not as a divider. Religion is an instrument of peace, not a vehicle of violence. It is therefore necessary to take religion out of the selfish ambitions of the politicians.

Economic Implications of Political Violence

Political violence has serious implications for the economic growth of Nigeria. This is because political stability and economic growth go hand in hand. Political violence wreaks overwhelming havoc on the Nigerian economy. A peaceful and secure society allows people to freely pursue economic activities and attract foreign investors. The reverse is the case where there is fear and insecurity. For many years, Nigeria enjoyed the presence of foreign investors and their contributions in various dimensions of the country's economy. In 1956, the Shell Oil Company discovered oil in Oloibiri in the Niger Delta (others include the Bonga Offshore field and the Agbami and Erha oil fields). Since 1956, oil production has grown steadily. Producing approximately 2.5 million barrels per day, Nigeria became the eleventh largest oil exporter in the world, the largest in Africa. As a strong member of OPEC, Nigeria derives substantial revenue from oil production, with approximately 80 percent going toward government revenue. With this large revenue, and its large deposits of oil, Nigeria has the potential to build a prosperous and sustainable economy. Nigerians are wondering how the huge oil revenue is being spent, since there are no physical and visible developments to show.

Despite its rich natural resources, Nigeria experiences several socioeconomic problems. Foreign companies not only dominate the oil sector, they also collude with political leaders on the revenue. On the issue of revenue allocation, many communities allege that the government has neglected them. They claim that the oil wealth is not being fairly redistributed to areas in which the oil is being pumped. There is inadequate infrastructure, insufficient macroeconomic management, and widespread poverty. In 1996, the poverty level was 46 percent, but according to figures in the *World Factbook*, approximately 70 percent of Nigerians were below the poverty line in 2007.[23] This figure, as revealed by the United Nations Habitat (an arm of the UN responsible for promotion of quality housing and urban planning around the world), had risen to 76 percent by 2009, making Nigeria one of the twenty poorest countries in the world.

The Niger Delta, where the oil is derived remains poor, with no corresponding physical infrastructure to indicate the economic wealth that the region possesses. Environmental problems and underdevelopment have triggered violence on several occasions, especially among the youth of the Ijaw, the main ethnic group in the Delta region. As mentioned earlier, the Abacha regime hanged Ken Saro-Wiwa and eight Ogoni activists on November 10, 1995, for speaking out against the environmental damage that the Shell Oil Company was causing. By conniving with the oil companies, the government of Nigeria rendered the people of Ogoni powerless. This atrocious act, which was condemned globally by human rights organizations, significantly damaged the international image of Nigeria and the integrity of the military government. It also sent the message of insecurity in Nigeria to foreign business people and multinational corporations.

The Commonwealth Action Group (which consisted of eight foreign ministers with the purpose of dealing with serious violations of democratic principles by member states), almost recommended the suspension of Nigeria from the Commonwealth of Nations in 1998.[24] Nelson Mandela, the then president of South Africa, called on the United States to apply oil exporting sanctions on Nigeria, but U.S. President Bill Clinton did not believe that a unilateral action on Nigeria would be effective. However, the U.S. did impose limited sanctions on Nigeria. For example, travel restrictions were placed on government officials and their family members. Arms sales and military assistance were also suspended. Perhaps underlying Clinton's decision to not impose economic sanctions against Nigeria's crude oil supply was influenced by the fact that the U.S. was so dependent on it.

The leader of the Ijaw activist group, Muhahid Dokubu-Asari, was formerly the president of the influential Ijaw Youth Council. The Ijaw youth became militant in their quest to know how the oil revenue was allocated and utilized, and demanded better environmental conditions. They engaged in many violent activities, including kidnapping oil workers and holding them for ransom. Dokubu-Asari and his cohorts believed that they could take the oil from the pipelines since it belonged to the people of the Niger Delta. In most cases of conflict with the oil workers, the youth carried and used weapons, but they also relied on the protection from their god of war, called Egbisu. They carried a leaf, which symbolized the presence of Egbisu with them and the power of his protection over them. This belief in supernatural power against bullets was commonplace in pre-colonial Africa. In post-modern times, such reliance on magical power has proven to be a suicidal strategy. Needless to say, many innocent lives have been lost.

A logical question to ask: Is the possession of petroleum a curse or a blessing to Nigeria? Historical facts show that in other parts of Africa, such as Angola and the Democratic Republic of Congo (DRC), the oil factor has created economic and political problems of a huge magnitude. In Chad, where oil was recently discovered, there has been violence over the distribution of the revenue. As in the Niger Delta, the possession of oil has not raised the people's standard of living.

Fundamental to correcting this situation is understanding the problems that are responsible for Nigeria's economic turmoil. The issues are many and complex. First is the mismanagement of resources and public funds with political underpinnings. While supplying oil to outside countries, Nigerians suffer from gas shortages, or the prices are frequently hiked. The scarcity and high price of gas make life more difficult for an average Nigerian. With the inflation rate at approximately 15 percent and increasing prices of petroleum, the Nigerian common people feel the impact. The standard of living continues to drop as a result of the government's mismanagement of economic resources. Public officers benefit from the oil revenue, while the common people have nothing to show for it. Second, the people of the Niger Delta engage in bunkering. Since independence, the Nigerian constitution stipulated that all mineral resources, including gas and oil, are owned and controlled by the federal government. This means that any oil extraction not permitted by the federal government is illegal-bunkering that involves cutting into pipes and siphoning off the oil through makeshift valves. Thereafter, the crude oil is shipped out and sold to pre-arranged tankers and smuggled out. Bunkering has been taking place in the Niger Delta, and the government has not been able to effectively control it, or hold the culprits responsible. It is having a negative impact on the nation's economy. Bunkering is not only illegal, it is also dangerous, and damages the oil installations. It affects the revenue that accrues from oil, for Nigeria is losing significant income due to bunkering activities. Figures from the major oil companies show that approximately 150,000 or 200,000 bpd are lost to bunkering in the Niger Delta. A writer indicated that:

> The vast profits available from illegal bunkering and from ransoming western oil workers have degraded the traditional tribal structures of the Delta peoples to the point that gangs now exert great social, political, and economic power. In the Delta it is a classic positive-feedback loop: a switch from political motivation to profit motivation is shifting the entire culture to one of guerrilla entrepreneurs. So while the strike and the ongoing attacks both impact the oil markets, one seems likely to be a short-term event, while the other is a growing and indefinite problem.[25]

Nigeria's successive governments have not succeeded in eradicating bunkering. This is partly because of the high level of corruption, and partly because of the increasing violence in the Niger Delta. Many countries warn their companies and investors against going to Nigeria.

Hostage Taking Saga

The Niger Delta is the main source of Nigeria's wealth; this area has become a problematic area for the government. Hostage taking has become a professional business for some people, and it is significantly damaging the country's economy. Kidnappers often demand millions of Naira to release their victims; the oil companies and their workers live in fear. The lack of security affects oil production, and multi-national companies are wary of investing in Nigeria. Western countries are warning their citizens about going to Nigeria either for business or for tourism. In 1998, some youths in Ilaje and Ese Odo in Ondo State held 200 oil workers hostage in protest for the neglect of their communities by both the oil companies and the government.

Outside of the oil producing regions, kidnapping of politicians, their family members, journalists, and celebrities is also pervasive. In Rivers State, the father of the Deputy Speaker of the House of Assembly was held hostage. In Bayelsa, the mother of a lawmaker was kidnapped. Popular actors such as Pete Edochie and Nkem Owoh (a.k.a. Osuofia) were kidnapped in August and November 2009, respectively. Traditional rulers have not been spared. For example, Igwe Mbamalu Okeke of Abagana in Anambra was kidnapped in 2009. Overall, approximately 200 foreign oil workers were kidnapped in 2006, while over 500 people were kidnapped by heavily armed militants in 2009.

The people of the Niger Delta see Nigeria's successive governments and the various oil companies as collaborators who sabotage their wealth. Hence, hostage taking is a reaction to how the government and the oil companies are treating them and their land. Hostage takers often come up with a packaged demand that insists upon more control of the oil wealth, compensation for environmental problems, and huge ransoms for the hostages. The militant groups sometimes threaten to damage pipelines in order to reduce production and the export of oil. In many cases, the threats are acted upon as demonstrated in the Ekeremor Local Government Area of Bayelsa State, where militants damaged a Shell oil facility in March 2006. As shown in Table 2 (on the following page), the Movement for the Emancipation of the Niger Delta (MEND) was responsible for most of the hostage taking.

Talking to CNN, "Tamuno God's Will," a leader of MEND declared: "We are going to descend on all foreign interests in the Nigerian economy, either in the river or in the land ... We are telling all expatriates to leave Nigeria, not only the Niger Delta, but to leave Nigeria. We will take lives, we will destroy lives, [and] we will crumble the economy."[26] It is important to note that kidnapping is not directed only at foreigners. The list of Nigerians who have been kidnapped is long. While claiming that they are fighting the government for their economic problems, the perpetrators of kidnapping misplace their frustration on foreigners. They kidnap in order to draw the government's attention to their political and economic demands. In doing so, they scare away oil workers and foreign multi-millionaire investors. This produces a negative impact on the politics and economy, and significantly damages the national prestige of Nigeria.

Table 2. A Selected List of Expatriates Kidnapped

Date	Number of Hostages	Responsibility
January 2007	2 (engineers)	MEND
January 2007	24 (Filipino sailors)	
February 18, 2007	9	MEND
May 2, 2007	5 (Americans)	
May 3, 2007	17	
May 9, 2007	4 (contractors)	
May 2007	11 workers of Daewoo Engineering (8 Filipinos and 3 Koreans)	MEND
June 2007	6 (Russians)	

Conclusion

This chapter has shown the devastating effect of political violence on the democracy and economy of Nigeria. Neither democracy nor the economy can thrive in a violent and insecure environment. Nigerian politics should embrace the politics of civility, politics without bitterness, and politics that promote nation building. The return to a democratic rule is purported to bring unity, political stability, and economic growth to the country. Nigerian politicians should respect democratic principles, and allow toleration to override violence and inordinate ambition.

Nigeria relies heavily on oil revenue. Approximately 90 percent of Nigerian export revenues are derived from crude oil. Unfortunately, this large revenue does not reflect in the overall economy, as it does not trickle down to the common people. Hence, everywhere there is poverty. The fiscal policies of successive governments have not strongly supported economic growth. The combination of high expenditures, failure to provide adequate infrastructure, and mismanagement has exacerbated economic problems. When oil prices began to collapse in the 1980s, Nigeria's foreign debt increased.

There are many conflicts over the distribution of political power and economic resources. With the boom in oil prices, there are high expectations of Nigeria receiving huge profits that would improve the domestic economy. For many years, Nigerians have been expecting successive governments to judiciously use the oil money to improve their standard of living, provide jobs, and build and maintain the infrastructure. The return to democratic rule in May 1999 did not produce any remarkable economic difference than the military regimes. Nigeria experienced more violence between 1999 and 2007 than previously. It was during this period that hostage taking found its way into the Nigerian system, thereby instilling fear in foreigners and oil companies, and hampering economic growth. A country cannot survive economically in a hostile and insecure environment. Writing on the political economy of Nigeria, Sani Musa summed up the problems:

> Nigeria has the appropriate credentials for greatness. But, mismanagement of the economy, lack of public accountability, insensitivity of the leadership to the yearnings and aspirations of the people, corruption, and insecurity of lives and property have been the critical issues in the nation's life and public debate. Consequently, low capacity utilization in the industries, an inefficient and inadequate power supply, decay in the education and health sectors, galloping inflation, the deteriorating value of the Naira against convertible currencies, unemployment, and mass poverty characterized the Nigerian society and economy in May 1999 when the Obasanjo administration took over the reins of power.[27]

Anything that does not lend support to political gain is ignored, marginalized, or forgotten.

Solutions have been suggested to improve political relations in an attempt to enhance economic growth. The government has a major role to play in securing that the necessary actions are taken. First, political leaders should be more sensitive to the needs, health, and economic welfare of the people. Second, to secure peace in the Niger Delta, international communities must intervene as mediators. Although political issues and economic growth are internal affairs, it becomes an international problem when foreign companies are involved and when Nigeria's international trade in oil is gravely affected. Despite Nigeria's volatile situation, there has not been much international pressure for peace and reconciliation in the Niger Delta. Third, oil companies in the Niger Delta must improve environmental conditions. With the enormous damage to the environment, the health of the people is jeopardized, and their livelihood is lost If the government has the policies to exploit land and oil, it should come up with policies and resources to protect the people and adequately compensate them. Fourth, the onus is on the government of Nigeria to provide employment for the youth who are often engaged in acts of violence since that seems to be the only source of livelihood for them. Fifth, the government should review its revenue allocation in order to benefit the people who live where the economic resources are derived. When speaking to journalists in Oyo State, the state Chairman of the Red Cross, Dr. Jane Adebusuyi, noted the potential violence that could erupt in the state. She declared that "We can live together in peace; we can resolve our conflicts amicably through dialogue."[28]

This is a civilized and peaceful strategy for resolving differences. Instead of resorting to violence, peaceful demonstrations could be organized. Less violence and political stability will serve to promote economic growth as well. The oil revolution, which produced an economic boom in the 1970s, engendered a false economic security and hope. The oil revenue was not expended on expanding commercial networks, industrial infrastructures, or a network of roads. The profit from oil gradually increased economic greed, especially on the part of the political leaders who had access to national funds. The recent suicide bombings, which have claimed many innocent lives, are clear manifestations of the prevalent insecurity and the vulnerability of Nigerians to acts of terrorism and violence. This new trend, no doubt, constitutes a major roadblock to development, unity, sustainable democracy, and good governance. The bombings threaten the security of the country and deter multinational companies from investing in Nigeria. It is imperative that the Nigerian government tighten up security measures in order to protect and preserve precious lives. There is always a backlash to such acts of violence, especially from the international community. For example, the U.S. immediately sent the Federal Bureau of Investigation (FBI) to investigate the bombing of the United ations (UN) building in Abuja. This latest incident, in addition to hostage taking, makes Nigeria an unsafe place, especially for foreigners.

It is the responsibility of the government to provide adequate political and economic security for its people. As things are in Nigeria, there is an urgent need for the government to focus on the security of its people. Politicians need to be tolerant of opposition, and Nigerians in general should be willing to allow peace and security to exist. The rate of political assassinations and the impact of godfatherism and hostage taking prevent the dividends of democracy from being richly realized. Political maturity must prevail in order to give the masses a level of confidence in their political leaders. The combination of freedom (in all its ramifications), observance and respect for fundamental human rights, credible elections, reduction of corruption, responsible leadership, and government's sensitivity to security will promote democracy, economic growth, and prosperity. The recognition of gender and ethnic equality and playing down of religion, as is indicated in the constitution, will support a democratic process. Democracy and good governance, rather than violence, should be interwoven into the political and economic identity of any nation, especially Nigeria.

Cameroon

CHAD

NIGERIA

CAMEROON

CENTRAL AFRICAN
REPUBLIC

Mora
Mokolo
Maroua
Kaele
Garoua
Tchollire
Ngaoundere
Banyo
Bamenda
Foumban
Betare Oya
Garoua-boulai
Kumba
Nanga Eboko
Batouri
Buea
Tiko
Bonaberi
Victoria
Douala
Doume
Mesamena
Yaounde
Yokadouma
Ebolowa
Sangmelima

ATLANTIC
OCEAN

EQUATORIAL
GUINEA

GABON

REPUBLIC
OF
THE
CONGO

Chapter 6

Cameroon: The Elusiveness of Democracy

Emmanuel M. Mbah

Located in West-Central Africa and perched just above the Bight of Biafra, Cameroon has a total land area of roughly 475,440 square kilometers with a population of 19.7 million people (2010 figures). There are upwards of 250 subgroups or "tribes" inhabiting its territorial land space. In total, the people of Cameroon speak more than 280 indigenous languages. Cameroon's population is composed of 20 percent Anglophones who live predominantly in the administrative provinces of the Northwest and Southwest; together they form the British Southern Cameroons (and later West Cameroon), which were colonized by Great Britain. Eighty percent of the population is French-speaking, and live predominantly in the eight other administrative provinces. The French-speaking section of former East Cameroon was administered by the French during the period of colonial rule as part of French Equatorial Africa. English and French are recognized by the constitution as the official languages, although the latter is more predominantly used in administration and other official state business than the former.

Cameroon's pre-independence contact with the outside world, particularly with Europe, has been varied. Its earliest contact with Europe occurred when the Portuguese first explored the coastal/Atlantic portions of the territory in the 1500s. The name Cameroon came from this initial contact when the Portuguese explorer Fernando Po used it to refer to the territories flanked by the River Wouri in present-day Littoral Province. The Portuguese called this river *Rio does Cameroes*, or "river of prawns," in reference to the abundance of prawns found in that river. The Portuguese did not, however, establish any permanency in the territory, which was officially occupied and eventually colonized by the Germans in 1884 following the colonial share-out of African territory that resulted from the Berlin Colonial Conference of 1884–85.[1]

German colonization of Cameroon lasted from 1884 to 1916. The Germans were kicked out of the territory in 1916 following their defeat by Britain and France during World War I. Following an unsuccessful Anglo-French condominium or joint administration, the territory was provisionally partitioned between Britain and France; this partition was confirmed by the Milner-Simon Agreement of 1919.[2] In the partition, the British took one-fifth of the territory composed of two small parcels of land, Southern and Northern Cameroons, which they administered as part of their Nigerian colony. As already stipulated, the remaining portion, East Cameroon, went to the French and was administered as part of their Equatorial African territory. These territories were, however, supposed to be administered as League of Nations Mandates beginning on June 28, 1919, and as United Nations (UN) Trust Territories after 1945. This was not in accordance with the arrangements that actually took place.

On the heels of the decolonization process that heightened in the post-World War II period, the French section of Cameroon became independent on January 1, 1960. For the two British portions (Northern and Southern Cameroons), a UN-sponsored plebiscite was conducted on February 11, 1961, to determine their fate. Despite the irregularities that marked the plebiscite, the results indicated that Northern Cameroons voted to join Nigeria, while Southern Cameroons voted to reunite with French Cameroon to become the Federal Republic of Cameroon, formalized on September 1, 1961. Following a 1972 referendum, the country's name was changed to the United Republic of Cameroon with the intention of promoting the unity that had been disrupted during the colonial period. Far from unifying the country, the referendum actually signaled the start of more serious problems.

Democratic Practice under a Single-Party Ideology

Multiculturalism has been both an impediment and a blessing to the practice of multiparty democracy in Cameroon. While the rich and varied colonial and early independent history of Cameroon appeared to show signs of promise, it is argued that the seeds of intolerance were sown during the early period of the Ahmadou Ahidjo regime, as manifested by the one-party ideology.

The establishment of modern political parties in Cameroon can be traced to the post-1945 period when both the British and the French gave permission for these parties in their respective colonial territories. Multiparty democratic practice in the British Southern Cameroons was marked by a heightened degree of tolerance among the respective parties, with little interference from the British. It was in this atmosphere that the Kamerun National Congress

(KNC) of Dr. Emmanuel Endeley, the Kamerun People's Party of N.N. Mbile, the Cameroon People's National Convention (CPNC), a merger of the KNC and KPP, and the Kamerun National Democratic Party (KNDP) of John Ngu Foncha strived to peacefully position themselves in the political struggles that culminated in the 1961 plebiscite. There was no chaos when the KNDP's ideal of reunification with French Cameroon succeeded in the plebiscite.[3]

In French Cameroon intolerance quickly set in as early as 1948 when the French, Ahmadou Ahidjo's Movement for Union of Cameroon (MUC), and other smaller parties decided to target Reuben Um Nyobé's Union of the Populations of Cameroon (UPC). What followed was armed resistance against the French, as well as against local authorities in French Cameroon. Even before this period, the French had encouraged the formation of about 90 political parties in the 1940s and 1950s. Many of these turned out to be of a regional and ethnic nature, as part of a plot to diffuse the UPC's popularity. Subsequently, UPC meetings were banned, and its sympathizers harassed. The party was outlawed in July 1955 by French authorities, and some of its leaders were ultimately assassinated.[4]

Just before 1958, French authorities had resolved to grant early independence to Cameroon. Meanwhile, the idea of reunification with Southern Cameroon was a popular ideal amongst many political groups in French Cameroon. This included the UPC, which was supported by French authorities in a bid "to prevent the rise to power of the radical UPC and to enhance [France's] position in a postindependence Cameroon."[5] In May 1957, the French appointed André-Marie Mbida as the first Prime Minister in French Cameroon, but because of disagreements with French authorities as well as some members of the Cameroon legislature, Mbida resigned in February 1958. Mbida's problem with French authorities derived from his stance against early independence and reunification for Cameroon, coupled with his reluctance to seek a political solution to the UPC insurrection. With French backing, Ahidjo's MUC party had succeeded against all odds, and he was selected by the French to replace Mbida in January 1958 because of his politics of moderation, his support for immediate independence and reunification, as well as his support for French influence in a post-independence Cameroon. Ahidjo became the first president of the new Cameroon republic (French Cameroon) when that territory attained independence on January 1, 1960.[6]

While the UPC continued to function underground or in exile, Ahidjo was ready to befriend Théodore Mayi-Matip, the leader of a moderate UPC faction known as the *rallié upeciste*, in order to destroy the main UPC Party and prevent it from ever becoming a "coherent political faction."[7] On February 25, 1960, Ahidjo repealed through decree the July 13, 1955 French law that banned the UPC. This gave it legal status once more, although his sole interest lay in propping up Mayi-Matip's faction. Armed with emergency powers secured from the legislative assembly in October 1959 (through which he could rule by decree until elections were held in March 1960), Ahidjo requested and received additional French troops to assist his government in suppressing resistance from radical UPC elements. It was with the assistance of French military personnel that Ahidjo was able to establish the *Service des Etudes et de la documentation* (SEDOC), the intelligence and torture service that assisted him in the intimidation that allowed him to have a firm grip over the new Cameroon nation throughout his tenure.[8] Thus, it was partly because of UPC opposition and Ahidjo's resolve in destroying it, as well as because of the multi-ethnic nature of the country, that the one-party ideology was introduced in the Federal Republic of Cameroon during the early 1960s. Before long, Anglophone Cameroonians, who previously had a peaceful experience in the practice of multiparty democracy, were subjected to Ahidjo's one-party logic.

From 1960 to 1972, Ahidjo took further measures to cement his grip on power, ensuring that one-party logic became the culture for the new Cameroon Republic. He used the emergency powers of 1959 to postpone legislative elections that were slated for March 1960 on grounds that the unstable political atmosphere resulted from radical UPC resistance. He then appointed 42 loyal members into a constitutional committee charged with drafting a new constitution. The result of this constitution was to strengthen the executive and weaken the legislature. The exorbitant powers accorded to Ahidjo by this constitution were confirmed at the Foumban Constitutional Convention of July 1961, which aimed to draft a federal constitution for a reunified Cameroon. Because Ahidjo and his East Cameroon delegation, with the backing of French experts and advisers, came prepared to subvert the entire procedure, the Southern Cameroon delegation at the convention were unable to negotiate even "a loose and decentralized federation that would have given greater authority to the different states in the federation...."[9] Thus, the constitution that ushered in reunification of the former British and French sections of Cameroon was highly centralized, with a heavy investiture of power in the executive.[10] The Southern Cameroon delegation did not anticipate how much preparedness was required for a constitutional exercise of that magnitude. The broad investiture of power accorded the president by this federal constitution gave Ahidjo the authority to introduce other repressive laws, including the anti-subversion law of March 12, 1962, and these were "used in depriving Cameroonians of their freedoms for the next two decades."[11]

Even before the Foumban Constitutional Convention gave Ahidjo broad powers over West Cameroon (former Southern Cameroon), he had already started consolidating his position and that of his party throughout East Cameroon (former French Cameroon) by manipulating electoral laws to ensure that his party, the Movement for the Union of Cameroon (MUC), secured a majority of the seats in the April 1960 legislative elections. In a bid to make that party the only viable party in a 100-seat legislative assembly, Ahidjo's plan was well on its way to success when the MUC won 51 out of the 100 seats. To ensure that it was the dominant party in East Cameroon, Ahidjo embarked on co-opting opposition party leaders and members into his government by offering them cabinet positions, and threatening, intimidating, and persecuting those unwilling to join his MUC. In 1962, four opposition politicians rejected Ahidjo's idea of a single unified party in a June 23, 1962, memorandum titled *Manifeste du Front National Unifié*, on grounds that the idea was detrimental to the practice of democracy. They were arrested on June 29, and tried and convicted under the new Law No. 62/OF/18 of March 12, 1962, that charged them with "threatening national security and spreading news liable to be harmful to public authority."[12] Unprepared to face the plight of the four imprisoned politicians, many opposition party leaders either joined the MUC or dissolved their parties, and Ahidjo was now free to proclaim the MUC as "the only political party in East Cameroon with a truly national character."[13]

Ahidjo's final step in institutionalizing a single party throughout the federation lay in convincing and manipulating political leaders in West Cameroon to join the MUC as the only national party in the country. These West Cameroon leaders were easily sucked into Ahidjo's plan due to greed and personal ambitions. For example, to minority party leader Dr. Emmanuel Endeley of the Cameroon People's National Convention (CPNC), Ahidjo's single-party platform was an opening that could propel him to the center of national politics and prevent his party from being taken lightly by the majority Kamerun National Democratic Party (KNDP) of John Ngu Foncha. For his part, John Ngu Foncha, who was also Prime Minister of West Cameroon at the time, was afraid that an Ahidjo-Endeley alliance could end up undermining his authority. For this reason, Foncha precipitously created a National Coordinating Committee that brought together Ahidjo's MUC and the KNDP in discussions on avenues through which both parties could merge into a single national party. Some have even argued "Foncha never seemed to fear losing his power and prerogatives to the federal government as much as losing it to his own opposition within the state [of West Cameroon]."[14] Ahidjo himself was afraid of an alliance between the KNPD and any of the parties in East Cameroon that he had co-opted into the MUC.[15]

Ahidjo used the rivalry between political leaders of West Cameroon to suggest the dissolution of their parties in place of a single national party, and successfully argued that "multipartism was not only a hindrance to effective execution of government policies," but could result in chaos and collapse of the nation.[16] With this success came the creation of a single national party, the Cameroon National Union (CNU) on September 1, 1966, with Ahidjo doubling as the first president of the party and head of state of the Federal Republic of Cameroon. He now had absolute power and authority to institutionalize his single-party ideology. But he had to first do away with the federation and the federal constitution that had been created at Foumban in 1961, arguing that the federation was expensive and inefficient, and that it slowed down economic growth and development. Additionally, Ahidjo maintained that the federation "undermined national unity and fostered cleavages and conflicts between francophones and anglophones who considered themselves as members of separate states."[17] After brief consultations with the rank and file of the CNU party, Ahidjo scheduled a referendum on May 20, 1972, for Cameroonians to vote on the dissolution of the federation, to be replaced by a unitary state. Accordingly, almost every Cameroonian voted for the proposal, and the United Republic of Cameroon became a political entity by Decree No. 72/270 of June 2, 1972. Ahidjo assured the Anglophone community that the adoption of a unitary constitution would guarantee "bilingualism and polyculturalism."[18]

Beginning in 1972, the one-party ideology became part of the culture of democracy and governance in Cameroon. While it is true that the consolidation of national unity was one reason behind that logic, it is equally true that the establishment of a single party was designed to eliminate any opposition to Ahidjo's regime, which increasingly became dictatorial as the days went by. Ahidjo had successfully institutionalized his ideology on Cameroonians through the building of coalitions, through repression and intimidation, as well as through a highly centralized administrative structure anchored in the hands of the chief executive, Ahidjo. "Ahidjo's control of all aspects of government was so complete that most members of parliament were not even aware that they had the right to initiate legislation. By contrast, the president was not accountable to anyone."[19] For 25 years following its formation in 1966, the CNU reigned unopposed as the lone political party in Cameroon.

On November 6, 1992, Paul Biya became President of the United Republic of Cameroon after Ahidjo resigned amidst allegations of poor health. Before becoming president, Biya had served under Ahidjo in various cabinet positions from 1962 and was very knowledgeable on how to manipulate patronage in the regime's favor.[20] Thus, despite Biya's promise to introduce change in Cameroon on his accession, he decided to pursue the single-party logic of Ahidjo by keeping all the power in his hands. The structure that Ahidjo had put in place was very handy, especially after a failed military take-over by some army officers from the Northern Provinces in April 1984.[21]

At the National Congress of the CNU in 1985, many of Biya's liberal supporters had advised him to reintroduce multiparty democracy in Cameroon. Cautiously, he declined, but subsequently changed the name of the national party to the Cameroon's People Democratic Movement (CPDM). According to Joseph Takougang, "the word 'democratic' was supposed to signify that the party would henceforth be more democratic."[22] That was, however, not the case. Just as in the days of Ahidjo, the Political Bureau of the CPDM continued to use co-option and patronage to support the status quo of the single-party hegemony. In 1983, a constitutional amendment was introduced which allowed multiple candidates to contest presidential elections. In practice, this was window dressing, for it was difficult for any Cameroonian to meet the list of qualifying criteria to run for the post.[23]

Biya decided to maintain the centers of repression, intimidation, and torture bequeathed by the Ahidjo regime to reinforce his grip on power. These include SEDOC, which became the *Centre National des Etudes et des Recherches* (CENER) and the BMM. After the 1984 failed coup d'état, their role in surveillance and intimidation increased when President Biya reappointed Jean Fochivé as head of CENER. Fochivé's expertise in surveillance, intimidation, and torture was unparalleled, considering for 15 years he was the head of SEDOC under Ahidjo. To many Cameroonians, his reappointment was an indication of what direction the country had taken.[24]

Far from introducing a change in politics, the CPDM had one goal, and that was to strengthen President Biya's grip on power.[25] It remained the only political party in Cameroon until the return of multiparty politics in 1990. Thus, between 1966 and 1990, the respective regimes of Ahidjo and Biya were contumaciously averse to any idea that called for multiparty democratic practice. During this period, they respectively sought to persecute proponents of political pluralism, including Marxist-Leninists, remnants of the UPC, and anyone who sympathized or advocated for alternatives to the party in power. Cameroonians with alternative political dispensations could not express their views in the open, and many went underground, or on self-exile in order to exercise that right. According to Francis B. Nyamnjoh, "the dual ideologies of national unity and national development were used to stifle initiative and creativity," and the respective regimes have recurrently and conveniently made the claim "that all was well and that Cameroon was a veritable island of peace and quiet in an Africa of turbulence."[26]

It was in this atmosphere of political repression, characterized by one-party ideology that John Fru Ndi launched the Social Democratic Front (SDF) in the Anglophone provincial headquarter of Bamenda. On May 26, 1990, he launched the SDF without government approval, challenging the erstwhile single party logic. Before, during, and after the launching of the SDF, Biya and his CPDM cronies imbued with the lone party mentality hastened to chastise both Fru Ndi and his party's zeal for pluralism with frivolous accusations aimed at discrediting the SDF, its leader, and the party's platform. They did this in many ways. For example, Fru Ndi was labeled a debtor of questionable integrity, and accused of owing 400 million FCFA to the defunct Cameroon Bank.[27] On the day the SDF was launched, students at the University of Yaoundé sympathized with the party by celebrating its birth on the university premises. They were accused by the government media of singing the Nigerian national anthem; it was indirectly purported that these students were suggesting cessation and solidarity with Nigeria.[28] Meanwhile, government officials falsely alleged that 10,000 Nigerians took part in the SDF's launch in Bamenda, and that Fru Ndi had sought refuge in Nigeria in the immediate aftermath of the launch. Additionally, the SDF was duped a regional and ethnic party composed mainly of Bamenda Grasslanders, while sympathizers and participants at the launch were said to have been manipulated by Fru Ndi.[29] From the above outbursts, we can surmise that the ruling CPDM party, plagued by the one-party logic, was unwilling to allow political alternatives.

Despite such government outbursts, Biya was pressured enough to hint in an address to the first extraordinary congress of the CPDM (duped the Congress of Freedom and Democracy), that multiparty democracy was on its way, albeit on his own terms, and at a pace set by his party. Emphasis on a set pace, Nyamnjoh contends, "would largely account for why every subsequent initiative at accelerated democracy would be dismissed by Biya and his party as a ploy by irresponsible 'purveyors of illusions.'"[30]

When Parliament convened in November 1990 to discuss the prospect of liberalization in Cameroon, it became clear to all that Biya would acquiesce to the country's demand for pluralism. What was not clear at the time was how far he would go to minimize the role of opposition political parties in a plural Cameroon. That being said, new decrees on rights and freedoms were introduced in November 1990, as well as one law (law No. 90/05 of December 19, 1990) that sanctioned the formation of political parties. This authorization saw the creation of numerous parties in Cameroon, beginning in 1990. By March 1992, there were already 68 opposition political parties in the country. Many of them were, however, weak parties with no official platform and were essentially composed of the family members of the founders. The appearance of these new parties, some of which were apparently sponsored by the CPDM, have led many Cameroonians to argue that their authorization demonstrates "the government's interest in dissipating real democratic opposition,"[31] by keeping the CPDM strong, thereby falling back to the one-party logic.

Democracy, the One-Party Ideology, and Fair Play

A democracy built on participation and the rule of law is a necessary prerequisite for transparency, freedom, and the minimization of corruption, and vice versa. Unfortunately, the constitutions adopted by many African nations south of the Sahara during independence did not include such provisions.[32] The absence of institutions that guarantee transparency is, therefore, a serious impediment to the practice of multi-party democracy in Cameroon. For example, Ahidjo's anti-subversion decree of March 12, 1962, forbade Cameroonians from making statements that were critical of the party, the government, and the president. It was in November 1966 that Victor Kanga, the then Minister of Information and Tourism, was dismissed, arrested, tried, convicted, and sentenced to four years in prison "for publishing information detrimental to the regime."[33]

The laws that regulate democratic practice in the country are lacking in both substance and fairness. Repressive laws have recurrently been promulgated to eradicate or clamp down on dissent. While Article 3 of the Federal Constitution made provisions for opposition parties to exist, security forces did not hesitate to disperse a meeting of some Anglophone political leaders including John Ngu Foncha and Augustine Ngom Jua in June 1972 when they were discussing the formation of a new party; some were arrested and detained.[34] The 1985 arrest and detention of Anglophone lawyer Gorji-Dinka for questioning Biya's constitutional authority in changing the country's name to the Republic of Cameroon, and the arrest and detention of lawyer Yondo Black and ten others on grounds that they had conspired to form a political party are examples of how far Biya would go to maintain the single-party ideology bequeathed by Ahidjo.[35] The new decrees introduced by Biya in December 1990 gave Cameroonians the right to create political parties, but had a major setback in that the CPDM Minister of Territorial Administration had the sole legal authority to scrutinize the registration of documents of all aspiring political parties before granting authorization to those he liked. Thus, "by acting as both umpire and player, the CPDM was in a position to redefine or bend the rules of the game of multiparty democracy in Cameroon."[36]

In 1993, the Biya regime commenced work on a new constitutional draft, which promised decentralization and a guarantee of genuine multiparty democratic practices. While that constitution was approved by the Parliament in

December 1995, and signed by Biya on January 18, 1996, opposition politicians in parliament had contributed little or nothing to its outcome. Moreover, the few changes contained in the constitution had to do with the inclusion of more dictatorial articles such as Article 55 Section 2, and Articles 58 and 59: These empowered the president to appoint regional delegates in opposition towns in a bid to supersede the authority of elected opposition councils.[37]

Article 9 of the 1996 constitution also deserves some scrutiny because it remained the same as Article 15 of the 1961 Federal Constitution. These articles gave the president the power to declare a state of emergency whenever the security and territorial integrity of the state was threatened, and the president alone determines what constitutes threats to the state. Thus, following the violence that resulted from the 1992 rigged presidential elections, Biya was able to declare a state of emergency in many of the provinces where post-electoral protests and demonstrations took place, and these were predominantly in opposition strongholds. Moving backward from the 1996 constitution, Takougang rightly contends that "very little was changed from the 1961 federal and 1972 unitary constitutions since the president remained the ultimate source of all authority in the country."[38]

The CPDM wants to remain the main political party in a multiparty Cameroon. Its leader, Biya (who doubles as the President of Cameroon), has not missed an opportunity to tweak the electoral code to its favor. The opposition has continuously complained about the country's electoral code, which it claims has been designed by the CPDM government to rig elections and subvert the will of the people by all means possible. It was for this reason that the SDF, the strongest of the opposition parties, boycotted the first multiparty legislative elections held in March 1992. Fearful that its political machinations would draw greater attention if other opposition parties followed the SDF's example, the CPDM government decided to grant 500 million FCFA to opposition parties that promised to participate in the elections. They also offered aid for campaigns and preparations.[39] To many clear-minded Cameroonians, this offer was more of a bribe than an aid.

Subverting the will of the people with a single-party ideology is what happened in the aftermath of the 1996 municipal elections, following opposition victories in a number of urban councils. To prevent the opposition from effective control over these councils, the Biya government imposed CPDM Government Delegates over elected opposition mayors to take charge of finances and all major economic projects in predominantly opposition councils. The CPDM government was unwilling to relinquish control of these economically rich councils, including those of Bamenda, Kumba, Buea, and Douala to the opposition who denounced the tactics but could do nothing.[40]

The legislative elections of 1992, 1997, and 2002 were marked by numerous irregularities, as well as the willingness and ability of the CPDM government to subvert the wishes of the electorate by enticing and coercing minor opposition parties into coalition deals. In the March 1992 legislative elections boycotted by the SDF, 32 parties contested, but only four won seats in the 180-person parliament: the CPDM won 88 seats, the National Union for Democracy and Progress (UNDP) 68, the UPC 18, and the Movement for the Defense of the Republic (MDR) 6 seats. Clearly, the opposition had a majority of the seats even under serious allegations of government rigging. But the CPDM government was able to induce the MDR with six seats into a governing coalition that lasted up until the next legislative elections in 1997.[41]

In the May 1997 legislative elections, the ruling CPDM party won 116 seats in parliament while the opposition barely won 64 seats divided between the SDF (43), the UNDP (12), the UDC (5), the MDR (1), and the MLJC (1). There were widespread allegations by the opposition that the government had rigged the election in its favor. While the ruling party did not need a governing coalition to rule in view of the huge margin of seats it won, it went ahead and negotiated one with the UNDP, a more popular party than the MDR in the northern portions of Cameroon.[42] Many consider this alliance as evidence that the election was rigged and that the CPDM party was conscious that it lacked the popular will of the people. The same allegations of rigging were registered in the 2002 and 2007 legislative elections. In 2002, the CPDM won 149 seats, while the remaining 31 seats were shared between the SDF (21), UNDP (1), UPC (3), and CDU (5).[43]

Allegations of rigging were also leveled at the Biya regime following the presidential elections of 1992, 1997, and 2004; the incumbent won all three elections. While many have argued that the opposition's failure to agree on a consensus candidate was, in large part, responsible for the outcome of the election, it is only fair to add that the ambiguities that characterized the voting did not offer opposition candidates a fair shot.

During campaigns for the October 1997 presidential election, incumbent President Biya was proclaimed by the national media as the best candidate despite reservations from many a Cameroonian. The elections were held under an atmosphere of mistrust following Biya's refusal to create an independent electoral commission to oversee the elections.[44] The parliamentary opposition, the SDF, UNDP, and UDC boycotted the presidential election in protest against the short campaign period allowed them, as well as consensus that the Ministry of Territorial Administration (MINAT) would not be fair, leaving Biya to claim a 92 percent victory. Despite opposition claims that 80 percent of the electorate abstained from voting, and predictions by political analysts and some western diplomats that the proclamation of Biya as winner would result in chaos, nothing happened.[45] There was no civil war despite the endemic power structure of the country which centered heavily on Biya's Beti ethnic group, the prevailing economic crisis, chronic economic mismanagement and corruption, and the unfair tactics used by the ruling regime to prevent the peaceful participation of all Cameroonians in the democratic process. Cameroon has proven to be politically different from other former French colonies where the absence of free and fair elections has resulted in violence.[46] The same picture was replicated in the 2004 presidential elections.

In the 2004 presidential elections, the 15 opposition parties were divided on many issues; they were again given only 30 days to campaign, this was the minimum allowed under Cameroon law. The idea of having a consensus candidate for the opposition through the Coalition for National Reconciliation and Reconstruction (CNRR), a loose coalition of opposition parties established in 2003 "by disaffected former ministers, rights activists and veteran opposition leaders," failed again when John Fru Ndi of the SDF withdrew from the coalition after its refusal to select him as their presidential candidate. As leader of the largest opposition and head of the most prominent party of the marginalized Anglophone Cameroon, there were arguably serious calculations behind his decision to withdraw from CNRR and contest the election independently of that coalition, which had elected Ndam Njoya as its candidate.[47]

Disappointed by the self-centeredness of those who talk of change, the Union for the Republic (UR), represented by Antar Gassagay withdrew from the presidential majority coalition (CNRR) not long after the SDF left. Opposition self-centeredness minimized their claim for change, and served to distract from key discussions that undergird elections. As a result, political debate was elusive during the 2004 presidential elections despite the diminution of the campaign period by the Biya regime to stifle effective opposition mobilization. The enthusiasm and vigor that characterized the elections of the 1990s were gone, and "the only reform issue that made it into the CRRN's election campaign—the computerization of the electoral register—was effectively dropped in September after it failed to attract significant support at unevenly attended opposition rallies."[48] The election campaign discussion switched to the death of an SDF activist in the South-West Province. The victim was alleged to have been murdered by a CPDM member of parliament, although the SDF was "unable to make the necessary connection between the killing and the perceived human rights abuses of the [CPDM] regime."[49]

Even before the 2004 presidential elections were held, there were concerns in Cameroon and abroad as to whether free and fair elections could take place in an atmosphere where a government ministry (MINAT) conducts and announces the results of elections instead of an independent body. MINAT refused to heed to opposition calls for voter registration to be computerized (despite complaints from many rural areas of lost registration cards) on grounds that it could not afford the $17 million (US) required for the exercise. In September 2004, barely one month before the election, the government established the number of Cameroonians who registered to vote at 4.3 million people; the opposition and foreign dignitaries in Cameroon challenged that number, putting it at 8 million. Even before the election was held, a report prepared by a Common Wealth Monitoring Group concluded that the entire process was unsatisfactory. The government, however, denied the allegation,[50] and Biya easily won that election.

The issue of creating an independent electoral commission has become a recurrent opposition demand in all elections. From day one, the opposition has been begging the government to allow the establishment of that commission to no avail. In 2000, the government offered an alternative in the name of the government-controlled National Electoral Observatory (NEO), whose members were appointed by President Biya, head of the CPDM government. In creating the NEO, the government said that its role would be to supervise elections in a fair and transparent manner so as to avoid electoral ambiguities. The NEO was anything but fair. It did not have powers to organize elections, a fact that became clear when Biya postponed the June 2002 elections and sacked the Minister of Territorial Administration who was actually in charge of organizing elections. When that election was finally held, the government's rigging machinery had been fully organized, allowing the CPDM to claim a big victory, winning 149 out of 180 parliamentary seats that year, and "reducing every other party to a dying regional flicker, and imposing the CPDM as the only national party."[51] By the time the 2007 legislative elections were conducted, it became clear to Cameroonians and foreign missions in the country that transparency in multiparty democracy remained a tall order. Many Cameroonians who cared about their livelihood, especially civil servants, had begun towing the CPDM party line as a survival strategy. They openly campaigned for the CPDM in hopes of advancement, despite the belief by many that the CPDM does not represent the majority will of Cameroonians. Businessmen and others followed for the same reasons. Thus, by 2007, the single-party logic, as promoted by the CPDM, seemed to have won the day.

Elections in Cameroon since the 1990 advent of multiparty democracy have taken place on the heels of other very controversial laws. For example, according to Section 8 of Electoral Law No. 92/010 of September 17, 1992, voters had to prove that they had lived in a particular locality for a continuous period of six months in order to vote. To be considered a candidate, you must be an indigene of that locality, or show proof of continuous residence in that locality for a long period of time. While the ruling CPDM government claimed that the law was aimed at protecting indigenes from being outvoted by recent migrants and others, the real purpose of that law was to whip up ethnic sentiments in opposition strongholds in order to create the type of atmosphere conducive for chaos. Rigging was steadily becoming easy for MINAT to orchestrate because it was the responsible authority that organized, supervised, and announced election results.[52] These laws were extended to the 2002, 2004, and 2007 elections.

Controversial laws such as the one discussed above were aimed at enabling the government to manipulate the process of electioneering in its favor. We see this process at work when opposition sympathizers are requested to vote only in their villages of origin, even those who were born elsewhere. When they descend to those villages to vote, the CPDM election supervisors in the different polling stations would instruct them to go vote at their places of residence.[53] Voters residing in predominantly opposition strongholds must be on the voter register and possess a voting card as well as an identification card to participate in the voting exercise. These registers are manipulated by the government while voting, and identity cards are usually not issued to opposition sympathizers. During elections, "newspapers are full of stories about opposition lists that have been disqualified by the Ministry of Territorial Administration, either for failure to 'reflect the sociological components' of the locality or for including candidates that did not 'quite belong' in the area concerned."[54] Moreover, Cameroonians living in the Diaspora, many of whom left because of their disenchantment with the Biya regime, are therefore strong sympathizers of the opposition, and are not allowed to vote.

In order to stifle the practice of a multiparty democracy and subvert the will of the people, the Biya regime is guilty of the withholding of electoral cards to home-based opposition sympathizers, the creation of polling stations in the homes of CPDM members, the cooption of traditional chiefs, important dignitaries, businessmen, and civil servants to guarantee victories for the CPDM, the creation of new electoral constituencies to guarantee such victories, and using "election violence ... to justify irregularities."[55] "Within the ranks of the opposition itself, the CPDM has encouraged carpet crossing, dissension, scandals, and various crises in its [favor], with tempting offers to key individuals and communities."[56] It is, therefore, not surprising that the opposition has consistently denounced the absence of fair play in all elections since the advent of multiparty democracy in the 1990s.

The same problems with organizing elections in Cameroon since the introduction of multiparty democracy are still there. It has been suggested that the opposition's failure to present a consensus candidate in the 1992 presidential election gave Biya the opportunity that has kept him in power till this day. "Subsequent elections since then," Nyamnjoh points out, "have made little difference, and the opposition parties, one after another, have displayed the same contradictions, the same disinclination to go beyond rhetoric in matters of democracy within their parties and in their constituencies, and the same craving for power without vision."[57] While some of this might be true, it is fair to add that given the totality of its actions before and during elections, the Biya regime is prepared to go to any length to win and stay in power irrespective of any opposition consensus candidate.

Cameroonians celebrated in 1996 when the government announced an amendment to the constitution, restricting the presidential term to seven years, allowing the president to be reelected only once.[58] Many were prepared to persevere with the CPDM regime for the next 14 years, hoping that because the incumbent would be ineligible to run in the 2011 presidential election, the regime would be replaced. These hopes were dashed in early 2008 when the president indicated that term limits would be scrapped, giving Biya the opportunity to seek additional terms to extend his 29-year rule. (By 2011, President Biya would have been in office for 29 years). Cameroonians took to the streets in protest, though nothing seemed to have come out of the riots, with the exception of the many killed.[59] A main reason for such controversial decrees is to maintain the CPDM government in power. Such decrees, together with the regime's avowed struggle to disintegrate the opposition, are major features of the conduct of multiparty democracy in Cameroon.

In fact, the gradual disintegration of the opposition was apparent even before the 1992 elections when it became clear that Cameroon's multiethnic situation would seriously jeopardize the ability of any party or group of parties to garner the interest of every group in the country. This was exactly what happened when four opposition coalition parties belonging to President Biya's Beti ethnic group withdrew from the Yaoundé Plan of Action of June 15, 1991, where the idea of a consensus candidate had been agreed upon. Multiparty democracy became an ethnic affair, and all elections conducted after 1991 testified to the fact "that Cameroonians were voting along ethnic and regional lines, and endorsing national leaders primarily through their ethnic and regional elites."[60] Ethnocentric multiparty democracy, Nyamnjoh contends, gives credence to the dispensation that "Africans might be more comfortable with a democracy in tune with their social [or cultural] background and their predicaments under the global economy."[61] Biya's single party logic has continued to pit ethnic groups in Cameroon against each other. Even radical opposition parties championing the course for change have not escaped this predicament, as was evidenced during the Ghost Towns Operation from April 1991 to June

1992 (discussed below), when those who disagreed with the opposition logic of crippling the economy to force the regime to convene a sovereign national conference were branded opponents of democracy.

Due to the absence of true democratic institutions and the lack of fair play in the electoral process, Cameroonians have lost interest in the practice of multiparty democracy. The Biya regime successfully obliterated those issues that heightened political debate in the 1990s. Voter registration has been reduced in part because of disillusionment, and in part because of government obstructions, and " … voting no longer seems to offer the possibility of improved living conditions and enhanced liberties."[62] Biya and his CPDM cronies have weakened the opposition to the extent that the CPDM now has the same level of firmness, notoriety, and disillusionment amongst Cameroonians that the CNU had on the eve of Ahidjo's resignation.[63] But, above all, it is the infringement on the liberties of Cameroonians through intimidation and abuses that account for much of the disillusionment in the practice of multiparty democracy in the country.

Intimidation and Abuses

It is fair to argue that Cameroon has been in a perpetual state of emergency since the advent of multiparty democracy in 1990. Intimidation and abuses have heavily marred the democratic process, as members of the opposition, students, and other influential groups have been harassed by government forces in constant crackdowns, and some have even been killed.[64] Many would agree that the Biya government is an opportunistic and predatory regime that uses perceived threats to peace as opportunities to intimidate, abuse, and kill citizens of Cameroon in order to retain power. On May 26, 1990, when the SDF was launched in the North-West Provincial capital of Bamenda, six innocent Cameroonians were killed by government security forces in Bamenda because Biya and his party were unwilling to accept an alternative political dispensation.[65] Since that incident, intimidation and abuse of opposition activists and sympathizers, as well as others who have practically nothing to do with politics have increased precipitously.

Intimidation, harassment, and repression have been pursued since independence through two very organized security units. The first, CENER (previously known as SEDOC before 1975), is a political force responsible for spying on Cameroonians. The second, and equally notorious, is the BMM, which is a torture center for the extraction of confessions. Workers of both units are highly compensated financially and through promotions, many of who are all the more willing to abuse their authority for additional rewards.[66] For his part, Biya has relied heavily on the military for support and has continued to compensate them handsomely. In the 1990s, for example, while the Biya Government drastically slashed salaries for all civil servants in response to calls for the implementation of Structural Adjustment Programs by the World Bank and the International Monetary Fund (IMF) as preconditions for further aid, salaries of uniformed officers remained the same. Meanwhile, in April 1991, three military operational commanders, all of whom were Army Generals, were given the responsibility for the maintenance of peace and tranquility. They were to use all available means at their disposal in seven out of ten provinces that had been afflicted by pro-democracy demonstrations. Their role in intimidating, harassing, repressing, and torturing Cameroonians who only desired to participate in meaningful multiparty democracy cannot be overemphasized. Furthermore, in the aftermath of the October 1992 highly contested presidential election, Biya increased the number of Army Generals in the country from four to fifteen, and none of the new generals was an Anglophone. Biya's reliance on the military has one objective, and that is to maintain not only his position of power, but also that of his CPDM party stalwarts. According to Takougang, "some observers have even argued that Biya's failure to institute genuine democratic reforms in Cameroon since the beginning of the pro-democracy movement in the early 1990s may be due to the support by the military and the security forces for the regime and the status quo."[67]

Newspapers, the watchdogs of fair play in societies with a culture of free and fair democracies, have been recurrently purged of writers and articles critical of the president in both the Ahidjo and Biya regimes. It is not unheard of in Cameroon for newspapers to be confiscated and sometimes banned, while editors and journalists critical of the regime have been imprisoned and tortured. A case in point was the arrest and detention of the editor of Le Messager, Pius Njawe, for publishing articles critical of Biya and his regime. Many others have suffered the same fate. Thus, while Law No. 90/052 of December 19, 1990 facilitated the process of establishing newspapers and magazines, it also restricted their freedoms.[68]

The Biya regime's high-handed actions can also be seen during its retaliation against the opposition coalition or the Ghost Towns Operation of 1991 that aimed to cripple the economy of Cameroon in hopes of pressuring the government to convene a sovereign national conference. The government used this opportunity to accuse the opposition of fomenting chaos through intimidation and intolerance by repressing, harassing, and torturing opposition activists and sympathizers as well as innocent Cameroonians residing in opposition strongholds. By the end of the strike, opposition accounts put the number of people killed by government forces at close to 40.[69] Cameroonians have protested in the capital Yaoundé, as well as in Bamenda and Douala, calling on the government to enact electoral reforms that would, amongst other things, guarantee fair and reasonable voter registration.[70] Government reactions to these protests have always come in the form of repression.

To be fair, the radical opposition has also been responsible for some of the intimidation and harassment. The anti-government coalition or the Ghost Towns Operation that was started in June 1991, almost led to the collapse of Douala (the economic and commercial). It was characterized by various forms of intimidation, harassment, and abuses. Some opposition activists were responsible for destroying stores in Douala and elsewhere in the country. The ports were empty, taxis were grounded and only a few cars and people were on the streets. This operation was aimed at pressuring the government to summon a sovereign national conference in which various national factions would be free to discuss the state of affairs of the country as well as its future trajectory. It was designed to bleed the Cameroon economy gradually, and bring about the collapse of the Biya government by making it impossible for it to be able to pay civil servants and honor other financial obligations. But because a national conference would have offered an excellent platform for the opposition to lambast the regime for abuses, Biya refused to acquiesce to the demand.[71]

The Ghost Towns strike had devastating economic effects for Cameroon as well as neighboring landlocked countries, such as Chad and the Central African Republic, which depend on the port of Douala for their import and export transactions. It introduced hardship in the country by effectively slowing down business transactions in seven out of ten Cameroon provinces. However, it failed to force the regime to introduce meaningful political changes because it was not directed against the leaders of Biya's ruling CPDM party. Businesses were closed from Monday to Friday, but opened on weekends for people to restock. Only Yaoundé, the capital, was spared. The strike revealed the extent to which the opposition coalition was prepared to intimidate and abuse ordinary Cameroonians. Despite general support for the strike, many Cameroonians were adversely affected as many stayed away from their jobs and businesses for fear of retribution from the opposition, and many began questioning the tactics used by the opposition.[72] Such tactics convinced some sections of Cameroon society that "the opposition simply wanted to substitute one form of intolerance with another."[73]

In February 2008, the government again accused the opposition of intimidating citizens during the deadly riots that resulted from the high cost of food and fuel. Biya also announced his decision to end term limits in presidential elections, which would allow him to stand as a candidate in 2011.[74] The irony in this accusation is that those who died during the riots were killed by government forces, and not by the opposition.

It is not fair to accuse the opposition of the type of intimidation and abuses, which the government perpetrated, because it (the opposition) is only struggling to have its voice heard, and lacks the ability and resources that the government has to intimidate, harass, and repress its citizens. Some journalists, such as Herbert Boh, who were angry with the regime's high-handed actions during the Ghost Towns operation, have observed that:

> Vandalism, provoked by the absence of dialogue and by brutal military repression, is the people's only way of speaking loud enough to be heard above the noise generated by the firing of tear gas and gunshots. It is a desperate message from millions of peace-loving countrymen enslaved by abject poverty.[75]

Boh's remark is a succinct representation of the frustrations of an opposition being targeted by a regime that refuses to relinquish power. By using the state's military to intimidate Cameroonians and violate their human rights, Biya's CPDM government has succeeded to cling to power, and there is every indication that they intend to continue to impose itself on Cameroonians as the recent creation of ELECAM seems to suggest.

Elections, Change, and Transition

In December 2006, President Biya announced the creation of Elections Cameroon (ELECAM), in Law No. 2006/011 to serve as a neutral supervising body in forthcoming elections.[76] Many Cameroonians, foreign diplomats, and civil society groups who saw a flicker of hope in this announcement were disappointed when the president announced ELECAM's composition. A majority of the 12 members of ELECAM who were sworn in at the Yaoundé Supreme Court on January 29, 2009, are members of the CPDM Central Committee, and despite their pledge to guarantee free and fair elections in Cameroon, no one believes them, considering their political affiliation. These members were appointed through a presidential decree, they serve at the pleasure of the president, and there is no indication that ELECAM would be different from NEO or MINAT.[77] Their lot is with the CPDM party, and there is every reason to believe that they intend to keep that party in power.

As Cameroonians prepare for the 2011 presidential election, it is unclear if there will be a transition or whether such a transition would be peaceful. This lack of clarity derives from the absence of veritable democratic institutions in the country that can guarantee transparency in elections. We have seen how arbitrary laws and constitutional amendments have been used by the Biya regime to flout popular will. Cameroonians have now been told that these same institutions in their unchanged form would guarantee transparency. That remains to be seen. What is clear, however, is that a transition in 2011 is eminent, in view of the fact that President Biya is aging, and it would be wise for him not to run. The question then is as follows: What would be the nature of the transition? Would the transition be marked by transparency, or would the CPDM—given its composition in ELECAM—attempt to maintain its grip on power by replacing Biya with another of its parties' cronies? The answers to these questions lie in what happens to the Cameroon Constitution, as well as the strict interpretation of constitutionalism, between now and 2011.

Writing about constitutionalism, Charles Fombad has argued that while the democratic process in post-1990 Cameroon, as elsewhere in Africa, has been characterized by attempts at reforming constitutions, these new constitutions do not in themselves constitute solutions to the numerous struggles that lay on the path of genuine multiparty democracy because they lack constitutionalism. Fombad argues that constitutions, or the set of rules that guide the action of government and the governed, are not synonymous to constitutionalism or "the idea of a government limited in its actions and accountable to its citizens for its actions."[78] If the goal of constitutionalism is respect for the dignity of humans, then the practice of multiparty democracy is not necessarily an indication of the existence of constitutionalism in a country because democracy has been used in numerous occasions to stifle constitutionalism. Constitutionalism, however, remains a standard for effective democratic practice in a country. It is apparent from Fombad's analysis that multiparty democracy in Cameroon has been elusive because of the absence of constitutionalism.

If economic situations are an indication of present and future political trends, then I agree with Christian Cardinal Tumi that the organization of free and fair elections in Cameroon would pave the way for a transition, be it peaceful or otherwise, as there is no doubt that the Biya regime would be defeated by the participation of young voters, many of whom are actually feeling the pinch of Biya's disastrous policies by way of chronic unemployment and the high cost of living. The new rules set by ELECAM, which have increased the voting age from 18 to 20 to deprive the opposition of the youth vote,[79] should serve as an indicator of how the regime intends to conduct the 2011 presidential elections. It should also alert the opposition to the fact that Biya and his cronies are still not ready to make room for change.

If Biya decides to run for another term as president, given the composition of ELECAM, there probably would be no transition as it is unforeseeable that the architect of one of the most successful electoral fraud machines and unfairness in multiparty democracies in Africa would suddenly give up his ambitions.

Conclusion

Multiparty democracy in Cameroon has been elusive since independence because of the entrenchment of a single-party ideology, the absence of fair-play, as well as intimidation, repression, and harassment. Should constitutional amendments and state laws be crafted by incumbents to suit their political dispensations? Given the ethnic heterogeneity in all African states (including Cameroon) that has so often been used to justify the single-party ideology, it is fair to suggest that multiparty democracy in Cameroon will continue to be ellusive until such a time when strict constitutionalism becomes part of the culture and a yardstick of democratic practice in the country. It is only then that all electoral ambiguities, intimidation, and other forms of abuse will be eliminated, or at best, minimized.

Rwanda

Chapter 7

Rwanda: Democracy and Political Change

Julius O. Adekunle

Rwanda is a country of beauty, one endowed with several physical features such as spectacular volcanoes, mountains, and lakes. Rwanda has been variously described as "a land of almost ideal beauty," "the Switzerland of Africa," "the Pearl of Africa," "the Land of a Thousand Hills," and "the Land of Gorillas."[1] Over centuries of existence, Rwanda has not only been transformed from a kingdom to a country, but also has had an intermixture of cultural and political practices. Due to the different waves of migration into the region, and the experience of colonization and modernization, Rwanda has passed through several political changes and faced many challenges.

In its political history, Rwanda began as a stateless society with the Hutu lineage heads acting as political leaders. This political arrangement changed with the establishment of the Tutsi dynasty. Colonialism engendered the transition from dynastic rule to the Western parliamentary system. Before Rwanda became a major focus of international attention due to the 1994 genocide, the country experienced socio-political changes, making the study of democracy relevant. Providing historical background with the pre-colonial political practice, this chapter will examine the level of democracy in Rwanda. It will focus mainly on the post-colonial period, and use the Status of Democracy Index (SDI).

Pre-Colonial Political System

Rwanda, located in east central Africa, shares boundaries with Uganda to the north, Burundi to the south, Tanzania to the east, and the Democratic Republic of Congo to the west. The Akanyaru River separates Rwanda from its sister state, Burundi. Although Rwanda is a relatively small country, covering an area of 10,169 square miles, it has a population of approximately 11.4 million (2010 figures), making it the most densely populated country in Africa. The population comprises of the Hutu, Tutsi, and Twa ethnic groups.

In pre-colonial times, the Rwandan people operated on a monarchical political system that was hierarchical. At the head of the structure was the *mwami* (sacred king), whose position was hereditary and offered enormous political and military powers. The concept of absolutism, backed up by the claim to "divine right of kings" (which was popular in Europe), applied to the African political system. Rwanda, like other African pre-colonial states, did not recognize or practice democracy as in the Western interpretation of democracy, although there were institutions and agencies of democracy. The Rwandan system appeared less democratic because the king was selected rather than elected, and the ruling line came only from among the Tutsi. There was a monopoly of political power and positions since other ethnic groups were denied access to political leadership. Like other African societies, religion was not totally separated from politics. For example, the *ubwiru* (royal ritualists) served not only as political advisors to the king, but were also responsible for performing regular rituals for the king in order to legitimize and consolidate his political power. Like the king, the *ubwiru* held hereditary positions.

The functions of the lineage heads among the Hutu, who existed before the arrival of the Tutsi dynastic founders, were reduced primarily to the collection of tribute and taxes for the king. On their arrival, the Tutsi redistributed power and undertook a restructuring of the political system. With this political change, the Tutsi dominated and controlled access to political offices and economic resources. All three ethnic groups (BaTwa, Hutu, and Tutsi) have a different historical narration of their settlement in the region, and have pursued different occupations and performed different socio-political functions. Their symbiotic relationship facilitated the political and economic structure of society. For example, the BaTwa controlled the forests as hunters, the Hutu claimed ownership of land as farmers, and the Tutsi dominated the economy as cattle owners. However, there have been frictions because the BaTwa and Hutu claimed that they have been exploited and marginalized by the minority Tutsi, who monopolized both political and economic power.

Colonialism, Democracy, and Change

A structure of power sharing did not exist in Rwanda before colonization. The Tutsi dominated politics and political positions. When the German colonialists arrived in 1897, they met the monarchical structure under the leadership of the Tutsi. This political arrangement fitted into the German colonial administrative system of indirect rule. Since the Germans believed in the "superiority" of the Tutsi over the other ethnic groups, they continued to utilize the Tutsi traditional rulers in their colonial administration thereby strengthening the already undemocratic political system. German imperialism gradually weakened the Tutsi power as the rulers were relegated in political hierarchy. Other factors also worked against the Tutsi hegemony. First, the opening up of Rwanda to international trade through colonialism drastically reduced the Tutsi's economic power, which basically depended on cattle ownership. Second, the Germans enforced their taxation policy on all Rwandans, which indirectly favored ethnic equality. In this respect, the Tutsi lost economic control. Third, the Germans were the effective political leaders, not the Tutsi. Although these factors partly helped the Hutu, they were unable to completely gain autonomy from Tutsi rule.

At the end of World War I, Germany had lost the war, and the League of Nations mandated Rwanda and Burundi to Belgium. Like the Germans, the Belgians relied heavily on the Tutsi rulers for the success of their colonial administration. Favoring the Tutsi in politics and education, the Belgians directly contributed to widening the ethnic division and hostility between Hutu and Tutsi. While the German colonial rule was short lived, the Belgians were considered harsher colonialists. Their political, economic, and social policies worked to divide the Rwandans rather than unite them. Being an imposed rule without active and direct participation of the Rwandans in the government, the Belgian colonial rule was as un-democratic as that of the Germans, or even the Tutsi oligarchy.

The Catholic Church played a profound role in shaping the socio-political direction of Rwanda during the colonial period. The church initially aligned with the Tutsi aristocracy, evangelized and educated them, and strongly supported their political leadership. Expectedly, the Hutu considered the cozy relationship between the Tutsi and the Catholic Church undemocratic, and unacceptable. A change occurred when King Yuhi Musinga fell out of favor with the Belgian colonial authorities as well as the church for refusing to be baptized. The church was displeased because it would hinder its evangelization efforts. The Belgian authorities wanted to check Musinga's power in order to consolidate their control. Confronting these two-pronged problems, Musinga seemed helpless. The Belgians deposed and exiled him. This action is a classic example of the collaboration that existed between Christianity and colonialism. It also reveals how powerful and controlling the Belgians were in Rwanda. It should be noted that the colonial powers exiled many of the African kings whom they felt were not cooperating with them.

Mutara Rudahigwa succeeded his father, Musinga. Mutara was a baptized seminary graduate. Presumably in the name of modernization, Mutara permitted the Hutu to gain political and educational power. It would appear that the Tutsi's gradual loss of power was the gain of the Hutu who found the favor of the church and the Belgian authorities. The Hutu gained further support from the Belgians when the *ubuhake* system and the carrying of ethnic identity cards were prohibited in the 1950s. Encouraged by the Western education received through the church, the Hutu gradually became empowered enough to challenge the Tutsi political and social dominance. When the church shifted support from the Tutsi to the Hutu, this led to colonial reforms, which prompted the Belgians to encourage "the growth of democratic political institutions."[2] As expected, the Tutsi resisted because they wanted to maintain the political status quo.

The Belgian colonial government has always used the policy of "divide and rule." They shifted their support from the Tutsi to the Hutu. The Belgians believed that, given the number power and the operation of democracy, power would go to the Hutu who were clearly in the majority. This thought presumably led to the deliberate weakening of the Tutsi power to transfer political control to the Hutu majority. Without adequate preparation and political experience for Rwandans, the Belgians granted independence. Led by Grégoire Kayibanda, the leader of the Parti du Mouvement de l'Emancipation Hutu (PARMEHUTU), Rwanda gained independence in 1962.

Independence and Nascent Democracy

Shortly after independence, tensions began to mount as a result of ethnic conflicts. There were also oppositions to Kayibanda's undemocratic policies, especially from the Tutsi. Re-elected in 1965 and in 1969 when the PARME-HUTU changed its name to Mouvement Démocratique Républicain (MDR), Kayibanda and his government gained enormous political power and became dictatorial, corrupt, and ethnically insensitive. His government broke away completely from the Tutsi monarch, causing an uneasy relationship between the Tutsi and Hutu. The Tutsi accused Kayibanda of marginalizing them, and democratic rule continued to elude Rwanda. Kayibanda's government was overthrown in a military coup led by Juvenal Habyarimana (Hutu) in 1973. With the successful change of government, Kayibanda was placed under house imprisonment, and condemned to death on June 29, 1974. He was eventually pardoned, and died on December 15, 1976.

Kayibanda's political experience demonstrates the difficulty in establishing a democratic process in a volatile situation where there is a sharp ethnic division. Like its predecessor, Habyarimana's regime was also criticized as undemocratic, partly because ethnicity dictated the type of power and position an individual held in government and because the military acquired so much power that people lived in fear of the government. Habyarimana's weakness was reflected in his inability to checkmate the ethnic activism of his political party. That is partly why many Rwandans, especially the Tutsi, went into exile in Uganda and the now Democratic Republic of Congo. In July 1990, facing mounting pressure from Western countries, Habyarimana agreed to adopt a democratic system of multi-party government.

The Genocide and Political Change

Habyarimana and Cyprien Ntaryamira, the President of Burundi, were killed in a plane crash on April 6, 1994, while returning from peace and political power-sharing talks. The plane crash and subsequent development altered the course of history in Rwanda. Soon after the unprecedented massive massacre of the Tutsi and moderate Hutu began in what later came to be called genocide. Approximately 800,000 were killed while million became refugees in neighboring countries. Rwanda was in political disarray.

The issue of democracy becomes more relevant in modern Rwanda because of the political changes that have taken place since the 1994 genocide. Because Rwanda had been the focus of international attention, Paul Kagame and his government wanted to prove to the world that they had a vision for a democratic system, which would change the status quo of ethnic, gender, and social inequality as well as embrace people's participation in political matters. According to John De Gruchy, democratic vision refers to ... "that hope for a society in which all people are truly equal and yet where difference is respected; a society in which all people are truly free, yet where social responsibility rather than individual self-interest prevails; and a society which is truly just, and therefore one in which the vast gulf between rich and poor has been overcome."[3]

One difficulty in achieving a smooth new political order is reconciling and restoring people's confidence in the administration. Pressure also came from the international community, which demanded political change. Although the government is determined to pursue peace, ethnic equality, and a democratic political system, it has not been an easy task given the deep-rooted distrust and the long process of reconstruction. Many African countries that did not experience tragedy in the magnitude of Rwanda's continue to grapple with the principles and practice of democracy. Hence, the task of establishing a sustainable democracy and good governance is an arduous one. In several political areas, the government has been criticized for its undemocratic policies, but has changed or improved in other areas.

Media Freedom

From a global perspective, the media has the function of circulating news and information to society. In the Rwandan culture, palace officials performed the functions of the media since society was predominantly non-literate in the Western model. Rwandan literature was essentially oral and royal. The activities of the rulers were well preserved in oral traditions, but there are also royal records in Kinyarwanda. The culture of a heavy reliance on oral information changed when written records began to emerge in the late nineteenth century with the arrival of the Europeans, especially the Catholic priests who introduced Christianity and Western education.

During the colonial period, the Belgians controlled the media, and since then, successive governments have done likewise. This suggests a lack of freedom of the press in Rwanda. The lingering effects of the ethnic divide and government control limited media operations. For example, the government owned and controlled newspapers and the only radio station (Radio Rwanda) until 1991. It is pointed out elsewhere that:

> As the mouthpiece of the government, the radio announced prima-
> rily political matters and speeches of Habyarimana, the president. The
> radio station did not have any significant impact on the life of the
> people in the rural areas because not many people owned radio sets,
> while in the urban centers such as Butare and Kigali, many house-
> holds possessed radios.[4]

As it was during the colonial period, there was no media freedom in the early years of independence. Because "he who pays the piper dictates the tune," there has been no objective reporting from the media. It was difficult to criticize the government, and the situation was further compounded by the ethnic rivalry between the Hutu and Tutsi. For example, the Rwandan Patriotic Front (RPF) founded Radio Muhabura and *Kanguka* ("Wake Up" in Kinyarwanda) newspaper in 1988 to present the voice of the Tutsi, while the Hutu established *Radio et Television Libres des Mille Collines* (RTLM) in 1993, and the *Kangura* ("Wake Up") newspaper. The cultural, ethnic, economic, and political climate that existed in Rwanda did not provide for a democratic and free media. Thus, the media played a biased and negative role in the outbreak and conduct of the 1994 genocide because it was used to spur and direct the massive killing.[5] The RTLM, a privately owned and run Hutu radio station, was particularly known for its prejudiced and hate broadcast.

There is no gainsaying the fact that media freedom is one of the pillars of a democratic society. Its absence is an indication of a shaky political system. The government's involvement in, and control of the media, shows there was no press freedom and no democracy.

In rebuilding Rwanda during the post-genocide period, the government has encouraged media freedom. This is a challenging task given the people's deep-rooted and lingering distrust of successive governments. Some media officials involved in propagating the genocide were found guilty. Sharon LaFraniere, reporting on the verdict, quoted the judges as saying: "The power of the media to create and destroy human values comes with great responsibility. Those who control the media are accountable for its consequences."[6]

Press freedom in Rwanda remains under heavy criticism. A 2009 report indicates that, "independent news coverage was minimal due to business woes and government intimidation."[7] It is claimed that because the government is authoritarian, there is a lack of political and press freedom. In his own argument, Safari Gaspard, the President of the Rwandan Journalist Association, contended that, "there is press freedom but no independent press to exercise it."[8] Paul Kagame is focused on transforming the Rwandan society, but press freedom remains an enigma as his government threatens to suspend some international and local media agencies in Rwanda. Rwanda is placed 140th in press freedom, as shown in Table 1.

Table 1. Rwanda's Rank in the World Order

Press Freedom	140
Corruption Rank	88
Economic Freedom	135
Civil Liberties	5 (2007); 5 (2006)
Political Score	6 (2007); 6 (2006)
Democracy Rank	136
African Union	Ranked 34 (Mauritius ranked 1)

Source: World Audit Organization at www.worldaudit.org/democracy.htm.

To improve journalism and media reputation, the School of Journalism and Communication of the National University of Rwanda (NUR) is partnering with Carleton University in Canada to provide training for Rwandan journalists. It is called the Rwanda Initiative. Through seminars and workshops, journalists and interns are being trained to improve their skills and the quality of their news reporting. The idea is to move away from the biased media reporting that characterized the genocide period. With correct and informative national and international reporting, the government is encouraged to grant more press freedom.

Corruption, Culture, and Change

Corruption takes different and various dimensions. There is evidence of corruption and all its ramifications in Rwanda, as it exists in other parts of Africa. Corruption may not be associated with African culture, but because of greed, bad governance, and poor economic management, it has penetrated every facet of the society. It is plausible to argue that political corruption emanating from undemocratic practices and lack of power sharing has been part of Rwandan history. This situation, however, is changing in contemporary times because the people and government of Rwanda are conscious of the ethics and philosophy of democracy. The same cannot be said of economic corruption, which is more difficult to eradicate. Judging from the performances of African states on corruption, it seems very clear that Rwanda is doing relatively better in checking corruption than other African states. According to the summary of a finding on corruption:

> Various governance indicators indicate that Rwanda performs relatively well in terms of corruption, compared to many African countries. The country has also achieved significant progress over the last years in terms of government effectiveness and transparency of the regulatory framework. In spite of these efforts, corruption remains prevalent in the country and there have been instances of tax and public funds embezzlement, fraudulent procurement practices, judicial corruption as well as high ranking officials involved in corrupt practices.... The Government is reported to conduct a firm fight against corruption and has put a number of measures and institutions in place such as the National Tender Board, the Office of the Auditor General and the Ombudsman's Office.[9]

While realizing the monumental task to check the various forms of corruption, the government set up some agencies to deal with the problem. For example, the Anti-Corruption Unit promotes the nation's integrity by raising a general awareness on corruption. Also, the Ombudsman Office, established in 2004, ensures that there is transparency to and compliance with the government's regulations in every sector of the administration. Indeed, "the Ombudsman has taken a strong stand against corruption and regularly exposes cases of fraud, malpractice, and corruption"[10] at all levels.

Economic Freedom

Rwanda is poor economically. Being a land-locked country that does not have important and sustainable mineral resources or industrial and technological development, it has experienced little economic flexibility. In the traditional setting, Rwanda's economy was based on agriculture and cattle rearing. There was little or no economic mobility or diversification. The Hutu were farmers, the Tutsi were cattle owners, and the Twa were hunters. There was a symbiotic economic relationship, but the Tutsi enjoyed the dividends of the economy more than the other ethnic groups. The change from the traditional economic culture of food production to the colonial economy of cash crop and wage system did not engender a rapid economic growth.

After independence, Rwanda continued to have a weak economic base. Coffee, which the German missionaries introduced to Rwanda in 1904, became the primary agricultural product, especially in the rural communities. The Belgian colonial government even directed farmers to produce low quality and high-volume coffee. However, coffee is subject to the vagaries of weather and prices are subject to the dictates of the world market. For many years, the revenue from coffee has not sustained the government primarily because of the fluctuating world market prices. For example, Rwanda's annual earnings fell significantly when the price of coffee dropped in the world market in the 1980s. The effect of the genocide on coffee production cannot be ignored, but since then Rwandan coffee has improved significantly in international market. Since Rwanda does not possess important economic resources, its international trade remains unbalanced. Like other African countries, Rwanda is an importer, not an exporter. Thus, the government has faced economic problems, and since the 1994 genocide, it has attempted some economic recovery measures.

Economic freedom involves the right, ability, and opportunity of an individual to pursue economic activities without coercion. The government is supposed to provide the infrastructure for economic growth and economic mobility for its people. In a country such as Rwanda, where there are limited opportunities and a lack of government support for small-scale businesses, there is evidently little or no commercial freedom. Trade is often restricted due to the inability of the people to accumulate enough capital, and absence of networks.

Facing many economic and socio-political problems, an accurate measurement of economic freedom in Rwanda may be a difficult exercise given the dearth of current data and the effect of conflicts. However, according to the 2009 Index of Economic Freedom, Rwanda's score is 54.2, making it the 124th country in the world. This score is below the world average, and leaves Rwanda in the category of mostly unfree economic countries.[11] In Africa, nevertheless, Rwanda is placed 22nd among 46 countries.

Religious Freedom

Religion is an integral part of African cultural life. As John S. Mbiti put it, "Africans are notoriously religious, and each people has its own religious system with a set of beliefs and practices. Religion permeates into all the departments of life so fully that it is not easy or possible always to isolate it."[12] In the pre-colonial times, the people of Rwanda enjoyed religious freedom. Indeed, a complex and interlocking relationship existed between religion and politics. While there was no clearly defined role for the interaction between religion and politics, it was apparent that governance was guided by religion. Since the Tutsi swept aside the Hutu lineage chiefs and instituted their own dynasty, the position of the king was held sacred. The *mwami* (king), through a group of *abiru* (priests), performed regular rituals and divinations for peaceful and successful reign. To express the aura of sacrosanctity that surrounded the king, the Rwandan people often say in Kinyarwanda, *Umwami si umuntu ni imaana* ("the king is not a man, he is a god").[13] This religious representation of the king as god is similar to how the Yoruba in Nigeria view the Alaafin (king) who was referred to as second in command to the gods. The Rwandan king was considered a rainmaker and Christopher C. Taylor adds that he was also associated with "productivity of the soil and milk, prosperity, fertility, and continuity."[14] Although the king did not impose his religious beliefs on his subjects, it was logical for the people to follow him, being a predominantly agricultural and pastoral people. Thus, there was complete religious freedom in the precolonial Rwanda.

Christianity was first introduced into the Rwandan society in the late nineteenth century through the Roman Catholic missionaries. Ordained a priest in 1878, Joseph Hirth founded the Roman Catholic Church in Rwanda in 1899. With the coming of Catholicism, there was no radical change in religious freedom; Christianity only offered an alternative religion for Rwandans. Christian missionaries tried to establish a working religious and political relationship with the ruling class, which was facilitated by the German colonial administration that allowed evangelization of the Rwanda people. By providing a Western education and a practical approach to cultural and social interaction with the Rwandan people, Christianity gained influence and dominated the life and politics of the country for many years. As it was under the Tutsi dynasty, the German and subsequently the Belgian colonial administrations did not place any restrictions on religious practices. Hence, Christianity and traditional religions went hand in hand.

Islam arrived through the coastal Arab and Swahili merchants in the eighteenth century, but it was not widely practiced. Spreading gradually over time, there is no historical evidence to support the enforcement of the religion on the people. This suggests that there was religious freedom. Because Catholicism had gained ground, Islam was unable to achieve significant inroads until after the 1994 genocide. During the genocide, "the Catholic Church was accused of playing a negative role ... because it did not do enough to stop the killing, and it is alleged that some of its priests supported the massacres."[15] This accusation of complicity dealt a devastating blow to the influence and growth of the church in particular, and Christianity in general, and it provided an opportunity for the expansion of Islam. In spite of this setback, adherents of the Catholic and Protestant churches have been working together not only to seek peace, but also to contribute to the political and economic development of Rwanda. The genocide has not affected the religious freedom that had been in existence.

As a continuation of the existing policy on religious liberty, the Constitution of Rwanda provides for freedom of religion. Political parties must not be formed on the basis of religion, and the government does operate on religious principles. Religious instructions are permitted in schools. Many Christian and Islamic religious organizations carry out their activities with some restrictions from the government. For example, in Gitarama, the Jehovah's Witness group has been denied the permits to build its Kingdom Halls because of its opposition to some government policies. Presumably, because of the genocide and the role religious leaders supposedly played, the government has limited "nighttime religious meetings and ... continued to require religious groups to hold services at their established places of worship and to ban the use of private homes for this purpose."[16] In spite of these restrictions, no religious group has had any major confrontation with the government, indeed, the government cooperates with numerous international religious organizations that are providing relief assistance and working on development projects. Religious organizations also cooperate with the government on unity and reconciliation initiatives. Although there are many Christian denomination and Islamic groups, religious conflicts are a rarity. This is proof of the existence of religious toleration and religious dialogue, which are fundamental to peaceful co-existence and to a successful democratic political system.

Women in Politics

Gender inequality was a feature of traditional Rwandan society. Rwandan culture limited women's role not only in politics, but also in access to economic resources such as land. The Rwandan proverb, "A woman does not have an identity, she takes her husband's" demonstrates the socio-political inequality that existed in the traditional Rwandan culture. Moreover, the monarchical system did not provide for the full participation of women in political life, except for the queen mother.

Colonialism did little to change the cultural practice of political inequality for women. The Germans, who first colonized Rwanda, adopted the indirect rule system by using the traditional Tutsi aristocratic class to govern. The Belgians who followed also did nothing to include women in politics. The Hutu women continued to be relevant economically because they were engaged in agriculture, but they held no political positions. Two factors began a process of political change for women. First, was the gaining of independence in 1962, and second, the abolition of the monarchical system. Rwandan political leaders were no longer selected, but elected, and women had the right to vote and be voted for, as guaranteed in the constitution. However, they were still expected to vote according to their husband's dictate. In this respect, democracy was still not at work since equal rights constitutes one of the fundamental aspects of democracy.

One of the challenges that the Rwandan political system has faced since independence is the non-participation of women—a continuation of the culture that marginalized the women. The unstable political environment, as a consequence of non-inclusion of women, in addition to frequent ethnic conflicts and military intervention, has made it difficult for democracy to thrive. For example, women were not represented in the cabinet of Gregoire Kayibanda, the leader of the Parti du Mouvement de l'Emancipation Hutu (PARMEHUTU) who led Rwanda to independence in 1962. Evidently, PARMEHUTU was an ethnically based and male-dominated party. Similarly, when Juvénal Habyarimana toppled Kayibanda in a military coup in 1973, ethnicity rather than gender dominated the politics of the day. Habyarimana embarked on practices that were unsuitable for democracy by intimidating political opponents and instituting a one-party system, which forced the people to adopt his National Revolutionary Movement for Development (MRND) party. Like Kayibanda, Habyarimana did not have equal ethnic and gender representation in his cabinet until his sudden death in 1994, which sparked the genocide.

The most significant political change for women occurred after the 1994 genocide. Partly as a result of cultural change and the gender imbalance resulting from the men being killed in the genocide, women became empowered as they assumed new status as heads of household and came to the forefront politically. In essence, the genocide (not the culture or deliberate political reform) became the catalyst for the political empowerment of the Rwandan women. For example, in 1994, the Rwandan parliament consisted of 70 seats and women occupied eight of them. However, women basically dominated politics by having approximately 50 percent of the parliament in the 2003 elections. In her study of the role of women in the transitional process in Rwanda, Elizabeth Powley indicated that:

> Rwanda's parliamentary elections in September 2003 officially ended a nine-year period of post-genocide transition. While the ruling Rwandan Patriotic Front (RPF) dominated the elections as expected and won a large majority of seats in the newly formed bicameral legislature, the political landscape was altered dramatically: nearly 50 percent of new representatives are women. This statistics places Rwanda among only a few nations in the world with such strong representation of women in parliament.[17]

With this development, there is evidence of a change in the political culture of Rwanda. In order to achieve lasting democratization and sustainable peace, women have to play active and important roles. This new turn is striking because according to Speciosa Mukandutiye, the president of the forum of Rwandan Women Parliamentarians, "Gender equality is not deep in our culture. Traditionally, women were supposed to be housewives. Their role was to take care of their husbands and produce children. It was a shame to appear in public and make comments."[18] This cultural position has shifted, and women have become relevant in nation building. Given the new political, reconciliatory, and economic roles that women are assuming in Rwanda, it is believed that the building of a strong democracy lies in their hands. The establishment of the Ministry for Gender and Women in Development also provides the opportunity for the women to take decisions and implement policies that are geared toward socioeconomic and political development. Cecilia Mzvondiva argues that the increasing participation of women in politics "calls for a challenge to the government of Rwanda to reform the educational system to ensure that girls have access to education, should women's empowerment and their role on peace-building and reconstruction be sustainable."[19] More education would lead women to gain more self-confidence, assertiveness, and leadership qualities, while strengthening the democratization process.

Human Development

Human development is a relationship between the government's action, income, and the welfare of the people, including life expectancy and education. The government of Rwanda actively engages in various programs that promote and improve the welfare of its people. The old patriarchal and social structure in which gender and social disparity negatively affected Rwanda's human relations has to be dismantled for the attainment of sustainable development. The poor economic status of the country limits the ability of the government to provide adequate health and educational facilities and services. This is partly responsible for the poor health services and limited educational opportunities. Table 2 shows Rwanda's Human Development performance between 1985 and 2002. Rwanda's rating of HDI in 2002 was 133. With the government's increased effort in human development, the index in 2005 reveals the following, as is shown in Table 3. With the gradual recovery from the genocide, Rwanda is improving in human development and general rebuilding of the country, as shown in Tables 2 and 3 on the following page. Empowering women and including them in development programs is one positive step the government is taking to achieve development.

Creation of employment opportunities is another difficult area for the Kagame Administration because Rwanda is a society deeply involved in a rural, agricultural, and labor-intensive economic system with a weak technological and industrial base for jobs. Poverty is widespread because of low economic development in rural areas. Rwanda has few natural or mineral resources that generate employment opportunities and attract foreign investors. Hence, the government remains the largest employer. Policies have also affected job creation. According to the 2005 Report of the Economic Commission for Africa:

> Generating employment opportunities depends not only on the existence of adequate policies, but also to a large extent on the existence of strong institutions capable of managing change with regard to employment issues and playing an intermediary role between supply and demand for labor.[20]

For the improvement of human development, and for the alleviation of poverty, job creation ought to be one of the top priorities of the government.

Table 2. Human Development Index for Rwanda, 1985–2002

1985	0.397
1990	0.351
1995	0.341
2000	0.413
2002	0.431

Source: Human Development Index, Rwanda at http://hdrstats.undp.org/countries/country_fact_sheets/cty_fs_RWA.html.

Table 3. Rwanda's Human Development, 2005

HDI	161 (0.452)
Life Expectancy	169 (45.2)
Adult Literacy Rate	112 (64.9)
Enrollment Ratio	145 (50.9)
GDP per capita	158 (US$1,206)

Source: Human Development Index, Rwanda at http://hdrstats.undp.org/countries/country_fact_sheets/cty_fs_RWA.html.

Elections

Elections are a means by which the people of a country have the opportunity to choose their own political leaders, promoting democracy and providing legitimacy to the government. Elections should not be held in a tense and hostile environment. Where elections are held with intimidation and harassment, the process is not democratic because the right of the people to choose their own form of government is infringed upon. The constitution also makes provisions for dealing with electoral malpractices.

Rwanda has been conducting elections since the 1950s, when the process of decolonization began all over Africa. Universal suffrage was introduced in 1956, but only adult males were able to vote. Since the monarchy was still in place, and women were disenfranchised, it is apparent that Rwanda, under the Belgians, did not practice complete democracy. It would appear that the elections were put in place to elect people who would ratify colonial policies. It should also be noted that the Hutu were at an advantage because of their number power.

The social Revolution, which the Hutu organized in 1959, and in which thousands of people were killed, demonstrated the climate of fear that attended the political atmosphere of Rwanda. The referendum of 1961 that was intended to do away with the monarchy and the parliamentary elections was conducted in an intimidating, manipulative, and violent environment. The result was a heavily Hutu-dominated (MDR-PARMEHUTU) parliament (*Inteko Ishinga Amategeko*), with Grégoire Kayibanda as head of state. It is no gainsaying that ethnic competition for power and conflicts, in addition to political ambition, have made elections in Rwanda fraught with manipulations. Reelected as an unopposed candidate in the 1965 and 1969 elections, Kayibanda continued to lead a one-party and oppressive government by marginalizing the few Tutsi oppositions. Juvénal Habyarimana, who succeeded Kayibanda in 1973, ran a one-party system like his predecessor. During Habyarimana's regime, elections were a sham. The political situation remained divided and tense until the 1990s, when it was compounded by the genocide in 1994.

Following the genocide, Pasteur Bizimungu, a Hutu, succeeded Habyarimana, as president of the new Government of National Unity, which focused on reconciling, rebranding, and reorganizing the country with the objective of national unity. Paul Kagame was chosen as the vice-president, commander in chief of the RPA, and minister of defense. The presidential election of 2000 ushered in Paul Kagame as the president. Thus, Kagame came to power at a very challenging time in the political history of Rwanda. He was re-elected in a multi-party system election in 2003. Kagame claimed legitimacy not only because of the landslide re-election victory, but because there was no serious challenger. Below is the summary of the political situation in Rwanda since independence.[21]

1962–1965	Restricted Democratic Practice
1965–1973	One Party State (MDR-PARMEHUTU)
1973–1975	Military Regime
1975–1978	[De Facto] One Party State (MRND)
1978–1991	One Party State (MRND)
1991–1994	Multiparty Transition
1994–2003	Transitional Government
2003–	Restricted Democratic Practice.

The government of Paul Kagame has been criticized for becoming militant and for being intolerant of the opposition. The continuation of this strategy may hinder free and clear elections. In the new Rwanda, where ethnicity is underplayed and national integration is the priority, there should be credible elections, which are devoid of ethnic or gender considerations.

Conclusion

There is no evidence of democracy in Rwanda before, during, or after colonialism. The regimes before the genocide were too ethnically and politically biased to pursue meaningful democracy. The process of power-sharing, which emanated from the Arusha Peace Accords, could have promoted democracy. The Accords were a conflict resolution strategy: it was to end the long standing conflict between the Hutu dominated government and the Tutsi guerrilla fighters (the Rwandase Patrotic Front, RPF). Apparently, the opponents of the power-sharing government did not embrace the Accords. It was in pursuit of that democratic process that President Habyarimana's plane crashed while returning from signing the Accords in April 1994.[22] The plane crash became the ostensible reason for the genocide, but looming at the background were ethnic differences and opposition to democracy. The genocide was a result of the lack of democracy. Since the end of the genocide, there has been relative peace and political stability, but no full democracy. The process towards democracy, as indicated by the Status of Democracy Index, is a slow one. That is why Kagame's regime continues to receive criticism for its undemocratic policies.

In the 2003 election, the opponents of President Kagame complained of irregularities in electoral practices. If the election was free and peaceful, it was not fair. Democracy is also lacking because the top government offices are held primarily by the Tutsi extraction (Kagame's inner circle), indicating that the concept of nationalism has not completely prevailed. An ethnically dominated government in a multi-ethnic society is not a democratic government.

Rwandan government has made impressive socioeconomic progress since 1996. For example, Paul Kagame and his administration have tried to promote ethnic and gender equality, which is a positive indicator of a democratic society. It has become taboo for Rwandans to identify themselves through ethnic affiliation; they all identify themselves as Rwandans. Perpetrators of the 1994 genocide have been prosecuted in the *gacaca* courts. The government is strengthening itself by de-emphasizing ethnicity and increasing the role of women in politics. Rwanda has the highest number of women in Parliament in the world. There has been an improvement in the quality and consistency of education, and an increase in the provision of health services.

In spite of these progressive records, the government faces some fundamental and formidable political and social challenges. President Kagame has been criticized for his high-handedness. He has been described as an "unapologetic authoritarian." His administration "has also developed a reputation for having as little respect for press freedom,"[23] which is a concern in a democratic system. Since the new political order is relatively young, Rwanda has the opportunity to move more closely to a democratic system. The elimination of the ethnic divide and corruption on the one hand, and the promotion of human development, ethnic and gender equality, and economic and freedom of press on the other will go a long way to improve democracy in Rwanda.

Eritrea

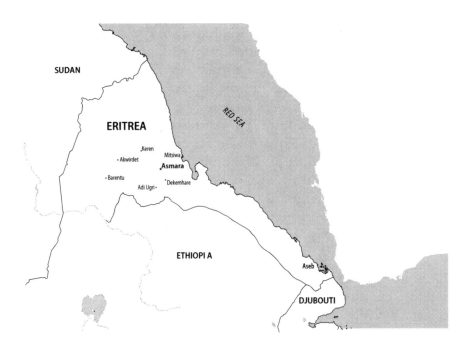

Chapter 8

Eritrea: A Weak Democracy

Saba Tesfayohannes Kidane

The concept and the practice of democracy in Eritrea should be explored in the context of the country's political history, which dates back to its formation as an Italian colony in 1890. This chapter, however, will focus on the years after Eritrea's independence, from the early 1990s to the present. The Eritrean independence struggle that lasted for three decades did not produce a democratic state. The leaders of the independence movement envisioned a state that is far from the modern concept of democracy. It has been a recurrent fact that many revolutionary and liberation movements come short of producing the promised 'freedom' that incorporates democracy as one of the outcomes expected after independence. It is within such observation that "great revolutionary hopes have been transformed into totalitarian nightmares or state bureaucracies."[1]

Despite the temptation to label Eritrea undemocratic from the outset, this chapter will analyze the status of democracy, and how democracy is understood or perceived in present-day Eritrea. It will give a historical overview of the country before it became a sovereign state in 1993. The Eritrean People's Liberation Front (EPLF), which later transformed itself into the government of the newly born Eritrea, masterminded the political philosophy and direction of the country. With active government involvement in the political, economic, social, and cultural lives of the people of Eritrea, the top-bottom style of leadership is the rule rather than the exception.

Eritrea developed as a political entity in the 1890s during the period of Italian colonization. It did not have independent political experience until the early 1990s. In 1991, EPLF forces defeated the Ethiopian forces, and liberated their country. A new chapter for the newly born country began, with very little experience in civilian governance. There were instances of political consciousness in the 1940s and 1950s during the British Military Administration (BMA), which led to political reforms by the BMA. The British forces built up the Eritrean industrial sector as the war was ongoing with Italian forces in Eritrea. However, as the war ended, it was compounded with the industrial slow-down in Eritrea. The British removed or sold an estimated 86 million pounds worth of industrial plants and equipments, including port facilities at the ports of *Assab* and *Massawa*.[2] This, combined with increased local taxation, resulted in large-scale unemployment, which, in turn, led to increased political consciousness of Eritrea's considerable urban working class.[3] The result was the proliferation of political parties.

Scholars such as Basil Davidson note that Eritrea was "derived from the imperial partnership and rivalry of two expansionist powers in the 19th century: Ethiopia and Italy."[4] The people of Eritrea had relations with other peoples of the region along the Red Sea and westwards beyond the *Mareb* valley. The Eritrean state formation that started with the Italian colonization intensified towards the end of the 1950s with the proliferation of many nationalistic parties. However, Eritrea was dissolved to be the fourteenth province of Ethiopia through illegal annexation by the Imperial régime in Ethiopia in 1962. After the defeat of Italy in World War II, the British forces that defeated the Italian forces in Eritrea assumed temporary administration of Eritrean territory. The BMA witnessed a growing number of political parties in Eritrean history for the first time. Parties of the then political situation had different views as to the future of Eritrea. Some preferred a union with Ethiopia, others, an independent state. The major political parties that developed during the British administration were the Eritrean Independence Party led by Wolde-Ab Wolde-Mariam, the Rabita Al Islamia led by Ibrahim Sultan, and the Unionist Party led by Tedla Bairu.[5]

The future of Eritrea varied according to the opinions of Britain, France, the Soviet Union, and the United States of America. When former colonizer Italy was defeated, the fates of her colonies, including Eritrea, were decided by the victorious Allied Powers. The chief British administrator had a very pessimistic view of independent Eritrea, which according to his opinion "could not but end in anarchy, or in renewed European control [because] there exists no imaginable governing or administrative class."[6]

With little agreement as to the future of Eritrea among the Great Powers of the day, a UN fact-finding mission was sent to Eritrea from November 1947 to January 1948 to learn about the desires of the Eritrean people. The five-member UN delegation included delegates from Burma, Guatemala, Norway, Pakistan, and South Africa. They were divided in their assessment of the situation in Eritrea, and came up with different recommendations as to what should be done. Norway favored a total union of Eritrea with Ethiopia, whereas delegates from Guatemala and Pakistan recommended complete independence of Eritrea after 10 years of UN trusteeship. The delegations from Burma and South Africa submitted their proposal allowing "Eritrea to be constituted a self-governing unit of a federation of which the other member shall be Ethiopia, under the sovereignty of the Ethiopian crown."[7] On December 2, 1950, the UN General Assembly voted that Eritrea should become an autonomous unit federated with Ethiopia under the Sovereignty of the Ethiopia Crown.

It did not take long for Emperor Haile Selassie of Ethiopia (who always had a vision of Eritrea's union with Ethiopia) to violate the federal arrangement, and declare the federation null and void while absorbing Eritrea into Ethiopian territory in 1962. The Eritrean people who witnessed the deterioration of the federal arrangement even before the final act of abolishing it altogether had already began in their protest. An armed struggle by the Eritrean Liberation Front (ELF) was sparked one year prior to annexation. Some ELF members were unhappy about the way the liberation movement had been run. That led to a power struggle and differences among ELF leaders on how to organize the liberation front. In turn, this led to the formation of a splinter group called the Eritrean People's Liberation Front (EPLF) in 1977.

The early stages in the EPLF formation succeeded in mobilizing the masses in support of the national liberation movement. The EPLF organized the Eritrean population into groups such as youth groups and women's groups at the village level. It was emphasized that the women's participation should be encouraged. By the end of 1978, the EPLF forces were in control of most of the country. Major cities in the Plateau and the Highlands, except Asmara (which was surrounded) and *Massawa,* were under offensive siege of the EPLF control.[8]

The EPLF had been committed to the strong notion of a centralist approach to organize the population into groups. The state is viewed as the principal vehicle of social change that mobilizes the people to engage in the process of nation building.[9] In the formative years, the EPLF political training stressed Marxism; in later years, as the military victory seems viable, the new emphasis became national and democratic issues.[10] After three decades of war for liberation, the EPLF-led forces forced out the Ethiopian army and took full control of Eritrea on May 24, 1991. After the UN-monitored referendum, Eritrea officially became a sovereign nation on May 24, 1993. Many countries recognized Eritrea's independence, and Eritrea joined the UN and the African Union (formerly the Organization of African Unity) in the aftermath of its formal independence.

Election of Head of State in Eritrea

Since the liberation, or de facto independence of Eritrea from Ethiopia in 1991 (and its formal or de jure independence in 1993 after an overwhelming vote for Eritrean independence through referendum), there has never been a free election for the Head of State in Eritrea's short political history. After the referendum result (99.8 percent), the Provisional Government of Eritrea (PGE) was established in May 1993 with executive, legislative, and judiciary branches. The Transitional National Assembly, by a majority vote, elected the then secretary general of the EPLF, Isaias Afewerki, to be the President of the PGE. The Transitional National Assembly has 150 members, of whom 75 are members of the EPLF, and the other 75 are non-EPLF popularly elected members. EPLF was replaced by the People's Front for Democracy and Justice (PFDJ) in February 1994, and established itself as the only political party in Eritrea. The PGE declared that during a four-year transition period it would draft and ratify a constitution, draft a law on political parties and press law, and carry out elections for a constitutional government.

In 1994, the PGE created a Constitutional Commission with a task of drafting a Constitution. The 50-member Constitutional Commission traveled throughout the country and even abroad to hold meetings and solicit people's input in the process of drafting the first constitution in Eritrea's history. Though acclaimed for being participatory in the process of its making, some argue that the Eritrean Constitution has some flaws, such as giving inordinate power to the executive branch. Nonetheless, after its ratification by the National Assembly in 1997, the Eritrean Constitution awaits being implemented.

Former liberation fighters assumed the leadership after Eritrea's independence with no experience in civilian administration or governance skills. They lacked the resources to sustain the ever-growing expectation of the people of the newly liberated nation. However, there were major achievements during the years of struggle for liberation. The EPLF made significant changes in the areas of land reform, village democratization, and gender equality, while simultaneously fighting for independence. Elected villagers, through their respective mass organizations, administered the liberated villages that is, peasants, women, workers, and youth associations.[11] Elections were held as often as every three-to-four months to assess and evaluate the performance of elected officials in order to make necessary changes. This was not the case, however, after Eritrean independence. Eritrean President Isaias Afewerki believes that it will take several decades before any national election happens in Eritrea. In an interview with Al-Jazeera English on May 22, 2008, the Eritrean President Afewerki, seemed pessimistic about holding elections, and stated that Eritrea will have to "wait three to four decades, maybe more"[12] for any sort of election.

Election of the Legislative National Council

The EPLF won Eritrean independence through military victory as the only front. It then established itself as the Provisional Government of Eritrea (PGE), and formed the provisional National Assembly in 1992. The People's Front for Democracy and Justice (formerly EPLF) led government has followed authoritarian political paths since its establishment as the ruling party in 1994. The government's authoritarian character became more palpable during the post-1998 period when the country had a border conflict in May of that year with neighboring Ethiopia. The PGE had postponed the election of the National Assembly that was scheduled to take place in December 2001. The national election, which was first scheduled for 1998, has been postponed to an unknown future date due to the border conflict that intensified during 1998–2000. It was halted after the two countries agreed in Algiers on Cessation of Hostilities on June 18, 2000. On December 12, 2000, a peace agreement was signed between the leaders of the two countries.

The Eritrean National Assembly met in September 2000, and 'debated' the ways in which the president handled the border war that Eritrea fought with Ethiopia during 1998–2000. The National Assembly also discussed the political transition. It was at this time that the National Assembly set up a Commission with a task of formulating and defining rules for multi-party election that was scheduled to happen in December 2001. The Commission submitted the party law that legalized a multi-party system in preparation for the national election. However, in September 2001, before any of its rules were put into action, the head of the Commission, Mahamud Sherifo, (the former Minister of Local Government), was arrested and imprisoned along with 11 dissident group members who opposed President Afewerki's undemocratic ruling. Unconfirmed sources reported that Sherifo was shot to death in prison, and that a few other dissidents met the same fate while in detention.

The group known as Group-15 (G-15) consists of members who are veterans of the ruling party; most are founding members of EPLF. In a formal letter on May 27, 2001, they asked President Afewerki to hold meetings of both the National Council and the Central Council of the PFDJ, of which they were members. President Afewerki responded by arresting and imprisoning 11 of the 15 signatories. Three of the G-15 were out of the country during the crackdown, while one withdrew her signature for safety reasons. The National Assembly met in January 2002 for the last time to denounce the dissidents as defeatist and treasonous. They also wanted to approve the President's agenda of cracking down on the opposition, to further extend the election date to an unknown future date, and to postpone of the formation of political parties.

Formation and Freedom of Political Parties

According to its Constitution, Eritrea is a one-party, unitary state that awaits the implementation of a multi-party system. Though Eritrea conducted regional and local elections with voting rights open to all qualified Eritreans, no other party except the ruling PFDJ could participate. People are not permitted to form other parties, or organize and campaign freely. The PFDJ cadres hold all the meetings during the election seasons. The PFDJ holds the monopoly in every aspect of the country's political, economic, social, and military life.

Opposition parties to the Eritrean government exist outside the country, with offices in neighboring Ethiopia, Sudan, and other African countries. There are also offices in Europe and the United States of America. However, the various opposition parties lack unity and collaboration as they differ in their views on "land policy, language, the role of religion in politics, and whether to reorganize the state through some form of ethnic or regional federalism."[13] The latest collaboration and unity meeting by the various Eritrean opposition groups was held on May 5–11, 2008, in Addis Ababa, Ethiopia under the umbrella of the Eritrean Democratic Alliance (EDA). It concluded by electing Tewelde Gebresselase as Secretary General of the executive council, and Abdella Mahmoud as chairman of the legislative council.[14]

Suffrage

The ratified Eritrean Constitution of 1997 provides general provision on the right to vote by stating "every citizen who fulfils the requirements of the electoral law shall have the right to vote and seek elective office."[15] The Constitution does not explicitly state universal suffrage, leaving the details for the Electoral Commission to set the age limit and other details. The electoral law would be responsible for clarifying the requirements. Considering the existing proclamations and decrees, it seems that the minimum age limit to vote would be 18 years of age and over. An example is the National Service Proclamation that requires every Eritrean between the ages of 18 and 40 to participate in compulsory national service for 18 months, including six months of military training.

Issues regarding race, gender, social status, and belief systems are not clearly stated in the constitutional provisions, leaving the task to the electoral law. Here again, one can draw a conclusion from the past performance of the Eritrean government in terms of its restriction on participation of its own citizens in civic matters. For instance, the Jehovah's Witnesses were denied Eritrean citizenship by the ruling party of Eritrea since they refused to participate in the 1993 Eritrean referendum on religious grounds. The Eritrean government justified its action on the grounds that the Jehovah's Witnesses failed to execute their civic duty by not participating in the Eritrea referendum that decided Eritrea's sovereignty. Furthermore, the government argues that by choosing not to participate in the referendum, followers of the Jehovah's Witnesses have opted out of their citizenship rights from the State of Eritrea.

Without a Constitution, there are no guarantees as to the definition of citizenship, or what the rights of citizens are. Without the rule of law and legal protection, citizens remain at the mercy of the government, as demonstrated by the treatment of the Jehovah's witnesses. This makes the Eritrean political system both highly unstable and undemocratic.

Media Freedom

In 1996, Eritrea adopted a Press Law that guaranteed freedom of the press. However, the government of Eritrea shut down all the private media (mainly newspapers) in September 2001, and arrested their journalists, with some of them being reported killed while in detention. The only media in Eritrea today are those that are controlled and run by the government. These include *TV ERI* and *Voice of the Masses Radio* (*Radio Dimtsi Hafash*). In the print media, *Hadas Eritrea* (*Tigrinya newspaper*), *Eritrea al Hadisa* (Arabic newspaper), and *Eritrea Profile* (English) are allowed. On the web, there is *Shaebia.org* for the PFDJ and *Shabait.com* for the State of Eritrea Ministry of Information. As the PFDJ and the State are two sides of a coin, they use their respective web sites to disseminate propaganda in the form of news and articles.

Eritrea was ranked the last of all the states that are rated according to the Press Freedom Index compiled by Reporters Without Borders since 2007. No independent media or civil society organizations exist in Eritrea. The existing local "non-governmental organizations" are initiated, and continue to be monitored and controlled by the government. Two such major associations are the National Union of Eritrean Women (NUEW) and the National Union of Eritrean Youth and Students (NUEYS). These mainly government-funded associations have been very instrumental in promoting the policy of the government.

Religious Freedom

Almost half of the estimated five million Eritreans follow Islam (mainly in the Eritrean Western and Eastern lowlands), and 40 percent practice Orthodox

Christianity, mainly in the highland areas. The remaining 10 percent of the population are Roman Catholics, Protestants, Seventh-Day-Adventists, Pentecostals, and Jehovah's Witnesses. Very few are Buddhists, Hindus, Bahai's, or atheists. The EPLF, as a Marxist-oriented movement during the independence struggle, has openly opposed religious groups such as Jehovah's Witnesses and Pentecostals. This was declared in the 1977 and 1987 National Democratic Program of the Front, which stated that the Front "strictly opposes all the imperialist-created new counter-revolutionary faiths, such as Jehovah's Witnesses, Pentecostals, Bahai, etc."[16]

When Eritrea achieved its independence in 1993, the new EPLF (PFDJ) led government continued the previous conviction of hostility toward other religious groups, with the exception of the four state-sanctioned religions, namely Orthodox Christianity, Roman Catholicism, the Federation of Lutherans, and Islam. The government harassed, arrested, and detained members of the Pentecostal churches, other independent evangelical groups, reformist movements from and within the Eritrean Orthodox Church, and Jehovah's Witnesses.

Following a May 2002 government decree that all religious groups must register or cease all religious activities, the government closed all religious facilities not belonging to the four state-sanctioned religions. Many leaders and pastors of the Pentecostal churches and independent reformist groups, as well as followers of the faith, remain in various prisons. They are imprisoned without any charges brought against them, and without permission for their families to visit them.

Prior to the government crack down on the Pentecostal and reformist Christian groups, the Jehovah's Witnesses were the first victims. The Jehovah's Witnesses who refused to participate in the 1993 Eritrean referendum on religious grounds were denied their right to citizenship. The Eritrean government defended its position, stating that the Jehovah's Witnesses refused to recognize the government, and refused to participate in the compulsory national service claiming that "they owed allegiance to no person, flags, or nation; they owed allegiance only to Jehovah."[17] Thus, the government argued "Jehovah Witnesses who have rejected the laws and refused to abide by them"[18] cannot invoke religious allegiance for their disobedience. Therefore, they have been punished for breaking the law not because they belong to a particular religious group.

Due to the grave persecution of minority religious groups, Eritrea was labeled as one of the Countries of Particular Concern (CPC) by the U.S. State Department International Religious Freedom Act for its severe violations of religious freedom in 2004 and remained a CPC, according to the latest report by the U.S. State Department.

Human Rights and Women's Rights

One of the goals for the EPLF during the years of struggle was to ensure equal participation of women. To ensure equality, quotas were set for women's participation in the village assemblies. Marriage laws were reformed to protect women from unequal treatment. The EPLF reasoned, "Women's full participation in the independence struggle was essential for the country's liberation."[19] This was a major step towards ensuring the equal rights of women in a society where women are relegated to subordinate position in all aspects of political, social, and economic life. The EPLF launched the National Union of Eritrean Women (NUEW) in November 1979 as one of the mass organizations to mobilize women for the independence war inside and outside of the country. The creation of such an organization, which was the first of its kind, attracted many women to join the liberation struggle and become indispensable assets to the movement. However, with the jubilee of Eritrean independence and celebration in 1993, much of the progress made during the liberation struggle was lost. The Eritrean "people became the objects of program rather than the agents of their own development"[20] where every policy was channeled in a top-down fashion.

Equal participation of Eritrean women in the political, social, and economic life was incorporated into the 1997 Constitution. This was expressed in the national service requirement for all women and men 18 years and older to participate in the 18-month national service that includes six months of military training. Another controversial constitutional provision is related to land reform. It was in 1994 that land reform was announced, which nationalized rural and urban land. All citizens over the age of eighteen, without gender distinction, were entitled to use the land for agricultural and residential purposes. Land reform was the first of its kind in Eritrean history, offering "women legal rights to own land."[21]

According to the 1997 pending constitution, thirty percent of the seats in the national assembly are reserved for women. Actually, very few women are in high-level governmental positions. The history and formation of the NUEW has made it a surrogate organization that operates within the approval ranges of the only ruling party in Eritrea, the PFDJ (EPLF before 1994). Therefore, the NUEW lacks the independence to execute its activities, and remains subservient to the State prerogatives. Also, the NUEW's lack of internal democracy and hostile tendencies toward other rival organizations has pushed many women with experience and skills from contributing to the progress of the organization. As a result, the NUEW "functions as a quiet, but effective lobby with government and the PFDJ in specific issues and policies."[22]

Other key issues in women's rights in Eritrea include harmful practices such as Female Genital Cutting/Mutilation (FGM), virginity-testing (*mikulal*) for prospective brides, and child marriage. Although these malpractices were banned in the fields during the liberation struggle, they were not easy to enforce in the larger patriarchal community. Many resisted the 1994 land reform that guaranteed equal rights to land ownership to all citizens of Eritrea 18 years and older without distinction to gender. Asserting women's right in a conservative society such as in Eritrea is not an easy task, even if the government is supportive of such causes. In an effort to eliminate FGM that had been commonly practiced for generations throughout the country (by all ethnic groups in Eritrea), the PFDJ government passed a declaration banning the practice on March 31, 2007. The proclamation stated "whosoever requests, incites or promotes female circumcision by providing tools or any other means, and whosoever, knowing that female circumcision is to take place or has taken place, fails, without good cause, to warn or inform the proper authorities promptly, shall be punishable with a fine and imprisonment."[23]

The government's human rights record remained poor, and authorities continued to commit serious abuses. These included the abridgement of citizens' right to change their government through a democratic process, unlawful killings by security forces, torture and beating of prisoners (sometimes resulting in death), arrest and torture of national service evaders (some of whom reportedly died of abuses while in detention), harsh and life threatening prison conditions, arbitrary arrest and detention, including family members of national service evaders, executive interference in the judiciary and the use of a special court system to limit due process, infringement on privacy rights, and roundups of young men and women for national service. Severe restrictions were imposed on basic civil liberties such as the freedoms of speech, press, assembly, association, and religion (particularly for religious groups not approved by the government), freedom of movement and travel for diplomats, the personnel of humanitarian and development agencies, the UN Mission to Eritrea and Ethiopia (UNMEE) and the activities of non-governmental organizations (NGOs).

There was also societal abuse and discrimination against women, such as the widespread practice of female genital mutilation (FGM). However, the new proclamation passed in 2007 by the Eritrean government banning FGM is the first step towards eradicating the wide spread practice. It is reported by Human Rights Watch that there are governmental and societal discrimination against members of the *Kunama* ethnic group; widespread societal discrimination based on sexual orientation, and reports of discrimination against those with HIV/AIDS. There are limitations on workers' rights. The government arrested three PFDJ trade union leaders who advocated for workers rights and better working conditions for two years and released them in 2007.[24]

The strict control of people's movements in and out of the country, combined with a lack of freedom and expression, and not having business opportunity and jobs, has caused thousands of youngsters to cross the border to neighboring Ethiopia and Sudan in hope of making their way to Europe, Canada, and the United States. However, many die before they reach their destination due to the treacherous and dangerous route they take to cross the borders. Some even get caught by the Eritrean border patrol and spend years in remote prisons inside Eritrea, others get deported back to Eritrea from countries like Egypt, Libya, Malta, and various European countries. The deportees end up in prisons and are inhumanly treated and tortured by the Eritrean government upon their arrival in Eritrea for leaving Eritrea illegally in the first place. A case in point is what happened to 223 Eritreans who were forcibly deported back from Malta in 2002. They were immediately taken to a military camp where they were detained and remained incommunicado.

In Ethiopia alone, there are about 25,000 Eritreans in the *Shimelba* refugee camp, and the number continues to grow. The number is even greater in Sudan, which resulted from the huge exodus of Eritrean youngsters crossing the border every day. These gross human rights violations affect the entire population because the government imprisons parents in place of their escaped children, and only releases them if they agree to pay a fee of 50,000 *Nakfa* (about $3,500). The parents of those who evade national service, and/or escape to neighboring countries are held responsible for the actions of their adult children. They are required to pay the fee or face imprisonment in place of an escaped son or daughter.

Human Development

According to the United Nations Development Program (UNDP), human development is about much more than the rise or fall of national incomes. It relates to creating an environment in which people can develop to their full potential, and lead productive, creative lives in accordance with their needs and interests. The concept of human development is that there should be opportunities for people to have a variety of choices, and that people are able to live a long and healthy life with access to available resources. In 2005, the Human Development Index (HDI) for Eritrea was 0.483, which places it 157th out of 177 countries, and in the low human development category.[25] According to the same report, the HDI provides a composite measure of three dimensions of human development: living a long and healthy life (measured by life expectancy), being educated (measured by adult literacy and enrolment at the primary, secondary, and tertiary level), and having a decent standard of living (measured by purchasing power parity and income). The same data indicates that the life expectance for Eritrea at birth is 56. Furthermore, the Human Poverty Index (HPI)-1 value of 36.0 for Eritrea ranks it 76th among the 108 developing countries for which the index has been calculated. The HPI-1 is rather a multi-dimensional alternative to the $1 a day (PPP US$) poverty measure.

Economic Freedom

According to a joint report by Eritrean National Development and UNDP, the Eritrean economy grew by 7.4 percent, and inflation was kept below 5 percent during the first few years of independence. However, after the 1998–2000 border conflict, the country's economy began to weaken. Combined with drought and poor economic performance, close to a million people are in danger of starvation. In 2006 the UN Human Poverty Index ranked Eritrea number 70 out of 102 countries. Private ownership is very much controlled and restricted, and most businesses are owned by the PFDJ.

Economic growth is one of the major manifestations of development. For any economy to grow, it needs a fertile ground in terms of economic freedom and rule of law. Policies that promote economic freedom provide a favorable environment that facilitates trade and encourages entrepreneurial activity, which, in turn, generates economic growth.[26] Schaefer further argues that the rule of law serves as the supporting structure of the economy, without which it cannot operate profitably. It does so by assuring entrepreneurs that policies will have a lasting power, and cannot change arbitrarily. Polices can be changed only through transparent, widely recognized procedures, permitting an environment favorable to long-term investment. Second, the rules will apply equally to all, rather than exempting some or being subject to change at the behest of the powerful. Thus, entrepreneurs will have legal recourse if policies unlawfully affect their activities, thereby reducing the risk of investments.[27]

The border war fought with Ethiopia during 1998–2000 and the subsequent stalemate have put major pressure on the country's economy. The stress on "fiscal aggregates and fuelled domestic and external imbalances, resulting in high inflation, low growth, low reserves, unsustainable debt and an overvalued exchange rate,"[28] is demonstrated by the International Monetary Fund (IMF) Report of 2007. According to the same IMF report, Eritrea's income from remittances declined from 41 percent of the Gross Domestic Product (GDP) in 2005, to some 23 percent in 2007. Moreover, it is expected that the Eritrean economy would continue to decline as the country faces interest rates below the rate of inflation, low private investment, limited outside support, and shortage of foreign exchange.

The IMF report also said that inflation increased to 12.3 percent in 2007 from 9 percent in 2006 due to imported food costs and monetary growth, and the banking sector was burdened by nonperforming loans, because "About half of all loans to borrowers other than the government were nonperforming in 2007."[29] The total public debt stood at 157 percent of GDP, and external debt was at 65 percent of the GDP as of 2007. The government is estimated to have the highest level of per capita military spending as a percentage GDP in the world, at 36.4 percent.[30]

According to the report of the U.S. Committee for Refugees and Immigrants, Ethiopia also hosted some 23,900 Eritrean refugees. About 16,800 of them lived in the *Shimelba* camp near the northern border. This group included some 4,000 ethnic *Kunama* (whom the Eritrean Government had accused of supporting Ethiopia in the 1998–2000 border dispute), evangelical Christians fleeing religious persecution, and newer arrivals fleeing forced conscription. Most of the *Kunama* turned down the option of U.S. resettlement after guerrilla leaders who wanted to keep them in the camp showed them the movie Roots and violent American television police dramas. They were told that Americans would "steal their organs." Another 7,100 ethnic Afar Eritrean refugees lived in the remote Afar region of northern Ethiopia.[31] On average, the U.S. Committee for Refugees and Immigrants states that about 300 to 600 ethnic Tigrinya Eritrean refugees entered per month amid growing fear about the possibility of a war between Ethiopia and Eritrea over their disputed border.

Conclusion

In Eritrea, the current conditions and lack of leadership make it very unlikely that a democratic administration will be seen in the near future in terms of allowing basic citizen rights by implementing the already ratified constitution. Moreover, the country lacks any kind of historical reference to good governance, there is a risk that the development of such a system might take decades, perhaps even more time than it took for the country to win independence.

The present leadership that came into power through military victory chose to continue violence as a means of resolving conflicts—both internal and external. The leadership continues to arrest, detain, and imprison critics, or whoever questions the excessive power and dictatorial, presidential régime. The fact that the government demands total compliance and obedience from all of its citizens in all aspects of life makes it very risky for anyone to deviate while still inside Eritrea. As a result, many leave the country through borders to find a better and safer place to live and, if possible, to fight the régime from afar. The lack of governmental institutions and civil society organizations makes the prospect of Eritrean democracy weak. This weakness can be overcome through responsible leadership and the hard work of many for a better tomorrow. Eritrean democracy can take root when the people are free to pursue their dreams as agents of change.

Insular Microstates

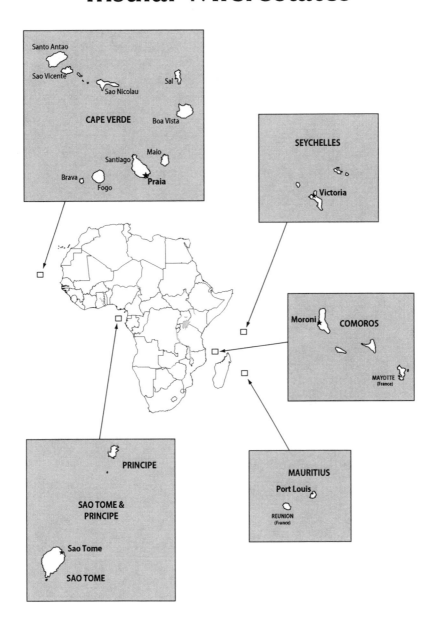

Santo Antao
Sao Vicente
Sao Nicolau
Sal
CAPE VERDE
Boa Vista
Maio
Santiago
Brava
Fogo
Praia

SEYCHELLES
Victoria

Moroni COMOROS
MAYOTTE
(France)

PRINCIPE

SAO TOME &
PRINCIPE

Sao Tome
SAO TOME

MAURITIUS
Port Louis
REUNION
(France)

Chapter 9

Insular Microstates: Democracy and Institutional Performance

Jose Adrian Garcia-Rojas

Territory is one of the elements that shape the State. Carré de Malberg wrote that a national community can only be part of a State when it owns the territory over which it rules in a sovereign and independent way.[1] The power of the State over its territory precludes any other one on the same space. An island microstate has a well defined border: the ocean. Sometimes, as in the case of the Comoro Islands, one of them can be part of another state, or can aspire to be an independent nation. This chapter will deal with the five African insular microstates. They have had, and continue to have, better democratic scores than the majority of the African countries since the beginning of the third wave of democratization that spread in the continent and all over the world during the 1990s.[2] In one case, free elections and multi-party politics are the only political systems that Mauritian people have known. Mauritius shares this oddity with Botswana. The Comoros, with its instability, continuous mercenary coups, and secessionist attempts, is the exception. However, things have improved in recent times.

Islands in Two Oceans

The African Insular Microstates consist of five islands, with two in the Atlantic Ocean (the former Portuguese colonies of Cape Verde and Sao Tome and Principe), and three in the Indian Ocean (the former British colonies of Mauritius and Seychelles, and the former French colony of Comoros). In the nineteenth century, two went from being colonized by France to being annexed by the United Kingdom. These microstates have different geographical features. Whereas Seychelles is an archipelago of around a hundred fifteen islands (most of them uninhabited), Cape Verde has ten main islands, nine of which are populated. The Comoros has three islands (because Mayotte decided, by referendum, to remain a French territory), and Mauritius and Sao Tome and Principe each have two islands. One of the physical characteristics of these countries is their size: they are microstates and islands. The largest of them is Cape Verde, followed by Mauritius and the Comoros, with a similar extension. The smallest one is Seychelles. Mauritius is the most populous, and the least populated is Seychelles, with only 81,500 inhabitants.

There is ethnic and linguistic diversity, but some form of religious homogeneity in each of the microstates. The Union of Comoros is a Muslim dominated country; Mauritius has a Hindu majority with a strong component of Christians, Muslims, and other religious groups. Cape Verde, Sao Tome and Principe, and Seychelles islands have a majority of Roman Catholic. Portuguese and Creole are the official languages in Cape Verde and Sao Tome and Principe. French, Swahili, and Arabic are spoken on the Comoros, and although English is the official language of Mauritius and Seychelles, Creole and French are spoken as well. The population is predominantly homogeneous and of African origin in Cape Verde and Sao Tome and Principe, and in the Comoros. Seychelles has many Creoles who descended from the French, English, and African colonizers. The population of Mauritius is diverse (the constitution recognizes representation according to communities), with people derived of African, Chinese, French, Hindu, or Muslim roots, as well as other origins.[3]

Evolution of the African Insular Microstates Political Systems until the 1990s

Mauritius was the first African insular microstate to gain independence in 1968: it became a Republic in 1992. The other four insular states gained independence in the mid-1970s, when a new wave of decolonization started in Africa, after the great one that took place at the end of World War II in the 1950s. In this second cycle of decolonization, all of the Portuguese colonies gained independence, among them were Cape Verde and Sao Tome and Principe.[4] These two countries became independent in 1975, the same year the Comoros gained independence from France. Mayotte was the exception, for it twice rejected (through a referendum) being linked to the new state, and that meant keeping its affiliation to France. The last country to join the independent nations was Seychelles in 1976.

In all these countries nationalist parties were formed; even in Cape Verde many people took part in the armed insurrection of Guinea-Bissau against Portugal.[5] In the former British possessions (Mauritius and Seychelles) there was self-rule before independence,[6] whereas the Comoros decided (by means of a referendum on each of the four islands) whether to keep the former status of being French possessions or to become a new state.

From the moment of reaching independence, until the third democratic wave that started in the late 1980s, only Mauritius held and still holds democratic elections, a multi-party system, and the replacement of political forces in office. The case of Mauritius and Botswana is exceptional in Africa because they have maintained free elections and a multi-party system since independence.[7] Cape Verde and Sao Tome and Principe, together with the rest of former Portuguese colonies in the continent, adopted the one-party system with Marxist-Leninist rhetoric and socialist political structure.[8] Seychelles chose a multi-party system that allowed an alternative presence in office, but in 1979, turned into a one-party regime that lasted until the end of 1991.[9] The Comoro Islands have a history of political instability; there have been several military coups, interventions of foreign mercenaries, and secession attempts on some of the islands. This began in 1975 when Ali Soilih[10] came to power after a coup d'état and stayed in office for three years. In another putsch by French mercenaries, Ali was toppled and killed. That paved the way for the takeover of President Ahmed Abdallah.[11] In his position as president, Abdallah built a one-party regime and established a close relationship with France. Rebel soldiers murdered Abdallah in a new mercenary coup in 1989. After some months of a government led by mercenaries, Mohamed Said Djohar (a.k.a. Papa Djo) took power through general elections. A series of military attempts to oust him from office took place, and even after he resigned there were other moves to overthrow the government.[12]

Institutional Design of the Insular Microstates

The 1968 Mauritius Constitution is the oldest of all the African insular microstates.[13] The constitutions of the Cape Verde,[14] Sao Tome and Principe,[15] and Seychelles sprang from the beginnings of the transition to democracy from one-party to multi-party states. In the Comoros, there have been different constitutional reforms since 1989 until 2001, the last one is still in force. All the African insular microstates except the Comoros have opted for unitary or centralized political systems, with the constitution solemnly declaring that condition. In the former Portuguese colonies of Mauritius and

Sao Tome and Principe, the constitution favors the federal system, but a special status is adopted for Rodrigues Island. As far as the Comoros is concerned, the constitution of 2001 strengthens the federal approach of the Union, endowing ample powers to the islands, which in some cases have separatist movements. The Comoros is an interesting case, because a series of mechanisms aimed at keeping the institutional stability among the three islands was implemented, but the separatist movements still persist.[16] Of the five African insular microstates, four have opted for the direct election of the Head of State, or president of the Republic. In Mauritius, the parliament elects the Head of State.[17] In the cases of Cape Verde and Sao Tome and Principe, however, the candidate directly elected by the voters must have the support of the majority of the votes at the first round, but if no presidential candidate receives more than half of the votes, a runoff election is held between the two front-runners (a two-ballot election system). In the Comoros and Seychelles,[18] no runoff election is held if there are no presidential candidates who gather more than 50 percent of the votes. In the Comoros, the president's office rotates among the three islands that belong to the Union. This means that the candidates are selected in each island and later on, all the citizens of the Comoros vote on them.

The post of vice-president exists in the Comoros (two vice-presidents), Mauritius, and Seychelles (since 1996), but not in Cape Verde and Sao Tome and Principe. The parliament elects the vice-president in Mauritius, but in the Comoros, the people elect both the president and the vice-president. In all cases, the president can be re-elected for a second mandate, although there are variations when it comes to the number of re-elections. For example, in Seychelles, there can be three consecutive re-elections. In Cape Verde, only one re-election is permitted, but a comeback is allowed after ten years or after two presidential elections. In Sao Tome and Principe, there is no chance of a third re-election except in the case of canvassing for a third mandate after five years of not being in office. The period of the presidential office is five years in all countries except in the Comoros, where there is only a four-year mandate.

The prime minister is the main political figure in Mauritius, where a Westminster-style model[19] has been applied, and that means a predominance of that post. In the Comoros and Seychelles, the president presides over the government and chooses his or her cabinet. In the other three insular political systems (Cape Verde, Mauritius, and Sao Tome and Principe), the parliament must vote for the prime minister. Therefore, two regimes are clearly presidential (the Comoros and Seychelles). Two are semi-presidential, modelled upon the French and Portuguese pattern (where the parliament holds a decisive role in the election of prime minister), and the other, Mauritius, is completely parliamentary. In Mauritius, the Head of State is elected by the parliament, but without being subjected as leader of one of the parties that compete in the general election. The prime minister's mandate, along with the cabinet, is five years, except in the case of the Comoros, where it is four years unless unexpected elections are held. The parliament, in all these African insular microstates, is called the National Assembly.

In all cases, it is a one-chamber institution. The mandate of the elected members is five years except in Sao Tome and Principe, with four; this, as already pointed out, depends on the eventuality of sudden elections in most cases. The number of representatives elected varies from seventy-two in Cape Verde, and seventy in Mauritius, to a minimum of thirty-three in the Comoros and thirty-four in Seychelles. The Comoros, Mauritius, and Sao Tome and Principe recognize the islands as different electoral districts in Rodrigues, Principe and each of the three islands of the Union of Comoros, whose insular Assemblies indirectly elect fifteen representatives in the National Assembly. Cape Verde and Sao Tome and Principe have a proportional electoral system with party lists,[20] whereas the Comoros, Mauritius, and Seychelles have a majority system. There is a runoff electoral system in the case of the Comoros, or to the most voted candidates in the different districts, as is the case of Mauritius and Seychelles. In these two countries, a group of members of parliament (eight in Mauritius[21] and nine in Seychelles) were proportionally allotted among those parties that did not get a clear representation in the districts, and that is done by means of the best losers system in Mauritius as a way to assign those additional seats.[22] It is also specified in Mauritius' constitution that the candidates must report to members of their constituencies. In Cape Verde, citizens in diaspora were allowed to elect six candidates.

Other than in Cape Verde and Seychelles, the rest of the insular microstates of Africa recognize the peculiarities of some of their islands, and therefore specific legal rules are included in their respective constitutions to regulate the election of the insular governments. Mauritius and Sao Tome and Principe recognize the specific characteristics of Rodrigues, and that implies having the status of electoral districts of insular range. It is also constitutionally recognized for these islands in the election of their Assemblies and regional governments. A further step regarding political decentralization can be found in the Comoros. The history of the Comoro Islands (as an independent entity) is the most unstable of the five insular microstates. Secession moves and the persistence of a strong pro independent component in some of the islands gave way to a relative agreement that led to the endorsement of the constitutional text, passed through a referendum, which endows ample powers to every island of the Union. First, the constitution establishes taking turns in office for

the presidential candidates of the three islands. Second, the Assemblies of each
island sends fifteen members to the National Assembly of the Comoros Union
(assigning five for each island). Third, the ministers have to be selected, taking into account the balance among the islands, and fourth, each and every
island endorses its own Fundamental Law, which must respect the limits stated
by the constitution.[23] The self-ruled islands of Grande Comore, Anjouan, and
Moheli[24] have a cabinet with an elected insular prime minister and an insular
Assembly, which is also elected by universal suffrage.

The Political Evolution since 1990s

Mauritius

Before the transition to democracy in the early 1990s, some African states,
such as Mauritius, had a consolidated multi-party tradition. Others, like Seychelles or the Comoros, tried that path with little success, and the outcome
was pseudo-democratic, or one-party regimes. Mauritius has adopted different combinations of government coalitions from the 1990s to the present time.
The main parties are the Mauritian Labour Party (MLP), the dominant party
in the early years of independence until the mid 1970s,[25] the Mauritian Militant Movement (MMM), the Militant Socialist Movement (MSM), and the
Mauritian Social Democratic Party (PMSD). All these parties have an ethnic
base; only the MMM emerged with the objective of being a national party.[26]
The MLP has a Hindu ethnic base, and its leaders are members of this community. PMSD was the party of the descendants of the French economic elite
and of the Creole community. The MSM was a split from a dissident group of
the MMM; other parties were also formed the same way.

The Mauritian electoral system has influenced the creation of electoral coalitions in order to maximize votes and to secure enough members of each party
into the National Assembly to support a prime minister and the government.
In practice, all the main parties have been partners in some electoral or government coalitions.[27] Coalition partners changed from general elections to the
other, and the adversaries of the past could be companions in a future electoral coalition.[28] Mauritius has had MLP-PMSD, MSM-MMM, MMM-MLP,
MSM-MLP electoral and government coalitions, and has switched one of the
parties in the following elections. All these coalitions have had other minor
parties as partners. A handful of leaders have dominated the Mauritius political life since independence. The first Mauritian prime minister was Sir See-
woosagur Ramgoolam, leader of the MLP and prime minister from before

independence until the 1982 elections. He ruled a coalition formed by MLP-PMSD (1976–1982). The second prime minister of Mauritius was Sir Anerood Jugnauth, president of the MMM (1983–1983). He governed in coalition with the Mauritian Socialist Party (MSP), a party created by dissidents of the MLP. He became the leader of the MSM when he and his supporters left the MMM, in a coalition with the old opponents of the MLP and PMSD (1983–1987). He was again the prime minister with the same partners, including the insular party Organization of the People of Rodrigues (OPR), from 1987 to 1991. With his former companions of the MMM and other minor parties, such as OPR and the Democratic Labour Movement (MTD), from 1991 to 1995; and again from 2000 to 2003 with the MMM, sharing the post of prime minister with his all life adversary Paul Berenger, leader of the MMM, and the only non-Hindu prime minister of Mauritius. Berenger led the government from September 2003 to July 2005.[29] The fourth and last prime-minister, Navinchandra Ramgoolam (MLP), son of the late prime minister, led an electoral and problematic coalition with the MMM, which lasted from 1995 to 2000. He also was the candidate for the post of prime minister for the electoral coalition Social Alliance (AS), formed by MLP and Xavier Duval Party, a split of the PMSD, that won the 2005 and 2010 general elections. In the 2010 general elections, the MLP formed a new coalition with the PMSD and the MSM.[30]

Seychelles

The rest of the countries have had a different political path. Seychelles returned to a multi-party political system in July 1993. The beginning of the transition to a more open political regime began with the constitutional commission election one year before (July 1992), and the two constitutional referenda in November 1992 and June 1993. The first constitutional referendum did not receive the majority of the needed votes (more than 60 percent in favor of the constitutional amendments) because the opposition voted *no*. In the second referendum, the party in office and the opposition parties agreed with the reform of the constitution that made possible the first democratic general elections since the 1970s.[31] The turnout was higher than in the rest of parliamentary and presidential elections. In the Seychelles elections, more than 80 percent of the electorate voted. The Seychelles have had four parliamentary and four presidential elections. All the elections have been won by the same old one-party, the Seychelles People's Progressive Front (SPPF). The SPPF, and its presidential candidate, France-Albert René (the president of Seychelles since 1977) won both elections in 1993 and 1998.[32] They also won the presidential elections of 2001 and 2006.[33]

In the 2006 election, the winner was René's successor, James Michel. The SPPF also won the 2002 and 2007 National Assembly election, and the main opposition parties changed through these years. In the first elections, the main opposition party was the Democratic Party (DP) and its leader, James Mancham, who was the first president of the independent Seychelles until France-Albert René led the coup in 1977. But since these first two elections, the Seychelles National Party (SNP) has been the major opposition party. The main presidential candidate has been Reverend Wavel Ramkalawan, who got 45 percent of the Seychelles people's electoral support in both the 2001 and 2006 presidential elections. This important percentage of votes decreased approximately by two points in the parliamentary elections. The Seychelles National Assembly electoral system (25 members are elected by single majority vote) did not offer many opportunities to the opposition to reach a proportional number of seats in the parliament, thus keeping its percentage of votes in terms of political representation. The SNP got an important number of its seats, because each party nominates one National Assembly member for every ten percent of their votes. For the SNP and other opposition parties, it is quite difficult to win in a constituency by a majority of votes because of the wide political control of the SPPF in the Seychelles' administrative, economic, and political life. The SPPF changed its name to Parti Lepep (People's Party) in July 2009.

Cape Verde

Cape Verde and Sao Tome and Principe are two of the more democratic and stable African political systems ever since their first free elections held in January 1991.[34] In both cases, the latest one-party lost both legislative and presidential elections, and in both cases those parties went to opposition in their National Assemblies and accepted the victory of parties that were banned shortly before elections. Cape Verde has held four parliamentary and presidential elections. An independent presidential candidate, participating with the support of the Movement for Democracy (MpD), won the first two elections by 73 percent of the popular vote against the first and only president of the independent Cape Verde, Aristides Pereira of the African Party of the Independence of Cape Verde (PAICV). The huge difference in the number of votes sent a message to the PAICV that the people of Cape Verde wanted a multi-party political regime with free elections and new men to lead the country.[35]

In the second presidential election, the first democratic president of Cape Verde, Antonio Mascarenhas Monteiro was the only candidate, and all main parties supported him. In a parliamentary regime such as that of Cape Verde, the prime minister is the main political figure. The prime minister needs a majority in the National Assembly. In the two first legislative elections, the MpD was the most popular. It won 56 of the 79 seats in the chamber in 1991, and 50 of 70 seats in 1996. The party in power changed in the January 2001 legislative election. In this election, the PAICV returned to power, but this time in a free electoral process. PAICV gained 40 of the 72 seats of the National Assembly, while the MpD only had 30.

In the third presidential election, held in February 2001, no single candidate obtained 50 percent of the vote in the first round. In the second round, the PAICV candidate and former prime minister during the one-party regime Pedro Pires won by only 12 votes more than the MpD candidate, Carlos Veiga, who was the first democratic prime minister of Cape Verde. The same candidates and parties obtained similar percentages of votes in the 2006 legislative and presidential elections; the PAICV candidate won in the first round but by a narrow margin of less than two points. Clearly, Cape Verde has a stable two-party system. Two main parties, PAICV and MpD, have been in power and in opposition. The difference between them in terms of votes is not too large; the only way to win and gain power is through free and fair elections. Since the 1996 legislative election, a third small party has had a seat or two in the National Assembly.

Sao Tome and Principe

Sao Tome and Principe have had a different history and a different party system than Cape Verde. In the first free elections (National People's Assembly) in January 1991,[36] the opposition party, Democratic Convergence Party-Reflection Group (PCD-GR), obtained the 54.4 percent of the votes and 33 of the 55 seats of the chamber. The old one-party Movement for the Liberation of Sao Tome and Principe (MLSTP) (that had added to its former name the name of Social Democratic Party, PSD), gained only 30.5 percent and 21 seats. The oldest opposition party, the Democratic Coalition of the Opposition (CODO), had only one, and 5 percent of the votes. In the first free presidential elections of March 1991, MLSTP-PSD did not present any candidate. The elected PCD-GR and CODO candidate Miguel Trovoada, who was a leading figure of the MLSTP during the one-party-state, was imprisoned and expelled from the MLSTP, and sent into exile in the last few years of the one-party regime. The first two prime ministers were from the PCD-GR party. In the second legislative election, the MLSTP-PSD won with 27 of the 55 seats of the chamber. A new party (the Independent Democratic Action, ADI) emerged in this election and a group of dissidents of the PCD-GR formed the president Trovoada political platform. This presidential party obtained the same number of seats as the PCD-GR, 14.

This type of presidential party or political platform has become one of the characteristics of the Sao Tome and Principe political system. The MLSTP-PSD entered the government in 1994, and it was a partner in the majority of the coalition governments until today.[37] The MLSTP-PSD was the majority party in the legislative elections of 1998 (31 of 55 seats), and 2002 (24 seats), but it lost the 2006 legislative election (20 seats). No MLSTP-PSD candidate won any presidential election. Miguel Trovoada of ADI won the second presidential election in the second round, and the ADI candidate and successor of Trovoada, Fradique de Menezes won the third election by 55.18 percent of the votes. President de Menezes also gained the last presidential election of 2006 with the 60.58 percent of the votes. His opponent in this election was the late Miguel Trovoada's son, Patrice. President de Menezes and a group of dissidents of ADI formed the Force for Change Democratic Movement (MDFM). In coalition with the PCD, they obtained second place in the 2002 legislative election, and first place in the 2006 National Assembly election.

The evolution of the Sao Tome and Principe party system shows some relevant features of the political regime. First, there is a weakness in the party system. In the case of ADI, the parties are devoted to the president of the republic and to the personality of Miguel Trovoada and his son. In the case of MDFM, the allegience is to President Menezes. Second, the MLSTP-PSD is devoted to the former president of the independent Sao Tome and Principe, Pinto da Costa. The MLSTP-PSD is, however, a more structured party than the other two. The PCD seems to be a party less devoted to leadership, because the MLSTP and the PCD were the oldest parties in the country. Sao Tome and Principe also show the ability of the political elite to reach agreements and to share power in different government coalitions. All the parties could become partners in a government coalition, and any party could hold the opposition place in the National Assembly.[38] In the August 2010 legislative elections, the electorate changed one more time and supported ADI, which had been expelled from government months before because pPresident Menezes and his party, MDFM, preferred to share power with MLSTP. ADI was the most voted party and gained 26 seats in the chamber; Patrice Trovoada, the party's leader, was elected prime minister.[39]

Union of Comoros

The Comoro Islands are a different case. The evolution of the Comorian political system from the beginning of the 1990s to 2010 follows similar features as the previous period: political instability, governmental weakness, secessionist attempts in some islands, foreign troop interventions to restore an elected president after a mercenary coup, and military coups. But they also have known, as other African countries, more or less free elections and the peaceful transfer of power from one president to another for the first time since independence. Since the election of President Ahmed Abdallah Mohamed Sambi in May 2006, and a new secessionist attempt in Anjouan (aborted with the African Union mediation and a military intervention), the country seems to be prepared for its new democratic presidential election. In its second round, the 1990 presidential election had as presidential candidates the two men who ruled the Comoro Islands for almost ten years: Saïd Mohamed Djohar and Taki Mohamed Abdoulkarim.[40] The years of President Djohar were marked by political instability, problems integrating the opposition parties and leaders in the the the new regime, constitutional change in 1992, attempts of a new mercenary coup d'état, and new French troops intervention to abort it. In the end, President Djohar was exiled.

In March 1996, the Comoros elected Taki as president.[41] The former minister, prime minister, president of the National Assembly, and old political plotter formed his first government with some of his former presidential rivals in the first electoral round. But, as Abdallah, of whom he was minister in the 1980s, had the authoritarian power of changing the constitution which had been approved in a referendum with the purpose of reinforcing the presidential powers and restricting the formation of new political parties. The opposition political forces boycotted the Federal Assembly election of December 1996 because of the mistake of President Taki to choose an independent electoral commission. The president's party (National Rally for Development, RND) won 36 of the 43 seats in the chamber, the moderate Islamic National Front of Justice got three and the rest was won by independent candidates. During Taki's presidency, Anjouan and Moheli decided to declare independence. The Organization of African Unity (OAU) and France refused both independence proposals, and urged the different parties to hold talks in Ethiopia. However, government troops tried to control Anjouan at the same time. That provoked a radicalization of the demand for independence in that island, the celebration of an illegal referendum on independence (October 1997), and a constitutional one (February 1998). Tadjidini Ben Saïd Massonde, who was the president of the High Council of the Republic (Constitutional Court), assumed the presidency in November 1998 after the sudden death of Taki. The presidential election was delayed because of the Anjouan situation.

In April 1999, representatives of the three independent Comoro Islands (with the mediation of OAU), reached an agreement in Madagascar to change the name of the country and rename it the Union of the Comoros, in order to pass through a referendum for a new constitution that would extend the autonomy and self-government of each island and have presidential elections in April 2000. The Anjouan representatives did not sign that agreement. On April 30, 1999, a military coup, led by the army commander-in-chief, allowed Colonel Assoumani Azali to take power. He suspended the constitution and all the constitutional powers, but at the same time, he accepted the Madagascar agreements. The OAU, France, and the international community condemned the coup d'état.

Azali ruled the Comoros by decree, but he was able to reach agreements with the separatist leaders of all the islands. The Comoros voted for a new federal constitution on December 23, 2001.[42] The strong men of Anjouan and Moheli accepted this new federal constitution that gave more autonomy to the three islands of the new Union of Comoros. In January, a new government prepared the presidential elections. Each island voted its own constitution and as the 2001 constitution prescribed. Grande Comore voted in the primaries for the presidential candidates. Azali won the first round with 39.81 percent of the votes. His two opponents who passed the primaries boycotted the presidential election in the second round in the three islands, because of the irregularities in the primaries. Azali was elected as the sole candidate, and the three islands voted their own insular presidents: Bacar in Anjouan, Fazul in Moheli, and Elbak in Grande Comore.

On December 20, 2003, President Azali and the three island presidents signed an agreement, which was negotiated in Pretoria, South Africa. In the April 2004 Assembly of the Union elections, the candidates of the island presidents Camp of the Autonomous Islands (CdIA) gained 12 of the 18 deputies of the chamber, and only six were of the presidential party, Convention for the Renewal of the Comoros (CRC). The island Assemblies nominated all of their 15 deputies in the federal Union of the CdIA.[43] The 2006 presidential election primaries were in Anjouan. Ahmed Abdallah Mohamed Sambi, a moderate Islamist candidate of the National Front for Justice (FNJ), won the primaries and the national presidential election with the support of the three island presidents. In April 2006, Azali transferred power to President Sambi peacefully. However, the separatist problem persists in Anjouan. President Sambi attempted to postpone the first round of the 2010 presidential election to November 27,[44] and to extend his presidential term until this date, but the constitutional court declared it unconstitutional in May 2010. In 2010, the rotary selection of candidates was held in Moheli. In this first round, 10 candidates competed. The three top-candidates were Mohamed Said Fazul (president of the island), Ikililou Dhoinine (who was President Sambi's vice-president and candidate), and Abdou Djabir. In the second round, the Comorian citizens voted for one of them. The winner was Ikililou Dhoinine, with 61 percent of the national vote.

Quantifying African Insular Microstates Democracy

Mauritius, as mentioned before, is with Botswana the oldest continuing democratic political system in Africa; it has the best five African island microstates score with its 18 points.[45] The lowest rankings went to the Comoros, with only 12.5 points. Cape Verde scored 17 points, only one point less than Mauritius, and Sao Tome and Principe and Seychelles scored 15 and 15.5 points, respectively. Mauritius is the only one of the five African insular microstates that got the 100 percent of the Status of Democracy Index (SDI). Some scores need to be deeply explained. In four microstates, democratic electoral processes seem to work out quite well. In the Union of Comoros, since the 2006 presidential elections, democracy seems to go in the right direction. The same four countries scored two points in the election of the head of state and in the legislative elections. They also scored two points in the development of the political parties and suffrage. The Comoros is an interesting case, because these four variables behave well at the national level and in two of the islands (Grande Comore and Moheli). This is not so in Anjouan, because the former island government president, Bacar, did not celebrate elections and declared the Anjouan secession of the Union. Since the Sambi era, a native of Anjouan, was elected new island president. With some difficulties, for the first time in the independent Comoros history, a native of Moheli was elected president of the Union because of the rotating federal president electoral system. In this case, the scores do not reflect the exact democratic process performance at the regional level.

The media freedom variable shows that Mauritius, Cape Verde, and Sao Tome and Principe also have two points, but the Comoros and Seychelles only scored one point. The same three countries and Seychelles have two points in religious freedom, except the Comoros, whose constitution's preamble states that Islam inspires the principles and laws of the Union. The Comoros guarantees the equality of all its citizens without distinction of race, gender, or religion, but in spite of that, authorities continue to limit other religions in practice. Human rights scores are high (two points) in the five countries. Mauritius and Seychelles got two points in human development, Cape Verde a score of one, and Sao Tome and Principe and the Comoros half of a point. Mauritius and Cape Verde got a two-point score from the economic freedom variable, and Sao Tome and Principe received one and a half points. The Union of Comoros and Seychelles only had a score of one point each. These scores and SDI indices have to be understood in the African context, and as this book shows, in general terms, four of the five African insular microstates (Mauritius, Cape Verde, Sao Tome and Principe and Seychelles) have better scores than the others African countries. Union of Comoros is the only exception, but, it also has better scores and institutional performances than other African political systems.

Table 1. Status of Democracy Index of African Island Microstates, 2010

Country	A	B	C	D	E	F	G	H	I	SDI	% SDI
Cape Verde	2	2	2	2	2	2	2	1	2	17	94
Comoros	1.5	1.5	2	1.5	1	1.5	2	0.5	1	12.5	69
Mauritius	2	2	2	2	2	2	2	2	2	18	100
Sao Tome & Principe	2	2	2	2	2	2	2	0.5	1.5	15	83
Seychelles	2	2	1.5	2	1	2	2	2est.	1	15.5	86

Legend: A: Free election head of State; B: Free election Legislature; C: Political Parties, D: Suffrage; E: Media Freedom; F: Religious Freedom; G: Human Rights; H: Human Development; I: Economic Freedom; SDI: Status of Democracy Index.
A: 0 = no, 1 = not totally free, 2 = yes. B: 0 = no, 1 = limited, 2 = yes; C: 0 = prohibited, 1 = controlled by government or need government approval, 2 = reasonably free; D: 0 = none,1 = some, 2 = yes; E: 0 = not free, 1 = partly free, 2 = free; F: 0 = none, 1 = some, 2 = yes; G: 0 = not observed, 1 = partly observed, 2 = full observed; H: 0 = low human development, 1 = medium human development, 2 = high human development; I: 0 = strong governmental interference, 1 = medium governmental interference, 2 = low governmental interference; est.: estimated.

Conclusion

Island microstates have some similar characteristics. These characteristics come from the peculiarities of people living in a limited space, and the singular relations that create dependence on foreign aid and food. There are also the special relations with the nearest continent, so far, and yet so close in many aspects. Moreover, geography makes insular people different in many ways, but similar in other important aspects. History and cultural tradition are important, but something else exists that is difficult to explain. Maybe it is because they lived so close and so far from the mainland in the past, and in some ways in the present, too.

The first years of these countries as independent nations were similar to the rest of the African countries. Only Mauritius, in this group of microstates, has preserved democracy, a multiparty system, and civil rights since independence The rest of the nations had an authoritarian one-state party system in their first decades as free countries. They have a different colonial past and different cultural heritages, but they also have lived a similar process of successful transition to a democratic system in three cases (Cape Verde, Sao Tome and Principe and Seychelles) since the early 1990s. These microstates also have better economic indicators, and most of them have stable party systems and have experienced different parties in power. This is one of the most outstanding differences between African island microstates and the majority of the African countries.

The Union of Comoros is the exception that conforms to the rule. However, this country, despite its tragic history of mercenaries, armed forces' coups d'état, and emergence of dictators, seems to follow the way of a democratic regime, even with the many dangerous problems of how to articulate the archipelago in a one nation-state. Indices aim to quantify and measure the democratic performance of a political system. History, political context, party systems, institutional design, and ethnic problems improve analysis and perception of democracy and democratic political change in Africa. In a continent where bad news makes the media front pages, no news in the African insular microstates is good news for a democratic future.

Tanzania

Chapter 10

Tanzania: Political Culture and Democratization

Shadrack Wanjala Nasong'o

From 1885, until the end of World War I, Tanganyika was a German colony. With the defeat of Germany in World War I, it was transferred to the British in 1919 under the League of Nations' Mandate System. In the run-up to de-colonization in 1961, Tanganyika had two major political parties. The first was the Tanganyika African National Union (TANU). It was formed in 1954 by Julius Nyerere from the Tanganyika African Association, which is a welfare association that he helped found as a student at Makerere University in Kampala, Uganda. In 1958, Zuberi Mtemvu split off from TANU, and formed the African National Congress (ANC) as a result of ideological differences with Nyerere. Mtemvu regarded Nyerere as too tame on issues of Africanization of the economy and the Tanganyika civil service, while Nyerere saw Mtemvu's extreme nationalism as the equivalent of racism.[1] In the 1960 Independence Elections, TANU won all parliamentary seats except one, and Nyerere won a landslide victory over Mtemvu, his sole opponent. This lopsided victory on the part of Nyerere and TANU laid the basis for a one-party state in Tanganyika.

At the same time of decolonization, there were two major political parties on the islands of Pemba and Zanzibar, each representing a specific cultural group—Zanzibar Nationalist Party (ZNP) for Arabs, and Afro-Shirazi Party (ASP) for Africans. As they did elsewhere, the outgoing British colonialists gerrymandered electoral constituencies on the islands to ensure that though the ASP won majority votes of 54 percent, ZNP, whose agenda was viewed as consistent with British interests, won majority parliamentary seats. This electoral fraud facilitated the Zanzibari Revolution of 1964, which was led, ironically, by Ugandan John Okello. After the revolution, all political parties except ASP were banned on the islands. The revolution resulted in the merger of Tanganyika and Zanzibar into the United Republic of Tanzania. Accordingly, by 1965, TANU reigned supreme on the mainland and ASP dominated the islands. In the 1967 Arusha Declaration, President Nyerere enunciated a centralized approach to development planning in Tanzania, which he dubbed *Ujamaa* (familyhood—an African variant of socialism based on the communalist ethos of the African family). In 1977, the two parties, TANU on the mainland and ASP on the islands, merged under the influence of Nyerere to constitute *Chama Cha Mapinduzi* (CCM) (Revolutionary Party), which has controlled the politics of Tanzania until today.

To further centralize political power, the regional administration was incorporated into the party structure because regional administrators doubled as local heads of the party at their respective levels, and Regional Commissioners were made ex-officio Members of Parliament.[2] The National Executive Committee (NEC) of CCM became the main policy making organ of the government, thus subordinating the legislature to the party NEC.[3] Parliamentary supremacy was further watered down through provisions on its election. Though the constitution provided for an Electoral Commission to conduct elections, its members were to be appointed by the president, who was also to confirm the speaker of the house as its chairman. Furthermore, the courts were stripped of the power to investigate the Commission's activities in the course of exercising its authority under the constitution. In this regard, the commission was only answerable to the president who appointed it, and its decisions were final, and could not be contested even in a court of law.[4] Furthermore, the constitution provided that the president, who was also chairman of CCM, could dismiss the legislature at any time and that parliament was essentially a committee of the party's Annual National Conference, whose task was to oversee the overall implementation of party policies.[5]

Clearly, therefore, Nyerere established an authoritarian political culture in Tanzania, albeit a relatively benign one compared to the authoritarian Kenyatta regime in neighboring Kenya.[6] Nyerere's regime was imbued with unquestionable integrity, and a commitment to the welfare of the people through the basic needs approach in his economic planning. Indeed, his *Ujamaa* socialist ideology enunciated six main principles, namely profession of faith in man by man, rejection of the exploitation of man by man, control of the major means of production and distribution by workers and peasants, popular democratic government of workers and peasants, faith and dedication to socialism (particularly on the part of leaders of the party), and *kujitegemea* (self-reliance) in the development process.[7] Although Nyerere forced his ideas on the people and made some policy errors, he enhanced national unity among the over 120 ethnic groups in Tanzania to the extent that the sense of Tanzanian nationhood was almost unparalleled in Africa at the time Nyerere left the political arena in 1985.[8] Nevertheless, Nyerere's voluntary retirement in 1985 paved the way for political and economic reform that has had major implications for the country. Tanzania has progressively moved away from its socialist experimentation to embrace both economic and political liberalism.

This chapter evaluates the impact and depth of this process of democratization in Tanzania with regard to issues of governance and political representation, freedom of the mass media, human rights and religious freedom, as well as economic freedom and human development. Utilizing the status of democracy index approach,[9] the chapter argues that though much has been achieved along the democratization trajectory in Tanzania, there is still a long way to go before the country reaches the democratic Promised Land.

Governance and Political Representation

Democracy as a form of political organization has never been attained in its pure form across the space of time and place. Although the Greek city-states, especially Athens and Sparta, are presented as the democratic *sine qua non* where citizens gathered in the town square to deliberate over public affairs, the kind of democracy therein was exclusive. Only propertied men could participate in public affairs. Women, men without property, and slaves were excluded. Perhaps it is on account of this reality that Plato once quipped: "I thank God that I was born Greek, not barbarian, freeman not slave, man not woman, and above all that I was born in the days of Socrates."[10]

The notion of representation in governance institutions is central to the idea of democratic governance. The essence of representative government is a government by the will, interests, and aspirations of the governed. In other words, people have the right to choose their representatives to constitute government in free and fair elections. Ironically, however, although elections are the "workshop at which popular rule is constructed ... voting creates an irony since through it the electorate both exercises its mandate to govern itself and cedes this power to the elected leaders."[11] Against this background, the democratic right to a limited mandate becomes critical. This entails a cap on political tenure in office, and the need to renew or revoke the mandate of elected representatives at regular intervals.

In the case of Tanzania, attempts at instituting this form of government began in 1992. Between 1985 and 1992, the politics of Tanzania were dominated by CCM, and prior to 1985, by Mwalimu Julius Nyerere. Although elections were held regularly between 1961 and 1992, these were less democratic to the extent that there was no competition between political parties,

nor was the president of CCM (the sole political party), ever challenged at
the electoral poll. CCM adherents dominated the politics of the country, and
anyone who did not adhere to the party line was marginalized. Universal suffrage was observed to the extent that anyone age eighteen years and above,
man or woman, had the right to vote as long as they registered to do so.
However, such voters did not have alternative choices in terms of competing
political alternatives and chief executive contenders. Their choice was cir-
cumscribed to a self-selecting group of CCM members at the legislative level,
and to a plebiscitary exercise at the presidential level. The only restriction
since 1992 is that for a political party to be registered, it must not be formed
on religious, ethnic, or regional bases and cannot oppose the union of Zanzibar and the mainland.

What has been achieved in the political culture of governance and representation in Tanzania since the onset of the process of democratization in
Tanzania? The first major breakthrough has been the institution of multiparty politics in the country. As of January 2011, six political parties were represented in Tanzania's Bunge (parliament) as a result of the 2010 general
elections (see Table 1 below), compared to only one between 1965 and 1995.
The parties represented in Bunge included Chama Cha Mapinduzi (CCM),
Chama Cha Demokrasia na Maendeleo (CHADEMA) [Party for Democracy
and Development], Civic United Front (CUF), National Convention for Construction and Reform (NCCR-Mageuzi), Tanzania Labour Party (TLP), and
United Democratic Party (UDP). Indeed, since the first multiparty elections
in 1995, the Tanzania legislature has been composed of at least five political
parties despite the dominance of the ruling party, CCM, as demonstrated in
Table 1.

Table 1. Proportion of Party Representation in Tanzanian Bunge, 1995–2010

PARTY	1995	2000	2005	2010
CCM	79.5%	87.0%	86.0%	75.2%
CHADEMA	1.5%	1.8%	3.6%	12.8%
CUF	10.4%	7.5%	9.8%	9.9%
NCCR-M	7.1%	0.4%	—	1.2%
TLP	—	1.8%	0.3%	0.3%
UDP	1.5%	1.4%	0.3%	0.3%
TOTAL	100%	100%	100%	100%

Source: Calculated from Tanzania National Election Commission figures.

Second is the fact that to a great extent, the free election of the head of state and members of the national legislature—the Bunge—has been instituted, and is the reality of contemporary Tanzanian politics. In this regard, Tanzania seems to have seamlessly transitioned into the political culture of a limited mandate for the chief executive of state in such a way that executive power passes from a Christian to a Muslim and vice versa—"the Christian" Nyerere handed over power to "the Muslim" Ali Hassan Mwinyi in 1985, who, in turn, gave way to the Christian Benjamin Mkapa in 1995, with the latter retiring in 2005 and handing over to the Muslim Jakaya Mrisho Kikwete. This, coupled with the freedom to form and join political parties, has tremendously supplemented the universal adult suffrage practiced since the one-party state. Tanzania is firmly on the road to democratic governance and responsive political representation. Third, with the increasing vibrancy of parliamentary debates in the multiparty political dispensation, democratization has signaled the end of parliament's role as the committee of CCM's Annual Conference. This was the case during the single party period, where its role was to confirm the decisions of the party's National Executive Committee.[12]

The downside to the process of democratization in Tanzania is that in spite of the fact that the new multiparty political dispensation has opened up political space and enhanced political debate and competitive electoral politics, CCM remains so dominant that the other political parties count for very little in terms of representation and impacting the governing process. Indeed, it could be argued that Tanzania is a multiparty system in name only. As shown in Table 1 on the previous page, the party enjoyed an unassailable majority of 75 percent of legislative seats following the 2010 elections, from 86 percent, 87 percent, and 80 percent following the 2005, 2000, and 1995 elections, respectively. CCM's predominance is further illustrated by its run-away victories in presidential elections, especially in mainland Tanzania. In the first multiparty elections of 1995, the party's Benjamin Mkapa won by 62 percent of the votes, increasing the tally to 72 percent in 2000. In 2005, the party's Jakaya Kikwete swept the election with 80 percent of the votes. However, in 2010, Kikwete's margin of victory dropped to 63 percent, signaling increasing competitiveness of the presidential contest (see Table 2 on the following page).

The predominance of CCM in Tanzania's political process is a function of a number of factors. First is the advantage of perennial incumbency of the party, which has enabled it to construct and maintain an elaborate and powerful bureaucratic network from the national level down through the regional, and district to the cell levels, hence its popularity and name recognition. Conversely, the new political parties remain largely unknown at the lower levels. Second, and as a corollary to the first factor, is CCM's control of the vast

Table 2. Share of Presidential Votes by Party in Tanzania, 1995–2010

PARTY	1995	2000	2005	2010
CCM	61.8%	71.7%	80.3%	62.8%
CUF	6.4%	16.3%	11.7%	8.3%
NCCR-M	27.8%	7.8%	0.5%	0.3%
UDP	4.0%	4.2%	0.3%	—
CHADEMA	—	—	5.9%	27.1%
TLP	—	—	0.7%	—
APPT	—	—	0.2%	1.2%
NLD	—	—	0.2%	—
TOTAL	100%	100%	100%	100%

Source: Calculated from Tanzania National Election Commission figures.

human, financial, and material resources in a conjuncture in which there is no difference between the ruling party and the government. Deployment of such enormous resources during electoral contests greatly advantages the ruling party vis-à-vis the opposition. Third, it could be argued that CCM benefits from the popular legacy of Mwalimu Julius Nyerere, the selfless and conscientious founding president of the country who wielded the 120 plus ethnic groups into a wholesome national identity.

The fourth factor is the lack of difference in the ideologies, or organizing principles, of the new parties compared to CCM. All the parties tend to espouse the same neoliberal policy framework recommended by the international financial institutions and hence they do not constitute an effective alternative to CCM. Against this background, the most intense electoral contests are to be found in the nomination of CCM candidates rather than in the general election.[13]

Finally, the fifth factor is the question of corruption. As Freedom House notes, corruption remains a serious problem in Tanzania, although the government has taken some steps to address it, including the development of a national anticorruption action plan.[14] Tanzania was ranked 93 out of 163 countries surveyed in Transparency International's 2006 Corruption Perceptions Index.[15] The country's High Court in 2006 ruled in favor of legal rights organizations that had challenged the formerly officially sanctioned practice of takrima (provision of free goods to voters by candidates) during election campaigns. In recognition of this malady, President Kikwete has stated that the government plans to strengthen the powers of the Prevention of Corruption Bureau, improve guidelines for concluding contracts, and reexamine procedures for procuring public goods.[16]

Freedom of the Mass Media

One of the key attributes of a democratic culture is the existence of alternative sources of news and information. Accordingly, freedom of the press is critical. During the single-party era in Tanzania (as elsewhere in Africa), such channels of political communication were tightly controlled by the state. Only one radio station existed—Radio Tanzania (Dar es Salaam and Zanzibar) and one television station—Zanzibar Television, in addition to three daily newspapers—*Daily News/Sunday News, Uhuru,* and *Mzalendo.* The latter two newspapers were owned by CCM, while the rest of the media were state owned. The press essentially served the propagandist purposes of the state as anyone expressing alternative views risked detention or deportation from their regions.[17]

Since the advent of democratization, media outlets have proliferated in Tanzania. These include 47 FM radio stations, 537 registered newspapers, and a dozen television stations. Fifty of the newspapers are regular, including eighteen dailies. The number of journalists has increased from roughly 230 in 1991 to more than 4,000 in 2008. Nevertheless, only four radio stations have a national reach, state-run Radio Tanzania and privately owned Radio One, Radio Free Africa, and Radio Uhuru. All these are viewed as sympathetic to the ruling CCM. The government reportedly continues to withhold advertising from critical newspapers, and those that report favorably on the opposition. Additionally, taxes on the media remain high despite presidential campaign promises that they would be reduced. Private firms keen to remain on good terms with the government allegedly follow suit, thus making it difficult for critical media outlets to remain financially viable. Nonetheless, even though the government occasionally pressures media outlets to suppress unfavorable stories, independent media outlets like *ThisDay* and even some state-owned newspapers regularly criticize official policies.[18]

As an indicator of increased media freedom, several independent media organizations have emerged to protect journalists in the course of carrying out their duties and also to enhance adherence to professional ethics by the media.[19] These include the Tanzania Journalists Association (TAJA) that takes care of the interests of journalists; the Association of Journalists and Media Workers (AJM) that broadly caters for all persons associated with journalism, the Tanzania Media Women Association (TAMWA) that brings together women journalists in the hitherto male-dominated profession (but has increasingly sought to address gender issues more broadly), Journalism for Environment in Tanzania (JET), which is for journalists who write or report on environmental concerns, the Tanzania Photographers' Association (TPA), the Freelance Journalists Association (FJA), and the Tanzania Sports Writers' Association (TASWA). In addition to such organizations formed through the initiatives of media workers, it is significant that international media organizations have also established chapters in Tanzania. An example is the Media Institute of Southern Africa (MISA). Its role is to facilitate and coordinate the development of genuinely free and pluralist media in southern Africa by helping to train media workers; strengthening the institutional capacity of media organizations through technical and financial support; and campaigning for media freedom in the region.[20] The activities of such international organizations in hitherto "closed" Tanzania contribute to the expansion of the frontiers of press freedom even though this is mainly limited to the urban areas.

The downside to media freedom, however, is that although the Constitution of the Republic of Tanzania provides for freedom of speech, it does not specifically guarantee freedom of the press. For instance, the establishment of the Media Council of Tanzania in 1995 to register journalists and regulate the press was an attempt to curb the freedom of the press. Similarly, the setting up of the Information Services Department (ISD) to distribute all news on the government is similarly a way of censoring the kind of government information that can be availed to the public. Indeed, in the mid-1990s, the government resorted to draconian laws and legal instruments of the one-party state to curb increasing media criticism of the state. These included the Media Professions Act (1994), the News Agency Act (1976), the Newspaper Act (1976), the National Security Act, and some sections of the Penal Code, to ban newspapers like *Cheka, Michapo, Rafiki, Mwanamama,* and *Dira.* Other papers were also threatened with the ban, such as *Tazama, Mwananchi, Majira,* and *The Express.*[21] In the electronic media, the government in Dar es Salaam adopted the strategy of allocating broadcast licenses preferentially, ensuring that broadcasters offered largely pro-government positions.[22]

Indeed, government crackdowns are permitted under the National Security Act, the Official Secrets Act, and the Restricted Areas Act on the basis of which, for instance, a dozen mainstream journalists were arrested briefly in August 2002 presumably to prevent the reporting of ethnic clashes in northern Tanzania.[23] Even the journalists who reported on the inadequate police response to a mine disaster in Arusha were detained, along with their colleagues who alleged an overreaction on the part of the police to a riot in Dar es Salaam.[24] This trend of harassing and intimidating journalists continued into 2005. On January 27, 2005, the editor of *Mtanzania Jumapili,* Badra Masoud, was summoned before the Registrar of Newspapers to explain a story that had exposed the use of money by government officials to buy support for their presidential bids in the 2005 general election.[25] In the same month, government officials subjected a reporter with *Mwananchi* newspaper in Zanzibar, Salma Said, to harassment in an effort to frustrate and silence her. Salma had been a reporter for *Dira* newspaper that was banned for "turning people against the government." Along with many other journalists, Salma was excluded from government functions, and forbidden from reporting on matters pertaining to the House of Representatives in Zanzibar without any reason.[26] In fact, media freedom rights in Zanzibar are much more constrained than is the case on the mainland. The 2001 media reforms that paved the way for media liberalization in Tanzania were not implemented in Zanzibar. Consequently, private newspapers and broadcasters are not permitted in Zanzibar, though most islanders receive mainland broadcasts and read the mainland press. The Zanzibari government often reacts to media criticism by accusing the press of being a "threat to national unity." In 2005, it banned the leading columnist Jabir Idrissa. The weekly newspaper *Dira* was banned in November 2003, with no reason provided until April 2006, when the government defended its decision on the grounds that the paper had been "publishing articles bent on destabilizing the unity and solidarity" of Zanzibar.[27]

Human Rights and Religious Freedom

Many of the arguments for human rights in democratization literature focus on political freedoms and civil liberties. In addition to press freedom discussed above, these include the freedoms of association, assembly, and religion. In the case of Tanzania, available evidence indicates that since the advent of democratization and the end of one-party rule in the country, constitutional protections for political rights and civil liberties are generally, but not always, respected. Only officially registered political parties are allowed to hold political rallies. Although many nongovernmental organizations (NGOs) are active, and some do influence the policy process in some cases, the government has managed to rein in and constrain their operations to a great extent. This reality manifests itself in the NGO Act legislated in 2002 that requires compulsory registration of all NGOs and provides for criminal sanctions, lack of appeal to the courts, alignment of NGO activities with government plans, and prohibition of national networks and coalitions of NGOs. This legal provision is inconsistent with other legislation, including the Tanzanian Constitution, the Universal Declaration of Human Rights, and the International Covenant on Civil and Political Rights.

Similarly, in spite of the fact that women's rights are guaranteed by the constitution and other corresponding statutes, the same laws are not uniformly guaranteed and protected across the divides between rural and urban terrains, formally and informally educated women, and the social spaces of religion and culture. For instance, President Jakaya Kikwete was hailed for elevating women to high profile cabinet positions, including ministers of finance and foreign affairs, following his election in 2005. Indeed, his foreign affairs minister, Ms. Asha-Rose Migiro, was tapped in January 2007 to become the UN Deputy Secretary-General, becoming only the third person and second woman in the history of the organization to be appointed to the position.[28] In spite of this rare achievement for Ms. Migiro, Tanzania is replete with traditional and Islamic customs and laws that discriminate against women. This is especially true in rural areas on the mainland, and on the islands of Pemba and Zanzibar. Generally, women have fewer educational and economic opportunities, as illustrated by the literacy rate of 77 percent for men as compared to 62 percent for women. Domestic violence against women in Tanzania is common, but is rarely prosecuted. More critical is the case of forced marriages, especially among the country's coastal populations and on the islands where the population is over 95 percent Muslim. Civil society activism for laws to bar such forced marriages are yet to bear fruit.

In contrast, as Freedom House notes,[29] freedom of religion is generally respected in Tanzania, and relations between the various faiths are peaceful for the most part. However, since the introduction of multiparty politics, a religious-based culture of political violence has emerged and significantly increased with each election cycle. These tensions resulted in the passage of the Mufti Law in 2001 by the Zanzibari government. The law provides for the island government to appoint a Mufti [an Islamic religious jurist who interprets Islamic law] to oversee Muslim organizations. Whereas the intent of the law is to ensure that such organizations operate within the rubric of their religious affiliation, critics of the same contend that the legal provision is permissive of too much governmental interference in the religious sphere, and thus is tantamount to violation of religious freedom.

Overall, because of the Tanzanian government's fear of its political opposition, it has sought to constrain the formation and operation of civil society organizations. One such constraint takes the form of cumbersome registration procedures, particularly for NGOs. The process involves different amounts of bureaucracy, waiting periods (some of up to two years), and likelihoods of being turned down. The latter is particularly the case if the mission or target group of the NGO parallels those of existing state or ruling party structures.[30] Additionally, the government occasionally bars NGOs from participating in activities it feels are "too politically sensitive" for its own survival. Its conflictual relationship with *Baraza la Wanawake Tanzania* (BAWATA) [Tanzania Women's Council] is a good illustration. In the run-up to the 1995 general elections, BAWATA initiated a strong civic education campaign to sensitize women and the general public about multiparty democracy that was new in the country, a move that the ruling CCM did not particularly like. Consequently, the party started to intimidate leaders of the organization for sensitizing the people, especially women, during the electioneering period; some of whom received death threats for their civic activities. When CCM sailed through the elections, relatives of BAWATA leaders were demoted from their government jobs.[31] Then, in January 1997, BAWATA was deregistered and banned by the government for "acting like a political party." However, the organization won a court appeal against its deregistration and against the constitutionality of the law that the government used to deregister it. Nevertheless, the government's determination to cripple BAWATA saw it convert the deregistration into suspension of its activities, which was now legal.[32] Though BAWATA subsequently resumed operation, it faced the pressure to avoid stepping into areas that could be deemed "political" by the state.[33]

Economic Freedom and Human Development

In terms of human development, Tanzania is among the least developed countries in the world. The 2010 United Nations Human Development Report ranked Tanzania 148th of 169 countries with available data for rankings, as shown in Table 3 on the following page. Tanzania's Human Development Index (HDI) of 0.398 is far below the world average as compared to Norway's number one rate of 0.938. It is even below other African countries such as Gabon at 0.648, Botswana at 0.633 and Kenya at 0.470 (Table 3). Similarly, according to the 2009 UN Development Report, Tanzania had a life expectancy of 52.5, which was better than neighboring Uganda's 51.5, but much lower than the world average at 67.2 years. Furthermore, it was lower than Kenya's 54.1 and Senegal's 63.1, continental sub-Saharan Africa's best.[34] In the same vein, Tanzania has an adult literacy rate of 72 percent and is ranked 138th in the world. This rate is below Kenya's and Uganda's, both of which are tied at the position of 135 with literacy rates of 74 percent. In sub-Saharan Africa, Zimbabwe is ranked tops at the 91 percent adult literacy rate, and is ranked 91st in the world. The world's number one country is Georgia, with a 100 percent adult literacy rate.[35]

According to the 2009 indices, Tanzania's economic freedom score is 58.3, making its economy the 93rd freest in the world.[36] This score illustrates that the country has improved over time, and currently places 11th out of the 46 sub-Saharan African countries so ranked. This eventuality has been a result of Tanzania's economic reform efforts and implementation of poverty reduction strategies. The economy has achieved an annual growth rate of seven percent since 2000, yielding improvements in various social and human development

Table 3. Tanzania's HDI in Comparative Perspective

COUNTRY	HDI	WORLD RANK
Norway	0.938	1
Gabon	0.648	93
Botswana	0.633	98
South Africa	0.597	110
Kenya	0.470	128
Ghana	0.467	130
Nigeria	0.423	142
Uganda	0.422	143
Tanzania	0.398	148

Source: Excerpted from the 2010 UN Human Development Report.

indicators. Remarkably, according to Freedom House,[37] Tanzania scores above the world average in fiscal freedom, investment freedom, and government size. Foreign and domestic investors receive equal treatment, although the main deterrents include poor infrastructure, government control, and corruption. Nevertheless, despite the country's remarkable improvement in economic terms, its economic freedom score remains below the world average.

Conclusion

In spite of the apparent back and forth initiatives in the liberalization of political and economic space in Tanzania, substantial gains have been achieved politically, socially, and economically relative to the one-party era. It is on the basis of these gains that the balance of scales falls decidedly on the side of increased freedom and democracy. However, the challenge that remains is how to sustain and improve on the gains made so far. One of the major impediments to democratization and the rule of law is apparently the impunity of official corruption. On the positive side, the anti-corruption bill passed in April 2007, provides for the creation of a board to coordinate and implement anti-graft efforts comprising of the police, the national intelligence service, and representatives from the private sector. These groups serve to further advance the frontiers of political and economic openness, assuming political will to implement the same.

On the downside, however, Tanzania faces one major democratic challenge. The country could be applauded for instituting the principle of limited mandate and sticking with the same. Accordingly, presidents serve two terms of five years, and retire with executive power passing from Christian to Muslim and vice versa, with each cycle since 1985 to 2010. Nevertheless, the challenge for democratic consolidation lies in the transfer of power from one political party to another. To the extent that CCM remains unchallenged, Tanzania is a long way from institutionalizing democratic governance. The challenge posed by the opposing political parties is merely token at best, and meaningless for the most part. On the Zanzibar and Pemba islands, where competition between the CCM and CUF has remained stiff since the reintroduction of multiparty politics in 1995, electoral malpractice, political violence, and intimidation have become the order of the day in every electoral cycle. These issues are marring the legacy of Nyerere, and the country where being Tanzanian was superior to being a Muslim or Christian, a Mchagga or Mhehe, or Mzanaki or Nyamwezi.

Namibia

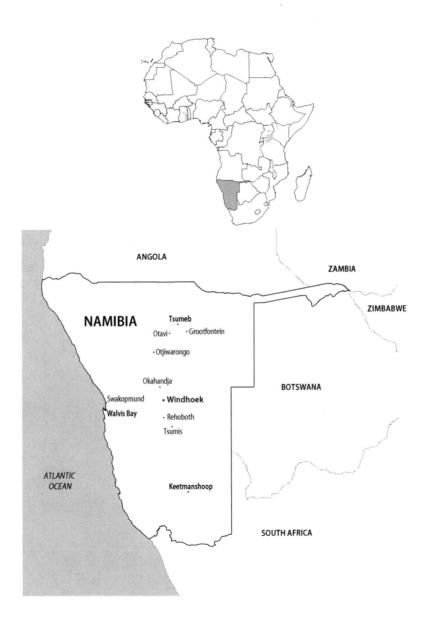

ANGOLA

ZAMBIA

ZIMBABWE

NAMIBIA   Tsumeb·

Otavi·   ·Grootfontein

·Otjiwarongo

Okahandja

·

Swakopmund   · Windhoek

Walvis Bay

· Rehoboth

Tsumis

BOTSWANA

ATLANTIC
OCEAN

Keetmanshoop

·

SOUTH AFRICA

Chapter 11

Namibia: A Successful Parliamentary Democracy

M. Fenyo

While all African countries boast of unique features, Namibia is probably more unique than most. Although a single political party has dominated its government since independence, Namibia has a rather successful parliamentary democracy. However, its wealth is the most unevenly distributed of any country in Africa, and perhaps even in the world. This introduction provides an account of the historical background that may help explain these paradoxes. A fairly elaborate presentation of its progressive and democratic constitution is followed by details regarding the application of constitutional laws, ownership of the means of production, services, education, health, and civil and human rights. Illustrations regarding Namibian reality are based on a range of publications in the social sciences and some personal reminiscences, affording the reader the insight that will allow them to assess the prospects of true democracy and social justice.

There are various attempts to rank African countries with one indicator or another. For instance, according to *The Economist* and the "Ibrahim Index of African Governance," a "new league table," dating from 2010, ranks Namibia among the "winners" when it comes to "governance;" it is ranked number 6. The Ibrahim Foundation, the leader in the assessment of governance, ranks African countries as to quality of services along 57 criteria. While Namibia has slid back somewhat in "safety and rule of law" and "participation and human rights," it has made further progress under the heading "improvement of sustainable development" and "decrease in the rate of inflation." Thus, Namibia ranks far above most African countries, but somewhat below the island-nations of the Indian Ocean, Botswana, and South Africa.[1]

According to the 2008 "World Democracy Audit," Namibia ranks 43rd overall, 39th in terms of freedom of the press, and 44th with regard to the "corruption index."[2] Namibia is judged less corrupt than the world average, but somewhat more corrupt than either Botswana or South Africa. Incidentally, Finland is ranked number one under all three headings, while the United States is ranked 15th under the heading "democracy."

Of course, there can be no absolute consensus when it comes to ranking countries according to whatever criterion, least of all when the dimension discussed is as vague and fluid as "democracy." Rather than impose a definition chosen by myself, I felt it might be more productive to present and examine the facts that appear relevant to a range of definitions, allow the reader and analyst to reach their own conclusions, and return to the subject of criteria at the end.

The Past

By taking public transportation (a small station-wagon), from Ovamboland in the North, to Windhoek, the capital, I was able to experience Namibian democracy at the grassroots level. There were thirteen of us passengers, not counting the driver, and we were all adults. I was sitting on someone's knee, and someone was sitting on mine. At times, I felt the panic of claustrophobia, but I was probably the only one. Everyone was considerate, but no one gave me special consideration, even though I was obviously a foreigner, my complexion was much lighter, I could not speak Ovishambo (which I assumed to be the language spoken by the others), and I was somewhat better dressed.

On another occasion, as I finished my lunch and was about to leave the restaurant, I was offered a ride by the leader of the party sitting at the next table. As it turned out, the person who offered me the ride was a minister in the cabinet of Sam Nujoma, who happened to be a rather attractive young lady. We boarded a LandRover; there were no limousines and no security force escorting us. The party was heading north, to attend the ceremony inaugurating a new high school. This time, I obviously owed the honor to the fact that I was a foreigner, and the space in the Landrover was somewhat less cramped than during my previous trip by "public" transportation. Still, I had to share the seat with the lady minister and a gentleman from the Netherlands. The minister, I gathered, was a former freedom fighter who, at some point, managed to find refuge in northern Europe. I was invited to join the group. Thus, I became part of the official delegation, enjoying the minister's hospitality and the hospitality of her hosts at the headquarters of the school district. Once again, I was experiencing Namibian democracy, but as a privileged person.

Thus, democracy, at least in the Namibian context, has several meanings. In addition to the political democracy advocated by American leaders and diplomats, there is democracy at the grassroots, extending far back in history. In fact, Western social scientists tend to refer to this period, when customs and social institutions were formed, as "prehistory." If they are Marxist (as several Namibian leaders claimed to be at one time), they may label this type of democracy "primitive communism." If they are African, they may refer to it as "African socialism." Regardless of the label, it can take many different forms. As the anecdotes above illustrate, democracy can mean hospitality, civility, kindness, consideration, tolerance, or even privileges. It can also mean egalitarianism and humanism. I am sure it can manifest itself in other ways as well.[3]

Eurocentric historians date the beginnings of African history—presumably making allowance for the priority of the Nile Valley civilization—from the arrival of Europeans; sometimes, however reluctantly, they date it from the arrival of Islam. Europeans did not penetrate into Namibia until the eighteenth century, perhaps because of the inhospitable Namibian desert.[4] Unfortunately, the arrival of Europeans also signified an end to democratic and communitarian traditions. In Western and Central Africa, the transatlantic trade involving European naval powers entailed endless warfare, the domination or exploitation of one group by another, and the enslavement of millions. While American historians do not always acknowledge it, there is an inherent contradiction between slavery and democracy.

"Namibia is one of Africa's least known countries," wrote Peter Katjavivi, an Oxford-trained historian, eventually appointed President of the University of Namibia.[5] Indeed, he is one of the few "insiders" to give a rather detailed account of certain aspects of the Namibian past. The present area of Namibia was occupied for thousands of years by Bushmen (San) and the Nama, who speak Khoisan languages. Bushmen rock paintings in the Kalahari Desert have been dated to as early as 28,000 years ago. The Herero, arriving in the sixteenth century, gradually moved toward the central region of Namibia, from Windhoek up to Otavi.[6] Nama groups, the Herero, and others were often in conflict over extremely scarce resources, such as water, but the conflicts were not always along ethnic lines.[7] Communitarian or democratic as African inhabitants and settlers may have been, Katjavivi—quoting Clarence-Smith—writes of the emergence of a feudal class structure in the nineteenth century, among the Herero and others, perhaps under the impact of the European presence.

Bantu kingdoms, particularly the Ovambo, occupied the northern third of the country, which was suitable for farming. They were to form the bulk of the freedom fighters who were fighting for decolonization, and against apartheid and the South African occupation. Now they represent about half of the total population of the country. Surprisingly, their diet, their main crops are corn (maize), beans, peanuts—relatively new arrivals from the Western Hemisphere.

The Germans moved in gradually, following the arrival of European missionaries and merchants. Although the first missionaries were English, the ones who left a truly lasting impression on the land were members of the Rhenish Lutheran Mission, who spoke German[8] and whose mission was to "civilize." Upon the demise of Otto von Bismarck, the recently united German Reich (the "Second") decided to participate in the scramble for Africa in order to find its "place in the sun." Except for the area around Walvis Bay, colonized by the British, present-day Namibia was claimed by Germany. Although the German invasion started in the nineteenth century, the discovery of diamonds in 1908 gave the German government and merchants an additional incentive.

Although the Germans at first seemed inclined to negotiate with the Herero and Nama leaders, even creating a buffer zone between the two, conflict eventually erupted, even before the discovery of diamonds.[9] Thus, in Südwestafrika as elsewhere, the Europeans encountered resistance, particularly from the Herero and Nama nations, who resented the expropriation of their land and cattle.[10] The Herero leader, Samuel Maharero, declared war in January 1904, provoked by the murder of ten Hereros kept in a German jail.[11] The German response to resistance was more brutal than anything ever experienced in Africa before, or even elsewhere during the period of imperialism (viz. the Sepoy "mutiny" in India and the abuse suffered by the people of the Congo during the administration of the Belgian ruler). Although the war was essentially over by 1905, guerrilla warfare and the extermination of the natives continued. While the slaughter of the Mahdi's army at Omdurman and elsewhere was an act of terror, and the ten million or so victims of King Leopold's regime in the "free" Congo was piecemeal murder, the genocide of the Herero was well organized, concentrated, and systematic. Seventy-five to 90 percent of the Herero population, and almost 50 percent of the Nama were exterminated between 1904 and 1907. Atrocities were also committed against occasional German "allies" such as the Bushmen. Apparently, the German military had orders to shoot "every Bushman that did not stand still when ordered to do so."[12] Although the perpetrators could not have known, it was a dress rehearsal for the Holocaust 40 years later.

There has been some talk in recent years about compensation to the Herero on the part of Germany, using the model of compensation for the Jewish victims of the Shoah during World War II. The Namibian government has made no concrete demands, and no concrete offers were specified by the Germans. It should be noted that the Herero and Nama were not the first to resist. In their outstanding study of the Bushmen, *The Bushman Myth*, Robert Gordon and Stuart Sholto-Douglas discuss Upingtonia, a country founded by Boer settlers trekking in from the Transvaal in 1885. By 1887, the white settlers had been killed or chased away by Bushmen who resented the white's attempt to take over the copper mining operations. This was the first Namibian war of liberation.

The German regime was short-lived, lasting only until World War I. When the British defeated the German *Schutztruppe* in July 1915. South Africa soon took over, on behalf of the British, and later as a "mandate," on behalf of the League of Nations. According to Article 2 of the Mandate, "The Mandatory shall promote to the utmost the material and moral well-being and the social progress of the inhabitants of the territory subject to the present Mandate."[13] This mandate was not taken seriously by the "Mandatory." Instead, a policy of divide and rule was applied. There were domestic servants, and even some clerks and teachers, who were relatively privileged. Many came from among the so-called Coloreds (Coloureds) and Rehobothers (also known as Basters).[14] The "contract" workers from the North, presumably Oshivambo-speakers working the mines, railways, and fisheries, were the most exploited. The railroad lines, incidentally, built by Africans commandeered by the colonial power, served the same purpose as elsewhere in Africa: to facilitate the extraction, exploitation, and export of the country's mineral resources.[15] People were forced into contract work by the imposition of taxes—"the poll tax, the hut tax, the grazing tax, and the tax on hunting dogs."[16] Strikes were fairly common in the period between 1915 and 1959.[17] In December 1959, during the "Windhoek massacre," some 13 strikers (or demonstrators) were killed, and fifty-two wounded in a confrontation with the South African police.[18] Although the strikes were illegal, they served to enhance a feeling of solidarity, maybe even a sense of nationhood.

The United Negro Improvement Association (UNIA) was another influential Black organization. Founded in faraway Jamaica by Marcus Garvey in 1914, it established a branch in Namibia in 1921, calling for black unity and a black administration.[19] It survived even as the UNIA lost much of its influence elsewhere. Also influential was the African Methodist Episcopal (AME) church, originally founded in the United States. The AME, and even the black members of the Lutheran church, often joined the patriotic movement.

The origins of the South West Africa Progressive Organization (SWAPO) can be traced to South Africa, where a group of Namibian students who were closely linked to South African organizations (such as the African National Congress), were able to operate.[20] During the armed struggle, SWAPO was often described, by both friend and foe as a Marxist organization, or even "a Marxist-Leninist organization," by at least one person trained in Marxist theory.[21] In 1964, SWAPO began to infiltrate the "remote" parts of northern Namibia, and in 1966, launched its "terror campaign" in Ovamboland near the Angolan border.[22] In 1973, both the Organization of African Unity and the United Nations recognized SWAPO as the "sole and authentic representative of the people of Namibia."[23] In 1965, SWAPO was fully endorsed by the OAU.

As the apartheid regime in South Africa became formal, rigid, and increasingly discriminatory in the 1960s and 1970s, Namibians were not spared. Although the United Nations, inheriting the resolutions of the League of Nations, enjoined the government of South Africa to prepare South West Africa for independence, these instructions were effectively circumvented. The Ovamboland People's Organization was formed in Windhoek in 1959, and Sam Nujoma was elected its leader.[24] The first armed clash between SWAPO fighters and the South African army took place in August 1966.[25]

The Terrorism Act of 1967 was directed at the patriots, prompted primarily by Namibian resistance. In 1967–68, it led to the show trials against 37 SWAPO leaders and rank and file in Pretoria. Twenty were sentenced to life in prison and detained at Robben Island (along with Nelson Mandela and other famous patriots from the South).[26] As Herman Toivo ja Toivo reminded the court in a speech from the dock, "David slew Goliath because he had right on his side...."[27]

The northern part of Namibia was declared a native reserve, in accordance with the recommendation of the Odendaal commission in 1962. The Odendaal report was issued two years later,[28] drawing clear demarcation lines between "white areas" and "homelands." The indigenous authorities administering the area preserved some of the traditional communal rights. These "communal areas" included much of the agriculturally productive land in the North belonging to the Ovambo, but also some of the lands of the Kavango, Bushmen, the Kaokoveld, the land of the Damara, the Nama, and so forth.[29] The areas to the south of this district were separated by what was called the "police line" or "veterinary cordon fence." The demarcation was justified on the grounds that cattle from the north, exposed to the tse-tse fly, should not be allowed to contaminate cattle in the south, which were owned almost exclusively by white ranchers.[30]

In 1975, when Angola obtained a precarious victory in its fight for independence, SWAPO was allowed to establish bases on Angolan territory and the struggle for the independence of Namibia intensified. In 1978, the United Nations adopted Security Council Resolution 435 for settling the Namibian problem. The South African government, disregarding some of its commitments, sponsored elections in Namibia unilaterally; these were boycotted by SWAPO and some other pro-independence groups and the liberation struggle continued. SWAPO had up to 18,000 men under arms at one point, and was capable of launching raids into Namibia with 800 men at a time.[31] South African forces—mostly black troops—penetrated into Angolan territory in 1978, killing nearly one thousand Namibian refugees[32] hoping to keep the struggle from spilling over into Namibia or South Africa itself. They met with effective Angolan resistance, reinforced by a sizable Cuban expeditionary force. While the South Africans represented an apartheid regime, the Cubans participated on the principle of internationalist solidarity.

The battle of Cuito Cuanavale in Angola is considered a turning point in the struggle. Here, the South African forces withdrew, after an exchange of artillery fire. An international agreement led to the withdrawal of all foreign forces, including the Cubans. The fighting continued with considerable casualties until 1989. The ensuing elections in Namibia resulted in a victory for SWAPO, which garnered 57 percent of the popular vote, while the Democratic Turnhalle Alliance—the opposition party—received 29 percent.[33]

Little has changed since independence. The situation is complicated by the fact that the Herero have historical claims on much of the land south of the line. The survivors did not push their claims until recently, because they were in alliance with the DTA party (Deutsche Turnhalle), which is dominated by farmers of German descent. That alliance, however, broke down in 2004,[34] and the Herero, encouraged in part by Robert Mugabe's Black assertiveness in Zimbabwe, have become more vocal, demanding compensation for the atrocities suffered at the beginning of the twentieth century.

Democracy on Paper

The Namibian Constitution has been highly praised internationally. Indeed, it incorporates some of the language of the Constitution of the United States, including the phrase "life, liberty, and the pursuit of happiness." It also incorporates ideas that can be traced to the French Revolution, including the phrase "liberté, égalité, fraternité." There are, however, several progressive features added. One of these would be the repeated appeal to "democracy." As might be expected, powers are divided among three branches—legislative, executive, and judicial. Enumerated below are some of the most basic provisions and salient features of this constitution, beginning with the Preamble.

The Preamble states:

> "Whereas recognition of the inherent dignity and of the equal and inalienable rights of all members of the human family is indispensable for freedom, justice, and peace;
> Whereas the said rights include the right of the individual to life, liberty, and the pursuit of happiness, regardless of race, color, ethnic origin, sex, religion, creed, or social or economic status;
> Whereas the said rights are most effectively maintained and protected in a democratic society, where the government is responsible to freely

elect representatives of the people, operating under a sovereign constitution and a free and independent judiciary;

Whereas these rights have for so long been denied to the people of Namibia by colonialism, racism, and apartheid;

Whereas we the people of Namibia:

Have finally emerged victorious in our struggle against colonialism, racism, and apartheid;

are determined to adopt a Constitution which expresses for our children and ourselves a resolve to cherish and to protect the gains of our long struggle;

desire to promote amongst all of us the dignity of the individual and the unity and integrity of the Namibian nation among and in association with the nations of the world;

will strive to achieve national reconciliation and to foster peace, unity, and common loyalty to a single state;

committed to these principles, have resolved to constitute the Republic of Namibia as a sovereign, secular, democratic, and unitary State securing to all our citizens justice, liberty, equality, and fraternity;

Now, therefore, we the people of Namibia accept and adopt the Constitution as the fundamental law of our Sovereign and Independent Republic."

Namibia has a parliamentary government, and the legislative is made up of the National Assembly and National Council. The executive includes both a president and a prime minister.

Article 1 of the constitution states, "The Republic of Namibia is hereby established as a sovereign, secular, democratic, and unitary State founded upon the principles of democracy, the rule of law, and justice for all."[35] English is declared the official language (Article 3, 3), although other languages are permissible as languages of administration, legislation, and the courts, as well as media of instruction, if spoken "by a substantial component of the population."[36]

The "fundamental human rights and freedoms," listed in Articles 5 through 25, include life (no death penalty, although this seems to be contradicted by Article 47), liberty, and human dignity. Slavery and forced labor are explicitly banned. This bill of rights also stipulates equality before the law and freedom from discrimination, no arrest or detention without cause (habeas corpus). Even illegal immigrants have the right to consult lawyers. All persons have a right to a fair trial and other safeguards.[37] Persons are entitled "to the privacy of their homes."[38] Marriage and family are a basic right, not limited by "race, color, ethnic origin" etc., presumably as a reaction against previous laws banning mixed marriages.[39] Children under the age of 16 have basic rights as well; child labor is prohibited since children may not be employed under the age of 14. The right to acquire property is also guaranteed, but property may be expropriated in the public interest, in exchange for just compensation.[40] Justice, culture, and especially education are also identified as basic human rights.[41]

Article 21 enumerates the "fundamental freedoms." These include freedom of speech and of the press, freedom of thought and "conscience"; moreover, freedom of religion is stipulated separately, as are academic freedom, freedom of assembly and of association, including the freedom to join unions, withhold labor (strike), move freely in the country, settle in any part of the country, leave and return to Namibia, practice any profession, trade, or occupation.[42] Apartheid is specifically prohibited by Article 23.[43] The same article also provides for affirmative action — presumably hiring and employment practices favoring blacks — and the encouragement of women.[44] These freedoms are irrevocable, according to Article 24, even in times of emergency. A "competent Court shall have the right to adjudicate challenges."[45]

Articles 27 through 34 define the powers of the president. He or she is elected by direct, universal, and equal suffrage. The term of office is five years, and *for not more than two terms*.[46] The powers of the president are spelled out in terms similar to those of the president of the United States, including the right to appoint "ministers" (rather than "secretaries").

Articles 35 through 43 spell out the duties of the prime minister and the cabinet. Although the members of the cabinet are appointed by the president (from the National Assembly), the National Assembly may vote "no confidence" in any member of the cabinet, and the president is then obliged to terminate the appointment.[47] Thus, the cabinet ministers are answerable to Parliament as well.[48]

The functions of the National Assembly are spelled out in articles 44 through 67. The voters vote for parties, rather than candidates who are selected by the parties and placed on a list. Articles 68 through 77 deal with the National Council, which is comparable to the Senate of the United States Congress, even though Namibia is not described as a federation of states.

Articles 78 through 94 address the administration of justice. They specify three levels of courts, including the Supreme Court, a High court of Namibia, and the Lower Courts. The main function of the Supreme Court is to interpret, implement, and uphold the constitution.[49] The High Court has the same responsibilities with regard to the constitution as the Supreme Court, but it also hears appeals.[50] Judges may not be removed from office, except for "gross misconduct" or mental incompetence.[51] There are provisions for an Attorney General and a Prosecutor-General.[52]

Articles 89 through 94 explain the functions of the Ombudsman, which include the right to investigate complaints against government officials or agencies. Moreover, he or she has the duty "to investigate complaints concerning the over-utilization of living natural resources, the irrational exploitation of non-renewable resources, the degradation and destruction of ecosystems, and failure to protect the beauty and character of Namibia."[53] Presumably, one of the "living natural resources" the founders had in mind was wildlife, remembering that the elephant population was almost completely eradicated by the beginning of the twentieth century as Namibia inevitably became incorporated into the world capitalist system. Moreover, under paragraph (f), the Ombudsman has the duty to investigate "vigorously" all instances of suspected corruption.[54]

Articles 95 to 101 deal with "Principles of State Policy." Paragraph (a) of article 95 once again addresses the issue of "women's rights."[55] Paragraph (c) encourages the formation of independent trade (labor) unions. Other paragraphs refer to fair labor practices,[56] benefits for senior citizens and the unemployed, a living wage, a "decent standard of living," preserving the ecosystem; "in particular, the government shall provide measures against the dumping or recycling of foreign nuclear or toxic waste on Namibian territory."[57] Article 98 specifies the "Principles of Economic Order." These principles are described as a "mixed economy," allowing public and private ownership, cooperatives, joint public and private enterprise, and so forth.[58]

Articles 101 through 111 deal with regional and local government, but the number, names, or boundaries of the regions and local jurisdictions are not given. Articles 112, 113, and 114, deal with the Public Service Commission and the Security Commission. Articles 115 through 123 focus on "The Police and Defense Forces and the Prison Service." The following chapters (16, 17, 18, and 19) deal with Finance, the Central Bank, the National Planning Commission, the Coming into Force of the Constitution, and the Amendment of the Constitution. Amendments would require the approval of two-thirds of both the National Assembly and the National Council although, in some cases, a national referendum would be in order.[59]

Chapter 20 — Articles 133 through 143 — is titled "The Law in Force and Transitional Provisions." "Final Provisions" — Articles 144 through 148 — prescribe dates and definitions. These provisions apply mainly or exclusively to the short period of adoption of the Constitution and the beginning of its implementation.

The text of the Constitution is followed by a series of appendices termed "Schedules." Schedule 4 specifies the manner in which the 72 seats of the National Assembly will be allocated, and the number of seats allocated to each political party.[60]

The schedules are followed by the names on the list presented by each party, and presumably elected as members: 41 for SWAPO, 21 for the Democratic Turnhalle Alliance (DTA—largely, but not exclusively, with a white membership), four for the United Democratic Front of Namibia, three for the Aksie Christelik Nasionaal, one for the National Patriotic Front of Namibia, one for the Federal Convention of Namibia, and one for the Namibia National Front—for a total of 72.

The Namibian Constitution First Amendment Act of 1998 is called "Act to amend the Namibian Constitution so as to provide that the first president of Namibia may hold office as president for three terms, and to provide for incidental matters." This amendment was designed to amend article 134 by adding a "Sub-Article," and it was signed by the president on December 7, 1998. This amendment, and the ease with which it was adopted, might have become a major blot on the picture of Namibian democracy were it not for the fact that Sam Nujoma relinquished the office at the end of his third term.

Implementation of the Constitution

The general picture of Namibia that emerges from the description and analysis of facts is as follows:

Politics

A democratic milestone was achieved in November 2004, when elections resulted in a change in presidential leadership. There is no reason to believe that the elections were anything but fair. Yet, the change was not dramatic: Sam Nujoma passed presidential power over to Hifikepunye Pohamba, who belongs to the same political party.[61]

In 1990, the cabinet posts of the newly independent regime were occupied mostly by SWAPO leaders, some of who returned after long years of exile from Europe or from other African countries in the region. The civil service, by and large, was the one that had been installed by the South African apartheid regime. Although SWAPO leaders, and the Constitution itself, mention affirmative action, the country was lacking competent black professionals and administrators. The new ministers did not venture to fire the rank and file civil servant. Government employees were to be replaced gradually, by attrition, provided competent black persons could be found. Obviously, this was, and still is, a slow process, given the fact that the civil service is 60,000 to 70,000 strong; furthermore, the government is also committed to increasing efficiency.[62]

Most top level white civil servants stayed at their post instead of seeking refuge in South Africa, where the apartheid regime seemed entrenched in the early 1990s. The SWAPO regime did not push affirmative action. It is clear that solidarity with the African National Congress (ANC) and the anti-apartheid struggle in South Africa was a major consideration. The guiding principle being any move that might scare the white minority rulers from making concessions from surrendering political power in South Africa should be avoided, while all action that might reassure the white population was to be embraced.

Demographics

The total population of Namibia was estimated at around 2 million in the first decade of the twenty-first century (2.1 million by 2011). The country is sparsely and unevenly populated, with a density of approximately two persons per kilometer square. Apart from Windhoek, the capital, much of the population is concentrated on the subsistence farms in the agriculturally productive north, along a swath of land within 50 kilometers from the Angolan border.

According to the 2001 census, Windhoek had a population of 234,000, although other estimates indicate as low as 161,000 and as high as in excess of 300,000.[63] The trend in Namibia reflects the general trend on the continent: a steady influx of population from the countryside to the urban centers. Obviously, the figures vary according to what is included within the city limits. Much of the city appears modern and rather European. When my colleagues and I landed there on a study tour a few years ago, our first impression was that, if our object was to "get a taste of Africa," we had picked the wrong country and the wrong city. Culturally speaking, Windhoek does not have the appearance of an African city; the only aspect that marks it as African is the predominance of African features among its inhabitants. It has a good infrastructure, and is kept scrupulously clean. African-American scholars who had the privilege of receiving funds to travel to Namibia (included many who had never been to any part of the continent before), must have been disappointed to see so little that was "typically" African.

The picture changes if we venture away from the downtown. Windhoek has not overcome the segregation imposed upon it during the apartheid regime. Black, unskilled workers were brought in from the north of the country to provide security and an industrial proletariat in black townships. In 1959, they were forced to congregate in Katutura and other suburbs with a high population density and high rates of poverty. In fact, Katutura was regarded as a place where the residents would never feel at home: the word Katutura itself meaning "we do not live."[64] There has been some integration in housing since, but it has affected mainly the black bourgeoisie, more exactly, the high-ranking officials.

Some demographic conditions and social indices have worsened since 1990. For instance, life expectancy has dropped from 61 years in 1991 to 47 by 2004, due to the high incidence of HIV/AIDS.[65] Approximately 25 percent of the population is affected by the HIV/AIDS epidemic (here, as elsewhere in Africa, the term AIDS covers a host of deadly infectious diseases). Another estimate places the rate of HIV/AIDS rate at over 22 percent.[66] Life expectancy is less than 50 years for both men and women—a considerable drop in the space of the last two decades.[67] There is also considerable disparity between health services in Windhoek and the South, contrasted with the services in the more heavily populated north.

Sociopolitical Conditions

Namibia has a multi-ethnic population in which one ethnic group is numerically and politically dominant. The Ovambo represent about 50 percent of the population,[68] while none of the other ethnic groups exceeds even ten percent of the total. The ratio given for the white population is 6 percent, while 7 percent are described as coloreds or of mixed race. The ratio of Herero and Damara is also about 7 percent each. Other ethnic groups are even smaller.[69] Politically, the Ovambo were numerically dominant in the struggle for liberation, and remain dominant in the ranks of SWAPO. The SWAPO movement and party have attempted to project the image of diversity and multi-ethnicity, more or less successfully, allowing individuals from other groups to become part of the power structure.

Economic Conditions

Despite the progressive ideology of the SWAPO leaders during the fight for freedom, Namibia has been pursuing policies friendly to investors, whether foreign or native Germanophone. These policies continue to favor investment by multinationals or transnationals. Companies that operate in the export-processing zone pay no taxes. Generous tax breaks are available for foreign investors in mining and the extraction of oil.[70] Hardly a trace of socialist thinking remains, even in the official rhetoric.

Namibia is locked in a neo-colonial relationship with South Africa, which is the economic bright spot of the entire continent. The Namibian economy is overshadowed by that of South Africa, which is about 40 times larger in terms of its GNP, and which accounts for almost all of Namibia's foreign trade and foreign investment.[71] In other words, Namibia's economic development is a function of South African development, and contributes to it.

The resources and means of production of Namibia, with few exceptions, remain in the hands of outsiders or of people of European descent. As everywhere in Africa, the multinational corporations have their headquarters in Europe or the United States, but unlike elsewhere in Africa, the South African corporations are ever-present. Thus, from an ethnic viewpoint, the European element dominates directly or indirectly via South Africa. Land, cash-crop agriculture, and husbandry are owned by whites (some of whom may be absentee landlords), most of whom feel safe enough to remain in the country.

Some definitions of democracy imply an equitable distribution of wealth. This is certainly not the case in Namibia, and the progress in achieving that objective—whether expressed or not—has been very slow. As Kees van Donge and his team note: "everyone concedes that the effects of land reform policies since the early 1990s have been disappointing."[72] These factors may explain, to a large extent, why Namibia has the highest Gini index of all countries in the world, and by a rather big margin at that (South Africa is a distant second). According to Kees van Donge (quoting the World Bank), the Gini index "is a staggering 0.80." According to estimates from the United Nations, the index is 74 (70.7 as of 2003). According to yet other sources, it is around 0.71, including the CIA World Factbook of 2010. Whichever set of figures we accept, it is clear that social inequality in Namibia is unparalleled anywhere in the world. The wealthiest 5 percent of the population has an average income of $14,000, which is comparable to that of the middle-class of developed countries in Europe.[73] To put this factor into perspective, the Gini index of the United States (with its growing unequal income distribution) is around 40.8 in 2010. The Scandinavian countries and Belgium are the most egalitarian, among the lowest on the Gini scale, at least in Europe.[74]

Although the appalling Gini ratio may be due, to some extent, to the methods used in collecting data on income, the unequal wealth is mostly a function of the unequal ownership of land. Namibia seems to be the country where economic privilege and complexion coincides most closely. The huge farms and grazing areas in the central and southern regions are owned by a few white farming families, whereas the majority Ovambo in the north owns little or no land. In other words, the top ten percent of the population, the owners of most of the wealth, corresponds fairly closely to the stratum of persons of European descent. The elite among the white population is proportionately more numerous than in South Africa, while the other 90 percent is almost uniformly impoverished. Perhaps recent events in Zimbabwe have started to embolden the black administration in Namibia to tackle economic privilege. A land reform program was initiated as late as 2005, with the expropriation of some white-owned farms. President Hifikepunye Pohamba, educated in the Soviet Union, following the principles enunciated by Sam Nujoma, continued the land reform program. He has warned of a possible "revolution" if white farmers refuse to sell to the government.[75] "Comrade" Pohamba was reelected in 2009, and still enjoys the support of the founding father, Sam Nujoma.

About 40 percent of the land is commercial, fenced land; nevertheless, some distinctions are in order.[76] While large tracts of land are "in the hands of Namibians of European descent," these lands are arid or semi-arid, and not suitable for commercial agriculture.[77] To be more accurate, the white-dominated commercial agriculture raises cattle, karakul sheep, goats, and ostrich, largely for export.[78] Indeed, in Namibia, considerable acreage is necessary to maintain a herd of cattle, sheep, ostrich, or any grazing animal. The acreage devoted to hunting preserves in private hands is growing. Obviously, game preserves in such a dry climate have to be huge in order to be economically viable and profitable for their owner.

Since independence, despite the repeated resolutions and pronouncements of the SWAPO-led governments, little has changed with regard to land tenure. The amount of communal land is estimated at 34 million hectares. The total amount of commercial land, as described above, is estimated at 36 million hectares. Commercial land in black African hands is estimated at 5 million hectares — a substantial increase since 1990, but only a small fraction of the 36 million total.[79] The productivity of land has not increased significantly because wells/water are as scarce as ever. Irrigation is not an option, and many of the large farms have been converted to game reserves for commercial hunting serving the tourist industry.

Namibia is next door to South Africa, and has a somewhat similar ethnic makeup, with a majority of blacks, a minority of whites, and coloreds in between (but no Indians). While South Africa has the world's highest rate of violent crimes, including assaults and rape, Namibia has a low crime rate. In 2003, it had slightly more than 4,800 prisoners in jail, a per capita rate of 267 per one hundred thousand, and a negligible number of female prisoners. On the other hand, the prisons are filled to capacity.[80]

Economic Resources Other than Land

According to one source, the GDP was $2,686.36 per capita in 2003, as compared to the African average of $681.[81] The US State Department listed the GNP per capita at $2,370 in 2004.[82] The GNI was listed at $4,338, and the GDP per capita at $6,600 in 2009. The growth rate over a five-year period — the last five years — is listed at 5.14 per annum, but the "real growth rate" — which takes account of the inflation rate, is 2.9 percent on the average, still a commendable performance. The human development index is 0.627.[83] Mining makes up almost half of the Namibia's export earnings, beginning with diamonds, copper, lead, and uranium. Namibia has been described as a most attractive country for investment in mining.[84] Tourism is a major resource for Namibia, and there seems to be some correlation between the stability and democracy of the regime and the growing tourism trade from outside Africa. About 12 percent of Namibia's land, including the Etosha National Park, is designated as conservation area.

Education

The country spends about 7.2 percent of its GDP on education [UNESCO report], or over 25 percent of its budget. More recently, by 2008, education's share of the budget dropped to 22.4%.[85] Children are required to complete 10 years of schooling (primary and secondary), that is, they are to remain in school until age 16. Yet, only about 58.4 percent of school age children are enrolled, half of whom are girls. In other words, girls are not at a disadvantage in schooling. In 1992, Miss Universe, Michelle McLean, was from Namibia. The literacy rate among the adult population is given as 81 percent, one of the highest on the African continent.

Although schools were among the first institutions to be integrated after (sometimes even before) independence, integration remains incomplete. Cultural distinctions are marked: as in the United States, schools cater to families in the neighborhood, and neighborhoods are segregated. The facilities are separate but not equal; there are obvious discrepancies. For instance, schools with a predominantly white or colored population emphasize rugby, while schools that cater to blacks play soccer. The history textbooks I have seen, intended for state (public) schools deal exclusively with political history. They are well presented, Afrocentric, and free of jingoism.

While the education picture appears somewhat promising, the unemployment figures are not. Only about 7,000 of the 20,000 who graduate from high school annually manage to find jobs.[86] The five centers of the University of Namibia, with its main campus in Windhoek, enroll about 3,500 students annually, which is not a favorable comparison to American enrollment of approximately two million.[87]

Healthcare

The healthcare situation is bleak, in spite of the continued presence of Cuban doctors offering their services at cost. According to information obtained in 2011, there are still about 80 Cuban doctors serving in Namibia, mainly in the countryside. The infant mortality rate is almost 70 per thousand, and the maternal mortality is 230 per 100,000. Tuberculosis is quite common, and malaria even more so. Only 3.3 percent of the national revenue is spent on health, which is rather a low proportion, thanks in part, to the Cuban contribution.[88]

Civil Rights

According to the BBC, there is freedom of the press, not just in the text of the Constitution, but also in practice.[89] The semi-official *The Namibian* has the largest circulation, with an edition in English and in Oshivambo. Most of the dailies are privately owned, except for the *New Era*, which is published by the government. There are dissonant notes in regard to freedom. For instance, we read in *The Namibian* that President Pohamba tried to deter the "traditional leaders" from political activity, particularly from association with the Rally for Democracy and Progress.[90]

Conclusion

The information and interpretations above do not suffice for predicting Namibia's future, not even the future of democracy in Namibia. Obviously, Namibia's politics and fate are tied to the region, particularly to the fate of South Africa—the economic and political powerhouse—and the fate of Zimbabwe, which is at the focus of much international attention. Should the economy of Zimbabwe become more independent, Namibia will face a fork in the road: to either follow the path of expropriations of the Zimbabwe model, or follow the path of "reconciliation" and continued dominance by the white minority, as in South Africa.

Since the focus of this book is on democracy, it is appropriate to argue that in that department, Namibia fares relatively well. It has a parliamentary, multiparty system that has never been really tested. While the founding father, Sam Nujoma, has relinquished his personal power, the ruling party, SWAPO, has not been truly challenged. Assessing democracy from the point of view of basic human and civil rights, Namibia ranks high.

Adopting other definitions of democracy and considering the degree of social justice and socioeconomic factors, the Namibian record would be patchy, or even dismal. The country can, and has been described as "a liberal capitalist society"[91] with few redeeming features. It is clear, however, that this disequilibrium cannot last for long, if only because of the contrast or contradiction between ideology, politics, and the economic base.

Zambia

Chapter 12

Zambia: Multiparty Politics in a Single Party Political Culture

Joshua Kivuva

The immediate post-Cold War period in Africa was one that was character-ized by spirited attempts towards democratization. After several cycles of elec-tions, these efforts have proved futile, as almost every country in the continent has either stagnated or regressed in the democratization experiment. Even coun-tries like Kenya and South Africa that had demonstrated strong potential for successful democratization have faced serious challenges that have put the whole process in serious doubt. One of the biggest challenges that the continent has faced since the 1990s has been that the beneficiaries of the democratization wave have turned out to be democracy's worst enemies. The leaders of the post-1990 period, many of whom had benefitted from the democratization efforts, ended up manipulating the electoral system and the constitution-making process in order to retain power. Thus, throughout the continent, elections that fol-lowed the first multiparty elections were characterized by what has been de-scribed as a "declining electoral quality" that has been marked by the absence of "democratic consolidation."[1]

Zambia presents one of the most interesting cases of the above. After the 1991 multiparty election that saw President Kenneth Kaunda set high standards of democratic fairness in the conduct of elections, the Chiluba government that had benefitted from Kaunda's democratic overtures turned out to be one of the least in terms of respecting the democratic practices. On coming to power, President Frederick Chiluba did everything possible to ensure that his Move-ment for Multiparty Democracy (MMD) Party did not lose power the way Kaunda's United National Independent Party (UNIP) did. Chiluba turned out to be one of the worst leaders of the post-Cold War democratizing Africa. In-deed, even after his futile attempts to manipulate the Zambian Constitution to allow him to run for a third term as president, Chiluba subverted the process of democratization by handpicking his successor whom he imposed on the MMD, and the country at large.

From Kaunda to Banda

The democratization process in Zambia began in the late 1980s. Soon after, the government of President Kaunda embraced the demands for plural politics, and conducted its first multiparty elections in 1991. Unlike other African leaders who resisted the demands for political pluralism, Kaunda did not wait for the demands of political pluralism to develop into a violent confrontation between the government and the opposition. Rather, he called for multiparty elections in 1991. These elections, which saw Kenneth Kaunda lose the presidency, have been branded a "model of democratization" in Africa.[2] However, Chiluba's MMD government, which replaced Kaunda's UNIP, did not maintain the high standards that the 1991 elections had bequeathed him. Instead, under Chiluba, Zambia's democratization process stagnated. In fact, during his first five years in power, the process of democratization in the country "regressed."[3] Throughout his first term in office, Chiluba became another Kaunda, "authoritarian" and "undemocratic," and was intolerant of any views that did not echo his own. Chiluba's regime became as corrupt as Kaunda's UNIP had been. Indeed, within five years, corruption and other political and economic malfeasance were as bad, if not worse, as they had been under Kaunda. Like Kaunda before him, Chiluba used the government's coercive machinery, namely the police and party youth wingers, to silence any opposition both within and outside the MMD.

The climax of Chiluba's first five years in power was the conduct of the October 1996 elections where he sought reelection as president. The 1996 elections were so flawed, that there hardly existed any opposition to Chiluba and the MMD. Indeed, the 1996 elections were in no way as free or fair as the 1991 ones. During the two terms that Chiluba was president, the level of political decay and economic corruption was quite high, as he manipulated electoral rules and regulations to ensure that he retained his position. The levels of economic corruption skyrocketed as well. It therefore came as no surprise when, after leaving office in 2001, Chiluba was arraigned in court on corruption and other abuse of office charges, which he has since been acquitted.

Chiluba was succeeded by Levy Mwanawasa, whom he single-handedly picked. Mwanawasa was inaugurated on January 2, 2002, to succeed Chiluba, even though his winning margin was less than 34,000 votes.[4] Unlike in 1991 and 1996, when the MMD won 125 and 131 seats, respectfully, in 2001, the MMD had only 69 of the 150 seats in Parliament; hence, the ruling party did not command a governing majority in Parliament. In fact, Mwanawasa got only 28 percent of the votes cast, while his closest challenger, Anderson Mazoka of the United Party of National Development (UPND), came in a very close second with about 27 percent of the vote. The turnout at only 37 percent of the legally eligible electorate was poor, and the worst in Zambia's electoral history.[5]

The transfer of power from Chiluba to Mwanawasa proved quite costly for the MMD. Soon after Chiluba handpicked Mwanawasa as his successor, a spilt occurred within the MMD. A disappointed Michael Sata, who believed he deserved to be Chiluba's successor, quit the party to form the Patriotic Front (PF) Party. Since then, Sata became Mwanawasa's greatest challenger until the latter's death in 2008. Indeed, Mwanawasa's poor showing during the 2001 election was the result of the split in votes between the MMD and Sata's PF. Mwanawasa sought reelection in 2006. The 2006 elections were, however, considered generally free and fair, and represented the will of the people. There were, for example, no challenges to the presidential vote, and there was no significant election boycott by any major party either. Indeed, all political parties were committed to taking part in the elections.[6] This notwithstanding, there were few challenges to the declared results, that is, there were signs of voter manipulation, especially in the registration of voters. The registration of voters seemed higher in areas that had supported the MMD, and lower in areas that were considered supportive of the opposition and opposition candidates.[7]

Mwanawasa, owing to his failing health, was unable to consolidate his power and hence after his death on August 19, 2008, the MMD was faced with a further split. The selection of Rupiah Banda as Mwanawasa's successor did not resolve the MMD's internal problems either. Mwanawasa's death caused internal wrangling that was dangerous for the party's survival. Although Banda, the acting president, emerged as the party's choice to succeed Mwanawasa, this too was a heavy blow to the party, as other senior members were fighting to be Mwanawasa's successor. When the MMD NEC chose Banda (with 47 votes) against Ngandu Magande's 11 votes,[8] another split almost took place within the MMD. The majority of senior party leaders did not favor Banda, whose rise to be Mwanawasa's successor resulted from being the acting president. As acting president, he was able to manipulate government resources and the media to his advantage.

Like Mwanawasa and Chiluba before him, Banda represented the old order, an order informed by UNIP's single party socialization and Chiluba's anti-democratic tendencies. The three post multiparty Zambian leaders—Chiluba, Mwanawasa, and Banda—were socialized by the single party political culture where the party leadership determined and dominated Zambian politics. A new generation of leaders seems to have come of age that is challenging the old order. This is a new generation of Young Turks who are opposed to the recycling of the former UNIP and MMD party's old guards.

Sata, Mwanawasa, and Banda had served in Kaunda's UNIP, though Chiluba was himself a senior trade unionist, which had a close relationship with the government. Even Sata, who had held a number of senior positions in UNIP's and the MMD governments, belonged to this old generation of single party culture Zambian politicians. For example, Sata believed that he had to be the party's nominee for the presidency, and when he was not nominated, he defected from the MMD.[9] Several other senior MMD Party members, also schooled in the pre-multiparty political culture, defected from the MMD when it became apparent that they were not going to be the MMD's nominees for the president.

Conceptualizing Democratization: An African Context

It is now almost universally accepted that democratization is both a process and a condition. There is, however, no agreement on the role that the state has, or could play in the democratization process. While the state plays an important role in the process of democratization, the state is neither the only nor the major determinant of democratization. There are other determinants of the process that are either internal (domestic) or external (international) which are more significant than the state. Internal determinants include the nation's political culture, the nature of civil society, and the nature of the political dispensation existing in the country. External actors include international NGOs, donor agencies such as the International Monetary Fund (IMF), the World Bank, and other bilateral donors such as the European Union, the United States, Britain, France, and Germany.

Most commentaries on democratization have looked at the presence or absence of institutions that are considered vital in the democratization process. Political scientists and practitioners of politics, for example, have so stressed the legal and institutional framework of democratization and multiparty politics that they have ignored the importance of culture and the political socialization that needs to take place if people's perceptions and perspectives on politics are to change. We can make all the legal changes and institute all the relevant institutional provisions for it, but democratization can only occur where there is a change in the population's political culture. It takes place when a change occurs in the way people process their ideas, beliefs, and attitudes about governance and the conduct of politics. Thus, sustainable democratization is not about the state or state institutions. It is about the people and their beliefs, politics, values, and ideas. It is also about their behavior towards politics, and the political culture they develop. This means that generational differences and age variations do contribute an important aspect to the nature of democratization in any society.

The above has important significance, especially for a country such as Zambia, where more than 60 percent of the population was born after independence, and where more than half of the population is below 15.[10] In Zambia, those who experienced colonialism are more nationalistic, and were more concerned about protecting their independence than those who did not experience colonialism. The political culture that developed after independence was one that tended to be more state-centric in that it was geared toward establishing a strong state. Initially, a strong state was considered necessary for development, and also to overcome the forces of neo-colonialism. Due to South Africa's threats to the survival of the country, a strong state was also considered necessary to overcome Apartheid South Africa's attempts to sabotage Zambia's economy.

In Africa, the excitement and euphoria for independence and the desire to protect what was a "hard won independence" led to the development of a political culture that did not care much about political pluralism. In Zambia, as was true of other African countries, the struggle for independence produced what came to be known as the heroes of independence—Jomo Kenyatta, Sedar Senghor, Kenneth Kaunda, Felix Houphoüet-Boigny, Ahmed Sékou Touré, and Kwame Nkrumah—which led to the development of a political culture that viewed opposition to these national heroes as being treasonable. The reverence and respect that Africans had, or believed their independence heroes deserved, were inconsistent with the practice of plural politics.

Democratization is a process of which an environment is created where disagreements over policies and politics are accepted as normal and legitimate, and where disagreements over resources and resource distributions are resolved within a generally accepted political process, such as elections. It is an environment in which the plurality of ideas, policies, and actors are not just accepted as legitimate, but one where a general framework is established in which politics and political differences are managed. It leads to the creation of a broad consensus about the rules and conduct of the political game. Democratization takes place when a plural society is created in which it is possible to come up with different political outcomes after an election. This can only happen when both the leaders and the rest of the population agree to the legitimacy of political pluralism.

Throughout Africa, there has been a tendency to confuse the introduction of multiparty politics with democratization. In many African countries, the mere introduction of multiparty political dispensation has been mistaken for democratization. Yet, in most of these African countries, the introduction of multiparty politics has only involved a change of the legal (or constitutional framework) of the country—from one that did not allow the existence of more than one political party, to one that does. This occurs without any corresponding change in the way politics are conducted, or without any efforts being made to re-socialize the people (and their leaders) in the ways that politics should be conducted in the changed, or changing, multiparty political environment. Indeed, in most of the countries, other than changing that aspect of the law that prohibited the formation of other political parties, no new laws were passed to guarantee the operations of the new parties.

Democratization also involves the weakening of the government's instruments of coercion. It involves increasing the level and amount of participation of the common citizen in the country's political affairs. In other words, democratization requires the development of a participatory political culture that encourages political competition. It must inculcate a culture of popular participation, and a culture that encourages quality participation from all. Democratization, therefore, entails what might be called "inclusive politics," where leaders and parties who may not even be in government are consulted or included in government committees and other government delegations. This is best exemplified in Nelson Mandela's practice of leaving his archrival, Mongosutu Buthelezi, as the acting president whenever he (Mandela) was out of the country.

Zambia's Undemocratic Culture

Zambia's democracy remains as what scholars have characterized "partial, undisciplined, and intolerant of dissent."[11] As Alastair Fraser and Miles Larmer point out, "Zambia's democratic culture—in the form of the public expression of popular social attitudes towards political, economic, and social change—is, at least in urban areas, healthily undisciplined." They add, "what has been lacking hitherto is any significant expression of these attitudes in electoral or legislative forums, something that the Patriotic Front (Sata's party), albeit in problematic ways, has began to offer."[12]

Thus, despite the change from a single party to a multiparty system, Zambia's political culture has not changed much. As Jan Kees van Donge points out, other than the fact that "another party is in power ... under another pres-

ident ... the major aspects of Zambian politics have not changed." Although democratization was supposed to lead to a parliamentary system of government,
in Zambia "power is still concentrated in the presidency." Also, Zambia is a
"multiparty state that is ruled by one party." The MMD dominates in all regions
of the country, except for the Eastern Province. There are "numerous opposition parties, but they are fragmented and ineffective."[13]

The tendency to mobilize support via appeals to community identity is yet
another characteristic of Zambia's political culture.[14] Ethnicity still enjoys an overwhelming influence over political behavior.[15] In the over twenty years that the
party has governed, the MMD has retained the advantage of incumbency previously abused by UNIP during the one party era.[16] The result has been that the MMD
has won all the multiparty elections since 1991, at times through means and
under circumstances that would not be considered free and fair. The 1991 and 1996
elections in Zambia, for example, were rigged, with much of it being done by
the state. This has happened in many emerging democracies in Africa; the incumbents have used all sorts of means to ensure that they remain in power. The
2001 elections were no exceptions. The MMD government took advantage of the
ineffectiveness of the Election Commission of Zambia (ECZ) to manipulate the
elections. First, the government not only underfunded the ECZ, but they also
failed, (or refused), to provide funds until June. This was a ploy by the MMD to
make interfering with the elections easier. The presiding and returning officers training was also poor as well.

The MMD government continually manipulated the ECZ to ensure that the
party reaped maximum benefits. Ordinarily, voters register in their places of
work, but the majority of them travel to their rural homes over major holidays. In Zambia, as is true in many African cities, the majority of urban workers travel to their rural homes to celebrate with their folks over the Christmas
holidays. In the 2001 elections for example, the MMD government colluded
with the ECZ to call for elections on December 27, a day that many of the
urban workers were returning to their place of work after the Christmas break.
However, the voting day was not made a public holiday. Secondly, on this day,
most schools and universities are normally closed for the December (Christmas) holiday, and teachers and students were away from their stations and
halls of residence on the campuses where they had registered. To make matters worse, the ECZ ruled that voters could only cast their votes where they
were registered, yet the elections were called when a large number of voters
were outside their normal workstations.

The MMD government manipulated the registration of new voters, and of
voters in different regions to ensure that voters in the areas that had supported
the MMD and MMD candidates were registered, or those that were from re-

gions that were likely to support the opposition were not registered. Like most African countries, youths did not get issued identity cards automatically when they attained 18 years of age. With the perception that the youth were supporting the "Young Turks" in the opposition, the MMD government was not motivated to issue Zambia's youth with the national identity cards that would have facilitated their being issued voting cards. This was complicated by the problems associated with the compilation of the registers. For example, voter registration started so close to the election day, that there was not sufficient time to register and make credible voter registers.

Other aspects of the voting and electioneering process were equally manipulated, including the authentication of voter registers, accreditation of election monitors, and the staffing of poll stations. Also, the distance between voting stations and populations in a particular constituency were gerrymandered to ensure that constituencies perceived to be pro opposition were overpopulated, and their poll stations manned by fewer officials than those in the MMD support areas. Election officials had a lot of discretion in conducting elections, and their actions greatly influenced the outcome. The presiding officers for example, determined when polling stations opened and closed (even when specific times were mandated), and also controlled the pace of voting which determined the number of people who could vote within the allocated time. This was especially significant in the urban areas where population density was high, and lines were long. A presiding officer, by just running his station slowly, could influence the number of voters to successfully cast their votes within the time allocated. This, coupled with disorganization on the voting day, left ample room for certain concerned elements to manipulate the process. For example, owing to the fact that many polling stations opened late for voting, the government and the ECZ decided to extend the voting hours to compensate, yet this information reached only a few presiding officers. Others deliberately decided not to extent the opening hours.

Nominations were not done in an open manner, and most of the parliamentary candidates were handpicked. This ended up with the selection of the old guard. Government officials were deployed to work for the MMD campaigns, some in so obvious areas as the registration of MMD members. The government and MMD leaders threatened that they were going to deny development funds to those opposed to the MMD. The government monopoly of media through state-owned television and radio aired biased broadcasting by the Zambian National Broadcasting Corporation radio, and television had negative broadcasts on opposition candidates. In the 2001 elections, observers noted with serious concern "the problem of access to public media throughout the electioneering period."[17] This was not only perpetrated by the MMD alone. Zambia has a number of independent media houses whose broadcast content also tended to be pro opposition parties.

Two factors account for the above. First, as is true with most other African countries, the shift from single party to multiparty political dispensation in Zambia was not accompanied by any significant change in the political culture and political socialization of the people or their leaders. Chiluba won the 1991 elections with such an overwhelming majority that opposition to the MMD government fizzled out, and Chiluba governed Zambia as if the country was a single party state with him as the sole leader. The second factor that explains this situation is the manner in which multiparty politics were reintroduced in the country. The short period, and the manner in which multiparty elections were introduced in Zambia (after an extremely short period of political agitation), saved Zambia from the politically instigated violence, chaos, and property destruction that other African countries have gone through, but it also hindered the process of democratization in the country.

When Chiluba came to power after a landslide victory in the 1991 elections, he did not face any major obstacles in consolidating himself in power. In the 1991 elections that brought him to power, Chiluba's MMD party won over 72 per cent of the votes, and 125 seats in the 150 seat Zambian Parliament. The MMD's closest rival, the UNIP (and the opposition in general), won a combined total of 25 seats. These were not enough seats to pose any significant challenges to Chiluba, and therefore his MMD party had no difficulties carrying his agenda forward. In 1996, Chiluba's victory was even more pronounced. Chiluba's MMD party got 131 seats and over 80 percent of the total votes. However, rather than use his mandate and his party's majority in Parliament to enhance the process of democratization, Chiluba proved Claude Ake prophetic.

Commenting about democratic transitions in Africa (from a single party to a multiparty system), Ake observed that the elections that precede such a transition only give the voter "a choice between oppressors." To Ake, since African states still remain "inherently anti-democratic," the multiparty systems that were introduced in the 1990s saw a group of "self-appointed military or civilian dictators being replaced by elected dictators."[18] Ake must have been thinking about Zambia when he made the above observations. In Zambia, elections have followed a trend commonly witnessed in Africa in which the problem of conducting free and fair elections within an environment of poverty has proven a hard task. Zambian politics are characterized by "personality politics, elite factionalization, and ethno-regional coalition building, rather than being a contest of alternative policies."[19]

Zambia's political parties have lacked ideological foundations, and their policies are also hard to discern. The MMD, for example, despite having ruled for over two decades, remains "an uneasy coalition of social forces that made temporary common cause to oust UNIP,"[20] but that has since not been able to chart its policy or ideological stand. Under Chiluba's first term, Zambia was not much different from the Kaunda government he had replaced. In fact, unlike Kaunda, who had negotiated with the MMD, and the opposition to smoothly transition Zambia into a multiparty political system, when Chiluba won the 1991 elections, he not only refused to negotiate with his opponents, but also took advantage of the MMD's overwhelming majority in Parliament to pass bills that enabled him and his MMD party to dominate Zambia's political landscape. As a result, the 1991 elections in the country only moved Zambia from a UNIP-Kaunda dictatorship within the single-party legal framework, to an MMD-Chiluba tyranny within a multiparty governmental system.

Zambia's initial change to a multiparty political system was a negotiated deal. Unlike other African leaders who violently resisted the demands for opening up the political system to competition, President Kaunda and his UNIP party showed an uncharacteristic willingness to bring change to Zambia's political system before the demands for political pluralism turned violent. With the mediation of the church and other civil society organizations, Kaunda was able to peacefully open up Zambia's political space. There were a number of meetings between the UNIP and the opposition, and hence the constitutional reforms that brought about multiparty politics in Zambia were the result of a negotiated package, not one won from the streets. In a sense, the return of a multiparty system in Zambia was the result of an "elite settlement," rather than the result of mass action against the government. To a great extent therefore, the UNIP's negotiated deal with the MMD leadership led to the perpetration of the status quo in the country. As a result, despite the transition from a UNIP-Kaunda leadership in a single party political environment to an MMD-Chiluba leadership in a multiparty one, no real change occurred to Zambia's politics. Although the UNIP and Kaunda were defeated, the MMD government simply replaced the Kaunda government without bringing about any meaningful changes to the political system inherited. Hence, the masses did not benefit from these changes. Despite the reintroduction of a multiparty political system in Zambia, political competition has "remained limited."[21]

In many African countries, the demands for change and the process of political liberalization in the immediate post cold war period were characterized by a protracted period of agitation and violent demonstrations against the government. The long process of agitation provided the people and opposition leaders with an opportunity to re-evaluate their demands, as well as the kind of change they needed. In Zambia, the change to a multiparty political system was so abrupt, that even the victorious majority (including the MMD leaders), many of whom were political novices, had not been fully socialized into the culture of multiparty politics. The change from the UNIP's monopoly of political space to one where the party had to compete with others occurred within such a short time that the change and the multiparty system itself was attained without any meaningful democratization taking place. In other words, unlike other African countries where the introduction of a multiparty political system was the result of, or was accompanied by, significant levels of democratization, the introduction of a multiparty system in Zambia was a mere *event*, not a *process*.

Unlike in other African countries, where advocates of political pluralism made several unsuccessful presidential bids, Zambia's democratization process was unfortunate in that the advocates of political pluralism were successful in removing Kaunda and the UNIP from power within a few months of serious agitation for political pluralism. Hence, no changes had taken place in the people's perception about politics or democracy. Though the changes from a single party to multiparty politics took place, no corresponding change took place in the political socialization of the people or leaders. As the above has shown, the multiparty system in Zambia was introduced, and operated, in a political system that was still dominated by a non-democratic political culture. To understand the above, there is a need to put Zambia's undemocratic culture in its proper historical context.

The political culture that existed in Zambia on the eve of the reintroduction of plural politics is one that can be considered undemocratic. The genesis of this culture goes back to the early 1970s when President Kaunda's UNIP government ended the multiparty system that had successfully worked for Zambia since independence in 1964. Zambia's undemocratic culture was perpetuated by Kaunda's UNIP party and its dominance of Zambian politics since independence. Even more specifically, after December 1972, the multiparty system was brought to an end, making the UNIP the only legal political party in the country.

Zambia's undemocratic political culture was the product of three factors. These are nationalism and the desire to protect the country's *hard-won-independence*, the status of Zambia as a Frontline State, and the symbiotic relationship between governmental political elites and their economic counterparts within the leadership of the Copperbelt mining industry. In the post 1990 period, this culture has been perpetrated by Chiluba and a group of self interested politicians who have taken advantage of their positions to manipulate the system in order to ensure the continued dominance of the MMD.

In 1990, when the clamor for plural politics and opposition to the UNIP's monopoly of power began, Zambia had been independent for over 35 years.

This meant that the majority of adult voters had experienced colonialism and witnessed the independence struggle. The political culture of the adult voter in Zambia by 1990 had been, to a great extent, informed by their colonial experience, nationalism, and the legacies that both colonialism and nationalism had bequeathed the country. This culture determined why the elite masses' attitudes, beliefs, and perceptions became more protective of their government. This was not just confined to Zambia. Most African populations developed the same reverence for their heroes of independence—Kenyatta, Kaunda, Nyerere, Senghor, and Nkrumah. The reverence that Africans had for these heroes led to the development of a political culture that viewed opposition to these national heroes as treasonable. The respect and reverence Africans had for their heroes of independence were inconsistent with the demands of plural politics.

An important aspect of Zambia's undemocratic political culture is derived from Zambia's geographic location. Zambia is a landlocked country whose economy is dependent on copper mining. Zambia was also one of the leading Frontline States, and therefore, was prone to sabotage from the Apartheid South African government. Since independence, there had been a genuine concern from both the political elite and a large majority of the Zambian population that the introduction of plural politics in the country would provide the Apartheid regime in South Africa an opportunity to infiltrate the country and sabotage its development. Faced with these genuine security threats from the South African government, and determined to protect the countries' hard won independence, a political culture of *nationalism* and *patriotism* based on the desire to remain united under a strong government developed among Zambian adults and politicians. Because of the seriousness of South Africa's threats to Zambia's survival as an independent nation, the political culture that developed from these threats obliged Zambians to make personal sacrifices for public gain and the maintenance of state security.

Since the government was also the major employer in the country, any threat to the state was also a threat to the middle class whose livelihood depended on government jobs. Therefore, as long as these threats to the government and the state persisted, the middle class was inclined to support the government, even at the expense of personal freedoms. Given a choice between support for a strong government that would protect them, and a government that allowed for political pluralism, the majority of adult Zambians preferred security (political and economic) to political pluralism. Since the majority of the economic elite derived their livelihood from their government controlled copper mining jobs, the elite did not pressure the government to democratize. In such an environment, it would have been very hard for the middle class to pressure the government to democratize or to open up the political system to plural politics.

There also existed two other aspects of the political culture that were uniquely Zambian. The first was derived from Kaunda's political leadership style. Kaunda's patronage system, rather than acting as the glue that bonded UNIP members, became a source of new conflict. As leaders tried to get closer to Kaunda to access a bigger share of the national resources for their constituents, some succeeded while others did not get what they considered adequate. Owing to the uneven rate of economic development and regional disparities in resource endowment, different leaders and their constituents expected much more from Kaunda's government than his patronage system could offer. This led to claims of favoritism and conflict. In the period preceding the introduction of multiparty politics therefore, the UNIP became the center of conflicts over Kaunda's patronage, and the political spoils on which it relied.[22]

The second aspect of Zambia's political culture that was uniquely Zambian pertained to the manner in which Kaunda "Zambianized" the economy and the civil service. This policy of "Zambianization" of the economy and civil service also created a large middle class of professionals working for the government, mostly in the lucrative copper minefields. Since independence, and owing to the high rate of urbanization in the country and the fact that the majority of the urban workers were employed in one sector of the economy (copper mining), the Zambian economic elite established an independence from the political elite that had not been witnessed elsewhere in the continent. The Copper Mineworkers Union, though a very influential organization politically, had since the colonial times resisted the government's attempts to co-opt it, or to render its leaders cronies of the political elite as had happened in other African countries.

As a result, a political culture developed within the labor movement that kept its leaders from interfering directly in matters that were purely of a political nature, while it exercised independence and a great measure of autonomy in workers affairs. A symbiotic relationship developed between the two in which the political elites controlled the country's governmental affairs, while the mineworkers controlled the economy. Since copper prices in the international markets were good, Zambia's civil servants and other workers had a better life than in other African countries and, hence, for almost two decades the middle class supported the government.

Things began to change when copper prices plummeted in the 1980s, shrinking the middle class. At the same time, things were also changing for the rural populations. The rural peasants were not spared the difficulties facing urban dwellers, and hence the symbiotic relations between the government political elites and their economic counterparts in the Copperbelt regions had far-reaching effects on the rural areas. The need to keep urban mineworkers content and supplied with cheap foodstuffs forced the government to keep the price of food (produced by the rural poor) low. This not only discouraged food production, but also curtailed the mobility of the rural peasants upwards into the middleclass. Unsuccessful agricultural reforms of the 1980s and early 1990s did not improve the plight of the rural folks either.

It was the problems facing the rural folks coupled with the plummeting prices of copper in the international markets and the effects of Structural Adjustment Policies (SAPs) that triggered the riots that set in motion the demands for social, political, and economic liberalization in the country. Indeed, the rise and development of the MMD, and the agitation that eventually led to plural politics in Zambia were a response to the economic malaise that was facing the country, and not the result of the prevailing political situation. Put in other words, the labor movement was responding to the economic collapse, not to the deteriorating human rights situation in the country. People were demonstrating against the shortages of essential consumer goods and against the skyrocketing prices of foodstuffs. The demands for political pluralism were therefore incidental, even as late as 1990. Most of the rhetoric about political pluralism came from a small segment of the economic elite that felt that the reforms they wanted in the economy could not be initiated without reforming the political environment first.

Demands for political pluralism in the country were started by a small segment of the elite (mostly outside the labor movement) that felt that an economic collapse was imminent unless drastic measures were taken to overhaul the way Zambian society was run. This is the group that linked the economic problems that Zambia was facing with UNIP's monopoly of political power. This group, which was constituted of employers in the private sector and a number of political elite that were no longer enjoying Kaunda's patronage, managed to convince the labor unions that the worsening economic situation in Zambia could not be salvaged without political reforms as well. It was this small group of political elites, supported by the economic elites, that was responsible for spearheading the demands for political pluralism.

The above views are supported by the composition of the MMD (the party that defeated Kaunda), which replaced the UNIP as the ruling party. Unlike elsewhere in Africa, where the euphoria for multiparty politics led to the formation of mass-based movements or political parties (at least before they broke into different ethnic or regionally based factions), the MMD was not a mass-based movement. Rather, it was composed mainly of trade union officials under the Zambian Confederation of Trade Unions (ZCTU), and the Zambia Industrial and Commercial Association (ZINCOM), an organization of employers mostly in the private sector. While the ZCTU provided the organizational leadership to the MMD, ZINCOM provided its funding. These two organizations were more concerned with economic reforms than with political liberalization. Their concern with political liberalization was their conviction that without political liberalization, economic liberalization and development could not take place. In other words, both the ZCTU and the ZINCOM saw political liberalization as a precondition for economic liberalization. Government mismanagement of the economy and the high levels of corruption could not be ended without political liberalization. Both the ZCTU and the ZINCOM were elitist; the ZCTU declared its support for the MMD in December 1990.[23]

The role of the trade union movement in Zambia in the agitation for political pluralism is different from the way it influenced the rest of African trade unions. Rather than joining demonstrators in the streets, or organizing industrial action against the government, the labor movement in Zambia expected change to come through the ruling UNIP party. A brief elaboration will suffice here. Like elsewhere in Africa, in Zambia the labor movement had played an important role in the fight for independence, and although labor unions were affiliated with the UNIP government (through the ZCTU), they still maintained a great measure of independence[24] and ensured that workers rights were protected. A mutual relationship developed between the governmental elites and trade union officials in which the political elite ran governmental affairs while the trade unions ran the economic matters.

Indeed, throughout the ZCTU's affiliation with the UNIP, the trade union movement walked the thin line between trying to organize workers and ensuring they were not perceived to be anti-government. Due to the ZCTU's long affiliation with the UNIP and the government, the MMD leaders (who were also long time ZCTU leaders), hoped that change could still come within the UNIP framework. That is, a change that would not only end single party politics and introduce a multiparty system, but also one that would continue the status quo—one that would only change the leadership of the country. Despite the ZCTU's affiliation to the UNIP during the era of a one party state, the union did not lose much of its autonomy or independence, and continued fighting for workers' rights. Together with the Christian churches, the ZCTU was the only other organ to occasionally oppose or criticize government policy, though within the generally well defined parameters of disagreement. The ZCTU did not in any way organize groups to oppose the government until it lent its support to the MMD in 1990.

Since the MMD was predominantly an organization of (former) trade union leaders, the manner in which the party demanded change also differed from the rest of Africa. Rather than getting supporters on the streets for demonstrations and riots (as was the case in other African countries demanding for plural politics), the MMD made appeals to the international community, to international labor organizations, and to the donor community. This reflects the naivety and socialization of the MMD leadership and their political beliefs. As elite groups, the ZCTU and the ZINCOM did not believe that change could be brought about by the masses through destructive street demonstrations, but by pressure from the international community. Therefore, rather than organizing the masses and local groups in demonstrations and street riots, the MMD established offices in London, Washington, and Stockholm. From these remote offices, they lobbied for international pressure and sanctions against the Kaunda government.

Frederick Chiluba, the long time trade union leader turned president, points out that support from the trade union organization in the West, particularly the AFL-CIO (American Federation of Labor-Congress of Industrial Organization) in the U.S.A., Britain's Trade Union Congress (TUC), and labor organizations from Norway and Finland, as well as the International Confederation of Free Trade Unions (ICFTU) to which Zambian trade unions are affiliated, were sought more openly from 1988. According to Chiluba, these affiliations, together with contacts developed with the Commonwealth Trade Union Council, were valuable in circulating news about the true state of affairs in Zambia, and also helped lobby for donor support to be pegged on improved human rights and democratization.[25] These appeals were quite significant, and played an important role in changing the UNIP and Kaunda's policies.[26]

Multiparty Politics in a Single Party Political Culture

The manner in which multiparty politics were reintroduced in Zambia prevented the re-socialization of the people into a multiparty political culture from happening. This section explores the challenges that the post 1990 governments in Zambia have faced in institutionalizing democracy, and the inability of the MMD leaders to bring about a different political culture in Zambia. Zambia's return to multiparty politics was a paradox. On the one hand, Zambia's re-introduction to multiparty politics was one of the least conflictive democratization processes in the continent during the post cold war era, yet on the other hand, the process has not been accompanied by any significant levels of democratization. Rather than violently resisting the democratization wave, or clinging to power like his contemporaries, President Kaunda allowed a return to multiparty democracy, and conducted what were definitely free and fair elections. To crown it all, when he lost in the 1991 elections, President Kaunda peacefully handed over power to his successor, the MMD's Frederick Chiluba.

Unlike the UNIP-Kaunda leadership that willingly negotiated with the MMD and Chiluba, the latter, after winning the 1991 elections, refused to negotiate with opponents, and took advantage of the MMD's majority in Parliament to pass bills that enabled Chiluba to monopolize Zambia's political landscape. In 1996, the MMD dominated Parliament passed constitutional amendments which granted President Chiluba powers over the legislature and the judiciary. Chiluba used these powers not only to consolidate his position, but to ensure that he controlled the electoral process in the country as well. Chiluba did not consult the major stakeholders on the electioneering process, harassed the media and journalists, and even silenced his own supporters and colleagues within the MMD and in Parliament.

Within the first five years of his rule, Chiluba rolled back most of the democratic gains achieved in the post cold war period. As Human Rights Watch (HRW) has documented in its various annual reports, the Chiluba years were no different from those of his predecessor in the treatment of the media, the opposition, or its citizens. The Human Rights Watch (1996/7), for example, detailed President Chiluba's government harassment of the press and political opponents. This, to a great extent, was the result of the manner in which multiparty politics in Zambia were achieved, which did little to change the undemocratic political culture that had existed since independence.

As pointed out earlier, in Zambia the change to plural politics occurred within such a short period that neither the leaders nor the masses had been socialized into the intricacies of plural politics. When the clamor for "multipartyism" began in the late 1980s, the advocates of political pluralism succeeded in removing Kaunda and establishing a multiparty government within a short time. This prevented them from reflecting on the kind of government or person they wanted to replace Kaunda with. To make matters worse, the first multiparty elections in the country were held at the height of the masses' euphoria for change; hence, the MMD's victory was overwhelming even to the MMD itself.

The problem was similar to a number of other countries in Africa — the people wanted change in the form of the removal of the Kaunda regime, but did not know the kind of government they wanted to replace the old regime with, let alone knowing how to install a working democracy. It has been the practice in many African countries that people are so eager to remove an oppressive regime, that they do not pay serious attention to the replacement government. The mentality of the African populations fighting political oppression has been that as long as the oppressive regime is removed from power, any replacement government is preferred. This mindset has turned out to be quite frustrating for democratization in many African countries. For Zambia, Chiluba did not turn out to be the agent of democratization that the country needed.

The above problem is not uniquely Zambian. In Kenya, the reintroduction of political pluralism led to the introduction of political practices that can only be classified as the "politics of insanity." During the 1992 and 1997 elections, one of the leading opposition presidential candidates (the one rumored to have been robbed of victory through rigging), was one whose mental stability was highly questionable owing to a stroke he had suffered in detention in the early 1990s. These "politics of insanity" in Kenya in the 1992 and 1997 elections were not confined to the presidential elections alone. In the 1992 elections in particular, the now infamous "three piece suit"[27] saw the elections of people completely unknown to the electorate—some of them social misfits. Because of the "ethnicization" and regionalization of politics in Kenya, each region voted as a bloc for a particular set of candidates (presidential, parliamentary and councilors).[28]

In the case of Zambia, the MMD's overwhelming victory gave its leaders a false sense of "legitimacy," and a free hand to do whatever they wanted. Since few of them had been socialized into the culture of political pluralism, many of the MMD leaders did not behave differently from Kaunda, and operated in the same manner as the UNIP had under Kaunda. The overwhelming support that the people gave the MMD leaders meant that there was not a significant opposition party to check the excesses of the MMD, and hence the party and its leader Chiluba simply replaced the UNIP and Kaunda, but did not behave or perform any differently. Due to the overwhelming support that the MMD got (winning the elections with over 72 percent of the vote in 1991, and 80 percent in 1996), there was no one in the significant opposition to check the MMD excesses. Hence, the MMD engaged in the same excesses that they had accused the leadership of the UNIP.[29]

Despite the 1991 Mwanakate's Commission recommendations for Zambia to change its political system from a single party to multiparty system, the constitutional changes that took place simply repealed the laws that prohibited the formation of other political parties, but left almost intact the legal framework that had supported the single party rule. No attempts were made to make the constitutional amendments that would have facilitated the establishment of a true multiparty political or legal framework. Even president Chiluba's 1995 constitutional changes left intact many of the laws that had protected the single party regime of Kaunda. Indeed, Chiluba's 1995 constitutional changes were made to protect the MMD's position in Zambia. Thus, despite the transition from single party to multiparty system, the political environment and the political culture of Zambia's democratization remained as it had been in the era of the single party.

The MMD leadership had another shortcoming. Most of its leaders were political novices. They brought their political naivety and inexperience to the leadership of the MMD, and to the country. Hardly any of the MMD leaders had any real experience in running a political institution, and hence they did not have a well-crafted political agenda for the country either. As a result, the leadership of the MMD became a "Tower of Babel." Threatened by its own internal scrabbles, the MMD leaders used the same tactics the UNIP and Kaunda had used to silence dissent and opposition. Within a short time, the MMD was at war with itself, leading to a number of break-ups in the party as well as the formation of rival "opposition" ones. These rival parties included the National Party (NP), the Agenda for Zambia Party (AZ), the Liberal Progressive Front (LPF), and Zambia's National Congress Party (ZADECO). Other MMD leaders quit the party to run as independents. When Chiluba picked Mwanawasa to replace him as president, a further breakup occurred when Michael Sata quit the MMD to found the Patriotic Front (PF) party.

Immediately after the 1991 elections, there was every indication that Chiluba's MMD could not hold together as a party for long. The National Party was the first splinter group from the MMD. The NP was founded in 1993 when over ten MMD Members of Parliament broke away to found their own party.[30] In addition to being both senior MMD leaders and popular politicians, those who defected to found the NP were from different regions of Zambia, which immediately gave the NP a national outlook. However, internal disputes, such as personality differences and leadership wrangles within the party, drove out much of the NP support. By the 1996 elections, the NP had been so weakened, that it had won only five seats.

The AZ was another MMD breakaway party. The AZ was founded by A. Mbikusita Lewanika,[31] a former cabinet Minister under the MMD government. Lewanika joined the NP, only to break away just a few weeks before the 1996 elections. Other splinter parties from the MMD included the Liberal Progressive Front (LPF) and Zambia's National Congress (Zadeco).[32] These breakaway parties joined the UNIP in their opposition to Chiluba. The UNIP was one of the oldest political parties in Zambia having been founded in 1958 by Kenneth Kaunda.[33]

Zambia's Changing Political Culture

In analyzing the rates and trends of democratization in Africa, Young rec-
ommends the need to take inventory of the contradictory processes that have
occurred in the process of democratization. As he points out, there is a need
to move away from focusing on the "initial transitional dynamics," towards
evaluating more important aspects of democratization, such as weighing the
consequences, evaluating the degree of consolidation, and speculating about
the sustainability of the altered practices of politics.[34]

Zambia, like many other African states, has moved beyond the initial phase
of transition to a more complex process of democratic consolidation and institutionalization. The process has been sidetracked, although not entirely abandoned. The euphoria and optimism that met the first multiparty elections in the
country in 1991 has since evaporated, owing to Chiluba's political manipulations.
Although Chiluba's manipulation of the electoral system slowed down the democratization process in the country, after the reelection of Mwanawasa in 2006
and the recent (2008) presidential elections to replace the departed Mwanawasa,
it is evident that the degeneration was not permanent. Zambia seems to be back
on the course of democratization. Although the 1996, 2001, and 2006 elections
were marred by incidences of violence and allegations of massive voter fraud, a
number of positive changes have taken place. Most notable was the position the
entire society took towards violence as a means of solving political disputes.

The country as a whole, particularly the opposition candidates and the police, seemed determined not to use violence or force to solve their political differences. The general conduct of the electioneering process since 2006 has been
peaceful, and when disputes arose during counting and the announcement of
the results, opposition candidates stuck to their promise to use only peaceful
and constitutional means to seek redress. The determination of the opposition not to resort to violence, and not to incite followers into demonstrations
(even in the face of numerous allegations of fraud in the country), was testimony to a changing political culture in the country. There were obvious cases
of a manipulated election by government officials in the 2006 General Elections, yet the opposition stuck to the promise that it was not going to incite its
followers into any form of violent reaction to the allegations of voter fraud.
Mwanawasa's government also did much to bring confidence to the electoral
process. Mwanawasa attempted to introduce biometrics into the conduct of
elections, and tried to map all constituencies using Geographical Information
Systems (GIS). Even though this technology was not so useful in the elections,
the fact that his government was determined to use them shows how much he
wanted to bring the country back onto the democratic path.

The conduct of elections is one of the key determinants of a democracy. According to Schumpeter, elections are the "defining institutions of democracy."[35] No country can claim to be democratic unless it holds regular elections. The quality of the elections (in terms of their fairness, freeness, and the manner in which the outcome reflects the free will of the majority) also determines the quality of that country's democracy. A key component of democracy is the establishment of political institutions within both the state and society to facilitate this. Throughout Africa, the institutional base of democracy is generally lacking, and Zambia is not an exception. This notwithstanding, the extent of Zambia's democratization in the last two decades can be measured.

According to Gould, the 1996 elections offered an opportunity to measure the degree of democratic consolidation or democratic slippage. In analyzing Zambia's democratization process, Gould concludes that by 1996, Zambia's democracy had fallen on the side of "slippage," since the MMD led by Chiluba had exploited its constitutional control over the legislative branch to eliminate any effective challenge to the MMD hegemony, and had openly manipulated existing constitutional and electoral rules to trip up their competitors.[36] Elections are also an important aspect of transitioning to democracy. As Samuel Huntington points out, democratic transitions end when a government that was not chosen freely and fairly is replaced by one that is elected in a free, open, and fair election.

An election is deemed democratic if it is competitive, and has been conducted in a free and fair environment.[37] According to Huntington, a good measure of assessing the level of democratization is by applying what he calls the "two turnover test."[38] To Huntington, a key determinant of a democratizing state is not just the holding of regular elections, but also the ability of the people to remove or change a government, and the willingness of those defeated in the elections to accept such a defeat. To Huntington, a democracy gets consolidated when a sitting president who loses an election accepts the defeat, and gives up power.

If we were to apply Huntington's test to Zambia, then we can conclude that Zambia qualifies to be a democratic or democratizing country. Since the late 1980s, Zambia has consistently held regular elections in the 1991, 1996, 2001, 2006, and 2008 presidential elections to elect a new president after the death of President Mwanawasa. However, an examination of Zambia's democratization process since the late 1980s reveals a rather bumpy and difficult experience. Although the initial multiparty elections were a reflection of true democracy (free, fair, and the results generally reflecting the will of the majority), the subsequent elections, especially during the Chiluba period, did not live up to the standards set by the 1991 elections. In fact, in the elections of 1996 and 2001, Zambia's standards of democratization either stagnated,[39] or degenerated.[40]

Like other African countries, despite Zambia's 1991 elections being considered a "model of democracy" in the continent,[41] Zambia's subsequent elections have been flawed and characterized by a "declining electoral quality" — a lack of internal democracy, abuse of governmental resources during campaigns, and the growing hostility of government to democracy monitoring.[42] The 2006 general elections and the 2008 presidential election to choose a replacement to the late President Mwanawasa were less un-democratic, and have set Zambia back on the path of democratization once again. The latter two elections have shown some signs of competitiveness, fairness, and openness. The results, although close and contested, were a fair reflection of people's choice.

The greatest democratic degeneration or regression in Zambia occurred during the 1996 elections, which were so flawed that the outcome was known well before the casting of the votes. The 1996 elections were the opposite of the 1991 because they were flawed. The 1996 election was rigged, and the process and results manipulated to ensure that a Chiluba victory was assured.[43] Zambia's political environment on the eve of the general elections in 1996 was not conducive to having free and fair elections either. Zambia, especially Lusaka and other major regional headquarters, was awash with demonstrators and other anti-government protests.

The climax of these protests was a series of bomb blasts that rocked the capital. The government blamed the opposition, while the opposition blamed the bombings on the government. A number of pro-UNIP leaders were arrested and tried for treason. Despite the involvement of the donor community, and threats that they were going to cut donor assistance to Zambia, government harassment of the opposition did not cease. This drew the ire of university students, who joined in the protests against the government. The effect of all this was that the government created an environment in which the opposition could not establish any formidable challenge to the MMD's dominance. The opposition reacted to this by boycotting the elections. Thus, in 1996, the major opposition parties decided to boycott the elections. This boycott influenced the decision by the majority of election monitoring teams, who declined to take place in the 1996 elections claiming that the process had already been manipulated.[44] According to Kirkwood, in the 1996 elections, the voter had nothing to choose from since Chiluba had already frustrated the opposition into boycotting the elections. As he points out, major opposition parties had decided to boycott the elections in protest over irregularities that Chiluba's MMD government had already engaged in, giving the ruling party enormous advantages.[45]

In the 1996 elections, Zambia's electoral body used outdated and unreliable registers to conduct the elections. The government did not carry out a fresh registration exercise. Rather, it used the 1987 registers, which it hoodwinked the people into believing they had updated. Furthermore, the secrecy with which the exercise was conducted left few people in doubt as to the government's commitment or intentions to use the registers to manipulate the election's outcome. The people's suspicion of the government's intent of rigging the elections were confirmed when the tender to upgrade voter registers was controversially awarded to an Israeli firm under suspicious circumstances.[46]

Like the 1996 elections, the 2001 elections were also contentious with allegations of vote rigging. The counting of votes was equally flawed, with different candidates being declared victorious. Initial election results had indicated that Anderson Mazoka of the United Party for National Development (UPND) was the winner, but this was reversed when Mwanawasa, the handpicked MMD leader, was declared winner and was eventually sworn in as president with a paltry 28 percent of the votes, and 69 out of 150 seats in Parliament. The 2001 elections were characterized by open and excessive election malpractices, allegations of vote rigging, and political interference in the electoral process. As was the case with previous elections, the state owned television and media houses were excessively biased in favor of the ruling party. As most observer groups noted, the excessive use of state resources, including public funds by the MMD, significantly distorted the playing field in favor of the ruling party and its candidates.

A significant level of election irregularities and mismanagement characterized the 2001 elections. Prior to the elections, biased and selective voter registration disenfranchised many areas that were considered opposition strongholds. Mwanawasa's very narrow election victory was followed by numerous petitions in court to nullify his election, as it was alleged that the elections were rigged in favor of the MMD. Despite the irregularities and outright voter fraud, efforts to have Mwanawasa's victory overturned were frustrated by the lack of an independent judiciary.[47] Other domestic and international observer groups made the same verdict. An important aspect of the 2001 elections was the marked absence of any significant post election violence despite the close elections, as well as the political disputes over the announced election results.

In the run up to the 2001 elections, there was a perception within the MMD that a low voter turnout would be to the party's advantage. Therefore, the MMD government manipulated the ECZ to ensure that the elections were not popularized. Burnell (2002) claims that the timing of the 2001 elections, for example, was meant to ensure a low turnout. According to Burnell, the elections were called during the rainy season, which complicated logistics of distributing election materials, as well as inconveniencing the majority of voters who walk to vote and who have to stand in long lines for almost half a day to vote. In the rural areas in particular, the rainy season normally limits the amount of work that peasants can do outside their farms. The onset of the rainy season in Africa confines the majority of peasant to farm related work; they hardly have the time, the means, or the luxury of voting.[48]

Mwanawasa's narrow victory in the 2001 elections turned out to be a blessing for Zambia's democratization process. Mwanawasa's narrow election victory forced him to consult more broadly, and to reach out to the opposition. He also worked hard towards changing his image as a Chiluba surrogate. In 2001, Mwanawasa had been handpicked by Chiluba to be the sole MMD presidential candidate. Chiluba had hoped that since Mwanawasa was sickly, and lacked popular support, he would be an easy person to manipulate. Hence, Chiluba and his cronies could count on Mwanawasa to protect them from prosecution for corruption. Mwanawasa's narrow victory, the many challenges to his election, and Chiluba's attempts to manipulate him all posed a big challenge to Mwanawasa's democratization efforts. However, things changed for the better with the 2006 elections.

The 2006 elections were an improvement on the 2001 elections, especially in terms of the outcome. The MMD's Mwanawasa, who had won with a paltry 28 percent of the votes and who formed a minority government, got a better tally in 2006. The forty-three percent of the votes that Mwanawasa got in 2006 enabled him to rule with a broader mandate than in 2001, although the combined opposition still held the majority of seats in Parliament. The conduct of the 2006 elections was also quite different from the previous ones. Voter apathy and election malpractices were drastically reduced. Voter fraud was also significantly lower. Election violence, especially during the campaigns period, was low, and police brutality was at a minimal. Indeed, as the Commonwealth Observer Mission in Zambia pointed out, the Electoral Commission of Zambia did a commendable job. The Commonwealth Observer Group pointed out that the 2006 overall process of the elections was "more open and had a satisfactory level of transparency and credibility." Overall, the Commonwealth Observer Group was satisfied with the conduct of the 2006 general elections. Although common before, violence broke out only at the counting and announcement of the results. The level of violence, however, was low and quickly died out when opposition leaders and civil society groups condemned it. The main presidential candidates in 2006 had pledged to use peaceful and constitutional means to end any disputes arising from the elections.

Unlike in 2001 where the opposition was divided, in 2006 the opposition fielded fewer candidates. The UPND managed to form an opposition alliance, uniting Kaunda's UNIP, the UDA, and the FDD. As in previous elections, attempts towards fielding a single opposition candidate failed, as Michael Sata (the strongest of the opposition candidates) did not join the opposition alliance. Two other opposition candidates also participated in the elections. They were Godfrey Miyanda of the Heritage Party, and Ken Ngondo of the All People's Congress Party.[49] The EISA Regional Observer Mission to Zambia's 2006 elections gave a press release in which it pointed out that in general, the constitutional and legal framework existed in the country under which credible elections could be held. The EISA mission's report concurred with the Commonwealth Observer Mission in accepting that the electoral process and campaigning were conducted in a generally peaceful atmosphere where all parties campaigned in a relatively free and tolerant environment.

Democratization amid Human Rights Violations

One of Zambia's achievements in the era of democratization was the 1995 constitutional review. President Chiluba, however, used the new constitution as a weapon to eliminate his opponents, and hence the new constitution became a source of more controversy and opposition. In what has generally been considered to have been aimed solely at Kaunda, the new constitution stipulated that any person running for the presidency had to be Zambian by birth. Kaunda, whose parents were Malawians, could not therefore contest. This was the basis for the UNIP's boycott of the 1996 elections. Another clause in the new constitution stipulated that no one who had already served two terms as president could run for the presidency again. Kaunda, who had already served for more than two terms, was therefore eliminated from future contests. Other sections of the new constitution were also manipulated to bar people who would have challenged Chiluba or his allies in the MMD. Chiluba made use of the MMD's overwhelming majority in the Parliament to pass through political acts aimed at ensuring executive dominance.[50]

Press and media personalities were harassed during Chiluba's period. The most ridiculous of the harassments came from the Speaker of the Zambian Parliament who ordered the arrest of three of *The Post* editorial staff members in February 1996 for contempt of the House. According to HRW-Africa, the three were arrested for failing to withdraw and apologize to the speaker for an article that appeared in *The Post*; the speaker considered the article "inflammatory and contemptuous," and meant to lower the dignity of the House. The three (the paper's Managing Director, Editor and Columnist), were arrested and spent three weeks in prison until the High Court of Zambia ordered their release.[51]

After the 1996 rigged elections, the crackdown on opposition supporters, which had been witnessed throughout the electioneering period, continued. In June 1997, police attacked the headquarters of the UNIP and arrested a number of the UNIP supporters.[52] According to HRW, live bullets were fired at Kaunda and Rodger Chokwe, injuring both of them in the process. Despite the denials by the government, chaos and protests continued throughout the capital, culminating in the October 28, 1997, attempted coup against the Chiluba government, which made the political environment become even more charged. A scared Chiluba declared a state of emergency throughout Zambia, and took advantage of the emergency regulations to carry out a campaign against the opposition and civil society organizations sympathetic to the opposition. More opposition activists, including Kaunda and many other UNIP supporters, were arrested and detained under the pretext that they supported or sympathized with the coup plotters.[53] Lawyers for those detained were also harassed. Many of them suffered a similar fate as the detainees.

Human rights violations by the government increased after the October 28, 1997, attempted coup. Following the declaration of a state of emergency, all public gatherings, even ones that had already been licensed, were banned. This ban continued until the emergency was ended on March 17, 1998, when Chiluba bowed to international pressure to restore Zambia into normalcy.[54] Over 100 suspects were arrested and detained, and many of them were tortured or subjected to inhuman treatment in jail. A number of opposition leaders, who did not play any part in the attempted coup, were arrested as well. In November 4, 1999, Major Wezi Kaunda, the son of Zambia's founding president, was killed in what people believe was a politically motivated murder by government agents. This occurred after a similar attack on Kenneth Kaunda in March, pointing the finger at Chiluba's government agents who wanted to silence the opposition leaders.[55]

Opposition to Chiluba was not confined only to domestic groups. Chiluba's non-democratic activities attracted international attention as well. Pressure was also exerted by Zambia's neighbors and trading partners within the Southern African Development Community (SADC) for the Chiluba government to end human rights violations in the country. Attempts by Human Rights Watch to gain access to the detainees were fruitless. This, and other human rights violations, prompted Zambia's bilateral and multilateral lenders to threaten to cut their financial aid to Zambia unless the government improved its human rights record. After the 1997 attempted coup, the European Union sent a stern warning to Chiluba not to perpetrate human rights abuses in the pretext of containing the coup. A United States' Special Envoy gave a similar warning to Zambia in December 1997.

The failure of Chiluba to heed the warnings of the U. S. A. and E.U. for his government to adhere to the internationally agreed human rights standards set in motion a chain reaction which saw donor financial assistance to Zambia reduced. Britain, Denmark, the E.U., Canada, Norway, and Japan all withdrew financial aid and conditioned any further assistance to the Zambian government to deliberate efforts by the government to improve the political situation in the country. The European Union, Canada, Norway and Japan set three conditions that the government had to meet before aid could be resumed. These three conditions included the charging or releasing of those accused of plotting the coup, the lifting of the state of emergency, and a full investigation of all allegations of torture of detainees.[56]

Chiluba's exit in 2001 did not improve the human rights situation in Zambia in any significant way. Chiluba's successor, Levy Mwanawasa, did much to reverse the democratic degeneration experienced during Chiluba's time. At the same time, he contributed significantly towards the degeneration of democracy in the country, particularly the first five years of his rule. In general, Mwanawasa's treatment of the press and the mediawas not different from Chiluba's. During his first regime, he harassed the media in a similar fashion to Chiluba's; between 2001 and 2006, the International Press Institute (IPI) documented numerous cases of Mwanawasa's harassment of the media. The IPI's report indicates that a number of journalists in Zambia were victims of police brutality in the course of their duties. In April 7, 2005, police in the Nakonde region arrested Zambia National Broadcasting Corporation members for exposing their corrupt practices.[57] MMD supporters attacked vendors of The Post, while The Post's Managing Editor was detained under sedition laws for an article that appeared in the paper that was critical of the president. The 2005 edition of the IPI pointed out that attempts to guarantee press freedom of Information in the Constitution Review Commission were shelved when the AG complained that such guarantee would endanger state security. The AG also opposed proposed provisions to guarantee freedom of all electronic and print media from interference, as well as a proposition that would have protected journalists from having to disclose the source of their information except in court.[58]

On November 25, 2002, the press and members of the public were barred from witnessing the election of the House Speaker. The reason for this was to prevent any "bad publicity" due to the anticipated competition that was likely to take place, owing to the government's narrow margin in Parliament.[59] There were a number of bomb hoaxes targeting news media houses that were thought to have been the work of the police or government agents to threaten or intimidate journalists. The residence of The Post's Editor was bombed. This, coming at a time when the editor and the staff of The Post were engaged in a number of accusations and counter accusations with the former president Chiluba, led many people to believe that government agents were responsible for the attack.

In January 2003, three journalists with *The Monitor* were arrested for claiming that the president's brother was corrupt. The Mwanawasa government also harassed journalists who tried to link his government to corruption perpetrated by his predecessor Chiluba. It is interesting that the Mwanawasa government was ok with journalists' coverage of the Chiluba arrest on corruption charges on February 20, 2003, yet harassed any journalists who pointed out that president Mwanawasa was once a member of the Chiluba cabinet. On November 1, 2003, the Mwanawasa government cancelled the operating license for Omega TV Station.

As a result of the many years of government control over the media during the one party regime, a culture of self-censorship developed within media houses. Journalists in government owned newspapers and government controlled television stations engaged in a deliberate bias reporting in favor of the government and government ministers. They deliberately distorted the opposition's records to give the government a better image, while blotting that of the opposition. This culture of self-censorship and biased reporting is not hard to understand. In a country as poor as Zambia, where unemployment is quite high, and where job security in almost every profession cannot be guaranteed, being viewed as against the government can be quite costly to an employee who is trying to feed his family. There are other financial incentives that the government used to ensure positive reporting and editorials by journalists. Journalists are bribed to accord certain individuals more coverage, and to ensure a news blackout for others. In addition to monetary incentives paid directly to journalists for positive reporting, the government also offers other tax incentives to those newspapers or television stations that cooperate. Other government policies significantly affect media houses directly. One example is the March 2006 proposed VAT Act that would have increased newspaper-printing costs by almost 25 percent. The government withdrew the tax after it became apparent that several newspapers would cease production.

The culture of biased reporting is not only encouraged by government functionaries, but opposition members also expect it, and have encouraged independent newspapers to engage in the same in favor of the opposition and against the government. Self-censorship was enforced by the management who punished and/or dismissed journalists for not exercising self-censorship. In May 1998, the management of the state owned *Zambia Daily Mail* (ZDM) instituted disciplinary action against one of its reporters for her exposure of the paper's editorial practice of censoring stories critical of the government. This disciplinary action was condemned by the Zambia Union of Journalists (ZUJ) and ZAMWA. According to Joy Sata, the disciplined journalist, the management of ZDM forced reporters to rely on "government sources" for their stories; reporters were forced to exercise self-censorship when they came across stories critical to the government. Any stories critical of the government were not going to be published. In another case, the news editor for the paper was put on indefinite suspension for leading an editorial protest against the management's decision to play down the attempted coup treason case. On January 24, 2000, the privately owned Radio Phoenix (RP) discontinued its live-call-in program "Let the People Speak: The Doctor's Strike," which was sponsored by Inter-African Network for Human Rights and Development (AFRONET) to provide a forum for striking doctors to air their grievances. RP suspended the program when the Ministry of Information complained about the content of the program.

On a number of occasions, journalists representing government-controlled state media were barred from covering functions organized by the opposition. One of the best examples of this was on May 24, 2006, when journalists representing the state-owned *Times of Zambia* were barred from an opposition United Party for National Development (UPND) press briefing that was called to announce the death of the UPND President, Anderson Mazoka. The reason given was that the government-owned newspaper reported only negative stories about the UPND leader. Harassment of reporters from government owned newspapers and television stations by opposition figures were also common. On August, 26, 2006, a reporter and a cameraman were harassed in an opposition rally called by the Patriotic Front (PF). The PF president Michael Sata accused the Zambia National Broadcasting Corporation of relying on people's taxes.

Conclusion

The conduct of multiparty elections in Zambia reveals undemocratic electoral practices that have become common in Africa. The first pertains to the conduct of the ruling parties that acted as if the electoral body was part and parcel, or an extension of the executive. In most African countries, the electoral bodies have been misused to ensure that the ruling party reaped maximum benefits, while the opposition was either deliberately inconvenienced or disadvantaged. The timing and the conduct of elections, for example, have been made to the advantage of the ruling parties. The second concerns presidential elections, which have become the most important political survival weapon for any ruling regime. Regardless of the margin of victory, there are all sorts of resources for a victorious candidate and party to purchase.[60] They coerce others to support the use of all means possible to ensure that they are declared winners in any presidential election. In Zambia, for example, despite Mwanawasa's narrow victory in 2001, he was still able to "buy a working parliamentary majority."[61] Despite this poor showing, Mwanawasa proceeded to form his cabinet with people drawn almost exclusively from regions that voted for the MMD. This was an act that was meant to punish the communities that did not support the party.

Zambia's democratization has taken place amid a worsening economy (declining incomes, falling copper prices, and declining living standards) and corruption. Formal sector employment fell by 24 percent between 1992 and 2004,[62] increasing the cuts in public expenditure which have led to a marked decline in living standards, and a marked decline in Zambia's rankings in the Human Development Index. Zambia slid from 110 of 136 countries in 1990 (0.465), and to 166 of 177 countries in 2005 (0.394) (UNDP 2006).[63] This has increased people's dissatisfaction with the MMD government, and has increased the "intensity of politicization at an early stage."[64] To retain power, the MMD resorted to the suppression of the opposition, the rigging of elections,[65] and ballot staffing. Incompetence and other bureaucratic problems within the ECZ have provided the MMD with even more opportunities to manipulate the elections.

In addition, the MMD resorted to making unilateral decisions and undertaking constitutional changes that enabled it to rule without majority electoral support.[66] Other undemocratic practices include the disqualification of Kaunda, Chiluba's attempt to change the constitution to allow Chiluba to run for a third term, and the failure of Zambian leaders to respect the constitution as manifested by the various attempts to manipulate it to suit their political ambition.

Since the introduction of the multiparty system in Zambia, power has been dominated by the old guard (the majority of who had served in Kaunda's UNIP government). Even in the run up to the 2008 by elections, the major candidates, and indeed, the eventual winner, Rupiah Banda represented the old guard of the UNIP and Chiluba days. Many of these people had been tainted by participating in Kaunda's *de jure*, and later in Chiluba's almost de facto one party state. Even after the election of Mwanawasa and Rupiah Banda, and after the former's death, Zambia did not experience a fully democratic transition, one which would facilitate the rise of a newer generation of politicians untainted by participating in either Kaunda's or Chiluba's governments with dominant party systems. As a result, though the country had experienced different leadership, the composition and attitudes of the political elites has remained unchanged.

Appendix

Data on African Countries*

Cameroon

Location	Western Africa, bordering the Bight of Biafra, between Equatorial Guinea and Nigeria
Population	19,294,149
Religion	Indigenous beliefs 40%, Christian 40%, Muslim 20%
Literacy	Definition: age 15 and over can read and write—total population: 67.9% male: 77% female: 59.8% (2001 est.)
Capital	Yaounde
Government Type	Republic; multiparty presidential regime
Suffrage	20 years of age; universal
Legal System	Based on French civil law system with common law influence; accepts compulsory ICJ jurisdiction
GDP	$44.65 billion (2010 est.)
Per capita	$2,300 (2010 est.)
Unemployment	30% (2001 est.)
Exports	$4.371 billion (2010 est.)
Imports	$4.869 billion (2010 est.)
Debt-external	$3.344 billion (31 December 2010 est.)

---

*Source: CIA, The World Factbook at https://www.cia.gov/library/publications/the-world-factbook/.

Military	Cameroon Armed Forces (Forces Armees Camerounaises, FAC): Army (L'Armee de Terre), Navy (includes naval infantry), Air Force (Armee de l'Air du Cameroun, AAC), Fire Fighter Corps, Gendarmerie (2010) 18–23 years of age for male and female voluntary military service; no conscription; high school graduation required; service obligation 4 years; the government makes periodic calls for volunteers (2010)

Egypt

Location	Northern Africa, bordering the Mediterranean Sea, between Libya and the Gaza Strip, and the Red Sea north of Sudan, and includes the Asian Sinai Peninsula
Population	80,471,869 (July 2010 est.)
Religion	Muslim (mostly Sunni) 90%, Coptic 9%, other Christian 1%
Literacy	Definition: age 15 and over can read and write—total population: 71.4% male: 83%, female: 59.4% (2005 est.)
Capital	Cairo
Government Type	Republic
Suffrage	18 years of age; universal and compulsory
Legal System	Based on Islamic and civil law (particularly Napoleonic codes); judicial review by Supreme Court and Council of State (oversees validity of administrative decisions); accepts compulsory ICJ jurisdiction with reservations
GDP	$500.9 billion (2010 est.)
Per capita	$6,200 (2010 est.)
Unemployment	9.7% (2010 est.)
Exports	$25.34 billion (2010 est.)
Imports	$46.52 billion (2010 est.)
Debt-external	$30.61 billion (31 December 2010 est.)
Military	Army, Navy, Air Force, Air Defense Command, 18–30 years of age for male conscript military service; service obligation 12–36 months, followed by a 9-year reserve obligation (2008)

Eritrea

Location	Eastern Africa, bordering the Red Sea, between Djibouti and Sudan
Population	5,792,984 (July 2010 est.)
Religion	Muslim, Coptic Christian, Roman Catholic, Protestant
Literacy	Definition: age 15 and over can read and write—total population: 58.6% male: 69.9% female: 47.6% (2003 est.)
Capital	Asmara
Government Type	Transitional government
Suffrage	18 years of age; universal
Legal System	Primary basis is the Ethiopian legal code of 1957 with revisions; new civil, commercial, and penal codes have not yet been promulgated; government also issues unilateral proclamations setting laws and policies; also relies on customary and post-independence-enacted laws and, for civil cases involving Muslims, Islamic law; has not accepted compulsory ICJ jurisdiction
GDP	$4.178 billion (2010 est.)
Per capita	$700 (2010 est.)
Unemployment	N/A
Exports	$25 million (2010 est.)
Imports	$738 million (2010 est.)
Debt-external	$NA (31 December 2010 est.) $961.9 million (31 December 2008 est.)
Military	Eritrean Armed Forces: Ground Forces, Navy, Air Force (2010) 18–40 years of age for male and female voluntary and compulsory military service; 16-month conscript service obligation (2006)

Insular States

Cape Verde

Location	Western Africa, group of islands in the North Atlantic Ocean, west of Senegal
Population	508,659 (July 2010 est.)
Religion	Roman Catholic (infused with indigenous beliefs), Protestant (mostly Church of the Nazarene)
Literacy	Definition: age 15 and over can read and write—total population: 76.6% male: 85.8% female: 69.2% (2003 est.)
Capital	Praia
Government Type	Republic
Suffrage	18 years of age; universal
Legal System	Based on the legal system of Portugal; has not accepted compulsory ICJ jurisdiction
GDP	$1.861 billion (2010 est.)
Per capita	$3,700 (2010 est.)
Unemployment	21% (2000 est.)
Exports	$114 million (2010 est.)
Imports	$858 million (2010 est.)
Debt-external	$325 million (2002)
Military	People's Revolutionary Armed Forces (FARP) Army, Coast Guard (includes maritime air wing) (2007) 18 years of age (est.) for selective compulsory military service; 14-month conscript service obligation (2006)

Comoros

Location	Southern Africa, group of islands at the northern mouth of the Mozambique Channel, about two-thirds of the way between northern Madagascar and northern Mozambique
Population	773,407 (July 2010 est.)

Religion	Sunni Muslim 98%, Roman Catholic 2%
Literacy	Definition: age 15 and over can read and write—total population: 56.5% male: 63.6% female: 49.3% (2003 est.)
Capital	Moroni
Government Type	Republic
Suffrage	18 years of age; universal
Legal System	French and Islamic law in a new consolidated code; has not accepted compulsory ICJ jurisdiction
GDP	$789.4 million (2010 est.)
Per capita	$1,000 (2010 est.)
Unemployment	20% (1996 est.)
Exports	$32 million (2006)
Imports	$143 million (2006)
Debt-external	$232 million (2000 est.)
Military	Army of National Development (AND): Comoran Security Force, Comoran Coast Guard, Comoran Federal Police (2010) 18 years of age for 2-year voluntary military service; no conscription; women first inducted into the Army in 2004 (2010)

Mauritius

Location	Southern Africa, island in the Indian Ocean, east of Madagascar
Population	1,294,104 (July 2010 est.)
Religion	Hindu 48%, Roman Catholic 23.6%, Muslim 16.6%, other Christian 8.6%, other 2.5%, unspecified 0.3%, none 0.4% (2000 census)
Literacy	Definition: age 15 and over can read and write—total population: 84.4% male: 88.4% female: 80.5% (2000 census)
Capital	Port Louis
Government Type	Parliamentary democracy

Suffrage	18 years of age; universal
Legal System	Based on French civil law system with elements of English common law in certain areas; accepts compulsory ICJ jurisdiction with reservations

GDP	$17.49 billion (2010 est.)
Per capita	$13,500 (2010 est.)
Unemployment	7.5% (2010 est.)
Exports	$2.041 billion (2010 est.)
Imports	$3.935 billion (2010 est.)
Debt-external	$5.043 billion (31 December 2010 est.)

Military	No regular military forces; Mauritius Police Force, Special Mobile Force, National Coast Guard (2009)

Sao Tome and Principe

Location	Western Africa, islands in the Gulf of Guinea, straddling the Equator, west of Gabon
Population	175,808 (July 2010 est.)
Religion	Catholic 70.3%, Evangelical 3.4%, New Apostolic 2%, Adventist 1.8%, other 3.1%, none 19.4% (2001 census)
Literacy	Definition: age 15 and over can read and write—total population: 84.9% male: 92.2% female: 77.9% (2001 census)

Capital	Sao Tome
Government Type	Republic
Suffrage	18 years of age; universal
Legal System	Based on Portuguese legal system and customary law; has not accepted compulsory ICJ jurisdiction

GDP	$316.9 million (2010 est.)
Per capita	$1,800 (2010 est.)
Unemployment	N/A
Exports	$13 million (2010 est.)
Imports	$99 million (2010 est.)
Debt-external	$318 million (2002)

| Military | Armed Forces of Sao Tome and Principe (Forcas Armadas de Sao Tome e Principe, FASTP): Army, Coast Guard of Sao Tome e Principe (Guarda Costeira de Sao Tome e Principe, GCSTP), Presidential Guard (2010) 18 years of age (est.) (2004) |

Seychelles

Location	Archipelago in the Indian Ocean, northeast of Madagascar
Population	88,340 (July 2010 est.)
Religion	Roman Catholic 82.3%, Anglican 6.4%, Seventh Day Adventist 1.1%, other Christian 3.4%, Hindu 2.1%, Muslim 1.1%, other non-Christian 1.5%, unspecified 1.5%, none 0.6% (2002 census)
Literacy	Definition: age 15 and over can read and write—total population: 91.8% male: 91.4% female: 92.3% (2002 census)
Capital	Victoria
Government Type	Republic
Suffrage	17 years of age; universal
Legal System	Based on English common law, French civil law, and customary law; has not accepted compulsory ICJ jurisdiction
GDP	$1.908 billion (2010 est.)
Per capita	$21,600 (2010 est.)
Unemployment	2% (2006 est.)
Exports	$464 million (2010 est.)
Imports	$831 million (2010 est.)
Debt-external	$1.374 billion (31 December 2010 est.)
Military	Seychelles Defense Force: Army, Coast Guard (includes Naval Wing, Air Wing), National Guard (2005) 18 years of age for voluntary military service (younger with parental consent); no conscription (2010)

Morocco

Location	Northern Africa, bordering the North Atlantic Ocean and the Mediterranean Sea, between Algeria and Western Sahara
Population	31,627,428 (July 2010 est.)
Religion	Muslim 98.7%, Christian 1.1%, Jewish 0.2%
Literacy	Definition: age 15 and over can read and write: 52.3% male: 65.7% female: 39.6% (2004 census)
Capital	Rabat
Government Type	Constitutional Monarchy
Suffrage	18 years of age; universal
Legal System	Based on Islamic law, and French and Spanish civil law systems; judicial review of legislative acts in Constitutional Chamber of Supreme Court; has not accepted compulsory ICJ jurisdiction
GDP	$153.8 billion (2010 est.)
Per capita	$4,900 (2010 est.)
Unemployment	9.8% (2010 est.)
Exports	$14.49 billion (2010 est.)
Imports	$34.19 billion (2010 est.)
Debt-external	$22.69 billion (31 December 2010 est.)
Military	Royal Armed Forces (Forces Armees Royales, FAR): Royal Moroccan Army (includes Air Defense), Royal Moroccan Navy (includes Coast Guard, Marines), Royal Moroccan Air Force (Al Quwwat al Jawyiya al Malakiya Marakishiya; Force Aerienne Royale Marocaine) (2010) 18 years of age for voluntary military service; service obligation—18 months (2010)

Namibia

Location	Southern Africa, bordering the South Atlantic Ocean, between Angola and South Africa

Population	2,128,471
Religion	Christian 80% to 90% (Lutheran 50% at least), indigenous beliefs 10% to 20%
Literacy	Definition: age 15 and over can read and write—total population: 85% male: 86.8% female: 83.5% (2001 census)
Capital	Windhoek
Government Type	Republic
Suffrage	18 years of age; universal
Legal System	Based on Roman-Dutch law and 1990 constitution; has not accepted compulsory ICJ jurisdiction
GDP	$14.64 billion (2010 est.)
Per capita	$6,900 (2010 est.)
Unemployment	51.2% (2008 est.)
Exports	$4.277 billion (2010 est.)
Imports	$5.152 billion (2010 est.)
Debt-external	$2.373 billion (31 December 2010 est.)
Military	Namibian Defense Force (NDF): Army, Navy, Air Force (2010), 18 years of age for voluntary military service; no conscription (2010)

Nigeria

Location	Western Africa, bordering the Gulf of Guinea, between Benin and Cameroon
Population	152,217,341
Religion	Muslim 50%, Christian 40%, indigenous beliefs 10%
Literacy	Definition: age 15 and over can read and write—total population: 68% male: 75.7% female: 60.6% (2003 est.)
Capital	Abuja
Government Type	Federal Republic

Suffrage	18 years of age; universal
Legal System	Based on English common law, Islamic law (in 12 northern states), and traditional law; accepts compulsory ICJ jurisdiction with reservations

GDP	$369.8 billion (2010 est.)
Per capita	$2,400 (2010 est.)
Unemployment	4.9% (2007 est.)
Exports	$76.33 billion (2010 est.)
Imports	$34.18 billion (2010 est.)
Debt-external	$11.02 billion (31 December 2010 est.)

Military	Nigerian Armed Forces: Army, Navy, Air Force (2008) 18 years of age for voluntary military service (2007

Rwanda

Location	Central Africa, east of Democratic Republic of the Congo
Population	11,055,976 (July 2010 est.)
Religion	Roman Catholic 56.5%, Protestant 26%, Adventist 11.1%, Muslim 4.6%, indigenous beliefs 0.1%, none 1.7% (2001)
Literacy	Definition: age 15 and over can read and write—total population: 70.4% male: 76.3% female: 64.7% (2003 est.)

Capital	Kigali
Government Type	Republic; presidential, multiparty system
Suffrage	18 years of age; universal
Legal System	Based on German and Belgian civil law systems and customary law; judicial review of legislative acts in the Supreme Court; has not accepted compulsory ICJ jurisdiction

GDP	$11.84 billion (2010 est.)
Per capita	$1,100 (2010 est.)
Unemployment	N/A
Exports	$226 million (2010 est.)
Imports	$1.047 billion (2010 est.)

Debt-external	N/A
Military	Rwandan Defense Forces (RDF), Rwandan Patriotic Air Force (2009), 18 years of age for voluntary military service; no conscription (2010)

Tanzania

Location	Eastern Africa, bordering the Indian Ocean, between Kenya and Mozambique
Population	41,892,895
Religion	Mainland—Christian 30%, Muslim 35%, indigenous beliefs 35%; Zanzibar—more than 99% Muslim
Literacy	Definition: age 15 and over can read and write Kiswahili (Swahili), English, or Arabic. Total population: 69.4% male: 77.5% female: 62.2% (2002 census)
Capital	Dar es Salaam
Government Type	Republic
Suffrage	18 years of age; universal
Legal System	Based on English common law; judicial review of legislative acts limited to matters of interpretation; has not accepted compulsory ICJ jurisdiction
GDP	$62.22 billion (2010 est.)
Per capita	$1,500 (2010 est.)
Unemployment	N/A
Exports	$3.809 billion (2010 est.)
Imports	$6.334 billion (2010 est.)
Debt-external	$7.576 billion (31 December 2010 est.)
Military	Tanzanian People's Defense Force (Jeshi la Wananchi la Tanzania, JWTZ): Army, Naval Wing (includes Coast Guard), Air Defense Command (includes Air Wing), National Service (2007), 18 years of age for voluntary military service (2007)

Zambia

Location	Southern Africa, east of Angola
Population	13,460,305
Religion	Christian 50%–75%, Muslim and Hindu 24%–49%, indigenous beliefs 1%
Literacy	Definition: age 15 and over can read and write English— total population: 80.6% male: 86.8% female: 74.8% (2003 est.)
Capital	Lusaka
Government Type	Republic
Suffrage	18 years of age; universal
Legal System	Based on English common law and customary law; judicial review of legislative acts in an ad hoc constitutional council; has not accepted compulsory ICJ jurisdiction
GDP	$20.03 billion (2010 est.)
Per capita	$1,500 (2010 est.)
Unemployment	50% (2000 est.)
Exports	$6.463 billion (2010 est.)
Imports	$4.949 billion (2010 est.)
Debt-external	$3.495 billion (31 December 2010 est.)
Military	Zambian National Defense Force (ZNDF): Zambian Army, Zambian Air Force, National Service (2009) 18–27 years of age for male and female voluntary military service (16 years of age with parental consent); no conscription; Zambian citizenship required; mandatory HIV testing upon enlistment; mandatory retirement for officers at age 65 (Army, Air Force) (2010)

Notes

Introduction

1. Saliba Sarsar, "Democracy in the Arab World." *Middle East Quarterly*, Vol. VII, No. 1 (March 2000): 39–48 and Saliba Sarsar, "Measuring Arab Democracy." *Middle East Quarterly*, Vol. XIII, No. 3 (Summer 2006): 21–28.

2. Saliba Sarsar and David Strohmetz, "Focus on Governance: The Economics of Democracy in Muslim Countries." *Middle East Quarterly*, Vol. 15, No. 3 (Summer 2008): 3–11.

Chapter 1

1. J. A. Atanda, "The Changing Status of the Alaafin of Oyo Under Colonial Rule and Independence," in Michael Crowder and Obaro Ikime, ed. *West African Chiefs* (Ile-Ife: University of Ife Press, 1970), 214.

2. Robert I. Rotberg, *A Political History of Tropical Africa* (New York: Harcourt, Brace and World, 1965), 112–113.

3. This saying originated from Lord Acton in a letter to Bishop Mandell Creighton in 1887. According to Lord Acton, "Power tends to corrupt, and absolute power corrupts absolutely. Great men are almost always bad men."

4. This became the most effective means of curbing a highhanded Alaafin. The system worked successfully for the empire.

5. Johnson, 70.

6. John Middleton and David Tait, eds., *Tribes without Rulers: Studies in African Segmentary Systems* (London: Routledge and Kegan Paul, 1958).

7. I. M. Lewis, *A Pastoral Democracy: A Study of Pastoralism and Politics among the Northern Somali of the Horn of Africa* (First published, London: Oxford University Press, 1961, reprinted International Institute, James Curry, 1999), 1.

8. Middleton and Tait, 6.

9. Joseph E. Harris, *Africans and their History,* Revised Edition (New York: The Penguin Group, 1987), 120–121.

10. Ibid.

11. Daryll Forde and G.I. Jones, *The Ibo and Ibiobio-Speaking Peoples of South-eastern Nigeria* (London: International African Institute, 1950, reprinted 1967), 15.

12. Harris, 122.

13. Paul Bohannan and Philip Curtin, *Africa and Africans*, Third Edition (Prospect Heights, IL: Waveland Press, 1988), 162–163.

14. Teresa A. Booker, "Peace, Spirituality, and Justice: Nigerian Style," in Julius O. Adekunle, ed. *Religion in Politics: Secularism and National Integration in Modern Nigeria* (Trenton, NJ: Africa World Press, 2009), 319.

15. Andersen, Roy R., Robert F. Seibert, Jon G. Wagner, *Politics and Change in the Middle East: Sources of Conflict and Accommodation*, Eighth Edition (Upper Saddle River, NJ: Pearson Prentice Hall, 2007), 14.

16. Richard W. Hull, Munyakare: *African Civilization before the Batuuree* (New York: John Wiley and Sons, 1972), 16.

17. Adu Boahen with J. F. Ade. Ajayi and Michael Tidy, *Topics in West African History*, Second Edition (London: Longman, 1986).

18. John Esposito and John Voll, *Islam and Democracy* (London: Oxford University Press, 1966).

19. Audrey Chapman Smock, *Women: Roles and Status in Eight Countries* (New York: A Wiley-Interscience Publication, 1977), 180.

20. John Middleton, *Encyclopedia of Africa*, Vol. 2 (New York: 1997), 196.

21. Robert W. July, *A History of the African People,* Fifth Edition (Prospect Heights, IL: Waveland Press, 1998), 154.

22. J. Omisade Awolalu and P. Adelumo Dopamu, *West African Traditional Religion* (Ibadan, Nigeria: Onibonoje Press and Book Industries, 1979), 86–87.

23. Christopher Fyfe, "West African Trade A.D. 1000–1800," in J. F. Ade. Ajayi and Ian Espie, eds. *A Thousand Years of West African History: A Handbook for Teachers and Students* (Ibadan, Nigeria: Ibadan University Press, first published 1965, reprinted 1970), 243.

24. For more information on the characteristics, methodologies, and values of African traditional education, see Julius O. Adekunle, "Education," in Toyin Falola, ed. *Africa: African Cultures and Societies before 1885*, Vol. 2 (Durham, NC: Carolina Academic Press, 2000), 59–72.

25. Vincent Obisienunwo Orlu Nmehielle, The African Human Rights System: Its Laws, Practice, and Institutions (The Hague: Kluwer Law International, 2001), 7–8.

Chapter 2

1. Daniel Brumberg, "Liberalization versus Democracy." In Thomas Carothers and Marina Ottaway, eds., *Uncharted Journey: Promoting Democracy in the Middle East* (Washington, DC: Carnegie Endowment for International Peace, 2005), 15–35.

2. See Hazem Beblawi and Giacomo Luciani, eds., *The Rentier State* (London: Croom Helm, 1987); Simon Bromley. *Rethinking Middle East Politics* (Oxford: Polity Press, 1994); and Eva Bellin, *Stalled Democracy: Capital, Labor, and the Paradox of State-Sponsored Development* (Ithaca and London: Cornell University Press, 2002).

3. See Nicola Pratt, "Identity, Culture and Democratization: The Case of Egypt." *New Political Science*, Vol. 27, No. 1 (March 2005): 69–86.

4. See CIA, *World Factbook 2011*, Egypt at https://www.cia.gov/library/publications/the-world-factbook/geos/eg.html.

5. Raymond A. Hinnebusch, Jr., *Egyptian Politics Under Sadat: The Post-Populist Development of an Authoritarian-Modernizing State* (Boulder and London: Lynne Rienner Publishers, 1988), 1.

6. Ibid., 86.

7. Steven A. Cook, *Ruling but Not Governing: The Military and Political Development in Egypt, Algeria, and Turkey* (Baltimore: Johns Hopkins University Press, 2007).

8. Jeffrey Fleishman, "How Long Can Egyptian Military Navigate Middle Ground." *Los Angeles Times*, February 6, 2011.

9. Ibid., 80.

10. See CIA, *World Factbook 2011*.

11. See Saliba Sarsar, "Quantifying Arab Democracy. *Middle East Quarterly* (Summer 2006): 21–28 and at http://www.meforum.org/970/quantifying-arab-democracy, and Saliba Sarsar and David Strohmetz, The Economics of Democracy in Muslim Countries. *Middle East Quarterly* (Summer 2008): 3–11 and at http://www.meforum.org/1921/the-economics-of-democracy-in-muslim-countries.

12. David Bukay, "Is the Military Bulwark against Islamism Collapsing." *Middle East Quarterly* (Summer 2009): 29.

13. Mona El-Ghobashy, "Constitutional Contention in Contemporary Egypt." *American Behavioral Scientist*, Vol. 51, No. 11 (July 2008): 1592.

14. For a perceptive analysis of the role of the judiciary, see Robin Wright, *Dreams and Shadows: The Future of the Middle East* (New York: Penguin Books, 2008), 89–97.

15. See the website of the National Democratic Party at http://www.ndp.org.eg/en/About Us/1.aspx.

16. For a discussion of Hizb al-Wasat within the context of inclusiveness and toleration, see Peter E. Makari, *Conflict & Cooperation: Christian-Muslim Relations in Contemporary Egypt* (Syracuse: Syracuse University Press, 2007), 130–137.

17. Andrew Hammond, "Though nominal Winner, Egypt's Ruling NDP Party Embarrassed in Parliamentary Elections." *Washington Report on Middle East Affairs* (January–February 2001): 31.

18. For an in-depth analysis, see http://www.freedomhouse.org/inc/content/pubs/fiiw/inc_country_detail.cfm?year=2008&c.

19. Mohammed Herzallah and Amr Hamzawy, "Egypt's Local Elections Farce: Causes and Consequences." *Policy Outlook*. Washington, DC: Carnegie Endowment for International Peace (April 2008): 1.

20. Freedom House, "Freedom in the World: Egypt 2008." At http://www.freedomhouse.org/inc/content/pubs/fiw/inc_country_detail.cfm?year=2008.

21. Brian Katulis, "Women's Rights in Focus: Egypt—Findings from May–June 2004 Focus Groups with Egyptian Citizens on Women's Freedom." Freedom House (October 19, 2004).

22. Human Rights Watch, "Egypt: Military Trials Usurp Justice System at http://www.hrw.org/en/news/2011/04/29/egypt-military-trials-usurp-justice-system.

23. Freedom House, "Freedom of the Press—Egypt 2008" at http://www.freedomhouse.org/template.cfm?page=251&year=2008&country=7387.

24. Freedom House, "Freedom in the World 2011: Egypt" at http://www.freedomhouse.org/uploads/fiw11/Egypt_FIW_2011.pdf.

25. Ghassan Rubeiz, "The Copts suffer from their state, but so do all Egyptians." *The Daily Star* (September 1, 2009) at http://www.dailystar.com.lb/article.asp?article_ID=105932&categ_ID=5&edition_id=10.

26. International Religious Freedom Report, 2008, http://www.state.gov/g/drl/rls/irf/2008/.

27. Charles Onians, "Supply and Demand Democracy in Egypt." *World Policy Journal* (Summer 2004): 78.

28. "Al-fashiya ad-diniya wa talbanat al-ta'lim al-misri" [Religious Fascism and the Tabilanization of Egyptian Education], *Watani* (December 2007 and January 2008).

29. Hala Mustafa, "A Policy for Promoting Liberal Democracy in Egypt." *White Paper Series: Voices from the Middle East on Democratization and Reform*. Washington DC: Foundation for Defense of Democracies (May 2006): 3.

30. Khairi Abaza, "Political Islam and Regime Survival in Egypt." *Policy Focus*, No. 51. Washington, DC: The Washington Institute for Near East Policy (January 2006).

31. Saliba Sarsar, "Citizenship, not religion, must be the basis for inclusion in the Middle East." *Common Ground News Service* (February 8, 2011) at http://www.commongroundnews.org/article.php?id=29240&lan=en&sp=0.

32. See the Amnesty International report on Egypt at http://www.amnesty.org/en/region/egypt/report-2008.

33. Ibid.

34. Ibid.

35. Michelle L. Browers, *Democracy and Civil Society in Arab Political Thought: Transcultural Possibilities* (Syracuse: Syracuse University Press, 2006), 194–195.

36. United Nations Development Program, "Egypt: A Country Profile of Human Development Indicators" at http://hdrstats.undp.org/en/countries/profiles/EGY.html.

37. United Nations Development Program, "Human and Income Poverty: Developing Countries" at http://hdr.undp.org/en/media/HDR_20072008_Table_3.pdf.

38. See CIA, *World Factbook 2010*, Egypt at https://www.cia.gov/library/publications/the-world-factbook/geos/eg.html.

39. http://www.heritage.org/index/Country/Egypt.

40. See Barry Rubin, "The Fallen Pharaoh" at http://www.qantara.de/webcom/show_article.php/_c-476/_nr-616/i.html.

41. Ibid.

42. Saad Eddin Ibrahim, "Liberalization and Democratization in the Arab World: An Overview." In Rex Brynen, Bahgat Korany, and Paul Noble.eds. *Political Liberalizationa and Democratization in the Arab World*. Vol. 1: *Theoretical Perspectives* (Boulder, CO: Lynne Rienner, 1995), 29.

43. Khairi Abaza, "Political Islam and Regime Survival in Egypt." *Policy Focus*, No. 51. Washington, DC: The Washington Institute for Near East Policy (January 2006).

Chapter 3

1. Jeremy M. Sharp, "US Democracy Promotion Policy in the Middle East: The Islamist Dilemma," *CRS Report for Congress*, June 15, 2006.

2. King Mohammed VI, Excerpts from Address to the Nation, Saturday, July 31, 1999.

3. Saliba Sarsar, "Quantifying Arab Democracy: Democracy in the Middle East," *Middle East Quarterly* (Summer 2006): 21–8.

4. For an insight in the historical development of this culture in Morocco, see M. Palazzoli, "The Evolution of Moroccan National Movement since Independence," in Michael

Brett, *North Africa: Islam and Modernization* (London: Frank Cass, 1973), 123–42; and P. Entelis, John O. Voll, "Sultans, Saints, and Presidents: The Islamic Community and the State in North Africa," in John P. Entelis, ed., *Islam, Democracy, and the State in North Africa* (Bloomington: Indiana University Press, 1997), 1–16.

5. C. R. Pennell, *Morocco since 1830: A History* (New York: New York University Press, 2000), 352–3. See also Yasin cited in Mohammed Darif, *Jama'al al-'Adlwa-Ihsan: qara't fi al-Masarat* (Rabat: Manshurat al-Majallat al-Maghribiyya I-'ilm al-ijtima' al-siyyasi: 1995), 11–14.

6. For a theoretical exploration of this argument in relation to Africa in general and Lesotho in particular, see James Ferguson, *The Anti Politics Machine: "Development," Depoliticization and Bureaucratic Power in Lesotho* (Minnesota: University of Minnesota Press, 1994).

7. See for instance Staffan I. Lindberg, *Democracy and Elections in Africa* (Baltimore: Johns Hopkins University Press, 2006).

8. Samuel P. Huntington, *The Third Wave* (London: University of Oklahoma Press, 1991), 109–315.

9. Ibid., 40–43.

10. Ibid., 46–7. According to Linz and Stepan, political violence is both an important indicator and a contributing cause of democratic breakdown. See Juan J. Linz and Alfred Stepan, eds., *The Breakdown of Democratic Regime* (Baltimore and London: The Johns Hopkins University Press, 1978), 14.

11. Huntington, 109.

12. Robert Pinkney, *The International Politics of East Africa* (Manchester, UK: Manchester University Press, 2001), 102; and Linz and Stepan, 15.

13. Huntington, 582–3. See also Geraldo L. Munk, "Democratic Transitions in Comparative Perspective," *Comparative Politics*, Vol. 26, No. 3 (1994): 363–4.

14. Huntington, 110–23. See also Guillermo O'Donnell, Philippe Schmitter, and Laurence Whitehead, eds., *Transitions from Authoritarian Rule: Prospects for Democracy, in 4 volumes* (Baltimore: The Johns Hopkins University Press, 1986), 19–20.

15. Huntington, 141–2.

16. Pinkney, 121.

17. Essbai Habib, email correspondence, January 13, 2009.

18. Pinkney, 150.

19. *The Economist* (US), July 31, 1999.

20. Abdeslam M. Maghraoui, "Democracy in the Arab World: Depoliticization in Morocco," *Journal of Democracy*, Vol. 13, No. 4 (2002): 28.

21. Constitution of the Islamic Kingdom of Morocco Article 24 [Appointment of Government] 1992.

22. Geoffrey Pridham and Paul G. Lewis, "Introduction: Stabilizing Fragile Democracies and Party System Development," in Geoffrey Pridham and Paul G. Lewis, eds., *Stabilizing Fragile Democracies: Comparing New Party Systems in Eastern Europe* (London and New York: Routledge, 1996), 4.

23. I. William Zartman, "Political Pluralism in Morocco," in I. William Zartman ed., *Man, State, and Society in the Contemporary Maghrib* (New York: Praeger Publishers, 1973), 245.

24. Seymour Martin Lipset, Kyoung-Ryung Seong and John Charles Torres, "A Comparative Analysis of the Social Requisites of Democracy," *International Social Science Journal*, Vol. 45 (1993): 155–75.

25. Pridham and Lewis, "Introduction: Stabilizing Fragile Democracies," 4–5. For similar views, see G. Bingham Powell, *Contemporary Democracies: Participation, Stability and*

Violence (Cambridge: Harvard University Press, 1982), 7; and Seymour Martin Lipset, "The Indispensability of Political Parties," *Journal of Democracy*, Vol. 11, No. 1 (2000): 48–55.

26. For details on the role of political parties in the transition in Spain, see Paul Heywood, "The Emergence of New Party Systems and Transitions to Democracy: Spain in Comparative Perspective," in Geoffrey Pridham and Paul G. Lewis, eds., *Stabilizing Fragile Democracies: Comparing New Party Systems in Eastern Europe* (London and New York: Routledge, 1996), 145–66. While the author adduced to the contribution of parties in Spanish transition, he cautions that "the Spanish example cannot be seen as prototypical even of the transitions to democracy which took place in southern Europe in the mid-1970s," including its contemporaries Greece and Portugal.

27. Victor M. Perez-Diaz, *The Return of Civil Society: The Emergence of Democratic Spain* (Harvard: Harvard University Press, 1993).

28. Martin Heper. "Transition to Democracy Reconsidered," in *Comparative Political Dynamics*, ed., D. A. Rustow and E. P. Erickson (London: Harper Collins, 1991), 201–2. For more details on Turkey, see also Martin Heper and Ahmet Evin, *State, Democracy and the Military in Turkey in the 1980s* (Berlin: de Gruytern, 1988).

29. Ibid., 202.

30. Pinkney, 28.

31. E. H. Stephens, "Capitalist Development and Democracy in South America," *Politics and Society*, Vol. 7, No. 3 (1989): 281–352.

32. Dris Ben Ali, "Civil Society and Economic Reforms in Morocco," *ZEF Projekt* (Center for Development Research) Jan. 2005, 4.

33. Lise Garon, *Dangerous Alliances: Civil Society, the Media and Democratic Transition in North Africa* (London: Zed Books, 2003).

34. U.S. Department of State, *Country Report on Human Rights, 2000* released by the Bureau of Democracy, Human Rights and Labor (Feb. 23, 2001), 1.

35. Raphael Chijioke Njoku, "Civil Society in the Islamic Kingdom of Morocco," in Robert Dibie, ed., *Comparative Perspectives on Civil Society* (Lanham: Lexington Book, Rowan and Little, 2008), 85–96.

36. Geoffrey Pridham and Paul G. Lewis, "Introduction: Stabilizing Fragile Democracies and Party System Development," in Geoffrey Pridham and Paul G. Lewis, ed., *Stabilizing Fragile Democracies: Comparing New Party Systems in Eastern Europe* (London and New York: Routledge, 1996), 2–3. For details on the Rustow's model, see Rustow, "Transitional Approach," 337–63.

37. Robert Dahl, *Polyarchy: Participation and Opposition* (New Haven, CT: Yale University Press, 1978), 203.

38. Pinkney, 29.

39. Binder, et al., 53.

40. Ibid., 65–70.

41. Geraldo L. Munk, "Democratic Transitions in Contemporary Perspectives," *Comparative Politics*, Vol. 26, No. 3 (April 1994): 357.

42. Daniel A. Wagner, *Literacy, Culture, and Development: Becoming Literate in Morocco* (Cambridge: Cambridge University Press, 1993), 36.

43. See also *Annuaire Statique du Maroc*, Annual Statistics of Morocco, (Rabat: Ministry of Communication, 1999; 2000).

44. For an expanded analysis along this line, see Ali, 3.

45. Rachel Simon, "Between the Family and the Outside World: Jewish Girls in the Modern Middle East and North Africa," *Jewish Social Studies*, Vol. 7, No.1 (2000): 81–108.

46. Amal Rassam, "Women and Domestic Power in Morocco," *International Journal of Middle Eastern Studies*, 12 (1980): 171.

47. IFAD, *Survival, Change and Decision-making in Rural Households: Three Village Case Studies from Eastern Morocco* (Rome: International Food and Agricultural Development, 1997), 1–2.

48. For an interesting account of the economic origins of this reform, see Pennell, 356–62.

49. Raphael Chijioke Njoku, *Culture and Customs of Morocco* (Westport: Greenwood, 2005), 10; Pennell, 365–6. For an interesting study on this royal affluence under Kind Hassan, see Jean-Francois Clement, "Morocco's Bourgeoisie: Monarchy, State and Owing Class," *Middle East Report* (Sept–Oct. 1986): 13–17.

50. Seymour Martin Lipset, *Political Man: The Social Basis of Politics* (London: Heinemann, 1960), 1–54. See also Michael Bratton and Nicolas van de Walle, *Democratic Experiments in Africa: Regime Transition in Comparative Perspective* (Cambridge: Cambridge University Press, 1998), 21. The authors note that writers in both the liberal and materialist intellectual traditions traced the sources of democracy as arising during Western European's transformation from an agrarian to industrial society, which has been highlighted by Lipset's classic works.

51. Leroy Vail, "Introduction: Ethnicity in Southern African History," in Leroy Vail, ed. *The Creation of Tribalism in Southern Africa* (Berkeley and Los Angeles: University of California Press, 1991), 1.

52. Frederick Cooper, "Africa and the World Economy," in Frederick Cooper, Florencia E. Mallon, Steve J. Stern, Allen F. Isaacman and William Roseberry, *Confronting Historical Paradigms: Peasants, Labour, and The Capitalist World System in Africa and Latin America* (Wisconsin: The University of Wisconsin, 1993), 90.

53. Adam Przeworski, in Larry Diamond, Marc Plattner, Yun-han, and Hung-mao Tien, eds., *Consolidating the Third Wave of Democracies: Themes and Perspectives* (Baltimore, MD: Johns Hopkins University Press, 1997), 297. The $6000 figure is expressed in purchasing power-parity to the US dollars.

54. Seymour Martin Lipset, "Some Social Requisites for Democracy, Economic Development and Political Legitimacy," *American Political Science Review*, Vol. 53, No.1 (1959): 69–105. Or Lipset, "The Social Requisites of Democracy Revisited," *American Sociological Review*, 59 (February 1994): 1–22.

55. Lipset, "Some Social Requisites for Democracy," 84.

56. Lipset, *Political Man*, 51.

57. Lipset, "Some Social Requisites for Democracy," 87–97.

58. Ibid., 1. As the theorist discovered, governments that defy the elementary laws of supply and demand will fail to develop and will not institutionalize genuinely democratic systems.

59. Samuel P. Huntington, "After Twenty Years: The Future of the Third Wave," *Journal of Democracy*, Vol. 8, No.4 (1997): 5. The theorist appraises the work of Lipset in 1960, with the remark that although the correlation between economic development and democracy is evident, yet, "correlation, as we know, does not prove causation," hence we are left with the questions whether economic growth produce democracy or vice versa? Or whether economic growth and democratization are "both products of some cause or independent variable?"

60. Huntington, 5. The author further asserts that as a result of the positive effect of economic growth on democratization, it is possible to identify what he in *The Third Wave* (Norman and London: University of Oklahoma Press, 1991), called a "transition zone."

This is the zone of intermediate level of economic development, where pressures develop within to open up and democratize their political systems. According to Huntington, most of the 40 or more transitions to democracy that have occurred in recent decades have been in countries that were in the transition zone. Therefore, the future of democracy will most likely occur in those countries in the world, such as East and Southeast Asia, that are experiencing rapid economic growth. See also Geraldo L. Munk, "Democratic Transitions in a Comparative Perspective," *Comparative Politics*, Vol. 26, No.3 (1994): 365.

61. Barrington Moore, *Social Origins of Dictatorships and Democracy: Lord and Peasant in the Making of Modern World* (Boston, Mass.: Beacon Press, 1966), 418.

62. See Richard A. Joseph, *Democracy and Prebendal Politics in Nigeria* (Cambridge and New York: Cambridge University Press, 1987).

63. Also members of the CGEM have participated in discussions with the European Union as partners in depoliticization and liberalization of the state.

64. See Maghraoui, 25.

65. Ibid., 24.

66. Ali, 3.

67. U.S. Department of Labor, "Request for Information Concerning Labor Rights in Morocco and its Laws Governing Exploitative Child Labor," *Federal Register*, Vol. 68, No. 76 (April 21, 2003): 19579–19580.

Chapter 4

1. *Nigerian Digest* (USA), April 24, 1992.

2. Jon Kraus, "Nigeria under Shagari," *Current History*, March 1982, 109.

3. Chinua Achebe, *The Trouble With Nigeria* (London: Heinemann, 1987), 58–59.

4. Ibid., 57–58.

5. Ibid., 45–46.

6. Ibid., 62.

7. Ibid., 63.

8. Jean Herskovits, "Democracy in Nigeria," *Foreign Affairs*, Vol. 58, (1979–80), 324.

9. "Awolowo V. Shagari and others," *Journal of African Law*, Vol. 23, No. 2 (Autumn 1979), 175–182.

10. Larry Diamond, "Cleavage, Conflict and Anxiety in the Second Nigerian Republic," *Journal of Modern African Studies*, Vol. 20, No. 4, 1982, 652.

11. International Monetary Fund (IMF) *Fact Sheet: Mexico-Nigeria* (1985).

12. Okello Oculi, "Dependent Food Policy in Nigeria," *Review of African Political Economy*, No. 15–16 (May–Dec., 1979), 64–74.

13. Daniel J. Elazar, "Contrasting Unitary and Federal Systems," *International Political Science Review*, Vol. 18, No. 3 (1977), 237–251.

14. Bill Freund, "Oil Boom and Crisis in Contemporary Nigeria," *Review of African Political Economy*, No. 13 (Sept.–Dec, 1978), 98. See also Richard A. Joseph, "Affluence and Underdevelopment: The Nigerian Experience," *Journal of Modern African Studies*, Vol. 16, No. 2 (June 1978), 224–230.

15. Sayre P. Schatz, "Pirate Capitalism and the Inert Economy of Nigeria," *Journal of Modern African Studies*, Vol. 2 (1984), 45–57.

16. Karin Barber, "Popular Reactions to the Petro-dollar," *Journal of Modern African Studies,* Vol. 20 (1982), 438.

17. Jibrin Ibrahim, "Religion and Political Turbulence in Nigeria," *Journal of Modern African Studies,* Vol. 29, No. 1 (1991), 115–136; See also Adamu Adamu, "Religious Rumblings," *African Events,* June 1991, 36–39.

18. Quoted in Oyeleye Oyediran and Adigun Agbaje, "Two-Partyism Quoted in *West Africa,* (December 1990), 3045.

19. Oyeleye Oyediran and Adigun Agbaje, 3045.

20. "Awolowo V. Shagari and others," *Journal of African Law,* Vol. 23, No. 2 (Autumn 1979), 175—182.

21. Adigun Agbaje, "Travails of the Secular State: Religion, Politics and the Outlook on Nigeria's Third Republic," *Journal of Commonwealth and Comparative History* (London), Vol. 28, No. 3 (Nov. 1990), 288–308.

22. Larry Diamond, "Cleavage, Conflict, and Anxiety in the Second Nigerian Republic," *Journal of Modern African Studies,* Vol. 20, No. 4 (1982), 629–668.

23. Quoted in Oyeleye Oyediran and Adigun Agbaje, "Two-Partyism and Democratic Transition in Nigeria," *Journal of Modern African Studies,* Vol. 29, No. 2 (1991), 221.

24. Nigeria, Federal Government of, *Report of the Political Bureau* (Lagos, Government Printers, 1987), 124–132. Quoted in Oyeleye Oyediran and Adigun Agbaje, 234. For a critique of two-party system in Nigeria, see Anthony A. Akinola, "A Critique of Nigeria's Proposed Two Party System," *Journal of Modern African Studies,* Vol. 27 (March 1989), 109–123.

25. Obinna Anyadike, "New Breed, Old Politics?" *Africa Report,* May–June, 1991, 47.

26. Government's Views and Comments on the Findings and recommendations of the political Bureau (Lagos: Government Printers, 1987).

27. Nigeria, Federal Government of, *Report of the Constitutional Review Committee* containing the reviewed constitution (Lagos, 1988), Vol. 1, xx, *Nigerian News (USA),* April 24, 1992, 3.

28. Keith Atkins "The Quest for Democracy in Nigeria: An Agenda for Political, Democratic and Economic Stability," *National Concord,* (27 February 1992), 18–19.

29. Keith Atkins, 18.

30. See Text of a press conference addressed by *Campaign for Democracy* at the Lighthouse, Lagos, on Thursday, March 5, 1992 as a response to the paid advertisement of the *Association for Better Nigeria.*

31. Francis Emelifeonwu, "Gasoline Shortage Triggers Violence in Oil Rich Nigeria," *The Washington Times* (15 May 1992), A8.

32. Retrieved on 02/13/2010 from Jude Igbanoi (14 December 2009). "NBA Backs Akeredolu Over Yar'Adua's Health". *This Day.* http://allafrica.com/stories/200912150767.html.

33. BBC News Online, "Nigeria cabinet told to rule on sick President Yar'Adua". Retrieved on 01/22/2010 from http://news.bbc.co.uk/2/hi/africa/ 8474669.stm.

Chapter 5

1. For more information on violence during the European conquest, the African resistance, and during the colonial period, see Toyin Falola, *Colonialism and Violence in Nigeria* (Indianapolis, IN: Indiana University Press, 2009).

2. Constance Ikokwu, ".5m Displaced in Nigerian Ethnic Conflicts," *This Day* Newspaper, http://odili.net/news/source/2006/apr/27/204.html.

3. Julius O. Adekunle, "Religion, Politics, and Violence," in Julius O. Adekunle, ed., *Religion in Politics: Secularism and National Integration in Modern Nigeria* (Trenton, NJ: Africa World Press, 2009), 178–179.

4. For more information on Ken Saro-Wiwa, see Craig W. McLuckie and Aubrey McPhail, eds., *Ken Saro-Wiwa: Writer and Political Activist* (Boulder, CO: Lynne Rienner Publishers, 2000).

5. Sonnie Ekwowusi, "One Murder Too Many," *ThisDay*, Vol. 11, No. 4120 (August 2, 2006): 16.

6. For a comprehensive analysis of assassinations in Nigeria, see Shehu Sani, *Political Assassinations in Nigeria* (Ibadan, Nigeria: BookCraft, 2007).

7. Afeaye Anthony Igbafe and O. J. Offiong, "Political Assassinations in Nigeria: An Exploratory Study 1986–2005," *African Journal of Political Science and International Relations*, Vol. 1, No. 1 (2007).

8. Ekwowusi, 16.

9. Ibid.

10. Ibid.

11. Israel Okoye, "Political Godfatherism, Electoral Politics and Governance in Nigeria," paper presented at the 65th Annual Conference of the MPSA held in Chicago, USA; April 12–15, 2007, 1–23.

12. O. Akinola Adeoye, "Godfatherism and the Future of Nigerian Democracy," *African Journal of Political Science and International Relations*, Vol. 3 No. 6 (June 2009): 268–272.

13. For more information on the Zikist movement, see G. O. Olusanya, "The Zikist Movement—A Study in Political Radicalism," *The Journal of Modern African Studies*, Vol. 4, No. 3 (1966): 323–333.

14. Dr. Jibrin Ibrahim, "The Rise of Nigeria's Godfathers," *BBC News*, November 10, 2003, *news.bbc.co.uk/2/hi/africa/3156540.stm*.

15. Adeoye, 269.

16. Isaac Umunna, "Democracy under Stress," *Africa Today*, April 28, 2006.

17. Debo Adesina, "Annan says no to Tenure Extension," *The Guardian*, http://www.guardiannewsngr.com/news/article01.

18. Wola Adeyemo, "The Way Out," *Tell*, October 8, 2001, 7.

19. Adegbenro Adebanjo, "Everyone is Sharpening His Knife." *Tell*, October 8, 2001, 18–20.

20. "Babangida Institutionalized Corruption, Says Ribadu." Ribadu made the speech at the 3rd Media Trust Annual Dialogue in Abuja on the theme "Corruption: The Trouble With Nigeria." *This Day* Newspaper, November 17, 2010.

21. Alex Last, "The Politics of Nigerian Corruption." *BBC News*, September 16, 2006, http://news.bbc.co.uk/2/hi/africa/5339030.stm.

22. The governors include: Orji Kalu (Abia), Boni Haruna (Adamawa), Chris Ngige (former governor, Anambra), Ayo Fayose (Ekiti), Chimaroke Nnamani (Enugu), Saminu Turaki (Jigawa), Muhammed Lawal (ex-governor, Kwara), Abubakar Audu (ex-governor, Kogi), Ahmed Makarfi (Kaduna), Adamu Abdullahi, Attahiru Bafarawa, and Jolly Nyame.

23. Central Intelligence Agency. *The World Factbook*, https://www.cia.gov/library/publications/the-world ... /ni.html.

24. The Commonwealth Ministerial Action Group included: Barbados, Botswana, Great Britain, Canada, Ghana, Malaysia, New Zealand, and Zimbabwe.

25. Nigeria: A Closer Look at "Above Ground Factors," http://www.theoildrum.com/node/2687.

26. "Nigerian Kidnappers Release Hostages," CNN Online. http://www.cnn.com/2007/WORLD/africa/02/13/nigeria.hostages/index.html.

27. Sani Musa, "The Nigerian Political Economy in Transition," http:// library.fes.de/pdf-files/iez/03522.pdf.

28. *Ola Ajayi, "Oyo, hotbed of political disaster-RED CROSS," The Vanguard.* http://odili.net/news/source/2006/may/11/318.html.

Chapter 6

1. A. Adu Boahen, *African Perspectives on Colonialism* (Baltimore: The Johns Hopkins University Press, 1987), 32–33.

2. Emmanuel M. Mbah, *Land/Boundary Conflict in Africa: The Case of Former British Colonial Bamenda, Present-Day North-West Province of the Republic of Cameroon, 1916–1996* (Lewiston, New York: Edwin Mellen Press, 2008), 89; Mathias L. Niba, "Bafut Under Colonial Administration 1900–1949," http://lucy.ukc.ac.uk/Chilver/Paideuma/paideuma-Introdu-4.html.

3. Tambi Eyongetah Mbuagbaw et al., *A History of the Cameroon*, New Edition (London: Longman Group UK Limited, 1987), 114–119.

4. Joseph Takougang and Milton Krieger, *African State and Society in the 1990s: Cameron's Political Crossroads* (Boulder, CO: Westview Press, 1998), 35–38.

5. Ibid., 35–37.

6. Ibid., 39; Basil Davidson, *Modern Africa: A Social and Political History*, Third Edition (London: Longman Group UK Limited, 1994), 128–29.

7. Takougang and Krieger, 38.

8. Ibid., 39.

9. Ibid., 40–41.

10. Ibid., 41.

11. Ibid., 41.

12. Ibid., 41–44. Law No. 62/OF/18 remained a major obstacle to the practice of multiparty democracy in Cameroon until it was replaced in 1990 with Law No. 90/046.

13. As Quoted in Takougang and Krieger, 43–44.

14. As Quoted in Ibid., 44–45.

15. Ibid., 45.

16. Ibid., 46.

17. Ibid., 46–50.

18. Ibid., 50.

19. Ibid., 51.

20. Joseph Takougang, "The Nature of Politics in Cameroon," in John Mukum Mbaku and Joseph Takougang, eds., *The Leadership Challenge in Africa: Cameroon Under Paul Biya* (Trenton, N.J.: Africa World Press, Inc., 2004), 82.

21. Takougang, "The Nature of Politics in Cameroon," 79.

22. Ibid., 78–79.

23. Ibid., 79.

24. Ibid., 79–80.

25. Francis B. Nyamnjoh, *Africa's Media: Democracy and the Politics of Belonging* (Pretoria: UNISA Press, 2005), 110–111.

26. Nyamnjoh, 111.

27. Ibid., 111.

28. This author was a student at that university at the time and participated in the celebration.

29. Nyamnjoh, 111.

30. Ibid., 112.

31. Ibid., 112–113.

32. Munyae M. Mulinge and Gwen N. Lesetedi, "Interrogating Our Past: Colonialism and Corruption in Sub-Saharan Africa," *African Journal of Political Science*, Vol. 3, No. 2 (1998): 24.

33. Takougang and Krieger, 53–54.

34. Ibid., 53–55.

35. Takougang, 80.

36. Nyamnjoh, 112.

37. Takougang, 84.

38. Ibid., 85.

39. Nyamnjoh, 113.

40. Ibid., 118.

41. Ibid., 113 and 117.

42. Ibid., 113.

43. Ibid., 114.

44. Howard W. French, "Outcome of Cameroon Vote: Fear of the Future," *The New York Times*, October 14, 1997, http://www.nytimes.com.

45. BBC News, August 10, 2004, http://news.bbc.co.uk/; Nyamnjoh, *Africa's Media*, 118; French, "Outcome of Cameroon Vote," *The New York Times*, October 14, 1997.

46. French, "Outcome of Cameroon Vote," *The New York Times*, October 14, 1997.

47. BBC News, August 10, 2004, http://news.bbc.co.uk/.

48. "CDD Election Brief: Cameroon Election 2004," Center for Democracy and Development, www.cdd.org.uk.

49. Ibid.

50. BBC News, August 10, 2004, http://news.bbc.co.uk/.

51. Nyamnjoh, 121.

52. Ibid., 121.

53. Ibid., 120–21.

54. Ibid., 120–21.

55. Ibid., 120.

56. Ibid., 121.

57. Ibid., 117.

58. BBC News, August 10, 2004, http://news.bbc.co.uk/.

59. David Lewis and Tansa Musa, "Interview—Cameroon: More Dictatorship than Democracy—Cardinal," *REUTERS*, March 21, 2009, http://www.reuters.com/.

60. Nyamnjoh, 114.

61. Ibid., 114.

62. "CDD Election Brief: Cameroon Presidential Election 2004," *Center for Democracy and Development*, http://www.cdd.org.uk.

63. Takougang, 85. The results of the 1997, 2002, 2004, and 2007 elections are testament to the weakness of the opposition.

64. BBC News, August 10, 2004, http://news.bbc.co.uk/.

65. Takougang, 80.

66. Takougang and Krieger, 54.

67. Takougang, "The Nature of Politics in Cameroon," 80–81.

68. Ibid., 81.

69. Kenneth B. Noble, "Strike Aims to Bleed Cameroon's Economy to Force President's Fall," *The New York Times, August 5, 1991*, http://www.nytimes.com.

70. BBC News, August 10, 2004, http://news.bbc.co.uk/.

71. Noble, "Strike Aims to Bleed Cameroon's Economy," *The New York Times, August 5, 1991*.

72. Noble, *The New York Times*. The author was in Cameroon at the time, and could give an informed opinion on how Cameroonians felt about the strike.

73. Nyamnjoh, 115.

74. Lewis and Musa, "Interview—Cameroon: More Dictatorship than Democracy—Cardinal," *REUTERS*, March 21, 2009, http://www.reuters.com/.

75. As Quoted in Nyamnjoh, 116.

76. Martin A. Nkemngu, "Cameroon: ELECAM—Action Now," in *AllAfrica Global Media*, February 3, 2009, http://www.allafrica.com.

77. Progressive Initiative for Cameroon (PICAM), "ELECAM or ELEC-CPDM: The Death of Democracy in Cameroon with the Acquiescence of the Commonwealth," PICAM Press Release, February 2, 2009, http://www.picam.org/press-releases.

78. Charles Manga Fombad, "Post-1990 Constitutional Reforms in Africa: A Preliminary Assessment of the Prospects for Constitutional Governance & Constitutionalism," in Alfred Nhema and Paul Tiyambe Zeleza, eds., *The Resolution of African Conflicts: The Management of Conflict Resolution and Post Conflict Reconstruction* (Athens: Ohio University Press, 2008), 179–182.

79. Lewis and Musa, "Interview—Cameroon," *REUTERS*, March 21, 2009.

Chapter 7

1. René Lemarchand, *Rwanda and Burundi* (New York: Praeger Publishers, 1970), 13.

2. "History of Rwanda—Colonial Influence," *Global Oneness*, http://www.experiencefestival.com/history_of_rwanda_-_german_colonialism.

3. John De Gruchy, "The Dialectic of Reconciliation: Church and the Transition to Democracy in South Africa," in G Baum & H Wells, eds., *The Reconciliation of Peoples: Challenge to the Churches* (Geneva/Maryknoll: WCC/Orbis Books, 1977), 6–29.

4. Julius O. Adekunle, *Culture and Customs of Rwanda* (Westport, CT: Greenwood Press, 2007), 55–56. In rural areas, approximately 27.3 percent of the households had radios by 1991, but in urban centers, about 58.7 percent households owned radios. *Recensement général de la population et de l'habitat au 15 août 1991* (Kigali: Service National de Recensement, July 1993), 31.

5. For more information on the role of the media, especially the radio in the genocide, see Christine L. Kellow and H. Leslie Steeves, "The Role of Radio in the Rwandan Genocide," *Journal of Communication*, Vol. 48 Issue 3 (1998): 107–128.

6. Sharon LaFraniere, "Three Guilty in Rwanda Genocide," *The New York Times*, December 4, 2003, A1.

7. "Report 2009 on Press Freedom: Rwanda," http://www.eurac-network.org/web/uploads/documents/20090213_11147.doc.

8. Gonzaga Muganwa, "The Enigma of Press Freedom in Rwanda," *The Tiziano Project*, http://tizianoproject.org.

9. "Overview of Corruption in Rwanda," *U4 Expert Answer*, http://www.u4.no/helpdesk/helpdesk/query.cfm?id=164.

10. Ibid.

11. 2009 Index of Economic Freedom, http://www.heritage.org/index/ranking.aspx.

12. John S. Mbiti, *African Religions and Philosophy* (London: Heinemann, 1969, reprinted 1980), 1.

13. Adekunle, 28–29.

14. Christopher C. Taylor, *Milk, Honey and Money: Changing Concepts in Rwandan Healing* (Washington DC: Smithsonian Institution Press, 1992), 33.

15. Ibid., 36.

16. U.S. Department of State, "Rwanda: International Religious Freedom Report 2007," Bureau of Democracy, Human Rights, and Labor, http://www.state.gov/g/drl/rls/irf/2007/90115.htm.

17. Elizabeth Powley, *Strengthening Governance: The Role of Women in Rwanda's Transition* (Cambridge, MA: Hunt Alternatives Fund, 2003), 2.

18. Quoted by Cathy Majtenji, "Women have Strong Voice in Rwandan Parliament," http://www.voanews.com July 16, 2007.

19. Cecilia Ntombizodwa Mzvondiwa, "The Role of Women in the Reconstruction and Building of Peace in Rwanda: Peace Prospects for the Great Lakes Region," *African Security Review*, Vol. 16, No. 1 (2007): http://www.iss.co.za/.

20. *Economic Report on Africa 2005: Meeting the Challenges of Unemployment and Poverty in Africa* (Addis Ababa, Ethiopia: Economic Commission for Africa, 2005), 110–111.

21. "African Elections Database," http://africanelections.tripod.com/rw.html.

22. For more information on the Arusha Peace Accords, see Joel Steltenheim, "The Arusha Peace Accords and the Failure of International Intervention in Rwanda," www.wilsoncenter.org/subsites/ccpdc/pubs/ … /8.pdf.

23. George Katito, "Rwanda: On Independence Day, Not Quite Free?" *All Africa*, July 1, 2009, http://allafrica.com/stories/200907010011.html.

Chapter 8

1. David Macey, trans. *What is Democracy?* By Alain Touraine (Boulder, CO: Westview Press, 1997), 1.

2. James Firebrace with Stuart Holland, *Never Kneel Down: Drought, Development and Liberation in Eritrea* (Nottingham, England: Spokesman for War on Want, 1984), 18.

3. Ibid.

4. Basil Davidson, "An Historical Note," in Basil Davidson Lionel Cliffe and Bereket Habte Selassie, eds., *Behind the War in Eritrea* (Nottingham, England: Spokesman for War on Want, 1980), 11.

5. Bereket Habte Selassie, "From British Rule to Federation and Annexation," in *Ibid*, 36.

6. Basil Davidson, in Ibid, 13.

7. Report of the United Nations Commission for Eritrea: General Assembly, Official Records: Fifth Session Supplement No. 8 (A/1285) Lake Success, New York, 1950.

8. Gerard Chaliand, "The Guerilla Struggle," in Basil Davidson, Lionel Cliffe and Bereket Habte Selassie, eds., *Behind the War in Eritrea* (Nottingham: Spokesman, 1980), 52.

9. Dan Connell, *Rethinking Revolution: New Strategies for Democracy & Social Justice: The Experiences of Eritrea, South Africa, Palestine and Nicaragua* (Lawrenceville, NJ: The Red Sea Press, Inc., 2001), xi.

10. Roy Paterman, *Eritrea: Even the Stones are Burning* (Trenton, NJ: The Red Sea Press, Inc., 1990), 125.

11. Dan Connell, *Rethinking Revolution: New Strategies for Democracy & Social Justice: The Experiences of Eritrea, South Africa, Palestine and Nicaragua* (Lawrenceville, NJ: The Red Sea Press, Inc., 2001), 28–29.

12. President Afworki's response as to the question of election has shocked concerned Eritreans as to the future of democracy in the country.

13. Countries at Crossroad 2007: Country Report Eritrea, Freedom House.

14. "EDA Congress Ended Today," *Awate.com's Gedab News*, May 11, 2008. http://www.awate.com/portal/content/view/4839/3/.

15. The Constitution of Eritrea, Article 20, ratified by the Constituent Assembly on May 23, 1997.

16. The National Democratic Program of the EPLF 1977, Section 7D.

17. Sophia Tesfamariam, "Eritrea: Challenges and Threats posed by Religious Movements," http://www.shaebia.org/artman/publish/article_5759.shtml, March, 2009.

18. Ibid.

19. Connell, 29.

20. Connell, 42.

21. Ibid.

22. Connell.

23. Tesfay, Tedros, "FGM Proclamation: Ending a Female's Sorrow," http://www.shaebia.org.

24. Human Rights Watch, 2007.

25. Eritrea The Human Development Index—going beyond income http://hdrstats.undp.org/countries/country_fact_sheets/cty_fs_ERI.html.

26. Brett D. Schaefer, "Economic Freedom: The Path to African Prosperity," Heritage Lecture No. 778, http://www.heritage.org/Research/Africa/hl778.cfm, February 20, 2003.

27. Ibid.

28. IMF sees Eritrea Growth hampered by border impasse, June 25, 2008. http://africa.reuters.com/country/ER/news/usnL25727108.html.

29. Ibid.

30. Freedom House Report, 2007, http://www.freedomhouse.com.

31. U.S. Committee for Refugees and Immigrants, World Refugee Survey 2008-Ethiopia, June 19, 2008. http://www.unhcr.org/refworld/country ... ERI,456d621e2,485f50d171,0. html.

Chapter 9

1. Raymond Carré de Malberg, *Contribution à la Théorie Générale de l'État: Spécialement d'après les Données Fournies par le Droit Constitutionnel Français* (Paris: Sirey, 1922), 324.

2. Samuel P. Huntington, *The Third Wave: Democratization in the late Twentieth Century* (Norman, OK: University of Oklahoma Press, 1991).

3. The four ethnic categories referred in Mauritius's Constitution are the Hindus (52 percent), the Muslims (16 percent), the Sino-Mauritians (3 percent) and the general population (29 percent). The latter is a residual category containing most of the Christians in Mauritius. But the real number of ethnic groups is between four and twenty-four, depending on the social context. For an analysis of the ethnic groups in Mauritius politics, see, among others, the following works by Thomas H. Eriksen, "Containing Conflict and Transcending Ethnicity in Mauritius," in *Internal Conflict and Governance*, ed., Kumar Rupensinghe (Macmillan: Basingstoke, 1992), 103–129, "A Future-Oriented, non-Ethnic Nationalism? Mauritius as an Exemplary Case," *Ethnos* 58 (1993): 197–221, *Us and them in Modern Societies: Ethnicity and Nationalism in Mauritius, Trinidad and Beyond* (Oslo: Scandinavian University Press, 1993), "Nationalism, Mauritian Style: Cultural Unity and Ethnic Diversity," *Comparative Studies in Society and History* 36 (1994): 549–574, and *Common Denominators: Ethnicity, Nation Building and Compromise in Mauritius* (Oxford: Berg, 1998). For more information, see Sheila Bunwaree, "Economics, Conflicts and Interculturality in a small Island State: The Case of Mauritius," *Polis. Revue Camerounaise de Science Politique* 9 (2002): 61–79, Barbara Wake Carroll and Terrance Carroll, "Accommodating Ethnic Diversity in a Modernizing Democratic State: Theory and Practice in the Case of Mauritius," *Ethnic and Racial Studies* 23 (2000): 120–142, and by the same authors, "Trouble in Paradise: Ethnic Conflict in Mauritius," *Commonwealth and Comparative Politics* 38 (2000): 25–50.

4. For this period in the two former Portuguese colonies, see Elisa Silva Andrade, *Les Îles du Cap Vert: de la Découverte à l Independance Nationale (1460–1975)* (Paris: L Harmattan, 1996), C. Benigno da Cruz, *Sao Tomé e Príncipe: Do Colonialismo à Independencia* (Lisboa: Moraes Editores, 1975), Richard A. Lobban, *Cape Verde: Crioulo Colony to Independent Nation* (Boulder, CO, San Francisco, CA and Oxford: Westview Press, 1995), 87–100, Tony Hodges and Malyn D. Newitt, *Sao Tome e Principe: From Plantation Colony to Microstate* (Boulder, CO: Westview Press, 1988), Jens E. Torp, L.M. Denny and Donald I. Ray, *Mozambique. Sao Tome and Príncipe. Economics, Politics and Society* (London: Pinter Publishers, 1989), and Paul M. Whitaker, "The Revolutions of Portuguese Africa," *Journal of Modern African Studies* 8 (1970): 15–35.

5. Alexander Keese, "The Role of Cape Verdeans in War Mobilization and War Prevention in Portugal's African Empire, 1955–1965," *International Journal of African Historical Studies* 40 (2007): 497–511.

6. For this period in the three African insular microstates in the Indian Ocean, see Hrudananda Mohanty, *West Indian Ocean Islands: Strategic Dimensions of Regional Cooperation* (Delhi: Kalinga Publications, 2000), 6–16 and 52–74.

7. Larry W. Bowman, *Mauritius: Democracy and Development in the Indian Ocean* (Boulder, CO: Westview Press, 1991), Ajay Dubey, *Government and Politics in Mauritius* (Delhi: Kalinga Publications, 1997), and Thomas Meisenhelder, "The Developmental State in Mauritius," *Journal of Modern African Studies* 35 (1997): 279–297.

8. For the case of Cape Verde, see Elisa Silva Andrade, "Cape Verde," in *A History of Post-colonial Lusophone Africa*, ed. Patrick Chabal et al. (London: Hurst & Co, 2002), 264–290, Basil Davidson, "Practice and Theory: Guinea-Bissau and Cape Verde," in *Africa: Problems in the Transition to Socialism*, ed. Barry Munslow (London: Zed Books, 1986), 95–113, and Basil Davidson, *The Fortunate Isles: A Study in African Transformation* (Trenton: Africa World Press, 1989), Humberto Cardoso, *O Partido Unico em Cabo Verde: Um Assalto à Esperança* (Praia: Imprensa Nacional de Cabo Verde, 1993), Falali Koudawo, *Cabo Verde e Gune-Bissaud: Da Democracia Revolucionária à Democracia Liberal* (Bissau: Instituto Nacional de Estudos e Pesquisa, 2001), Jose Vicente Lopes, *Os Bastidores da Independência* (Praia: Spleen Ediçoes, 2002) and *As Causas da Independência* (Praia, Spleen Ediçoes, 2003).

For Sao Tome and Principe, see Tikum Mbah Azonga, "Time for Change," *West Africa* 3 (1993): 142–143, Manuel Pinto da Costa, "Towards an Alternative Development Policy for Sao Tome and Principe," in *The Political Economy of Small Tropical Islands: the Importance of Being Small*, ed. Helen Hintjens and Malyn Newitt (Exeter: University of Exeter Press, 1992): 112–122, Gerhard Seibert, "Sao Tome e Principe," in *A History of Postcolonial Lusophone Africa*, ed. Patrick Chabal et al. (London: Hurst & Co, 2002), 291–315, and Laurie S. Wisenberg and Gary F. Nelson, "Africa's New Island Republics and U.S. Foreign Policy," *Africa Today* 24 (1977): 6–30.

9. Deryck Scarr, *Seychelles since 1770: History of a Slave and Post-Slavery Society* (Trenton, NJ: Africa World Press Inc, 1999), 164–172. Also see Jean Houbert, "The Mascareignes, the Seychelles, and the Chagos, Islands with a French Connection: Security in a Decolonised Indian Ocean," in *The Political Economy of Small Islands: The Importance of being Small*, ed. Helen Hintjens and Malyn Newitt (Exeter: University of Exeter Press, 1992): 93–111, Raphael Kaplinsky, "Prospering at the Periphery: A Special Case, the Seychelles," in *African Islands and Enclaves*, ed. Robin Cohen (Beverly Hills: Sage Publications, 1983), 195–215, William F.S. Miles, "Socialist Society in the Seychelles," *Contemporary Review* 287 (2005): 340–350, and Donald R. Wright, *The World and a Very Small Place in Africa* (Armonk, N.Y.: M.E. Sharpe, 1997).

10. For an analysis of the Ali Soilih's regime, see Jean Charpantier, "Le Pouvoir d'Ali Soilih: Ngazidja, 1975–1978," *L'Afrique et l'Asie Modernes* 157 (1988): 70–89, Jean-Claude Maestre, "L'Expérience Révolutionnaire d'Ali Soilih aux Comores (1976–1978)," *Annuaire des Pays de l'Océan Indien* 4 (1977): 25–41, Youssouf Saïd Soilih and Elmamouni M. Nassur, *Ali Soilih, L'élan Brisé?* (Paris and Libreville: L Harmattan and Editios Ndzé, 2000), and Emmanuel Vérin and Pierre Vérin, *Histoire de la Révolution Comorienne: Decolonisation, Idéologie et Séisme Social* (Paris: L'Harmattan, 1999).

11. For the presidency of Ahmed Abdallah, see Alain Deschamps, *Les Comores d'Ahmed Abdallah: Mercenaries, Révolutionnaires et Coelarcanthe* (Paris: Karthala, 2005), Denis Venter, "La Tragicomedie Comorienne: Rideau sur le Systeme Abdallah?," *Année Africaine* (1989): 387–415, and Pierre Vérin, "Les Comores Indépendantes sous Ahmed Abdallah (1978–1989)," *Mondes et Cultures* 50 (1990): 217–223.

12. For a general vision of this years and the evolution of the Comoro Islands political system, see Abdou Djabir, *Les Comores: Un État en Construction* (Paris: L'Harmattan, 1993), Nakidini Mattoir, *Les Comores de 1975 à 1990: Une Histoire Politique Mouvementée* (Paris: L'Harmattan, 2004), and Pierre Verin, *Les Comores* (Paris: Karthala, 1994).

13. For a good and synthetic description of the main characteristics of the Mauritius Constitution and the development of its democratic institutions, see Parvez Dookhy y Riyad Dookhy, "Le Constitutionnalisme Mauricien," *Revue Juridique et Politique* 52 (1998): 288–299, M.J.N. Meetarbhan: "L'évolution de la Constitution Mauricienne Depus 1968", *Annuaire de Pays de l'Ocean Indien*, 14 (1995–1996): 23–40, and Richard Sandbook, "Origins of the

Democratic Developmental State: Interrogating Mauritius," *Canadian Journal of African Studies* 39 (2005): 549–581.

14. For an analysis of the Cape Verde Constitution, see Michael Bogdan, "The Law of the Republic of Cape Verde after 25 Years of Independence," *Journal of African Law* 44 (2000): 86–95, Wladimir Brito, "Um Balance da Constituiçao de 92," *Direito e Cidadania* 4 (1998): 181–198, Jorge Carlos Fonseca, *O Sistema de Governo na Constituiçao Cabo-Verdiana* (Lisboa: Associaçao Académica da Faculdade de Direito de Lisboa, 1990), José Lopes da Graça, "Balanço de Cinco Anos da Vigência da Constituiçao," *Direito e Cidadania* 4 (1998): 205–208.

15. For the institutional design of Sao Tome and Principe, see Gerhard Seibert, "Sao Tome and Principe," in *Legal Systems of the World. A Political, Social and Cultural Encyclopedia*, ed., Herbert M. Kritzer (Santa Barbara: ABC-Clio, 2002), 1403–1409, and Françoise Gaulme, "Sao Tomé Dix Ans Après la Démocratisation: ou les Apories D un Libéralisme Systématique," *Lusotopie* (2000): 47–58.

16. For the constitutional regulation of Rodrigues and Principe islands in the Mauritius and Sao Tome and Principe Constitutions, and the federal Constitution of the Union of Comoros, see Jose Adrian Garcia-Rojas, "La Especificidad Insular en el Constitucionalismo Africano: los Casos de Santo Tome y Principe, Mauricio y Comores" (paper presented at the 7th Iberian African Studies Conference, Lisboa, Portugal, September 9–11, 2009).

17. Parvez Dookhy, "Les Institutions Politiques de Maurice," *Revue Juridique et Politique* 51 (1997): 291–298.

18. André Sauzier, "L influence du Módele Juridique Français aux Seychelles," *Revue Internationale de Droit Comparé* 47 (1995): 154–158, and of the same author "Les Processus de Changaments Constitutionnels en République de Seychelles," *Annuaire de Pays de l Ocean Indien* 14 (1995–1996): 51–55.

19. Barbara de Smith, "L'exportation du Modèle Westminster et la Constitution Mauricienne," *Annuaire des Pays de l'Océan Indien* 14 (1995–1996): 41–49.

20. J. de Matos Correia, "Eleiçoes e Sistemas Eleitorais: Os Casos de Sao Tomé e Príncipe e de Cabo Verde," *Politica Internacional* 1 (1991): 38–48.

21. Raj Mathur, "Parliamentary Representation of Minority Communities: The Mauritian Experience," *Africa Today* 44 (1997): 61–82.

22. Michael Dyer and Jean Houbert, "Doors and Windows: the Bloc Vote and Best Losers in Mauritius," *Annuaire des Pays de l'Océan Indien* 14 (1995–1996): 347–371.

23. Saïd Mohamed Saïd Hassane, "Les Institutions de l'Union des Comores," *Revue Juridique et Politique* 4 (2005): 444–477, Binty Mady, "Le Crise Commorienne et le Droit," *Revue Juridique de l'Océan Indien* 2 (2001–2002): 7–16, and Abdelaziz Riziki Mohamed, *Comores: Les Institutions d un État mort-ne* (París: L Harmattan, 2001). For the troubled constitutional past of the Comoro Islands, see Jean-Paul Negrin, "Le Féderalisme à la Comorienne," *Annuaire des Pays de l'Océan Indien* 7 (1980): 131–144, and of the same author, "Les Changements Politiques et Constitutionnels de 1982–1983," *Annuaire des Pays de l'Océan Indien* 10 (1984–1985): 167–178, and Michel Pineau y Lucien Audibert, "La République Fédérale Islamique des Comores, Panorama des Années 1982–1983," *Annuaire des Pays de l'Océan Indien* 10 (1984–1985): 128–134.

24. I use the French names of the islands. The native names are Ngazidja (Grande Comore), Mwali (Moheli), Nzwani (Anjouan), and Mahore (Mayotte).

25. L. Amedee Darga and Gilles Daniel Joomun, "Mauritius," *South African Journal of International Affairs* 12 (2005): 95–110. See also Catherine Boudet, "Émeutes et Élections à Maurice: La Mort de Kaya, Aléa Échec de la Construction Nationale?" *Politique Africaine* 79 (2000): 153–164, Gavin Cawthra, "Mauritius: An Exemplar of Democracy, Develop-

ment and Peace for the Southern African Development Community?" *Africa Insight* 35 (2005): 14–19, and for the ethnic cleavage in politics, see Eliphas G. Mukonoweshuro, "Containing Political Instability in a Poly-Ethnic Society: The Case of Mauritius," *Ethnic and Racial Studies* 14 (1991): 199–224.

26. Pierre Livet and André Oraison, "Le Mouvement Militant Mauricien," *Annuaire des Pays de l'Océan Indien* 4 (1977): 43–93.

27. Henry Srebrnik, "Full of Sound and Fury: Three Decades of Parliamentary Politics in Mauritius," *Journal of Southern African Studies* 28 (2002): 277–289.

28. See Denis K. Kadima and Roukaya Kasenally, "The Formation, Collapse and Revival of Political Party Coalitions in Mauritius: Ethnic Logic and Calculation at Play," *Journal of African Elections* 4 (2004): 133–164.

29. Neil Ford, "Mauritius: Island Unruffled by Leadership Change," *African Business* 292 (2003): 40–41.

30. The MSM had formed an electoral coalition with MMM in the 2005 general elections. The National Assembly elected his leader, Sir Anerood Jugnauth, President of the Republic of Mauritius in 2003, when he left the prime minister tenure, and reelected in 2008.

31. John Hatchard, "Re-Establishing a Multi-Party State: Some Constitutional Lessons from the Seychelles," *The Journal of Modern African Studies* 31 (1993): 601–612.

32. Hrudananda Mohanty, "Seychelles: A Transition from One-Party State to Multi-Party Democracy," *Africa Quarterly* 39 (1999): 89–103.

33. 23 Nell Ford, "Seychelles: Model Elections but Questionable Democracy," *African Business* 324 (2006): 52–53.

34. For these first elections, see Michel Cahen, "Archipels de l'Alternance, la Victoire de l'Opposition aux Iles du Cap-Vert e Sao Tome e Principe," *Année Africaine* (1990–1991): 347–381, and by the same author, "Une Afrique Lusophone Libérale? La Fin des Premieres République," *Lusotopie* (special number dedicated to Liberal Transitions in Lusophone Africa) (1995): 85–104.

35. Bruce Baker, "Cape Verde: The Most Democratic Nation in Africa?" *Journal of Modern African Studies* 44 (2006): 493–511, and Peter Meyns, "Cape Verde: An African Exception," *Journal of Democracy* 13 (2002): 153–165.

36. Gerhard Seibert, *Comrades, Clients and Cousins: Colonialism, Socialism and Democratization in Sao Tomé e Principe* (Leiden and Boston: Brill, 2006), 399–496. Also see of the same author, "A Política Num Micro-estado: Sao Tome e Príncipe, ou os Conflitos Pessoais e Políticos na Genese dos Partidos Políticos," *Lusotopie* (1995): 239–250.

37. The continuity of the political system was threatened when young officers staged a military coup in August 1995. The military, feeling marginalised, neglected, and impoverished since the democratic transition, justified the coup attempt on the grounds of widespread corruption and government incompetence. The military returned to barracks after one week of negotiations, a general amnesty, and international pressures. See Gerhard Seibert, "Sao Tome and Principe: Military Coup as a Lesson?" *Lusotopie* (1996): 71–80. Another coup attempt also was aborted in July 2003. For an analysis of the July 2003 coup see Joao Gomes Porto, "Coup d'État in Sao Tome and Principe," *African Security Review* 12 (2003): 33–35, and Gerhard Seibert, "The Bloodless Coup of July 16 in Sao Tome e Principe," *Lusotopie* (2003): 245–260.

38. Macartan Humphreys, William A. Masters and Martin E. Sandbu, "The Role of Political Leaders in Democratic Deliberations: Results from a Field Experiment in Sao Tome and Principe," *World Politics* 58 (2006): 583–622.

39. In these 2010 legislative elections, MLSTP-PSD gained 21 seats in the National Assembly, PCD 7, and MDFM only obtained 1 seat.

40. Saïd Mahamoudou, "Les Comores et la Démocratie," *Politique Africaine* 67 (1997): 122–129.

41. S. Soudjay, "L'Arrivée au Poivoir de Mohamed Taki. Mécanisme d'Paradoxe: les Comores, un An après les Élections Présidentielles des 6 et 16 Mars 1996," *Annuaire des Pays de l'Ocean Indien* 14 (1995–1996): 581–587.

42. About the Azali's regime, see M'Sa Ali Djamal, *Luttes au Pouvoir aux Comores entre Notables Traditionnels, Notables Profesionalices et Politiques Profesionnels: Les Cas Azali*, (Levalois-Perret: De la lune, 2006).

43. Neil Ford, "Comoros: An Unstable Triangle," *Africa Business*, No. 300, 56–57.

44. The constitutional date was November 7 for the first round ,and December 26 for the second and nation-wide electoral day.

45. There are problems with some Microstates data because the smallest countries did not appear in many surveys. This is the case with the Index of Economic Freedom (the Heritage Foundation), where the Comoros, Sao Tome and Principe, and Seychelles were not present in the past years, and it also happened with Sao Tome and Principe and Seychelles in the Human Development Report, but most of them appear in the latest reports. Seychelles is the only one of the five countries analyzed in this chapter that does not yet appear in the 2010 Human Development Report.

Chapter 10

1. Fredrick O. Wanyama "From Socialist Experimentation to Liberal Democracy: Democratic Transition in Tanzania," in Shadrack W. Nasong'o, ed. *The African Search for Stable Forms of Statehood: Essays in Political Criticism* (New York: Edwin Mellen Press, 2008), 101–140; K. W. von Sperber, *Public Administration in Tanzania* (Munchen: Weltforum Verlag, 1970).

2. Ludeki Chweya and Wanjala Nasong'o, "Contemporary Kenyan Politics: A Structuration Theoretic Approach," in Nasong'o, ed. *The African Search for Stable Forms of Statehood: Essays in Political Criticism*, 47–100; Rok Ajulu, "Politicized Ethnicity, Competitive Politics and Conflict in Kenya: A Historical Perspective," *African Studies*, 61, 2 (2002), 251–268.

3. K. Ngombale-Mwiru, "The Arusha Declaration on 'Ujamaa Na Kujitegemea' and the Perspectives for Building Socialism in Tanzania," in Lionel Cliffe and John S. Saul, eds. *Socialism in Tanzania*, Vol. 2 (Dar es Salaam: East African Publishing House, 1973), 53; Wanyama, Note 5, 108–109.

4. Naomi Chazan, *Political and Society in Contemporary Africa* (Boulder, CO: Lynne Rienner, 1988); Samuel Wangwe, "Culture, Identity and Social Integration: The Tanzania Experience in Social Integration," in Conference on 'New Frontiers of Social Policy' (Arusha, Tanzania, December 12–15, 2005).

5. See Saliba Sarsar, "Quantifying Arab Democracy," *Middle East Quarterly*, Vol. XIII, No. 3, 2006, 21–28.

6. Homer W. Smith, Homer, *Man and His Gods* (Boston: Little, Brown, and Company, 1952), iv.

7. Amon E. Chaliga, "Management of the Elections: The Role of the National Electoral Commission," in S.S. Mushi and R. S. Mukandala, eds. *Multiparty Democracy in Transition: Tanzania's 1995 Elections* (Dar es Salaam: TEMCO, 1997), 25; Nasong'o, 203, note 4.

8. Wanyama, note 1, pp. 114–118.

9. Max Mmuya and Amon Chaligha, *Political Parties and Democracy in Tanzania* (Dar es Salaam: Dar es Salaam University Press, 1994); Michael Bratton, Robert Mattes and E. Gyima-Boadi, *Public Opinion, Democracy and Market Reform in Africa* (Cambridge: Cambridge University Press, 2005).

10. See Freedom House, http://www.freedomhouse.org/template.cfm?page=22&year=2007&country=7285.

11. Transparency International, http://www.infoplease.com/ipa/A0108028.html.

12. See Freedom House, 14.

13. Nestor Luanda, "The Role of the Media in the Transition to Multiparty Politics and the 1995 General Elections," in S. Mushi and R. Mukandala, eds. *Multiparty Democracy in Transition* (Dar es Salaam: TEMCO1997); Wanyama, 114–118, note 12.

14. Freedom House, http://www.freedomhouse.org/template.cfm?page=363&year=2008&country=7502.

15. Aili Mari Tripp, "Forging Developmental Synergies between States and Associations," in Nicolas Van de Walle, Nicole Ball and Vijaya Ramachandran, eds. *Beyond Structural Adjustment: The Institutional Context of African Development* (New York: Palgrave Macmillan, 2003).

16. Luanda, note 13; Wanyama, 114–118, note 12.

17. Luanda, Ibid; Jesse Kwayu, "Tanzania," in MISA, *So this is Democracy? Report on the State of Media Freedom in Southern Africa 2004* (Windhoek: The Media Institute of Southern Africa, 2005).

18. Richard Sandbrook, *Closing the Circle: Democratization and Development in Africa* (Toronto: Between the Lines, 2000).

19. Freedom House, http://www.freedomhouse.org/template.cfm?page=22&year=2002&country=2249.

20. Kwayu, note 17.

21. Wanyama, note 2.

22. Kwayu, 111, note 17; Wanyama, 127–131, note 2.

23. Freedom House, note 14.

24. UN News Center, "Tanzanian Foreign Minister Named UN Deputy Secretary General," http://www.un.org/apps/news/story.asp?NewsID=21166&Cr=Deputy&Cr1=Secretary.

25. Freedom House, note 14.

26. Aili Mari Tripp, "Political Reform in Tanzania: The Struggle for Associational Autonomy" (unpublished paper, 2000); Sarah Michael, *Undermining Development: The Absence of Power among Local NGOs in Africa* (Oxford: James Currey & Bloomington, IN: Indiana University Press, 2004).

27. Tripp, Ibid.

28. Tripp, Ibid.

29. Freedom House, note 14; Ajulu, Rok, note 2; ARD, Inc., "Democracy and Governance Assessment of Tanzania," Report to USAID/Tanzania, 2003.

30. United Nations Development Program, *Human Development Report* (New York: Oxford University Press, 2008).

31. Freedom House, http://www.freedomhouse.org/uploads/WoW09/WOW%202009.pdf.

32. Ibid.

33. Paschal B. Mihyo, "Chama Cha Mapinduzi (CCM): A Revolutionary Party in Transition, Tanzania," in Mohamed Salih, ed. *African Political Parties: Evolution, Institutionalisation and Governance* (London: Pluto Press, 2003), 66–93.

34. UNDP, 2009 Human Development Report.

35. Ibid.

36. Freedom House, http://www.freedomhouse.org/uploads/WoW09/WOW%202009.pdf.

37. Ibid.

Chapter 11

1. "It's Better to be Out to Sea," 1. www.allafrica.com/stories.

2. http://www.worldaudit.org.

3. As regards the "prehistory" see www.everyculture.com/Ma-Ni/Namibia.html, 2–3.

4. U.S. Department of State, 3.

5. Peter Katjavivi, *A History of Resistance in Namibia* (Trenton: Africa World Press, 1988), xiii. Also published in Paris by UNESCO Press, 1988.

6. Katjavivi, 3.

7. Katjavivi, 4.

8. Katjavivi, 6.

9. Katjavivi, 9.

10. http://www.everyculture, 2.

11. Katjavivi, 8.

12. Robert Gordon and Stuart Sholto Douglas, *The Bushman Myth: The Making of a Namibian Underclass* (Boulder: Westview Press, 2000), 52. See also, Allan D. Cooper, "Reparations for the Herrero Genocide: Defining the Limits of International Litigation," *Africa Affairs*, Vol. 106, No. 422 (2007): 113–126.

13. John J. Katzao et al. *Understanding History: Namibian Junior Secondary Textbook* (Namibia: Longman, 1993).

14. Katjavivi, 15.

15. SWAPO Department of Information and Publicity, *To be Born a Nation: The Liberation Struggle for Namibia* (London: Zed Press, 1987), v and 16–56.

16. Katzao, 7.

17. Katjavivi, 21.

18. Katzao, 15.

19. Katjavivi, 24–25.

20. Katjavivi, 30.

21. Morgan Norval, *Death in the Desert: The Namibian Tragedy* (Washington DC: Selous Foundation Press), Chapter 6.

22. Norval, 5.

23. Getachew Metaferia, "Namibian Bureaucracy: Beyond the Colonial Legacy," *Proceedings: Association of Third World Studies* (Georgia Southwestern University, 1995), 199–208.

24. Katjavivi, 22.

25. Katzao, 17.

26. http://www.historyofwar.org/articles/wars ... 1.

27. *To be Born a Nation*, 181–82; 311–16.

28. Kees van Donge, "Land Reform in Namibia: Issues of Equity and Poverty," The Hague: Institute of Social Studies, 2005, 285; also Katzao, 24–25.

29. See map in Kees van Donge, 288.

30. Kees van Donge, 285.

31. http://www.historyofwar.org/articles/wars … 1.

32. Katzao, 19.

33. http://aceproject.org/ace-en/topics/es/esy/onePage.

34. Kees van Donge, 289.

35. Ministry of Information and Broadcasting, *The Constitution of the Republic of Namibia* (Windhoek, n.d.), 2.

36. *Constitution,* 3.

37. *Constitution,* 9–10.

38. *Constitution,* 10.

39. *Constitution,* 10.

40. *Constitution,* 11.

41. *Constitution,* 12–13.

42. *Constitution,* 13–14.

43. *Constitution,* 14.

44. *Constitution,* 15.

45. *Constitution,* 16–17.

46. *Constitution,* article 29, 20.

47. *Constitution,* 27.

48. *Constitution,* article 41, 28.

49. *Constitution,* article 79, 44.

50. *Constitution,* article 80, 44.

51. *Constitution,* article 84, 46.

52. *Constitution,* articles 87 and 88, 47.

53. *Constitution,* 49.

54. *Constitution,* 50.

55. *Constitution,* 51.

56. Ibid.

57. *Constitution,* 52.

58. *Constitution,* 53

59. *Constitution,* 64.

60. *Constitution,* 76.

61. For a comparative analysis of the constitution of Namibia, see chapter 4 on Namibia in Kenneth Good's *Realising Democracy and Legitimacy in Southern Africa* (Pretoria: Africa Institute of South Africa, 1997), 67–75. The analysis has its limitations, however, since the author's focus is on Botswana, and he is only indirectly acquainted with circumstances in Namibia.

62. USAID: Democracy and Governance, 2008. See also enwikipedia.org wiki, articles on Namibia and Windhoek.

63. Metaferia, 202.

64. http://www.nationmaster.com/country/wa-namibia.

65. Katzao, 15.

66. USAID, Democracy and Governance.

67. U.S. Department of State, Background Note on Namibia, http://www.state.gov/r/pa/ei/bgn, 1.

68. http://ness.bbc.co.uk/1/hi/world/Africa.
69. U.S. Department of State, Background Note on Namibia, 1.
70. U.S. Department of State, Bureau of African Affairs, 1.
71. E:\Namibia stable economy ... htmp. 2—Africa Recovery, vol. 12 #4, 1999.
72. Africa Recovery, Vol. 12, No. 4, 1999, 18–19.
73. Kees van Donge, 306.
74. Kees van Donge, 289.
75. http://www.nationamaster.com/graph/eco_dis_fm_inc_gin_ind ...
76. http://news.bbc.co.uk/1/hi/world/Africa ... 3.
77. Mosimane, "Land Reform in Namibia" in Kees van Donge, 284.
78. Ibid., 284.
79. U.S. Department of State, 7.
80. Kees van Donge, 292.
81. http://www.nationmaster.com/country/was-namibia, 1.
82. Kees van Donge, 289.
83. U.S. Department of State, 2.
84. http://www.nationmaster.com/country/wa-namibia.
85. Rossing, *Namibia Newsletter*, Winter 1993. See also, http://www.tradingeconom-
ics.com/namibia, downloaded January 18, 2011.
86. USAID: Democracy and Governance.
87. Ibid.
88. Country Higher Education Profile, http://www.bc.edu/bc_org.
89. http://www.nationmaster.com/country/wa=Namibia.
90. Constitution, 3.
91. *The Namibian*, January 10, 2008. http://www.namibian/com.na.

Chapter 12

1. M. Bratton and D. Posner. "A First Look at Second Elections in Africa with Illustrations
from Zambia" in R. Joseph, ed. *State, Conflict and Democracy in Africa* (Boulder, CO: Lynne
Rienner, 1998), 377-407.
2. R. Joseph, Ibid.; M. Bratton and D. Posner, Ibid.
3. Bratton and Posner, Ibid.
4. P. Burnell. "Zambia's 2001 Elections: The Tyranny of Small Decisions, "Non-deci-
sion" and "Not Decisions," *Third World Quarterly*, Vol. 23, No, 6 (2002):1103–20.
5. Ibid., 1118.
6. Ibid., 1106.
7. N. Cheeseman, and M. Hinfelaar. "Parties, Platforms, and Mobilization: The Zambian Presidential Elections of 2008." *African Affairs*, 1009/434, (2009): 51–7.
8. Ngandu Magande was the Finance Minister during Mwanawasa's government.
9. Cheeseman and Hinfelaar, 619.
10. Frederick Chiluba, *Democracy: The Challenge of Change* (Lusaka, Zambia: Multi-
media Publications 1995), 79.
11. C. Baylies, and M. Szeftel, "The 1996 Zambian Elections: Still Waiting Democratic
Consideration." *Review of African Political Economy*, Vol. 24, No. 71(1997): 113–28.

12. M. Larmer. and A. Fraser. "Of Cabbages and King Cobra: Populist Politics and Zambia's 2006 Elections." *African Affairs*, Vol. 106, No. 425 (2007): 614.

13. K. Van Donge. "Reflections on Donors, Opposition Parties and Political Will in the 1966 Zambian General Elections." *Journal of Modern African Studies*, Vol. 38 (1998): 71–99.

14. N. Cheeseman, and M. Hinfelaar, 53.

15. D. Horowitz. *Ethnic and Groups in Conflict* (Berkeley, CA: University of California Press, 1985).

16. C. Baylies and M. Szeftel, 113–28.

17. Southern African Development Community Parliamentary Forum (SADC-PF), (2002), Interim Statement on the EUEU website http://www.eueu-zambia.org.

18. C. Ake, "The Political Question," in O. Oyediran ed. *Governance and Development in Nigeria: Essays in Honour of Professor Billy J. Dudley* (Ibadan: Oyediran International/Agbo Ero Publishers, 1996), 6.

19. M. Larmer and A. Fraser, 612.

20. A. Mbukusita-Lewanika. *Hour of Reunion, Movement for Multiparty Democracy: Conception, Dissension and Reconciliation.* (Limulunga, Mongu-Lealui: African Lineki Courier, 2003), 54.

21. Cheeseman and Hinfelaar, 57.

22. This helped to increase discontentment within UNIP and as the divisions increased, Kenneth Kaunda was forced to increase his powers as party and government leader to be able to reign on party deserters. Thus as party conflicts increased, Kenneth Kaunda strengthened the office of the president by making the executive more powerful in the day-to-day running of the country. This elevated the executive vis-à-vis the legislative and on the process encouraged Kaunda to make unilateral decisions on important matters, which alienated supporters further.

23. During the one party system, ZCTU had been an affiliate of UNIP. This continued until ZCTU became the major advocate of political pluralism in Zambia in the 1990s. As a way of weakening it, Zambia's labor law was changed requiring trade unions not to be affiliated with ZCTU. UNIP and Kaunda hoped that such a move would not only divide the labor movement, but would also reduce its significance in Zambian politics.

24. This was continued for a long time. Even in the run up to the re-introduction of multiparty politics in 1990, Timothy Walamba, Chairman of the Mineworkers Union of Zambia was ousted as Chairman when he accepted a position with UNIP's Central Committee.

25. Chiluba, 58.

26. For example, in April 1991, Zambia lost the Most Favored Nation trading status with the United States. In Britain, attacks on Kaunda's politics were more direct. At a meeting of the Commonwealth Heads of Government, Britain's Prime Minister condemned Kaunda's hypocrisy in condemning South Africa's Apartheid regime and its human rights abuses, yet, Kaunda himself was practicing the same. For more details, see Chiluba, 59–60.

27. The three piece suit required voters to cast their votes for a complete set of three; that is, if one chose to vote for KANU, one had to vote KANU in the presidential, Parliamentary seats and for councilor as well. Since the major prize was the presidential candidate, many people voted for a parliamentary and councilor candidate they did not know.

28. The choice of the set of candidates to vote for in each region was either determined on party lines or the presidential candidate (whose political party was easily identifiable with him). There was for example, Moi's KANU, Odinga's FORD-K, Matiba's FORD-A,

and Kibaki's DP. This pattern of voting has been witnessed in the country in subsequent elections, and has been one of the greatest challenges to democratization in the country.

29. For the ten years that Chiluba had been in power, MMD leaders embarked on a frenzy to enrich themselves quickly so that Chiluba's cronies got quite wealthy and as corrupt as Kaunda's had, if not more. To protect their wealth and to shield them from any criticism, the MMD government muzzled the press and harassed the independent media houses by imprisoning its editors, accusing its opponents (especially in UNIP and Kaunda) of all sorts of tramped up charges.

30. The group of defectors included Chilufya Kapwepwe, from the Northern part of Zambia and Baldwin Nkumbula, from the South. Both were MMD Members of Parliament elected during the 1991 multiparty elections. Both Kapwepwe and Nkumbula families were at the center of the anti-colonial movement, and were quite respected families in their own provinces. Other notable founders of the NP were Humphrey Mulemba and Arthur Wina. These two were not just senior MMD MPs, but had also been respected figures of the Zambian nationalist movement, which had deep grassroots support. Wina was Chairman of the National Interim Committee for Multi-Party Democracy (had been Finance Minister and Education Minister (1964–68), while Mulemba was UNIP Secretary General in 1981–5. Wina and Mulemba left the MMD and founded the National Party in August 1993. See Chiluba, 73.

31. Lewanika had organized the 1990 Garden House Conference that launched the MMD as an opposition party (Gould 2002:309). He had resigned from the cabinet after only a few months protesting the level of corruption and greed in Chiluba's government. He left MMD and was re-elected to Parliament on an NP ticket. He broke away from the NP to found the AZ about a month before election time. In the 1996 elections, AZ got only two seats.

32. Zadeco's founder, Dean Mung'omba (another former MMD cabinet minister) broke away from MMD in protest over Chiluba's corrupt government. Zadeco was able to gain substantial support from the youth. After his dismal performance in the 1996 elections (in which Zadeco did not win a single seat), Mung'omba started an anti-government campaign, which later landed him in detention in 1997 (Amnesty International Report 1998 (see Zambia Misrule of Law: Human Rights in State of Emergency, Amnesty International Report,—@ www.amnesty.org/ailib/aipub/1889/AFR/16300498.htm. March 1998/63/04/98.

33. More details on this can be found in Chiluba, 1995.

34. C. Young, "The Third Wave of Democratization in Africa: Ambiguities and contradictions" in R. Joseph, ed., 16.

35. Joseph Schumpeter as quoted in O. van Cranenburgh, "Democratization in Africa: the Role of Election Observation", in Jon Abbink and Certi Hesseling, eds., Election Observation and Democratization in Africa (New York: St. Martin's Press, Inc., 2000), 23.

36. Bratton and Posner.

37. Bratton and Van de Walle, 1997.

38. Huntington, 1991.

39. Ibid.

40. Young, 15–38.

41. Bratton and Posner.

42. Bratton and Posner, 399.

43. Jim Kirkwood, "Not yet an Election": Zambia 1996, South Africa Report, Vol. 12, No. 2 (1997): 28.

44. Most international observers refused to participate in the observation of the elections in 1996 because they considered them to have been manipulated long before the ac-

tual voting date. In the period before the elections were held, the Chiluba government and the MMD conduct had ensured that the outcome of the elections would be in their favor.

45. Ibid.

46. Ibid., 30.

47. Attempts by the opposition to petition the High Court of Zambia and to the Chief Justice to have even the announcement of the results delayed until investigations into the allegations of massive voter fraud were rejected on account that they were premature. This notwithstanding, the Carter Center that monitored the elections got the MMD off the hook on rigging allegations by claiming that the election irregularities and voter discrepancies cut across party lines and did not favor any particular candidate.

48. Burnell, 1110–1112.

49. Once again it was the division within the opposition that enabled MMD's Mwanawasa to retain the presidency, although as usual, amid allegations of voter fraud. There were serious cases of vote tallying problems with opposition candidates' votes being under tallied by the thousands in several stations. These irregularities put to question the entire exercise and made it hard for the losing candidates to accept the election results.

50. Changes were made in Parliament without any meaningful debates while regulations were put to benefit Chiluba and his cronies. For example, Chiluba's decision to declare a state of emergency in 1993 was supported by Parliament. The Criminal Procedure Code (Amendment) Act of 1993 was passed by Parliament allowing Chiluba to harass his opponents. Using it, journalists and other government critics were imprisoned or silenced.

51. Human Rights Watch/Africa 1996, 19–21.

52. A UNIP rally in Kabwe was also stopped despite UNIP having been issued with the required licenses to hold the meeting. This encounter led to an escalation in the level of violence as the police clashed with UNIP supports. In the encounter a number of people were arrested and many more were injured in the ensuing melee and as rioting and violent confrontations spread to the streets.

53. According to HRW-Africa, by the time the coup plotters were rounded up and the coup threat put down, over 100 activists and military personnel had either been arrested or detained. Efforts to have lawyers to be granted access to the detainees were not successful. Successive HRW publications have documented claims of torture of detainees in government custody. A number of the detainees, including Corporal Robert Chiulu died in detention. Charges against Kaunda were dropped when he agreed to retire from politics, which he announced in a speech to UNIP Central Committee meeting on July 3.

54. Not all the tortures went unpunished. In July seven police officers were arrested and tried for the torture and later death of an inmate they had arrested. HRW, 1999.

55. The prevalence of human right abuses in Zambia has given rise to the establishment of a number of NGO to monitor and campaign against human right abuses in the country. The most important of them is the Inter-Africa Network for Human Rights in Zambia (AFRONET), the Zambia Independent Monitoring Team (ZIMT), and the Zambia Civic and Education Association (ZCEA).

56. HRW, 1999, *World Report*, 2001.

57. Mukuka was forced into exile; the police constantly harassed his family.

58. See IPI, 2005:12.

59. It was publicly believed that President Mwanawasa did not win the election fairly, and that the opposition was likely to unite to field a candidate against the government. The fear was that if the press or members of the public were allowed in the chambers, they might

witness the government's maneuvers to impose a Speaker on the opposition. The view that the government intended to manipulate the election of the Speaker was given credence by the fact that the government preferred the election of the speaker to be by secret ballot while the opposition wanted an open balloting, IPI, 2002, 2.

60. To most African leaders, cabinet positions have been distributed as "electoral rewards and punishments" to ensure support for the ruling group.

61. M. Larmer and A. Fraser, 634.

62. Government of Zambia, "Quarterly employment statistics," at http://www.zamstats.gov. zm/qtr/labor.asp.

63. UNDP, "Human Development Index trends," at http://hdr.undp.org/statisitics/data/ indic_12_1_1.html.

64. Pastor, 1999: 7–8.

65. In 1996 and 2001, elections were marked by significant rigging; much of it was organized by State House, Larmer and Fraser, 620. The 2001 elections were judged by international observers as having been "unfree" and "unfair." EU, 2002.

66. Larmer and Fraser, 616.

Editors and Contributors

Saliba Sarsar is Professor of Political Science and the Associate Vice President for Global Initiatives at Monmouth University. He earned his doctoral degree from Rutgers University in Political Science, with specialization in International Relations and Middle Eastern Affairs. Sarsar is the author of several articles and commentaries on the Middle East; editor of *Palestine and the Quest for Peace* (American Task Force on Palestine, 2009); and co-editor (with Hussein Ibish) of *Principles and Pragmatism: Key Documents from the American Task Force on Palestine* (ATFP, 2006) and (with Drew Christiansen) of *Patriarch Michel Sabbah—Faithful Witness: On Reconciliation and Peace in the Holy Land* (New City Press, 2009).

Julius O. Adekunle, Ph.D., is Professor of African History at Monmouth University, New Jersey. He is the author of *Culture and Customs of Rwanda* (Greenwood Press, 2007); editor of *Religion in Politics: Secularism and National Integration in Modern Nigeria* (Africa World Press, 2009); and co-editor of *Color Struck: Essays on Race and Ethnicity in Global Perspective* (University Press of America, 2010).

Mario Fenyo received his Ph.D. from The American University, Washington, D.C. He is a Professor of History at Bowie State University where he teaches Third World and European History. Dr. Fenyo is the President-elect, Association of Third World Studies and is fluent in Spanish, French, and Hungarian. He has authored and co-authored several books, in addition to numerous journal articles.

Fuabeh P. Fonge is Associate Professor in the Department of History at North Carolina Agricultural and Technical State University, Greensboro. He was born in Cameroon and earned his B.A. degree from the University of Yaoundé, M.A. from Georgetown University, and Ph.D. from Howard University. Professor Fonge teaches courses in the history of Africa, Africana studies, and the African diaspora. Among his books are *A Concise History of Africa from Ancient Times to 1800, Modernization Without Development in Africa,* and *A Concise History of Africa Since 1800.* Dr. Fonge also edited the *Journal of North Carolina Association of Historians,* and is current editor of the *Journal of International Studies and Development.*

Jose Adrian Garcia-Rojas, Ph.D., is Associate Professor of Political Science and Public Administration and the Secretary of African Studies Center at the University of La Laguna, Spain. Dr. Garcia-Rojas is member of the editorial board of the Revista General de Derecho Comparado. He served as director of the Canary Islands Institute of Public Administration. He has been a visiting scholar at the African Studies Center of Michigan State University, the Center for African Studies at the University of Florida, and a visiting professor at CEAN (African Studies Center), Political Studies Institute (IEP) in Bordeaux, France. His research interest focuses on elections, parties and party systems, regional and local governments in Spain and EU countries, and African politics and public administration, particularly in the African microstates. He led an interdisciplinary research project about decentralization and local government in Cape Verde (2009–2010). He teaches Public Administration, Comparative Politics and African Politics and edited *Temas de Política y Gobierno en Canarias* (Dijusa, 2004).

Ngozi Caleb Kamalu is a Professor and Director of the MA Program in Political Science at Fayetteville State University, N.C. Kamalu received his Bachelor of Arts and Master of Public Administration degrees from Texas Southern University, and a Ph.D. degree in Political Science from Howard University. Kamalu also served as a Teaching and Research Fellow at Howard University and as a Research Assistant at the Woodrow Wilson International Center for Scholars in Washington, D.C.

Saba T. Kidane graduated with a Master's Degree from the University of California, Los Angeles (UCLA) in 2006, where she majored in African Area Studies with an emphasis on Political Science. Her first graduate degree was from the University of San Diego (USD) in Peace and Justice Studies in 2003. Her research interests include peace and conflict resolution, ethnic conflicts, human rights and democracy, and sustainability and development. Her research focus is Africa, particularly the Horn of Africa. Kidane also studied Political Science and International Relations at the University of Asmara and Addis Ababa from 1995 to 2000.

Joshua M. Kivuva received his Ph.D. in Development and Public Policy from the University of Pittsburgh, Pittsburgh, Penn. He is currently a lecturer in Political Science in the Department of Political Science and Public Administration at the University of Nairobi, Nairobi, Kenya. He is also a Consultant/Researcher for South Consulting (monitoring the Implementation of the Kenya National Reconciliation Dialogue). Dr. Kivuva has published several articles on ethnicity, violence, and post-conflict experience. His latest publication is "Reversed

Transition: From a Non-Democratic Multiparty System to a 'No-Party' Democracy in Uganda" in *The African Search for Stable Forms of Statehood: Essays in Political Criticism* ed., Shadrack Wanjala Nasong'o (New York: The Edwin Mellen Press, 2008). One of his works in progress is about globalization and the changing face of regional integration in Africa.

Emmanuel M. Mbah, Ph.D., is Assistant Professor of History at the City University of New York, College of Staten Island. His research focuses on conflict, ethnicity, and the socioeconomic and political life of Africans in colonial and postcolonial Africa. He is the author of *Land/Boundary Conflict in Africa: The Case of Former British Colonial Bamenda, Present-Day North-West Province of the Republic of Cameroon, 1916–1996* (The Edwin Mellen Press, 2008), "Disruptive Colonial Boundaries and Attempts to Resolve Land/Boundary Disputes in the Grasslands of Bamenda, Cameroon" (*African Journal on Conflict Resolution*, Vol. 9, No. 3, November 2009), and several chapters in edited volumes.

Shadrack Wanjala Nasong'o earned his Ph.D. in Public and International Affairs from Northeastern University, Boston. He is Associate Professor of International Studies at Rhodes College, Memphis, where he teaches courses in Comparative Politics, International Relations, and African Politics. Dr. Nasong'o is the author of *Contending Political Paradigms in Africa: Rationality and the Politics of Democratization in Kenya and Zambia* (Routledge, 2005) and *The Human Rights Sector in Kenya: Key Issues and Challenges* (Kenya Human Rights Institute, 2009). He is also the editor of *The African Search for Stable Forms of Statehood* (Edwin Mellen, 2008) and co-editor of *Kenya: The Struggle for Democracy* (Zed Books, 2007).

Raphael Chijioke Njoku, Ph.D., is Associate Professor of African History at the University of Louisville, Kentucky. He received his doctorate in African history from Dalhousie University Canada in 2003. Dr. Njoku had earlier earned a doctorate in Political Science from Vrije University, Belgium in 2001. His research specialty is African history and politics. He is the author of *Culture and Customs of Morocco* (2005), *African Cultural Values: Igbo Political Leadership in Colonial Nigeria 1900–1966* (2006) and co-editor of *Missions, States, and European Expansion in Africa* (2007), *War and Peace in Africa* (2010), and *Africa and the Wider World* (2010). Dr. Njoku has also published 31 scholarly articles in international journals and edited volumes. His most recent awards include: the University of Louisville Distinguished Research Award in the Category of Social Sciences (2009), the Indiana University Library Residency Award (2009), the Victor Olurunsola Endowed Research Award (2007), and the Schomburg Center Award for Research in Black Studies (2006–07).

Index